Report of the
Federal Cultural Policy Review Committee

Report of the Federal Cultural Policy Review Committee

Canada

Published by:

Information Services, Department of Communications, Government of Canada

© Minister of Supply and Services Canada 1982

Available in Canada through Authorized Bookstore Agents and other bookstores
or by mail from

Canadian Government Publishing Centre Supply and Services Canada, Ottawa, Canada, K1A 0S9

Catalogue No. C052-1/1982E   ISBN 0-660-11228-0

Canada: $9.95   Other countries: $11.95   Price subject to change without notice ·

Material from this document may be quoted or reproduced without permission.

Cet ouvrage est également disponible en français sous le titre de *Rapport du Comité d'étude de la politique culturelle fédérale.*

Companion volume to this Report:

Federal Cultural Policy Review Committee, *Summary of Briefs and Hearings.*
Published by: Information Services, Department of Communications, Government of Canada.
January 1982.

Cet ouvrage est également disponible en français sous le titre de *Compte rendu des mémoires et des audiences publiques.*

Federal Cultural Policy Review Committee

Comité d'étude de la politique culturelle fédérale

The Honourable Francis Fox
Minister of Communications
Ottawa, Canada

November 1982

Sir,

We, the undersigned, members of the Committee you established on 28 August 1980 to review cultural policies for Canada, have the honour to submit the following report.

Louis Applebaum, Chairman

Jacques Hébert, Co-chairman

Albert Breton, Vice-chairman

Ted Chapman, Vice-chairman

Joy Cohnstaedt

Guy Robert

John M. Dayton

Jean-Louis Roux

Denis Héroux

Sam Sniderman

Robert E. Landry

Alain Stanké

Elizabeth Lane

Thomas H.B. Symons

Hilda Lavoie-Frachon

Max Tapper

Mary Pratt

Rudy Wiebe

Contents

Foreword

This Report is a collective effort. It is the result of the deliberations of a large committee, assisted by a talented and loyal staff and a network of able and knowledgable consultants. But it is also the product of those thousands of people who took the trouble, and cared enough, to give us their views on culture and the arts in Canada. This is a committee report, in the widest sense: the account of a collective experience. And we think it is the richer for all that.

When we began this exercise some two years ago, neither of us fully anticipated the force of the ideas and the strength of the enthusiasm we were to encounter throughout the country. As we said in our previously published *Summary of Briefs and Hearings**, we were deeply impressed with the quality, variety and energy of Canadian cultural life. Of course we also found discord and disagreement, which was amply documented in the Summary. But that is only to be expected in a country as diverse as Canada. In any case, culture and the arts flourish best when no one point of view prevails. The variety of views we encountered, itself an indication of the vitality of Canadian cultural life, has contributed immeasurably to the shaping of this Report. So our thanks in the first instance must go to those many, many Canadians whose interest in, and dedication to, culture and the arts have been such a source of inspiration for us.

Our colleagues on the Committee have laboured congenially with us for many months. All of them are busy people with active lives who have cheerfully given of their time and expertise to this enterprise. The many hours spent reading briefs and background papers, the days given over to public hearings and other consultations, the days and weekends devoted every month to meetings and intense discussion – all these show the measure of their own dedication. Each brought to this project a different set of strengths, talents, experience and knowledge, giving to the Committee as a whole a sense of balance and proportion. Much the same could be said of our staff

---

*Federal Cultural Policy Review Committee, *Summary of Briefs and Hearings* (Ottawa: Department of Communications), January 1982.

and consultants. They came to us with many different backgrounds: the arts, representing nearly every discipline; government at all levels; private industry; the world of scholarship. To them we owe much.

This Report is the result of a long process of arriving at a collective stance on issues which, in some instances, elicited widely divergent views. We know that all Committee members have worked hard at reaching general agreement on broad principles and on main issues. That of necessity means that most if not all of them will still hold varying views on specific topics. This is not at all surprising or unusual; it is a reflection of Canada itself.

Although this Report concludes the work of the Federal Cultural Policy Review Committee, it is not regarded by us, nor should it be regarded by anyone else, as the end of work in cultural policy. We expect and hope that it will trigger lively discussion and dialogue. It is through informed public debate that sound public policy emerges. If this Report succeeds in inspiring such a continuing debate – and concerted action on the issues we set out in these pages – we shall count our efforts well rewarded.

Louis Applebaum   Jacques Hébert
Chairman   Co-chairman

Federal Cultural Policy Review Committee

*Louis Applebaum, Chairman
Toronto, Ontario

*Jacques Hébert, Co-chairman
Montreal, Quebec

*Albert Breton, Vice-chairman
Toronto, Ontario

*Ted Chapman, Vice-chairman
Calgary, Alberta

Joy Cohnstaedt
Winnipeg, Manitoba

John M. Dayton
Vancouver, British Columbia

Denis Héroux
Montreal, Quebec

Robert E. Landry
Ottawa, Ontario

Elizabeth Lane
Vancouver, British Columbia

Hilda Lavoie-Frachon
Nigadoo, New Brunswick

Mary Pratt
Mount Carmel, Newfoundland

*Guy Robert
Ville Mont-Royal, Quebec

Jean-Louis Roux
Montreal, Quebec

Sam Sniderman
Toronto, Ontario

Alain Stanké
Montreal, Quebec

*Thomas H.B. Symons
Peterborough, Ontario

Max Tapper
Winnipeg, Manitoba

Rudy Wiebe
Edmonton, Alberta

---

*Members of the Planning Committee.
Biographical notes will be found in Appendix B.

1
Cultural Policies and the Public Will

1

Cultural Policies and the Public Will

This book is about the shape and future of cultural policies for Canada. Its aim, through the collective voice of this Federal Cultural Policy Review Committee, is to make recommendations addressing immediate and long-range problems, and to propose a set of guiding principles which will give governments a basis for decision-making in the years ahead in fields of cultural activity that reach into the lives of all Canadians.

In our *Summary of Briefs and Hearings*, published in January 1982, we noted that the proper place for the formulation of our own conclusions and recommendations was our planned Report. With the publication of the present document, we are pleased to be able to bring our views – distilled through public consultation, research and internal debate – before the people of Canada. We shall begin by making a few general observations about the principles that have guided our work, before going on to lay the groundwork for formal recommendations in the main text.

Artist and Audience

The reader will discover, first of all, that we have placed great emphasis on artistic creativity, over and above any of the other facets of our cultural life. Creative talent can take many forms, and is by no means confined to the traditional arts – such as literature, painting and music. There are few fields of human endeavour which do not depend in some measure on the application of creative insights. Even within the relatively restricted scope of our own inquiry, we have looked beyond contemporary artistic activity to the preservation of our man-made and natural heritage and the cultural industries of broadcasting, publishing, film and sound recording. We believe in particular that no cultural policies aimed at promoting contemporary creation can possibly succeed unless they are firmly rooted in a respect for our artistic and intellectual heritage.

The Committee came to believe, through its months of deliberation, that the role of creative artists should be given special priority in consideration of cultural policies in order that the public might benefit from the results of creative work. Artistic creativity has two sides for us – the creative act of the artists themselves and the response of audiences and spectators, whose sensitivity and imagination allow the work of art to take on a public life of its own. The best test of an artist's work lies in its exposure to the critical gaze of discriminating audiences, with well-developed standards of aesthetic judgment, a desire to share artistic experiences with creative people, and an openness to new and innovative work. Audiences have to be discriminating in order to provide the artist with constructive responses. And audiences need to be open to new experiences in order that original work may emerge. It is these qualities of the audience, rather than sheer size alone, that must become the measure of successful artistic endeavour. We therefore believe that one of the chief goals of cultural policy must be to establish strong and stable lines of communication between artists of all kinds and those who will see, read or hear their messages.

We believe, moreover, that culture and the arts will best flourish in Canada when our artists are able to present their work to audiences with a fair measure of freedom from social, economic and political constraints. When we speak of freeing artists from social constraints, we are calling for a heightened recognition of the role they play in Canadian society. We are suggesting there must be a change in attitude and that the artistic professions must be placed on the same footing as any other honourable and vital vocation. When creative artists, and what they create, receive recognition and esteem commensurate with their contributions to our community and culture, much else will follow.

Recognition will also mark the beginning of a process in which the artist is freed from what are now unreasonable economic constraints. A few artists at the very top of their fields are, of course, materially well rewarded. However, the evidence is overwhelming that Canada does not provide an adequate living for most of its professional artists. It is clear to us that the largest subsidy to the cultural life of Canada comes not from governments, corporations or other patrons, but from the artists themselves, through their unpaid or underpaid labour. When creative activity is diminished because many artists are unable to earn a decent living, something is lost to us all, and our entire culture fails to fulfil its promise.

When we speak of the removal of political constraints, we mean that artistic activities must be sheltered as much as possible from the imperatives of government. This idea has clear implications for the effects of public policy on cultural life; above all, that policy should facilitate self-expression, rather than control or organize it. It has been one of the main tasks of our Committee to document and justify the vital role of the federal government in sustaining artistic and cultural activity in this country. But such a role for government does not extend to the exercise of artistic judgment – except where government relies on public trustees and professional adjudicators who stand outside the political process. However desirable it may be, state support of the arts can have a liberating effect on creative energies only if such support is allocated through "arm's-length" mechanisms, about which we shall have much to say in this Report. Without these mechanisms, we would put at risk not only the diversity of cultural expression, but also the fragile and unpredictable creative process itself. Happily, the Government of Canada has recognized and accepted the arms-length principle, which guides its relations with most of its cultural agencies.

Three Decades of Growth

In a more practical vein, we have interpreted our mandate as requiring us to pick up the threads of cultural inquiry where our predecessors, the members of the Royal Commission on National Development in the Arts, Letters and Sciences, left off in 1951. As we explained in the opening lines of the *Summary*, ours is the first comprehensive inquiry of its kind since Vincent Massey, Georges-Henri Lévesque, Norman MacKenzie, Hilda Neatby and Arthur Surveyor published their report (to which we shall refer in this book as the Massey-Lévesque Report) over 30 years ago. In its decision to follow, at least in part, the path surveyed in that report, the federal government wisely placed Canada among the fortunate nations of the world by recognizing and funding post-secondary education, heritage, the arts and artists. Some of that report, therefore, did much to alter the cultural landscape of Canada, even though the cultural growth in the period since 1951, which we have recorded at various points in this book, might well have taken place spontaneously, with or without the encouragement of formal policy recommendations. And we are fully aware that the roots of cultural development of which we write stretch back for many generations. In any case, we look upon the early postwar years as a major watershed, and feel it is instructive to take the measure of Canada's cultural growth in the intervening period.

When we look back on the past 30 years, we see much the same pattern of development in virtually every field of cultural life: new facilities for the performing arts, new museums and galleries, new community arts centres, new libraries and archives, new film and recording studios, new publishing ventures, new universities. Naturally there is more to this infrastructure than physical plant, important as that may be. There are also the orchestras, theatre and dance companies, film and television production groups, artistic and crafts cooperatives, and service organizations and professional associations of all types. The record of the past 30 years is one of which Canadians can be proud, not least because with the growth of this infrastructure has come a substantial growth in the artistic community itself – there are simply many more artists working in 1982 than were working in 1952, or even 1972 – and a marked flowering of artistic achievement. In a very real sense, Canadian cultural life can be said to have gained maturity and distinction. Sheer individual initiative, private donations, corporate sponsorship and various other kinds of aid have contributed to this growth, but any fair-minded person would have to acknowledge the important role played by governments at all levels in providing financial and organizational support.

Yet cultural policy has not been entirely successful in encouraging the best use of the human creative resources Canada has in abundance. As a democratic and cosmopolitan country, we have thrown open our borders to foreign cultural products and not given ourselves sufficient opportunity to enjoy the fruits of our own cultural labour. It is a telling state of affairs that our broadcasting system boasts the most sophisticated transmission hardware in the world – satellites, interactive cable, teletext – while Canadian viewers spend 80 per cent of their viewing time watching foreign programs on television. Broadcasting may provide the most striking illustration of this point, but it is by no means the only one. Our response to this dilemma is not, however, to come down on the side of protectionism, but rather to press home the point as forcefully as we can that federal cultural policy has largely favoured physical plant and organizational development over artistic creativity and achievement.

While the results of this policy orientation have been beneficial, it must be acknowledged that putting up buildings and establishing organizations are relatively simple tasks. For one thing, the accomplishments of such activity are measurable and therefore more easily explained to electorates and interest groups. This is one of the reasons why Canadians, when speaking of the growth and development of their culture and the arts, leap with alacrity to the comfort of numbers: concert halls built, theatre troupes created, television stations constructed, publishing firms founded. These can all be counted and added up. But what they add up to is more an industrial and employment policy than a cultural policy, properly understood. The bricks and mortar are necessary, but they are not the end product, the purpose of it all. The new task which we as a committee of inquiry into federal cultural policy now invite Canadians to undertake is a different and in some ways more difficult one. We have come to believe that federal cultural policy must place a new emphasis on encouraging the best use of our concert halls, theatres, cinemas, galleries and airwaves for the presentation to Canadians of the finest works of Canada's own creative artists. If we fail to make the stimulation of our own creative imagination the heart of our cultural policies, we will continue to live in a country dependent on the products of other cultures and we will never elevate life in Canada to a space essentially its own.

The stimulation of Canadian creativity will require that the knowledge base of culture and the arts be firm. Knowledge and information, and the means for their creation, storage and transmission, are fundamental to culture and the arts. Knowledge and culture are so closely intertwined at so many points that we find it awkward and artificial to treat the relationship as a separate subject. For this reason, the reader will find the matter treated at various places throughout this Report, often under the headings of education, training or research.

One aspect of knowledge, however, merits special attention here. Canada, and indeed the world, is in the throes of a technological revolution which will drastically affect the ways knowledge is created, stored and transmitted. By the year 2000, according to a recent report of the Science Council of Canada, most homes will have computer terminals, through which information can be summoned up and exchanged. The effect of this and related innovations on our economy and styles of living will be enormous, giving rise to what some have called the "information society." The effect on culture and the arts is less clear, but is likely to be equally dramatic.

Given current economic conditions, we cannot overemphasize the importance of seeing many of the recommendations made in this Report as part of a series of long-range solutions. It is true that in virtually every artistic discipline, practitioners and policy-makers are faced with urgent problems requiring immediate attention. Frequently these are problems associated with an acute shortage of funds, and this Committee remains convinced that, even within the present level of federal government expenditures, the proportion of the federal budget devoted to cultural activities in the broadest sense – 1.9 per cent in 1982* – is too low for a society such as ours. We have attempted, however, to address ourselves with equal vigour to the less visible but often more serious structural, organizational and legislative difficulties which may stand in the way of healthy cultural growth over the next two or three decades. If this Report can help to lay the groundwork for a rational set of cultural policies for Canada between now and the year 2000, then we will have done what we set out to do.

The Goals of Cultural Policy

The original task we set ourselves was to investigate not culture itself but rather federal cultural policy. Cultural policy is a concept that bears some explaining. We should say at once that the reader who anticipates a history of Canadian art or literature or music will be disappointed. What came within our purview was not so much the cultural materials and ideas themselves as the institutions and policies that have allowed them to flourish – or stunted their growth, as the case may be. If we pretend to offer few insights into the aesthetic significance of Canadian arts and letters, this does not mean that we have no vision of Canada's cultural future. It means only that our vision must of necessity be couched in institutional rather than aesthetic terms.

---

*This figure is based on the official *Estimates for the Fiscal Year Ending March 31, 1983*, and is calculated as a percentage of Government Net Costs. These include expenditures for the Communications portfolio – Arts and Culture sector of the Department of Communications (including the subsidy to Canada Post Corporation for handling "cultural mail"), plus the expenditures of 10 cultural agencies. They also include expenditures for the Secretary of State Multiculturalism program, Official Language Minorities program, and the Historic Parks program of Parks Canada. These expenditures for 1981-82 totaled $1.2 billion, compared with total Government Net Costs of $66.6 billion.

Cultural policy is a relatively new phrase in the Canadian lexicon, and not a universally accepted one either. To some, the term has negative or monolithic connotations, as if it implied that government should bend culture to its own purposes, or pursue some all-encompassing goal through closely coordinated means. Whereas we shall frequently refer to cultural policy, singular, as a terminological convenience, it is of course more accurate to speak of policies, plural, that mixture of goals and means which constitutes the political reality – a heritage policy, a film policy, a television policy and so on. It is true that the sum of these policies can be said to constitute an overall policy, even if the different goals pursued sometimes seem to be inconsistent. The only real question in this respect is whether those policies support and encourage people's natural creative instincts or whether they frustrate and neglect them.

In recent years, preoccupation with policy coherence and coordination has led to what we believe has been a dilution of cultural policy goals. We have observed a tendency to treat cultural policy as a means to other ends – social, economic and political. The apparent belief by some that culture is an instrument, not an end in itself, has consequences which this Committee must regard as undesirable. First, it contributes to a muddling of cultural goals with other national goals. We have been told throughout our inquiries that culture employs people, that it expands the economy, that it democratizes society, that it contributes to mental health, that it unites the country, that it advances the national interest in the world. These are all laudable goals, ones which we support, but we must respectfully observe that as much as possible they should be kept distinct from cultural goals.

Furthermore, when cultural policy is couched in terms that seem to suggest it has purposes other than the purely cultural, it arouses doubts about its true purpose. When some new cultural policy is justified on the grounds that it promotes national unity, for example, it raises the suspicion that its purpose is to homogenize the different cultural traditions that Canadians so cherish. These suspicions do nothing to enhance the believability of either the federal government in general, or its cultural policy in particular. Whether such anxieties are well-founded or not is beside the point; the very fact that they exist at all should serve as a warning to the federal government to choose both its goals and its terms more carefully. We therefore urge the federal government to make and administer cultural policy as much as possible with a view to the implementation of cultural objectives. No doubt a successful cultural policy will achieve desirable economic, social and political results as byproducts, as we shall note in Chapter 2. But these should not be allowed to dictate the aims or content of cultural policy itself.

On the other hand, since art and cultural materials are made by people, cultural policies must have a social policy component: the emergence and refinement of talent must be encouraged and barriers to the full participation of all in cultural life removed. Children with artistic talent are sometimes discouraged by parents from pursuing careers in the arts because of the minimal economic rewards and uncertain status these occupations sometimes afford. The schools themselves, far from nurturing such talent, often work to discourage or dissipate it. Some individuals are denied the expression of their full creative potential because they are disabled. Still others find their artistic aspirations blocked because they live in a region where few opportunities for development present themselves. Women are often prevented from making a greater contribution to arts and culture because they are inadequately represented at all levels of the cultural agencies, including juries and other selection committees. Developing artistic talent is primarily the responsibility of the individual. It remains our view, however, that governments must pursue a vigorous social policy aimed at eradicating discriminatory barriers to the full participation of all Canadians in cultural life.

The elimination of discriminatory barriers is an imperative of social policy. Our Committee believes it is also an imperative of cultural policy. *We should like to draw special attention to the fact that the present inequitable access of women to all levels of responsibility and activity in the cultural sector deprives Canadian society as a whole of a vital dimension of human and artistic experience.*

Culture in the Social Fabric

This Committee feels there is reason to rejoice in our differences – regional, ethnic, linguistic – rather than to treat them exclusively as problems for solution. Diversity is an essential cultural resource. As a country with two official languages, each a link to several different cultural traditions, and with many other traditions that are all part of the fabric of a complex society composed of regions, Canada offers a unique setting for the creative process. Taking the fullest advantage of this resource requires that we allow our various cultural traditions to reach out freely to each other. Diversity can be closed, in which case it is merely a collection of varying solitudes, or it can be open, in which case its value as a source of creative inspiration is most fully realized. As a general rule, we believe Canadian cultural policy should come down on the side of open diversity.

This principle has a number of implications. It means that federal cultural policy should be shaped by the fact that we have two official languages, but it should not partition Canadians into two linguistic compartments. Today, Canadians who speak primarily English have still too little awareness of cultural developments among Canadians who speak primarily French, and vice versa. Although both linguistic communities are open to international culture, they are relatively little aware of each other's achievements. The Committee believes that the federal government should design cultural policy so as to facilitate cultural contact between the two official language groups. The purpose of such contact should be to take best advantage of Canada's linguistic duality, in such a way that policies are not seen to have any other objective than the mutual cultural enrichment of both linguistic communities.

For more than three centuries there has developed in Canada a cultural tradition of French expression, centred in Quebec, which has survived and flourished, which has enriched Canadian cultural life and which experienced a new surge of vitality as a result of Quebec's "Quiet Revolution." Elsewhere in the country, in Acadia especially, and in Ontario and certain Western communities, the French language continues to be the vehicle of cultural expression for hundreds of thousands of Canadians. This great tradition must be nurtured and cherished.

For its part, regional diversity has an impact on Canadian cultural activity in at least three ways. First, it provides to the artistic community as a whole a number of different regional traditions from which to draw inspiration. As with language, region shapes our culture by creating distinct areas of cultural discourse. Second, regional diversity offers a number of different frames of reference, providing that ferment of ideas, values and perceptions which we have acknowledged as an important source of creativity. Finally, the presence of different regions provides a challenge for the distribution of cultural products of all types, a fact of particular consequence for those regions distant from the main population centres. There is no clear agreement among Canadians about what the regions of Canada are, or whether there are six or sixty-six, for there is no region of Canada which, on closer examination, does not resolve itself into still more regions. Be that as it may, we believe that the cultural interests of Canada as a whole are best served when all Canadians, regardless of their region of residence, have maximum access to cultural products and to the means of cultural expression. The fact of regional diversity should inform cultural policy from beginning to end.

Another important component of Canada's diversity is ethnicity. Canadians are descended from almost every ethnic group in the world, making Canada a meeting place for the world's cultural traditions. These traditions, moreover, are not mere replicas of cultures developed somewhere else; rather, they have taken root in Canadian soil, blossomed and taken on a life, a Canadian life, of their own. This has occurred at least in part because Canadian society provides a supportive atmosphere for cultural diversity. More recently that attitude has been embodied in the 1971 federal policy of multiculturalism and reinforced by Section 27 of the Charter of Rights. Throughout its public hearings, the Committee encountered considerable public confusion about this policy. Some measure of misunderstanding may come from the fact that, while the policy is described as being cultural in nature, in reality it is only partly so, since the Secretary of State's Multiculturalism Program has tended to take on the character of a social rather than a cultural policy. Confusion may also arise because the 1971 policy is framed in relatively general terms, but in practice has had a relatively narrow focus – ethnicity. Ethnicity is one important dimension of Canada's cultural diversity, but it is not the totality of it. Any policy of multiculturalism which is based solely on ethnicity runs the risk of ignoring other types of diversity, such as those deriving from language, religion, age, place of residence and so on. *The federal government should therefore enlarge its present concept of ethnic multiculturalism, to take into account the many different types of cultural diversity that exist in Canada.*

In the formulation of principles for cultural policy in general, and with special regard to cultural diversity in particular, it is important that no one group have privileges, priority or precedence over others. We have come to believe, however, that a special place in cultural policy should be reserved for peoples of Indian and Inuit ancestry. This should be so for several reasons. To begin with, the cultural traditions of the original peoples are uniquely rooted in this country, as compared with those more recently derived from other cultures. In the second place, the federal government has by treaty, law and custom a special responsibility for the well-being of these peoples. Finally, and most important of all, the original cultural traditions have a set of values and aesthetic standards which have not been easily accommodated within the usual structures and practices of federal cultural institutions.

The Native peoples of this country are sometimes incorrectly thought by other Canadians to form a homogeneous cultural group. But these Canadians in fact derive from many different cultural traditions. It is an important fact for the cultural history of Canada that they enjoyed for centuries a rich and varied cultural life formed by encounters with the physical environment, by migrations and by extensive exchanges among their different communities. Accordingly, federal heritage policies should put a new emphasis on the preservation, development and exhibition of the products of our original cultures. Even so, the point was repeatedly made to us by Native artists and others that the art of the original cultures is all too often treated as if it were part of a now dead past. *This Committee is convinced that Native artists must be recognized first and foremost as contemporary Canadian artists, whatever their field, and that federal policy should give special priority to promoting both traditional and contemporary creative work by artists of Indian and Inuit ancestry.*

About This Report

The principles we have underscored in this introductory chapter do not purport to exhaust this Committee's concerns, and the reader is now invited to turn to the main text for further elaboration. To a large extent, we have been able to shape the vast amounts of material that have come to our attention to correspond either to certain professions and disciplines, or else to government programs and policies. This correspondence explains why the reader will find many parallels between the structure of this Report and that of our *Summary*. On the other hand, we experienced more difficulty structuring our comments on certain subjects that cut across disciplinary lines, such as tax questions, community arts, national service organizations and so on. We have therefore provided a detailed index of subjects and proper names, to enable the reader to make the best possible use of this document. Other material of an interdisciplinary or more general nature will be found in Chapters 2, 3, 4 and 11.

Finally, we wish to make it clear to whom this Report is addressed. In the first instance, it is addressed to the Minister of Communications and his colleagues in the federal government, as well as to the numerous officials who will play a role in the evaluation and possible implementation of our recommendations. We believe that other readers – artists, administrators, critics, anyone with a professional interest in arts and culture – will find useful information and, we hope, stimulus in these pages. But we also address our fellow citizens, whose lives are touched by the many facets of cultural activity. Our recommendations are addressed to them, as much as to the men and women of government. Decision-makers will muster the political will to transform our cultural landscape when they have read the shape of the future in the will of those who elect them.

2
Government and Culture

_____

_____

_____

_____

_____

_____

2

Government and Culture

Society, Culture and Government

We start from a view of Canadian society that sees it as an aggregate of distinctive spheres of activity. Each of these has its own values and purposes and its own network of institutions, interacting with one another in myriad ways but equal in their social importance. The political order – the state – is one of these great spheres and institutional systems; the cultural world is another. Both are expressions of the society in which they are rooted but both, at the same time, are major forces in shaping that society. Inevitably, they intersect. The human wants, perceptions and prejudices by which governments are driven or constrained are, in large part, expressions of the culture. Conversely, the system of government influences all social activity, and all spheres of society, including the cultural, tend to develop their characteristic institutions in patterns that fit the political system and to define their own wants in terms that invite responses by governments.

Up to a point, the strength of each sphere is dependent on the strength of the other. Certainly the phenomenal surge of artistic activity in Canada over the past three decades has not been unrelated to the expansion of government operations (at all levels) during the same period – and especially to the growth of resources at the disposal of Canadian governments. And, as governments discovered in the year of the Centennial, cultural activity – by strengthening the cohesion of society – can strengthen the social underpinnings of government itself.

But there is a danger, too, in this seemingly happy interdependence of government and culture, for they do not pursue the same ends. Government serves the social need for order, predictability and control – seeking consensus, establishing norms, and offering uniformity of treatment. Cultural activity, by contrast, thrives on spontaneity and accepts diversity, discord and dissent as natural conditions – and withers if it is legislated or directed. The wellbeing of society is threatened if the state intrudes into the cultural realm in

ways that subordinate the role and purposes of the latter to the role and purposes of government itself – or of any other spheres of activity. Moreover, the
cultural sphere, embracing as it does artistic and intellectual activity, has as
one of its central functions the critical scrutiny of all other spheres including
the political. On this score alone it cannot be subordinated to the others.

This critical function suggests an analogy with religion, as an autonomous source of moral judgment resting on its own authority. After a protracted struggle, the separation of church and state was achieved, despite
lingering uncertainties from time to time about the proper role of government
in regulating or constraining the actions of particular sects or cults. Nor has it
proven impossible to reconcile this separation with government practices
which give legal force to religious sacraments or, through the tax laws, provide material support to religious institutions. A comparable separation of
culture and the state, it might be argued, is no less necessary.

A similar parallel might be drawn with the relationship of government
to the institutions of public information and comment – which may, in fact,
be seen as a segment of the cultural sphere. Limitations are imposed by
government on the media of expression in the form of libel laws (subject to
varying doctrines of fair comment), but the threat of Sedition Acts is a thing
of the past – and critics of the Report of the Royal Commission on
Newspapers (Kent Commission), with whatever justification, find an easy
recourse to historic arguments for an arm's-length relationship between
government and the press. In short, by these analogies, "freedom of cultural
pursuits" might claim equal standing in a bill of rights with "freedom of
religion" and "freedom of thought and expression."

But against these analogies, others may be cited in which the role of
government has taken a very different course. There was a time when the
sphere of economic activity was widely considered to be beyond the range of
legitimate political authority, but exponents of uncompromising laissez-faire
are rarities today. And in the matter of public education – more closely allied
to the question of cultural life, perhaps – the model developed at the end of
the 18th century in Prussia has become the near-universal model, in which all
significant aspects are subject to direction by ministers and their departmental bureaucracies: not just financing, but the choice of educational objectives,
the planning of curricula, the selection of texts, and the training and certification of teachers. The strong element of community control that characterized
public education in our own earlier tradition has given way progressively to
provincial direction, and the Committee encountered widespread support for
the criticism of the Organization for Economic Cooperation and Development
of Canada's failure to develop national educational goals and standards. It is
by no means certain that the autonomy enjoyed historically by post-
secondary institutions will not suffer the same erosion.

Is there a stronger case to be made for the autonomy of the cultural
sphere than for that of public education and its institutional system? The
answer may lie in the distinction made by the Massey-Lévesque Commission

beween Formal Education – schooling – and General Education, of which schooling is only one element. (Culture, in the Commissioners' definition, represented the intellectual and aesthetic aspects of general education.) Schooling, the concern of public systems of education operated under government direction, is a compulsory activity which is largely instrumental in character, in that it serves the needs of other spheres of social activity, including the economic and political. By contrast, culture involves spontaneous or at least voluntary activity by all members of society, and its value and satisfactions are essentially intrinsic, rather than instrumental.

How far is it reasonable to expect government to deal with culture in terms of its own intrinsic values rather than as an instrument for other ends? In some circumstances, it will clearly be used for the purposes of government itself. Architectural design – whether on Parliament Hill or in the Toronto city hall – makes a statement about the place of government in society. International cultural relations serve diplomatic objectives as does participation in international sporting events and expositions. If tapestry collections and talent competitions can be used to sell cigarettes, it is to be expected that governments will use similar devices to further their own version of brand loyalty.

The question of purposes arises when the government intervenes in the cultural sphere in ways that can have a decisive influence on cultural life – as patron, regulator, producer or provider of services. Our cultural life has become dependent on these interventions, and not the least of this Committee's tasks is to suggest how, in the process, cultural values and purposes can best be reconciled with the imperatives of government itself.

The Imperatives of Government

The working of government entails the balancing of specific public demands not only against the resources available but also against other competing and sometimes contradictory public wants. In considering alternative responses to a demand for action, government must calculate in effect the degree of public satisfaction likely to result from each possible response, measured against the degree of public dissatisfaction likely to be engendered. In the process it must weigh not only the direct effects (both benefits and costs) of each course contemplated, but also the indirect effects on courses of action pursued or contemplated in response to other demands. In all its aspects it is a political process in that, although costs and benefits may be discussed in economic or social terms, the ultimate calculation must always be made in terms of votes rather than dollars or jobs or morbidity rates. To say that a policy must win more votes than it loses is not a cynical quip; it is simply a shorthand way of saying that it must yield the most favourable possible balance of public benefits and must be felt by the public to do so.

The processes of government involve the interplay of two institutional systems. The first is political, involving all the instruments and processes of public expression, including interest groups and the media, together with the specialized institutions for mobilizing and channeling public views: parties, Parliament and the cabinet. The other is administrative, comprising the executive machinery of government: cabinet, and all the departments and agencies under its direction. What is most significant for the development, execution and adjustment of policy is the one element common to both: the ministers.

The characteristic instrument through which ministers act is the department. The conclusion of the 1960-63 Royal Commission on Government Organization (Glassco Commission) was that "the departmental form of organization is admirably suited to the needs of government in a parliamentary democracy. It is adaptable to almost any conceivable purpose and unrivalled in its sensitivity to public wants." Its versatility is reflected in the fact that it has been employed for every conceivable purpose: within the cultural realm alone, it has been used to provide schools, libraries, archives, museums, parks, exhibitions, entertainments, and laboratories, and to assist artistic, educational, and scientific or scholarly activities of every kind by institutions and persons throughout our society.

Within the departmental form, the role of ministers is crucial. All actions of any consequence are taken in their name and their powers enable them to ensure that all actions conform to the "public interest" as interpreted by them and their colleagues in response to their constant exposure to the political process. Moreover – although it is frequently overlooked – the departmental machinery is itself very much a part of that political process, providing as it does a powerful and continuous feedback to the minister about the wants, opinions and reactions to government operations from those sectors of the public with whom the department deals from day to day.

Within recent years, the evolution of government has reflected a growing preoccupation with the collective role of ministers. Sheer growth in the size and complexity of operations gave rise to what might be termed managerial concerns with administrative consistency and the allocation of resources. The history of these preoccupations can be traced in the development of such central authorities as the Treasury Board, the Public Service Commission, and more recently the Comptroller General, and in the growing array of common service departments such as Public Works, and Supply and Services. The search for better control over the allocation of resources is reflected in the creation of coordinating ministries of state for economic and regional development and for social development, and in the associated "envelope" system of expenditure control.

Until the mid-1960s, these managerial matters were the dominant concerns in the development of the machinery of government. But in the past 15 years, two other preoccupations have risen to the fore, both of them essentially political: policy coherence and accountability.

The operative idea behind the concern for policy coherence was summed up a few years ago by a Secretary to the Cabinet: "Governments must look to the public interest as a whole, and must have a comprehensive overview in which specific problems are seen as they relate to the whole." By various means of internal consultation and coordination – with the cabinet system as the central element – governments try to ensure that all their objectives are accommodated, as far as possible, in everything they do; the ideal is that the entire range of aims is brought to bear on every decision of consequence involving the policies and programs of each ministry. Because what is reflected in the array of objectives being pursued at any given moment is the complexity of public demands and attitudes, it is characterized by inner contradictions and conflicts. As a result, decisions made in response to any one set of wants are inevitably modified – or "contaminated" in the eyes of those intended to benefit directly – by motives that may seem at best tangential to the problems to which those decisions are ostensibly addressed. This means that although cultural policy will be *about* government action affecting cultural activity, it may tend not to be a policy exclusively *for* culture, but to be influenced in varying degrees by considerations of, say, economic growth, or social justice, or national unity. And the more completely any sphere of activity is brought within the regular framework of collective ministerial direction, the more it will be subjected to the interplay of these divergent aims.

The final matter of concern – accountability – is as old as the parliamentary system itself, having taken many forms throughout the centuries: in the British parliamentary contests with the Tudors and Stuarts, in the impeachment process of the century following the Restoration, in the evolution of cabinet responsibility (and in North America in the struggle for responsible government), and in the office of the Auditor General of Canada and the parliamentary scrutiny of public accounts.

As Parliament developed its instruments for exacting an accounting from ministers, the latter faced a growing problem of ensuring accountability within their burgeoning bureaucracies. From the 1930s to the 1960s, heavy reliance was placed on the Comptroller of the Treasury, armed with the formidable but cumbersome power of pre-audit. Financial control was further systematized in 1951 by the Financial Administration Act – still, with subsequent modifications, the basis for government control of expenditures and accounts. When the Comptroller of the Treasury was swept away, following the Glassco Commission Report, new measures were tried, including revised formats for the expenditure estimates and annual accounts. Complaints by the Auditor General in the 1970s that the government was losing control of expenditures led to the Royal Commission on Financial Management and Accountability (Lambert Commission), the creation of the office of Comptroller General, and the enlargement of the investigative and evaluative role of the office of Auditor General itself.

The Cultural Agencies of Government

For the regular departments of government, the adjustment to increased emphasis on policy coherence, accountability, resource allocation and expenditure control has not involved any drastic departures from their accustomed ways. Ministerial direction has, after all, always been a basic fact of life for them, and the switch in emphasis toward a more collective exercise of the ministerial function is a relatively minor complication. Similarly, they have long been used to working within a framework of administrative direction designed and applied by such central agencies as the Treasury Board, the Public Service Commission and, until the 1960s, the Comptroller of the Treasury.

By contrast, however, the Crown corporations, boards, councils and commissions that have proliferated in recent decades have not shared fully in the tradition of central direction, and as a consequence, the developments of the past few years have focused attention on their status and relationships with ministers and central agencies. Included among these nondepartmental bodies are a number of organizations that have served as the principal instruments of federal government action in cultural matters. Their status and relations with government are crucial questions in any review of cultural policy.

These cultural agencies differ from government departments in a number of ways, with little consistency among them. For most – including the Canada Council, the Canadian Broadcasting Corporation, the Canadian Film Development Corporation, the Canadian Radio-television and Telecommunications Commission, the National Arts Centre, the National Museums of Canada, the Social Sciences and Humanities Research Council, and, for some purposes, the National Film Board – the existence of a directing board implies a curtailment of the role played by a minister in relation to a department, and is an impediment to the collective ministerial pursuit of policy coherence. Administrative consistency, as it applies to departments, is breached by varying exemptions from the Financial Administration Act, the Public Service Employment Act and the Public Service Staff Relations Act. For some agencies, ministers retain control over the allocation of resources only in terms of the very broad program headings identified in the spending estimates approved by Parliament. And each variation in the ministerial role and administrative practice carries with it, if not a diminution of accountability, at least a variation in its application.

To quote again from the Glassco Report, "In effect the use of a nondepartmental form involves a decision that the ministerial function be restricted – and parliamentary acceptance of a corresponding diminution of ministerial responsibility. Because the departmental form offers the maximum in flexibility and responsiveness to public wants, there must clearly be special reasons for such a decision."

Historically a number of "special reasons" became generally accepted as sufficient justification for exceptions to the departmental pattern, including circumstances such as the following:

- assignment of quasi-judicial responsibilities;
- the necessity of conforming to commercial practice in the conduct of operations of a commercial character;
- responsibility for decisions on sensitive questions of taste and quality;
- generally, a need for freedom from partisan political pressures.

In recent years, however, questions have been raised about the nature and extent of the exemptions ascribed to the nondepartmental agencies. These challenges can be identified under two headings: policy direction and administrative controls, bearing in mind that the traditional distinction between policy and administration is, in important respects, an artificial one.

Policy Direction and the Cultural Agencies

The essential question about policy is whether matters of public policy, involving the expenditure of public funds, must for all purposes and in all respects be subject to ministerial direction. The challenge to the traditional view that cultural agencies should be free from such direction was exemplified in a speech given to the Canadian Conference of the Arts on May 4, 1979, by the Honourable John Roberts, then Secretary of State and the minister responsible at the time for the cultural agencies. After reaffirming the responsibility of the Canada Council for creative excellence, of the Canadian Broadcasting Corporation for programming, of the National Film Board for production and of the National Museums of Canada for acquisitions, the minister went on to assert his own responsibility for a wider range of decisions about policy, using the Canada Council as an example:

> "Beyond the raw decision about amounts of money, the government must also develop its views on many other matters of public policy: in what parts of the country should cultural institutions be? should economically deprived and geographically remote areas get special attention? to what extent should Canadian content be a factor? what proportion of total revenue should come from the box office? does the federal government have an educational role in culture? how to relate provincial government priorities to federal government priorities? These and many other questions are essentially questions of public policy. The government must answer them [and] . . . must be held responsible by Parliament and the country for the result."

The Lambert Commission in 1979 reached the same view. "Because Crown agencies are instruments of public purpose, just as are departments, ultimately the doctrine of individual and collective responsibility must be preserved.... Since in the last analysis, the policies being implemented are those of the Government, which must bear responsibility for them, there must be an instrument available to the Government to resolve the inherent tension that may develop between it and the Crown agency."

The instrument proposed by the Lambert Commission was the formal ministerial directive. When a proposed Crown Corporations Act was introduc-ed in the fall of 1979 as Bill C-27, it included provision for such a device. Sec-tion 9 of the bill provided that "the Governor in Council may, by order, give to any Crown corporation such directive as in his opinion is necessary or desirable for the better advancement of the national interests of Canada." Several qualifications were included: directives could not relate to the "perfor-mance of duties of an advisory nature" (since it would clearly be ludicrous to direct an adviser concerning the advice he was to give), or to "the provision of financial aid or other assistance...to or for the benefit of any particular per-son." In other words, the directive could not say which person is or is not to get grants. But the directives could relate, for example, to any of the ques-tions listed by Mr Roberts in the passage quoted from his speech of May 4, 1979 – or, for that matter, to those questions of judgment which he had iden-tified as agency responsibilities, including Canadian Broadcasting Corporation programming decisions, National Film Board production decisions, acquisi-tions by the National Museums, and Canada Council judgments of "creative excellence" involving performing arts companies or other organizations rather than individual artists.

The draft Crown Corporations Act was not, in the end, enacted, and in June of 1982 the government took a different legislative approach, in Part V of Bill C-123, the Government Organization Act, 1982. (The bill was not in fact passed before adjournment for the summer recess of that year, but it re-mains in the government's legislative program for the future.) Under the pro-visions of this draft statute, the Financial Administration Act would be amended to give the government the powers conferred on a sole stockholder under the Canada Business Corporations Act to give binding directions on any matter.

It has been the view of successive governments, and of the Lambert Commission, that the use of such a power of direction would be exceptional. It should be noted that the government of the United Kingdom has long had comparable powers in relation to its cultural agencies, including the British Broadcasting Corporation, but has used them rarely and without arousing fears of untoward political interference. Canadian cultural agencies are already subject to ministerial direction under the Official Languages Act on matters of language policy. The earlier draft Crown Corporations Act provided that such direction be exercised only after consultation with the board of the agency concerned, and would have required that orders-in-council containing directives be tabled in Parliament. By contrast, the new approach adopted in the draft Government Organization Act of 1982, which would confer an unlimited power of direction, makes no provision for either prior consultation or subsequent tabling.

While accepting the propriety of ministerial direction, when authorized by Parliament, on such specific questions of public policy as language requirements and conflict-of-interest rules, the cultural agencies – and much of the cultural community throughout the country – have expressed anxiety about the creation of a directing power in matters involving judgments of cultural needs and standards. The necessity of shielding cultural activity from the power of the state was a recurring theme in representations made to this Committee. The "tensions" that the Lambert Commission would resolve in favour of the government are depicted, in effect, as tensions between the government's concern with order and unity and the frequently anarchic character of cultural activity, which can by their nature only be accommodated (but not resolved) within autonomous bodies.

In the face of objections such as these, the government has deferred action. In announcing the introduction of Bill C-123, the President of the Treasury Board stated that, pending completion of the government's review of cultural policy, the proposed changes in ministerial powers of direction would not be applied to "corporations with a cultural mandate." This Committee had, in fact, been asked to examine the implications of such powers in relation to the earlier proposals contained in the draft Crown Corporations Act.

Is it realistic to expect that cultural agencies in the conduct of their operations will or should be insulated from major preoccupations of the government, whether the latter relate directly to cultural matters or to other matters? Or can a case be made for a broad exemption of some cultural agencies – for purposes going beyond the awarding of grants – from the power of ministerial direction? These are the questions which have confronted this Committee.

Administrative Controls

Long before policy direction became the live issue it is today, the federal government sought to systematize its relations with its nondepartmental organizations in matters of administration – especially financial administration. The Financial Administration Act of 1951 – which continues to provide the basic framework for the management of government finances – included a cluster of sections headed "Crown corporations" in which an effort was made to categorize the corporate agencies for purposes of financial control. Two of the categories – the "Agency" and "Proprietary" corporations listed in Schedules C and D – were given a general exemption from the provisions of the Act relating to departments. They are able to manage their own funds, including those provided by parliamentary appropriations, to maintain their own accounts and to follow accrual accounting practices instead of the cash accounting practised by the government – being spared the lapsing of unspent balances at the end of the fiscal year. They are, nonetheless, required to submit their annual capital budgets for ministerial approval, and Agency corporations must, in addition, secure approval of their annual operating budgets. For a third category, however – listed as "Departmental corporations" in Schedule B – the financial controls and practices are identical to those applied to departments.

Among the cultural agencies of most direct interest to this Committee, two, the National Museums of Canada and the Social Sciences and Humanities Research Council, are Departmental (or Schedule B) corporations, the Canadian Film Development Corporation is an Agency corporation (Schedule C), and the Canadian Broadcasting Corporation is a Proprietary corporation (Schedule D). Two others, the Canada Council and National Arts Centre, are totally exempt from the Financial Administration Act, and four others, the Canadian Radio-television and Telecommunications Commission, the National Film Board, the National Library of Canada and the Public Archives of Canada, lack corporate status and are treated as departments.

The Lambert Commission devoted a good deal of attention to the classification of agencies and the prescription of administrative relationships.

For two cultural agencies – the National Library and the Public Archives – the governing characteristic in the eyes of the Commission was that the "care and management" of operations was assigned to a senior official, "under the direction of a minister who reports to Parliament." The conclusion was that these should operate in every respect like a department of government – as, in fact, they now do.

For a second group – including the Canadian Radio-television and Telecommunications Commission, the Canada Council, the Canadian Film Development Corporation and the Social Sciences and Humanities Research Council – the "care and management" of administrative operations was ascribed to the chairman or permanent head. "The board or commission in this instance plays no part in the management of the agency," and "for all financial and personnel matters, the head of the agency, as chief executive officer, has a relationship with the central agencies akin to that of a deputy minister of department." They should, in consequence, be subject to the Financial Administration Act and the Public Service Employment Act.

Only within a third group – which included the Canadian Broadcasting Corporation, the National Arts Centre, the National Film Board and the National Museums of Canada – was the "care and management," the responsibility for administration, considered by the Commission to be the responsibility of the board and therefore exempt from the normal relationship with central agencies under the Financial Administration Act.

The other critical element of administrative practice relates to personnel administration. Agencies that are classified as departments or Departmental (Schedule B) corporations under the Financial Administration Act are subject to central controls over the numbers of their staff, the classification of positions and rates of pay. All of these agencies are bound by the Public Service Employment Act and must therefore observe the staffing rules and procedures prescribed by the Public Service Commission. The Public Service Staff

Relations Act also applies to this group. Two of these bodies, however – the National Film Board and the Social Sciences and Humanities Research Council – are designated as "separate employers," and as such undertake their own staffing and negotiate their own collective agreements with their staff.

The other agencies – the Canada Council, Canadian Broadcasting Corporation, Canadian Film Development Corporation and National Arts Centre – are exempt not only from the establishment and classification controls of the Treasury Board, but also from the Public Service Employment Act and the Public Service Staff Relations Act. They do, however, report their actual and projected manpower levels, which are published in the expenditure estimates presented annually to Parliament. And in determining the classification and rates of pay of their personnel, they are heavily influenced by the standards of the public service applying to comparable skills and duties, where these exist. All four of these agencies, however, draw their professional – and increasingly much of their managerial – staff from the cultural sector, often on relatively short contracts, and would find it inappropriate, if not difficult, to be treated as part of the public service.

It must be accepted that, although all controls are irksome and may, if excessive, create what is seen as a cocoon of "red tape," an agency is in no worse position than a department unless some particular control can be shown to impede the pursuit of its objectives. Even the latter condition may not be a sufficient argument if the "impediment" suffered by the agency is experienced equally by departments and is considered by ministers and Parliament to be an inescapable cost of doing public business.

To illustrate: that parliamentary control of budgeting and accounting must be on a cash rather than an accrual basis and that all funds appropriated must be disbursed within the fiscal year for which they are approved, are, in effect, matters of dogma. The strength of this principle was demonstrated by the Adjustment of Accounts Act of 1980 which abolished certain non-lapsing special accounts that had facilitated the operations of several cultural agencies. For the National Film Board, the loss of the Special Operating Account meant that, from April 1981, all film production expenditures have had to be made out of parliamentary appropriations and within the year for which the appropriation was made, and that any earned revenues go to the Consolidated Revenue Fund with no benefit to the Board. At the same time the four national museums lost their Special Purchase Accounts which had enabled them to husband acquisition funds in order to exploit market opportunities as they arose.

Any argument against a change to cash accounting for agencies such as the Canada Council or the Canadian Broadcasting Corporation might encounter the objection that it could be applied with equal force to departmental operations. And it would be naive – and futile – to suggest that the centuries-old pattern of budgetary control and accounting practice embedded in the tradition of parliamentary control of the public purse should be radically altered, even if it can be shown that very large and complex organizations in the private sector achieve equal if not better control over financial operations using accrual budgeting and accounting. The same kind of difficulty is encountered – although with less intensity – by any argument for exemption from government-wide standards and practices in personnel administration.

In the last analysis, demands for administrative consistency can be countered only if it can be shown, first, that there is a case for shielding an agency's operations from normal ministerial policy direction, and second, that the imposition of normal government practices relating to financial and personnel administration would significantly impair that operational autonomy in substantive matters.

Criteria for Defining Cultural Agency Status

As nondepartmental organizations have proliferated, the federal government has tried to devise a classification system that would serve to maintain an orderly system of relationships between the agencies on the one hand, and Parliament, ministers and the central machinery of government on the other. For all the effort expended, the results have been unsatisfactory – and particularly for the cultural agencies, which form a very small subset within a total of some 170 Crown corporations identified in Bill C-27 of 1979.

The two major attempts at a rational classification to date are to be found in the Financial Administration Act of 1951 and the Lambert Report of 1979. In both of these the essential criterion was the nature of the operation engaged in by the agency and, in particular, its degree of resemblance to operations found in the private sector.

The Financial Administration Act, as noted above, established three schedules of Crown corporations. Departmental corporations, listed in Schedule B, were defined as those providing "administrative, supervisory or regulatory services." Agency corporations, listed in Schedule C, embraced "trading or service operations on a quasi-commercial basis" and "the management of procurement, construction or disposal activities." The Proprietary corporations (Schedule D) were characterized by "the management of lending or financial operations or...of commercial operations involving the production of or dealing in goods, and the supplying of services to the public," and these agencies were "ordinarily expected" to conduct their operations without appropriations. The latter enjoy the greatest freedom from central controls; the first group are assimilated to departments.

From the start it proved difficult to fit all agencies into this classification. The Canadian Broadcasting Corporation has remained under Schedule D despite its dependence on appropriations. The Canada Council and National Arts Centre were simply excluded from the Act. Yet when the Canada Council's activities in support of the humanities and social sciences were withdrawn in 1978 to form a new agency – the Social Sciences and Humanities Research Council – the new organization was assigned to Schedule B, on the analogy of the Medical Research Council.

The Lambert Commission, employing a similar approach, proposed that all agencies be fitted into two categories. The first, which they termed "Independent Deciding and Advisory Bodies," would comprise organizations having "adjudicative, regulatory, granting, research and advisory functions," including the Canada Council, the Canadian Film Development Corporation, the Canadian Radio-television and Telecommunications Commission and the Social Sciences and Humanities Research Council. For these, as noted, the chief executive officer, charged with the "care and management" of the agency, would be subject to the central agencies in the same way as the deputy head of a department. Only the other group was classed by the Commission as "Crown corporations," and these would be characterized by having "tasks akin to private sector entrepreneurial undertakings in a market setting." The Canadian Broadcasting Corporation, National Arts Centre, National Film Board and National Museums of Canada were included in this group, which would be exempt from financial control by the central agencies.

This preoccupation with similarities and differences between the operations of public agencies and those of private commercial organizations was also reflected in the proposed classification of agencies contained in the draft Crown Corporations Act of 1979, but no attempt was made in that bill to define the criteria for classification. Instead, the drafters of the bill seemed reconciled to a view put forward in a "Blue Paper" on Crown Corporations, published by the Privy Council Office in 1977, which had abandoned the notion of a descriptive classification. "It is the Government's view," according to this document, "that,

> "those parts of the present criteria for Schedules B, C and D relating
> to the type of operation conducted by the corporations listed
> therein are unnecessary and make accurate classification more dif-
> ficult. It is proposed, therefore, that those parts be removed.... -
> Crown corporations would then be listed in a particular schedule,
> not by what they do but by the degree of financial management
> and control over them required by the government."

The source of the difficulty, it seems to us, lies in trying to ascribe degrees of autonomy solely on the basis of the character of the operations. For the cultural agencies, it is our view that an acceptable accommodation of government imperatives and cultural values can be achieved only by simultaneously employing two approaches: first, an examination of the operational character of the agencies, and second, an examination of the cultural impact or significance of each agency's activities – by a blending, in effect, of the insider's and outsider's view of the agency's functions. Only in this way can one determine whether cultural values are equally vulnerable and the imperatives of government equally strong in relation to all kinds of operations and in all domains of the cultural sphere. Or whether it is possible, by varying organizational forms and relationships along a spectrum of alternatives ranging from full autonomy to full ministerial control, to strike a satisfactory balance of political and cultural objectives.

Character of Operations of the Cultural Agencies

Operational roles can be categorized in several ways. The approach most commonly adopted is to distinguish between different types of activity: advisory, regulatory, sustaining, operating, and developmental.

On closer analysis, however, any such classification proves inadequate as a basis for determining the degree of autonomy required by an agency. An advisory body must obviously make its own decisions about the advice it will give; to suggest that it be subject to any kind of direction on this score would clearly be absurd. But the relationship with government appropriate to all other kinds of activities is a good deal less clear.

For regulatory activities – such as those of the Canadian Radio-television and Telecommunications Commission – opposing considerations must be weighed. Studies of the regulatory process have frequently stressed the need for some safeguard against the disturbing tendency of regulatory bodies to become insensitive to interests broader than those of the industries they regulate. And it is frequently argued that on regulatory decisions that raise major questions of public policy, ministers should exercise a power of direction, reflecting their public accountability for interpreting the public interest. Against this, however, must be set the countervailing principle, equally valid, of the importance of maintaining the integrity of the regulatory process, which requires that the process be (and be perceived to be) fair and impartial and conducted at arm's length from the political process. In short, the fact of engaging in a regulatory activity may not, by itself, provide an adequate guide in determining the relationship.

For sustaining activities, which provide financial support for cultural activities, a number of questions arise. As will be seen, whether that support is directed to individuals, to industrial or nonindustrial organizations, or to communities, may make a difference in deciding what measure of political direction is necessary or tolerable. Whether the support is granted automatically if certain objective criteria are satisfied, or by some politically determined formula, or only after a process of selection involving a judgment of cultural merit or entitlement, is another crucial question. What must be borne in mind is that the sustaining role of government – no less than the regulatory – is an aspect of its immense coercive power, which embraces both the power to compel or prohibit on threat of punishment and the power to entice and cajole by promise of reward. Rewards are as coercive as punishments, even if less painful to those coerced.

Developmental activities may employ the same range of methods as sustaining activities and in the same range of circumstances; consequently all the questions identified under that heading apply with equal force in this category of activity. It should also be noted that government programs under this heading (the Cultural Initiatives Program of the Department of Communications is a case in point) include a large measure of capital assistance to enlarge or improve the facilities for various modes of cultural expression. Whether the subsequent use of those facilities will raise politically sensitive

issues is not – and cannot be – a consideration in the developmental program itself in the same way in which it might affect sustaining activities.

An alternative approach to the analysis of operating roles involves the
examination of the different kinds of decisions required of public authorities
or agencies engaged in cultural programs:

- jurisdictional
- resource allocation
- standards and criteria
- adjudication of claims or performance.

Decisions involving the assignment of jurisdiction must clearly be
taken by ministers backed by parliamentary authority. But lack of clarity, or
differing interpretations within different programs or agencies, can raise new
questions of jurisdiction that ultimately require ministerial judgment – the
dispute between the National Library and Public Archives over the music collection and map collection being a case in point. Jurisdictional overlaps may
be unavoidable, and again ministers must either reserve the right of umpire
or grant primacy to one of the contestants. Instances that come to mind are
the CBC-CRTC relationship in broadcasting, the Canada Council Touring Office
and National Arts Centre, and the existence within the Canada Council (and
other agencies) of interests in the international ramifications of their programs that overlap those of the Department of External Affairs. Overlapping
jurisdiction is also responsible for much of the agitation – both within government and outside – for coordination. But because coordination in the end can
only be ensured by an exercise of ministerial powers, it may present dangers
to programs requiring a high degree of insulation from political direction. A
different kind of problem arises when, as a result of divided jurisdiction and
because of the ways in which the agencies involved interpret their mandates,
an area of cultural activity – industrial arts and crafts, for example – finds its
interests largely neglected. Again, in this situation, corrective action can only
come from ministers in the form of new and more precise definitions of
jurisdiction.

The primary allocation of resources – which matches the assignment of
jurisdiction – is just as obviously a ministerial responsibility. Once this decision has been made, however, and authorized by parliamentary appropriations, how much autonomy should an agency have in deciding on the allocation of resources within its area of jurisdiction? Should the judgment of the
Canada Council be overridden in determining the relative shares to go to, for
example, individual artists or arts organizations? or to the several arts
disciplines? What freedom is required by the National Museums of Canada –
or its constituent museums individually – in the apportionment of resources
for such purposes as conservation, research, or the mounting and touring of
exhibitions? As we have seen, according to one view these are policy
judgments for which ministers should be responsible and over which they

should have a corresponding degree of control. The Canada Council has resisted this view and has, in effect, asserted the right to exercise its own judgment in the application even of earmarked funds. The evidence also suggests that the Social Sciences and Humanities Research Council – perhaps partly because it is subject to the financial management requirements of the Treasury Board – has had to accept an allocation of resources that diverges increasingly from what its own judgment or that of its academic advisers might dictate. In assessing, in strictly cultural terms, the relative importance of competing claims on the resources available to an agency, ministers and their advisers can seldom if ever match the agency itself in competence. In fact, the differences that arise involve, almost invariably, a conflict between cultural and other considerations. In determining whose judgment should prevail, recourse must be made to other approaches to the analysis of government-agency relationships.

The same is true of the third class of decisions – those concerning criteria and standards – which have proven to be the other major source of friction between agencies and ministers. These are the judgments that raise such issues as the definition of community standards, the imposition of Canadian content requirements, and sensitivity to regional interests and to the claims of interest groups and of particular communities and audiences. All of these are politically charged issues, on which ministers feel a strong compulsion to intervene. But the judgments involved may seem, to the agencies responsible, to be crucial to the shaping of their programs to the cultural needs of the country. Decisions of this sort frequently bring into sharp relief the contradictions between political and cultural objectives.

The fourth class of decisions is essentially administrative: the day-to-day judgments that must be made at various levels within an organization in the conduct of its programs. Because these are the judgments that make the most direct impact on the public at large, they tend to determine the public responses that feed back through the political process. In asserting their claims to a greater voice in the making of decisions of the second and third categories, ministers are usually careful to deny any wish to intervene in these day-to-day judgments. But because the latter reflect, in fact, the more general prior decisions on questions of resource allocation or of standards and criteria, ministerial interventions on those more general questions will inevitably circumscribe and may even preempt an agency's freedom in making such administrative judgments.

Cultural Impact of Government Programs
The cultural impact of government programs can be examined in a number of ways to see what variations might be detected in the effects of political direction.

The first categorization to be considered is that adopted by the Committee in organizing its own work, which considers cultural activity sector by sector:

- Heritage
- Visual and applied arts
- Performing arts
- Literature
- Cultural industries

As a basis for gauging vulnerability to political direction, this is not a particularly useful approach. Within any of these sectors it is possible to find grounds for apprehensions about the baneful effects of government control or influence. The written word – including both literature and scholarship – has historically played the key role in the transmission, interpretation and enlargement of the intellectual content of culture, and in the process its function has embraced the illumination and critical analysis of the values, institutions and processes of society, including those of the political sphere itself. Consequently, literature and scholarship might claim a special insulation against political control. But increasingly, the written word reaches its audience through other forms of cultural expression – involving stage or screen (including the video screen). To this extent, then, the performing arts and cultural industries exhibit a comparable sensitivity.

It is not hard to find historical instances in which the visual and applied arts have assumed the role of political and social critic and suffered repression at the hands of the authorities of the day. Even music can become politically charged in exceptional circumstances – as were the polonaises in czarist Poland, or *Finlandia* in czarist Finland.

But social criticism is only half the problem. The other half concerns the thorny issue of taste – and the propensity of cultural activity in all its forms to outrage the sensibilities of varying segments of the public. Because of the sensitivity of elected governments to cross-currents of this sort, the threat of official censorship becomes the uninvited companion of government support for cultural activity, whether it be literature, or the performing arts, or the visual and applied arts, or the output of cultural industries. But the propensity to offend lies not in the mode of expression but in the content – not in the medium but in the message. For this reason it is difficult to assign degrees of vulnerability among cultural sectors.

The one possible exception to this conclusion concerns those activities considered as heritage. But then heritage is not a sector like the others. In its broadest sense, heritage is simply that part of culture that is received from the past. It therefore includes not only written records and artifacts, but also the bulk of our classical music and much of our literature, performing arts and visual and applied arts. And however offensive it may have seemed in its day to political authority or public taste, it has gained respectability and acceptance (if not sanctity) from the passage of time. As a consequence, apart from conflicts with plans for commercial development, heritage activities have relatively little to fear from governments, except from revolutionary regimes determined to erase the evidence of a rejected past.

A second cut at the cultural pie (which on closer examination seems to defy clean slicing and crumbles like a nut cake) focuses on the functional analysis of cultural activities, under four broad headings:

- the preservation and transmission of inherited elements,
- new creative and interpretive activity,
- what is essentially entertainment,
- training and development.

The first of these corresponds roughly to the heritage domain in the preceding classification, and may have little to fear from political intrusion for the reasons suggested. It should be noted, however, that a cultural heritage does not consist only of tangibles – structures, landscapes, artifacts and documents. Of at least equal importance are the intangibles: the ideas, values, attitudes and shared body of knowledge acquired by each generation from the past and reflecting its varied antecedents. How this intangible element of heritage is transmitted – and, in the process, reinterpreted – may be a matter of considerable sensitivity.

The second functional sector – creative and interpretive activity – which represents the growing fringe of culture, has clearly the greatest vulnerability to political direction and the greatest need for autonomy. It is in this domain that the pluralistic argument – already expressed in the opening section of this chapter – applies with greatest force, for it is here that the function of social criticism is concentrated and the controversies over taste and community standards are generated.

The third functional sector – entertainment (and recreation) – overlaps the two preceding ones and cannot, strictly speaking, be considered in complete isolation. But there is clearly a very large sector of activity of which the primary function is to satisfy varying demands for entertainment and recreation, transmitting little from the past, leaving little residue in the form of future heritage and showing little conscious concern with the interpretation of society to itself. As entertainment, it relies primarily on market mechanisms, and its characteristic problems tend to be associated with this orientation – developing and protecting markets, strengthening supply, circumventing obstacles that inhibit access to the market, optimizing the sharing of returns among those involved in production and distribution. From government it demands courses of action that involve at least as much industrial (or, more broadly, economic) policy as cultural policy, and the principal apprehensions about the role of government concern the serving of specialized markets and the sharing of returns.

The fourth sector – training and development – functions, in a sense, as a service sector to the other three. It embraces, as one element, the training in skills needed for cultural transmission, creation and interpretation, and for the recreation and entertainment aspect. In addition, it serves to animate, to develop a capacity for appreciation, enjoyment and, in the widest sense, participation. On both counts, it is closely linked with education policies and objectives (although it obviously extends beyond the system of formal education) and the problems it raises are those that have always been central in the planning and administration of education: the balancing of skill training against cultural transmission, or the extent to which government through the education process should try to shape public values and interests. It is questionable whether these problems can be resolved by insulating this sector from political direction. It can even be argued that, on the contrary, these are essentially political problems that can only be addressed through the political process, and the essential question concerns the extent to which they should be assigned to the community, provincial or federal level.

The third classification of cultural domains to be considered involves examination of the clientele to which different kinds of government programs and policies are primarily directed:

- Individual creative and interpretive artists and scholars;
- Nonindustrial organizations – performing arts companies, universities, museums, galleries, libraries and the like;
- Industries;
- Communities – geographic, ethnic, etc.

When cultural domains are distinguished on this basis, a further set of considerations emerges. Because the creative and interpretive function of culture relies so heavily on the individual artist or scholar, programs directed to individuals tend to involve the greatest vulnerability to political direction or influence, and to require the greatest degree of insulation.

Nonindustrial organizations are in an ambiguous position. On the one hand, there is a tendency for many of them – performing arts companies and galleries, for example, and to a lesser extent universities – to inspire strong community interest and loyalties, which inevitably find expression through the political process. Programs directed to the support of such institutions cannot in fact be shielded from such community-based political forces (which the institutions themselves tend to encourage). On the other hand, these institutions are frequently the instruments through which the creative and interpretive efforts of individuals are sponsored or expressed. To this extent programs directed to their support are no less vulnerable than those in the preceding category.

This last argument may apply with equal force to government programs directed to cultural industries – broadcasting and publishing come immediately to mind. But to the extent that these industries are preoccupied with the entertainment function identified in the previous classification of sectors, their operations will be bound up more closely with the market considerations noted in that context, and programs in their support will exhibit a characteristic blend of industrial and cultural policy which may require a greater degree of political direction.

Finally, programs directed to community interest seem inextricably linked to the political process. It would seem foolish to suggest that they be insulated from political direction, especially when they involve capital assistance for community facilities.

One additional consideration must be weighed in judging the cultural impact of government programs and their vulnerability to political direction: the external context within which they operate. Where a program is the sole source of a service or holds powers of life and death over a cultural activity, both its impact and the effect of political intervention are obviously greatest. For the same reason, adverse reactions to the way a program is conducted will have the greatest tendency to find political expression and thereby generate political interventions. One might conclude, in fact, that the best guarantee of autonomy is irrelevance. But, by the same reasoning, it is precisely where the impact is greatest that the need for autonomy is most acute.

Recommendations and Conclusions

The implications of the foregoing analysis will be reflected at various points in later sections of this Report dealing with particular cultural sectors, or specific agencies. But certain general conclusions can be recorded here, including the Committee's views, requested by the government, on the questions of status raised by Bill C-123, the proposed Government Organization Act, 1982.

As will be seen, these conclusions affect the status of different agencies in different ways, in respect of policy direction, administration controls and measures for ensuring accountability, but they draw coherence from a recognition of the fact that government operations in the cultural sphere are subject to special considerations. It therefore seems appropriate to us that the changes we propose in the status of a number of these agencies and in their relationships with ministers and the central machinery of government should be implemented through an omnibus Cultural Agencies Act, which would serve to emphasize the common underlying principles on which they rest.

1.   The status of federal cultural agencies should be defined in a new Cultural Agencies Act, in recognition of the fact that government activity in culture and the arts is subject to special considerations requiring a distinctive measure of autonomy. The provisions of this statute should prevail wherever they may conflict with those of the Financial Administration Act or the proposed Government Organization Act.

Policy Direction

In judging what degree of insulation from ministerial direction is appropriate to each agency, the Committee attaches paramount importance to the cultural impact of their programs – considering the cultural sectors served, the focus of the cultural activity, and the character of the clientele. For several organizations, this assessment is decisive in itself, regardless of the classification of their operations and the extent of their dependence on parliamentary appropriations. For other agencies, the cultural impact seems less sensitive to the usual processes of government direction; particular aspects of their work may require shielding from political forces, but in some instances this may be accomplished through exemptions from particular kinds of administrative controls. These are examined in the next section.

For five agencies, the Committee has concluded that the safeguarding of cultural values and purposes requires, as a matter of public interest, that their operations be immune from political direction. This group comprises the Canada Council, the Social Sciences and Humanities Research Council, the Canadian Broadcasting Corporation, the National Arts Centre, and the National Film Board.

The first two of these – the Canada Council and the Social Sciences and Humanities Research Council – are identical in all those aspects that are material to the question of their form and relationship with government. In terms of their cultural impact, both serve a number of cultural sectors including some of great sensitivity in their critical function; both are heavily engaged in the support of creative and interpretive activity essential to the health of our society; both direct their support to individual artists and scholars, or to nonindustrial organizations that sponsor or present the work of such persons; and both operate in an external environment in which, for artists and scholars, alternative sources of support are scarce or nonexistent and at best inadequate to their needs. In terms of their operating roles, both are engaged in sustaining activity that requires judgments of merit, and both are vitally interested in the determination of standards and criteria. All these considerations suggest that the high degree of autonomy possessed by the Canada Council since its inception is entirely appropriate to its circumstances and, by the same reasoning, that the relatively severe restrictions on the autonomy of the Social Sciences and Humanities Research Council are ill-advised.

The Canadian Broadcasting Corporation and the National Arts Centre require comparable shielding from political control but for different reasons. The fact that they might be considered to perform "tasks akin to private sector entrepreneurial undertakings in a market setting," as stated in the Lambert Report, is essentially irrelevant. What is important is that both are major channels for presenting the work of individual artists, and are deeply involved in program and production decisions that involve culturally important and controversial issues of taste and quality. For the Canadian Broadcasting Corporation this includes the selection and presentation of news and comment about public affairs.

The same considerations apply to the National Film Board in the production undertaken on its own account. The differences between it and the Canadian Broadcasting Corporation in status and relationships with the government have been anomalous; nor has its role as film procurement (or production) agent for the government justified the anomaly, as its obligations to its government clients could be defined satisfactorily within the contractual relationship. The changes proposed for the Board in Chapter 9 will curtail its production activity significantly but if it is to be, as contemplated, a centre of experimentation and innovation for film production, there will be a continuing need for freedom from government direction.

The role envisaged for the Canadian Film Development Corporation requires treatment similar to that required by the Canada Council and the Social Sciences and Humanities Research Council. Its support is of course directed to commercial film ventures, but these ventures, like the productions of the Canadian Broadcasting Corporation are (and should become increasingly) important outlets for the efforts of Canadian creative and interpretive artists and will raise sensitive or controversial issues of taste or social criticism. Moreover, our recommendations for the future development of the agency will require that, in its granting operations, cultural judgments should at least equal if not outweigh commercial ones. In the light of these circumstances, we conclude that the operations of the Canadian Film Development Corporation qualify for the same degree of autonomy as the other five agencies treated above.

For the Canadian Heritage Council recommended in Chapter 4 a mixture of functions is contemplated, but the principal one is developmental and sustaining, through programs of grants to a variety of organizations, both public and private. Because the Council will be concerned essentially with the preservation and transmission of cultural heritage, its activities will not be as vulnerable to political forces as, say, the activities supported by the Canada Council; nor will they be as likely to provoke adverse reactions through political channels. However, there will be culturally important questions of standards, criteria, and resource allocation to be made by the Council, and it would seem appropriate that it be exempt from policy direction by ministers. This conclusion is reinforced by a further consideration: the client organizations will almost certainly include provincial and municipal institutions, and any exercise of policy direction by the federal government would likely provoke provincial protests and distrust of the agency itself.

The relationship of the National Museums of Canada to ministers is complicated by the fact that the agency itself is viewed by this Committee (and was, in fact, initially conceived) as being, in essence, a service organization to its member organizations, each of which should have a major say in defining its own role and priorities and in allocating its own resources. Clearly, if it is undesirable that the Board and central staff should exercise a heavy-handed control over the operations of the individual museums, it is even more objectionable that this be done at a further remove. With one exception, however, the activities of this agency and its constituent parts are less vulnerable to political direction – and, for much the same reasons, less likely to attract it. The existence of a ministerial power, conditional on prior consultation and the subsequent tabling in Parliament of any formal directions, appears to us to raise no serious threat to cultural values. The exception concerns the decisions of the agency about the development of its collections, and any grant of a directing power should expressly exclude its use in respect of additions to or deletions from the collections.

The Public Archives of Canada and the National Library are, for practical purposes, indistinguishable from departments in most respects. This has, in practice, created no problems for the two organizations, nor does this Committee see any reason to be apprehensive. For certain specific functions, however, both the Dominion Archivist and the National Librarian should be exempt from ministerial direction. The Dominion Archivist, as the control officer of the government for records management, is responsible for approving all proposals for the destruction of records or for their removal from the ownership of the government. Although the Dominion Archivist's decisions on the destruction or disposal of records appear to be in no way subject to ministerial direction, the authority of the position rests only on an order-in-council, the Public Records Order of 1966. It would be preferable to establish the Dominion Archivist's powers and responsibilities by statute – as has, in fact, been contemplated as part of a revision of the Public Archives Act. The National Librarian, it is concluded, should be similarly free of ministerial direction in the management of the Library's collection, in order to avoid any possibility, however unlikely, of government censorship.

As was noted earlier in the section on criteria for defining status, the Canadian Radio-television and Telecommunications Commission is in a class by itself among the cultural agencies as the sole regulatory body. Its regulatory functions in the cultural sphere (leaving aside its responsibilities for communications) include the supervision of the Canadian broadcasting system to ensure compliance with the broadcasting policy as enunciated in the Broadcasting Act, and, within this context, the granting, renewing and termination of broadcasting licences.

In its general supervisory role, the Commission might be considered to be an instrument of government policy and consequently properly subject to policy direction. But as an adjudicative body, in the licensing of broadcasters, it must be and be seen to be free of political control. If this view is accepted, the provisions of the existing Broadcasting Act would seem to have matters reversed. There is now no provision in the Act for general policy directions (although it contains provision for direction on several specified matters), but it does provide in Section 23 for a challenge by government of the Commission's decisions on the award or renewal of licences. This anomaly should be corrected. The power to set aside or refer back licensing decisions should be removed. On the other hand, the Committee sees no objection to a general power of policy direction – as was contemplated in the draft revision of the Broadcasting Act introduced as Bill C-16 in 1978 – subject to certain conditions. First, the requirements of prior consultation and subsequent tabling should apply. And, in addition, where the Commission, on being consulted about a proposed directive, considers that issues are raised on which public representations should be heard, no directive should be given until the Commission has been able to conduct public hearings.

2.   To the extent that the functions of cultural agencies and offices require the exercise of impartial, critical judgment in the support of cultural activity, they should be exempt from political direction in the form of ministerial directives of either a general or specific nature.

Administrative Controls

The defects of past approaches to the classification of agencies are clearly evident in relation to the exercise of administrative control by the central agencies of government. In the view of this Committee, the primary test must again be the impact of an agency's operations on the cultural sector, not the degree of resemblance to "private sector entrepreneurial undertakings in a market setting." The Lambert Report compounded this classification error by advancing the view that only those boards that directed operations meeting its entrepreneurial test should have the "care and management" of operations. The other category of boards were represented as performing only a collegial task of deciding cases. The fact is that these boards – the Canada Council, the Social Sciences and Humanities Research Council and the Canadian Film Development Corporation – are deeply involved in crucial decisions about resource allocation and the definition of standards and criteria, and are as vitally interested as, say, the Canadian Broadcasting Corporation board in the "economy, efficiency and effectiveness" of the operations they direct. In these circumstances it is a serious mistake to ascribe the care and management of operations to a chief executive officer subject to direction by a minister and the central agencies of government. The arguments presented by the Lambert Commission in favour of autonomy in financial and personnel administration for such bodies as the Canadian Broadcasting Corporation and National Arts Centre apply with equal force to all the other cultural agencies which were judged, in the preceding section, to require immunity from policy direction: the Canada Council, National Film Board, Canadian Film Development Corporation, Social Sciences and Humanities Research Council and the proposed Canadian Heritage Council.

3.   Freedom from ministerial and central government agency direction in financial and personnel administration should be granted to all cultural agencies which, under their mandates, exercise a high degree of responsibility for the economy, efficiency and effectiveness of the operations they direct – namely, the National Film Board, Canadian Film Development Corporation, Social Sciences and Humanities Research Council and the proposed Canadian

Heritage Council – in the same manner as is now granted to the Canada Council, the National Arts Centre and the Canadian Broadcasting Corporation.

Obviously, in approaching the government with requests for annual appropriations – as all cultural agencies must – each organization must provide adequate explanations of its requests. But, as the Lambert Commission urged, the Treasury Board processes for the preparation of spending estimates should not be applied in such a way as to control the "policies and direction" of any of these agencies.

For the National Museums of Canada, the role of the board should again include the care and management of operations – a responsibility to be shared with the directors of the constituent museums and their advisory committees. This is of particular importance in the allocation of resources within the individual museums and in the development of their collections; restoration of the non-lapsing Special Purchase Account seems to us a minimal requirement. The Canadian Radio-television and Telecommunications Commission, National Library and Public Archives, on the other hand, can continue to operate satisfactorily with their departmental status, within the government regime of financial administration.

The care and management of an organization embraces personnel administration no less than financial management. To the extent that responsibility for the operation of an agency is assigned to a board, it must be accompanied by a corresponding degree of autonomy in such matters as staffing levels, classification of positions and hiring and firing.

As has been seen, the Canada Council, Canadian Broadcasting Corporation, Canadian Film Development Corporation and National Arts Centre already have this autonomy in all essential respects and, in the opinion of the Committee, this should continue. We are strengthened in this view by the fact that, for these agencies, most of the professional and managerial personnel develop their careers within the cultural sphere of society rather than within the public service, and this is as it should be. The goal of a unified public service, which plays so large a part in the centralized control of staffing matters, is simply not relevant to these organizations. The same consideration, in our view, applies to the National Film Board, which now requires Treasury Board approval of its staffing plans (in respect of its "continuing positions"), and we therefore conclude that the National Film Board should have the same autonomy in staffing matters as the other four agencies.

The Social Sciences and Humanities Research Council – which is now in much the same position as the National Film Board – differs from the others in the character of its personnel, most of whom are as much at home in the public service as in the academic world of their clientele. Given this fact, and the designation of the Council as a "separate employer" for purposes of the Public Service Employment Act and Public Service Staff Relations Act, the present staffing arrangements appear to pose no major difficulties. On the other hand, restraints imposed by the Treasury Board on staffing levels have forced the agency to modify its operating procedures in ways that may significantly impair their efficiency and effectiveness – at some slight gain in economy. We consider this to be incompatible with the board's responsibility for the care and management of the agency's affairs. The same may be said of the National Museums of Canada – with the added consideration that, for much of its professional and directing staff, this agency must employ people whose interests and careers lie outside the public service.

Apart from the general exercise of administrative controls in financial and personnel matters, government-wide requirements relating to specific matters may be imposed on the cultural agencies. This is now true of language policy under the Official Languages Act, and the draft Crown Corporations Act included conflict-of-interest provisions that were judged to be necessary and appropriate for all federal activities. It appears to us quite proper that cultural agencies should be subject to specific constraints of this kind, involving important issues of public policy clearly enunciated in parliamentary enactments.

There are instances, however, in which legislative measures adopted for unexceptionable reasons of public policy may affect the operations of particular agencies in ways that jeopardize other public interests to an extent outweighing the benefits conferred. For example, the extension of the Privacy provisions of the Human Rights Act to granting agencies such as the Canada Council and the Social Sciences and Humanities Research Council – which had been proposed in the draft Access to Information Act passed in July 1982 – would have seriously damaged the processes of peer adjudication on which the operations of such bodies depend. Granting agencies, while endorsing the principle of freer public access to government information, asked for, and received, exemption from the legislative provision that would have required them, on request, to divulge the names of assessors. The Committee commends the government's action in this matter. It confirms our view of the necessity, when such measures of general application are being considered, of assessing their impact on operations designed to serve cultural ends and weighing carefully the balance of public advantage wherever divergent public interests are found to exist.

Accountability Requirements
Immunity from ministerial direction and central administrative controls cannot absolve the cultural agencies of their accountability to Parliament and the public for the conduct of their operations. What the Lambert Commission had to say about government accountability applies with equal force to cultural agencies: that "the process of scrutiny, surveillance, public exposure, and debate helps to legitimize [their] actions...to the public."

For those agencies, such as the Canadian Radio-television and Telecommunications Commission or the National Library, which function like an ordinary department of government, no special measures are needed to ensure accountability. For the others, operating with the immunities we propose, the measures recommended by the Lambert Commission for Crown corporations seem to us to be generally appropriate. It should be the responsibility of the board of every agency to approve each year a corporate plan for the next three-to five-year period, which would serve both as a rationale for its annual request for an appropriation and, through the inclusion of its essential features in the annual report, as a basis for parliamentary and public scrutiny and discussion. Such corporate plans should not, however, require government approval, as contemplated in Bill C-123 of 1982.

Capital budgets, which for most of the cultural agencies are unnecessary, would continue (as now provided by the Financial Administration Act) to require approval by the government, as would any plans for capital borrowings (an even unlikelier occurrence). Operating budgets, however, although an annual responsibility of the boards, need be submitted to the government only in sufficient detail to provide an adequate explanation of appropriation requests, and should not require ministerial approval. The same should be true of manpower budgets.

Each board should be required to adopt bylaws governing the conduct of its activities, and all bylaws should be submitted to the designated minister for information. The Committee does not consider, however, that bylaws should require ratification by the Governor in Council, as was proposed in the Lambert Report and could be required by the government under Bill C-123. Boards must also develop and maintain adequate procedures for internal audit, and should establish an audit committee composed of external members of the board. For all these agencies external auditing should be conducted by the Auditor General, as is now the case.

Finally, the Committee endorses wholeheartedly the importance attached by the Lambert Commission to full disclosure through annual reports as a guarantee of accountability. In the words of the Lambert Report,

> "It should be through the quality and contents of the annual report that a board's performance is judged, both internally by Government and externally by Parliament and the public. In the end it is the persuasive power of disclosure and publicity that forces a responsible body to pay attention; and paying attention...is the attitude that a regime of accountability is designed to foster."

4. In recognition of the accountability of cultural agencies to Parliament and the Canadian public for the interpretation and execution of their respective mandates, each agency must develop appropriate measures for the disclosure of its plans and performance, including the preparation and publication each year of a corporate plan and an annual report which, in their form and content, will stimulate public interest and permit informed judgments.

Boards and Chief Executive Officers

The Lambert Commission also gave wise advice about the boards of directors of federal agencies. Quoting Thomas Macaulay's aphorism that the essence of responsible government is "to choose wisely and confide liberally," the Commissioners commented:

> "Although Government continues to espouse the corporate form of organization, it has sometimes been remiss in honouring Macaulay's dictum 'to choose wisely' and, in recent years, has more explicitly demonstrated a reluctance to 'confide liberally' by reasserting controls that countermand the original direct delegation of powers to its board of directors."

The two requirements are obviously related. To confide implies confidence, and without wise choice there can be no confidence. But to try to remedy defective choice by a curtailment of powers is simply to compound the initial error.

The selection of board members is clearly crucial in those cultural agencies which, in the view of this Committee, must be free of policy direction and administrative controls. What is required is that, for these agencies, the boards must bear most of the responsibility for defining the public interest which, in a departmental setting, would be borne by ministers. The board must therefore consist of persons who will be regarded, by ministers and members of Parliament and by the public at large, as qualified to act in lieu of political authority in prescribing policies and priorities and directing operations – especially when those operations venture into controversial realms of opinion or taste. As public trustees they must be alive to the forces to which political leaders are subject, but their overriding purposes must be cultural.

The record of the cultural agencies strongly suggests the need for some board members who have had direct experience of the kind of affairs with which the agency is involved and who are known and respected by their colleagues in the cultural world. We make reference to this in the section below on the Canada Council. But boards must be broadly based, with a decisive element drawn from other occupations, although members must have in each instance a demonstrated interest in cultural matters and community service. To ensure public confidence, all members must be persons of some standing within their geographic and occupational milieus.

In a general sense, boards are representative bodies – mini-parliaments, as the Canada Council was often characterized by one of its directors. Each must reflect, in the character of its membership, a balanced diversity – of place, language, sex, age, occupation – neither constant nor rigidly prescribed, but always needing to be weighed and adjusted as vacancies have to be filled. But members should not be regarded or regard themselves as delegates or spokesmen of particular interests or localities. If specialized expertise is needed, boards must look to others, within their staffs or in advisory bodies such as the Advisory Arts Panel of the Canada Council, or the advisory committees attached to the museums and National Gallery. If user interests are to be consulted, boards should turn to consultative committees like those proposed for particular interests or audiences in the broadcasting world.

We share the conclusion of the Lambert Commission that "the most potent instrument in the hands of the designated Minister or Governor in Council is the power to appoint and change boards." Regretfully, based on the record of the past and on submissions made to us across the country, we must also share their conclusion that this most potent instrument has not always been wisely used. Indeed, in the views of some intervenors, it has been grossly abused.

We hasten to add that most board members are able and conscientious, and many have made outstanding contributions. Given that on some boards they must serve without remuneration, their devotion to the public good at times verges on the heroic. But there have been too many instances in which political service in the ranks of the party faithful has seemed the dominant, if not the only, explanation of an appointment. Nor is it surprising that a number of those appointed with little record of cultural interests or of commitment to the purposes of the agencies take little active part in the work of their boards. Clearly, the use of board memberships as consolation prizes or status symbols not only impairs the competence of the boards, but also undermines public confidence and removes the prerequisite for the essential delegation of powers by government itself.

Not only must governments choose wisely; it is important that vacancies be filled with the least possible delay. There will, of course, be unexpected vacancies, for which the finding of good replacements may take time. But it has been a recurring complaint that even when terms of members have run their normal course, there have too often been persistent delays – of as much as a year and a half – before new appointments have been made. Not only does neglect of this kind weaken the direction of the agencies concerned, but it also suggests an attitude of indifference on the part of government that demeans the role and status of the boards.

The defects of past practice are more easily described than cured. No alternative method of constituting boards and filling vacancies suggests itself. If ministers are to repose the high degree of confidence in boards that seems to us essential, then ministers must retain the power of appointment. *This Committee can only urge, in the strongest terms possible, that this key ministerial function be discharged with due regard to the essential role and crucial importance of boards.*

Systematic consultation can be useful in broadening the range and strengthening the calibre of candidates to be considered. The cultural sphere has its own intricate and richly varied network of organizations that can be canvassed for suggestions – not as specific vacancies occur but on a continuing basis as a means of maintaining a roster of potential talent. And as vacancies are anticipated, the chairmen of the boards concerned should be consulted for their knowledge of the kinds of experience and competence of which their agencies are most in need. This is not to suggest that the boards themselves should be self-perpetuating. The final recommendation must be the minister's, and although he owes the normal courtesy of consultation to his political colleagues, his judgment should not be guided by political considerations, such as that which flows from parliamentary caucuses.

5.   Appointments to the boards of directors of cultural agencies should be made with an overriding concern for the appointees' experience in the fields of concern of the agency and their demonstrated broad-ranging interest in cultural matters. Attention should also be paid to ensuring that the boards as a whole are generally representative of Canadian society.

Like the Lambert Commission, we believe that chairmen of boards must bear a special responsibility for relations with the government and Parliament on matters such as the corporate plan of the agency and its record of operations as disclosed by annual reports, and they should serve as the formal link between the board and the designated minister. We subscribe, therefore, to the view that they should be appointed by the Governor in Council. There should be prior consultation with the board by the minister, and, as a general rule, the chairman should be selected from among incumbent or recent board members.

We further agree that, to ensure continuity in the direction of the cultural agencies, members of boards should be appointed for staggered terms of three years each, with the possibility of reappointment once. The provision in the draft Crown Corporations Act that would have limited initial terms to one year but allowed indefinite extensions thereafter seems to the Committee to be singularly devoid of merit. However, in the absence of any special circumstances requiring protected status – as in an adjudicative body such as the Canadian Radio-television and Telecommunications Commission – members should be removable by the Governor in Council at pleasure, in order to preserve the government's one essential power of controlling the composition of the boards.

The Committee also feels that members should not be required to serve without recompense for their time, as is now required of some boards. To expect this service – demanding as it often is, and in our view must be – to be rendered as a matter of public duty inevitably tends to limit the field of choice to people who are able to absent themselves from their regular pursuits with no loss of income. Given the diversity of backgrounds desirable within a board, any such limitation is to be avoided.

Finally, the Committee supports the view of the Lambert Commission concerning the chief executive officers of autonomous agencies:

"Just as we feel that the Government must use the instrument of appointment to control the composition of a board of directors and declare who shall be its chairman, so we believe that the board of directors should use the instrument of appointment of the chief executive officer to manifest its responsibility for the care and management of the corporation."

Only in the National Arts Centre is this now the case. Among the other agencies the existing requirement varies: the executive director of the Canadian Film Development Corporation is appointed by the government "on the recommendation of the board," the director and associate director of the Canada Council and the Secretary General of the National Museums of Canada are appointed by order-in-council with no provision for participation by the board, and in the Canadian Broadcasting Corporation and Social Sciences and Humanities Research Council, the offices of chairman and chief executive officer are merged, with the selection vested in the government.

The Committee strongly endorses the opinion of the Lambert Commission that the offices of chairman and chief executive officer be clearly distinguished, and that the selection of the latter be entrusted to the board in recognition of the board's responsibility for the care and management of the agency and also to forestall any confusion about the accountability of the executive officer. We further concur in the Commission's recommendation that the remuneration of the chief executive officer be fixed by the board within a range approved by the Governor in Council.

6.   Chairmen of boards of cultural agencies should be appointed by the Governor in Council, after consultation with the board, to ensure an effective working link with the government and Parliament. Chief executive officers should be appointed by agency boards, or at the very least appointed on their recommendation, as witness to the responsibility of the boards for agency care and management.

Ministerial Coordination
Even without powers of policy direction and administrative control over cultural agencies, ministers still bear major responsibilities in cultural matters. In relation to the autonomous agencies, as has been seen, the crucial tasks of defining jurisdictions, allocating resources and appointing board members must rest with ministers. In addition, ministers will continue to bear a wide range of program responsibilities that, either directly or incidentally, affect cultural development. Some of these – such as the direction of the National Library or of much of the Cultural Initiatives Program of the Department of Communications – involve activities directed to essentially cultural purposes but in which the nature of the cultural impact is not such as to require or justify insulation from the political process. In other instances, programs directed to the needs of particular populations include, within a wider

context, a strong cultural component – such as the programs responding to the needs of Native peoples. Finally, there is the wide variety of policies and programs of incidental but often crucial importance to cultural activity, such as taxation policies or industrial assistance measures.

The existence of this extensive and varied assortment of government activities affecting cultural life raises the question of whether one minister should be responsible for the coordination of all cultural matters: serving as the designated minister for all cultural agencies; housing within his or her department all government operations directed to cultural ends, other than those that are incidental to wider concerns such as Native peoples' affairs or industrial development; and monitoring the impact on cultural life of government activities generally. In effect, the assignment of ministerial responsibilities in the federal government over the past 20 years has evolved in this direction, to the point where, in the opinion of many, all that is lacking now is the formal designation of the responsible minister – now the Minister of Communications, and formerly the Secretary of State – as Minister of Culture.

It is evident, however, from representations made to the Committee from across the country, that there are mixed feelings about the concentration of all responsibility for cultural matters in the hands of a single minister. In one view, it is a mistake to conceive of all the cultural activities of government as being so interconnected as to require unified direction or even overseeing. At any given moment, the problems and needs of, for example, writing and publishing, are likely to be quite different from and unrelated to those of the performing arts, or museums, or historic sites and parks. Even within a single cultural sector the fact that, for example, both the Canada Council and Canadian Broadcasting Corporation are major instruments in sustaining the performing arts, requires little coordination of their activities. There may be utility – as we trust there will be – in periodic inquiries like that entrusted to this Committee, or to its predecessor, the Massey-Lévesque Commission 30 years ago. But it is argued that such comprehensive approaches are needed only as periodic stock-takings. For the day-to-day (or year-to-year) development of federal policies and programs, all that is required is that there be organizations within the machinery of government that are sensitive to the evolving concerns and needs of each part of the cultural life of the country, and are empowered to take such action as is appropriate to the federal government – each organization having its specific responsibilities.

The experience of the Committee bears out this view – to an extent. (We resist the temptation, to which some other commissions have succumbed, of recommending the creation of machinery to perpetuate, as a continuing activity, the task with which we have been charged.) But we are nonetheless persuaded that there is value in having one minister preeminently concerned with cultural matters. This minister would not devise a unified cultural policy or direct all cultural programs, but rather would serve as a central reference point and a channel to cabinet colleagues to ensure that cultural considerations and the views of the cultural community and of cultural agencies are given due attention in the formulation and execution of all policies having significant cultural implications. This would be a minister *for* culture, rather than a minister *of* culture. And in recognition of the fact that these responsibilities include only marginally the direction and control of policies and programs – which are the normal distinguishing marks of the ministerial role – it seems to us inappropriate that they should be the sole or even the principal concern of the minister's portfolio.

In this latter conclusion we reflect, in some measure, several apprehensions that were expressed to the Committee about the idea of a cultural ministry. One of these concerns the need to guard against the undue subordination of cultural aims to other government purposes. The fact that ministerial functions tend increasingly to be exercised collectively means that, in relation to their respective portfolios, ministers cannot be – and should not be – expected to serve as single-minded champions of the interests with which they deal. As was noted before, they are increasingly preoccupied with ensuring that the policies and programs under their supervision reflect *all* the objectives and concerns of the government. We would emphasize, however, that the primary safeguard of cultural values and purposes is to be found in our recommendation that those cultural activities most vulnerable to the intrusion of noncultural objectives be confided to boards of trustees insulated from political direction and entrusted with the full care and management of operations.

A further concern is that because a minister exercises greater control over departmental operations, he or she will be tempted – and encouraged by departmental officials – to distort the allocation of resources in their favour and to extend them into areas that are more appropriate to the autonomous agencies. Associated with this is the apprehension that a cultural ministry will tend to develop a large bureaucracy which, while lacking the direct experience acquired by the agencies of the conditions and needs of cultural activity throughout the country will, because of its relationship with the minister, exercise a disproportionate influence on government policies, priorities and programs.

That these apprehensions are widely shared is clear from statements made to the Committee in briefs and at our public hearings. It should, moreover, be clear that the Committee agrees that the jurisdiction of the agencies should be protected against departmental encroachment, that the resources necessary to their tasks should not be diverted to other channels more susceptible to political direction and control, and that the agencies' experience and understanding of cultural needs should carry due weight in the development of cultural policies and programs. But no juggling of organizational forms and relationships can effectively ensure that these conditions are maintained. The inescapable reality remains that the role and status appropriate to cultural agencies depends, in the last analysis, on ministerial and parliamentary acceptance, of which the best guarantee is a productive, spontaneous and confident cultural life permeating society.

7.   The Government of Canada should include in the portfolio
      of the minister responsible for the cultural agencies a man-
      date to act as a central reference point in cabinet for
      cultural matters – in effect, an advocate before government
      on behalf of the arts and culture community. This mandate
      would leave with cultural agencies and other departments
      – particularly the Department of the Secretary of State –
      the responsibility for developing cultural policies and pro-
      grams within their respective areas of concern.

Department of Communications

The mandate suggested in Recommendation 7 for the minister responsible
for the cultural agencies implies certain functions for the minister's department. If the minister is to be an effective advocate for the arts and culture
within government, departmental officials must provide him or her with
sound and well-informed counsel on broad cultural policy objectives. One
function clearly not implied by the mandate is the design and administration
of programs requiring specific value judgments and consequent funding of artistic and cultural achievement. Nevertheless, when an Arts and Culture
Branch was formed within the Department of the Secretary of State in 1972
(the branch having been transferred along with ministerial responsibility for
the cultural agencies to the Department of Communications in July 1980), a
process began of building up within the department a staff whose interests
sometimes tended to duplicate those in the cultural agencies. That process
has prompted the concern, stated above, over the inherent departmental
tendency to regard the department itself as the appropriate vehicle for
delivery of new forms of cultural funding.

We acknowledge the fact that some cultural programs may be more
suitably placed within the department than within any of the existing agencies, such as programs providing assistance with capital projects or
disseminating the results of cultural research. But by delineating, earlier in
this chapter, the essence of the arm's-length relationship of cultural agencies
to the political process and therefore to the department itself, we have explained the reasons why programs to benefit the cultural and artistic life of
society should be confided in normal practice to the relevant agency. This is
hardly an idea original to our Committee, but is a tradition which we believe
has so great a value that it should be sustained and protected.

*Only if a funding program is manifestly inappropriate for any cultural
agency to undertake, and is sufficiently impervious to being subjugated to
political ends, should it be undertaken by the department. And even then,
the department should assume the program only after consulting fully with
the agency(ies) concerned, in order to take advantage of their professional
expertise and contacts and to clarify respective program roles.*

*For cultural policy purposes, the department's chief function resides in
providing an environment in which Canada's cultural life and the federal
cultural agencies themselves may best flourish.*

This is a responsibility whose significance extends far beyond the more specific influence exercised by any particular agency. We see this departmental responsibility being exercised through cabinet advocacy, as described in Recommendation 7, but additionally in three broad and important ways, through:

- regular consultation with the arts and culture communities and with other levels of government, ensuring that lines of communication are kept open in order to bring to bear on cultural policy development the broadest possible range of informed concerns;
- development and maintenance of a vigorous program of cultural research;
- exploitation on behalf of artists of the department's expertise in new communications technology.

In pursuing the first of these three functions, the minister and departmental officials have immediately available a major resource of knowledgable advice in the cultural agencies themselves. Through the exercise of wise choice in agency board appointments, the minister can be assured of receiving the commensurate degree of insight required in the weighing of cultural policy alternatives. Beyond the agencies, however, the minister has the broader constituency of the arts and culture communities throughout the land. A continuous flow of information and advice to and from these communities, on the part of both the cultural agencies and the department, is essential to the development of cultural policies and programs that genuinely serve the needs of society.

In sustaining that flow of information and advice, a special role is played by the many national and regional service organizations in the area of arts and culture. These organizations, ranging from trade and professional associations of artists and cultural producers to more general umbrella organizations, can be highly effective liaison and advocacy bodies on whom the minister and departmental officials should rely for experienced opinion.

For service organizations related to particular disciplines and operating with true representativeness and effectiveness on behalf of their members, federal funding should be assumed or maintained by the cultural agency in the best position to judge the quality of the organization's work. For umbrella organizations representing diverse disciplines and activities, such as the Canadian Conference of the Arts, assistance commensurate with performance should be continued by the department.

The existence of effective service organizations at both the disciplinary and general level is essential, in the Committee's view, and can greatly enlarge and improve the value of the advice available to the minister.

Two-way communication need not and should not be restricted by the department to the cultural agencies and service organizations. During our public hearings it became amply clear that many Canadians were dissatisfied with their ability to obtain either information or an adequate hearing on cultural matters of concern to them. When the Department of the Secretary of State had responsibility for the Arts and Culture Branch, its regional offices performed a valuable service in fostering liaison with local citizens and cultural groups. Now that the responsibility resides with the Department of Communications, *we urge that department to use its existing network of regional offices not only to implement technical functions in the communications sphere, but also to serve the equally pressing information needs of culture and the arts.* A department specializing in the development of the latest technological means of communication will assuredly be able to fill this communications gap.

On a more formal and political plane, there is a constant need for consultation on cultural matters among federal, provincial and municipal authorities, a need that grows year by year as provincial and municipal governments step up their cultural programs. In addition to the talks held each year by ministers responsible for culture and heritage, a group known as the Assembly of Arts Administrators brings together provincial and federal cultural officials to discuss mutual concerns and exchange information. We are also aware of the effectiveness of working consultations that sometimes occur between staff of cultural departments and agencies of all three levels of government, and we feel encouraged by the prospects for improved intergovernment dialogue emerging from the West with the establishment of the Tri-Level Arts Liaison Group in British Columbia in 1977, followed by formation of a similar group in Alberta in 1980. The Committee warmly commends these types of initiatives, bringing together as they do all levels of government, private foundations and the business community to promote informal discussion and information exchange on issues in the arts. While we recognize that the Department of Communications cannot alone represent the federal government in such consultations, and we acknowledge the impossibility of uniform and binding federal positions because of the cultural agencies' autonomy, nevertheless we urge the department to encourage and even to coordinate the consultation process.

In the conduct of cultural research, too, the department plays an important coordinating role. By cultural research, we mean development of a knowledge base about arts and culture activities in Canada – not research into artistic or cultural material, which is usually carried out by scholars and critics, often with the financial support of the Social Sciences and Humanities Research Council.

The Cultural Statistics Program is currently operated by Statistics Canada in close cooperation with the Department of Communications. The key elements in this program are timeliness, reliability and comprehensiveness. Data must be collected and published on a regular cycle, soon enough after the time period studied to be relevant and useful; the form and content of data must provide an accurate reflection of the field under study and be generally accepted as such; and the various sectors of arts and culture must be comprehensively covered, requiring the program to be extended to sectors not yet served. The department has the responsibility for ensuring that these conditions are met and that the data are monitored and interpreted knowledgably, a task in which the involvement of the cultural community is essential if the community is to be served well. The Committee is pleased to note that such consultation is increasing.

Both the department's research and statistics directorate and its policy sector conduct their own research studies, the latter in the area of broadcasting and electronic communications. These departmental research units should increase the amount of research by independent outside researchers, in order to fill information gaps and to keep open a variety of information sources. Wide-ranging research, resulting in reliable information, is essential to successful policy development in the arts and culture as in any other area. Equally essential is that the information be widely and effectively disseminated to those who need it.

Over the past 10 years, a base has been laid for collecting and interpreting cultural statistics. This important work must continue in order to bring this service to the necessary level of effectiveness. We believe that Statistics Canada should continue to assume responsibility for the collection of cultural statistics as an essential part of its ongoing program and to allocate the required funds for this activity from its own appropriations. In order to confirm the needs and priorities of the program, full consultation should be established with government departments, agencies and the cultural community, all of which have a great need for reliable statistics in determining their own policies.

We also consider it essential that the attendant analysis and research be conducted by the Department of Communications as a service integral to its policy development process. Similarly, most agencies must interpret and analyze aspects of their fields in their own way, whether through their own research departments or through outside contracts or commissions. The cultural agencies should therefore expand their research activities, and ensure that the Statistics Canada program serves their needs and those of their clients.

There is an additional contribution that the department is in a unique position to make to cultural and artistic life. When responsibility for cultural affairs was transferred to the department also responsible for telecommunications and broadcasting, it was felt, correctly in our view, that communications technology should no longer be allowed to develop in isolation from the cultural implications of its use. The evolution of what is called "hardware" – such as Telidon, satellite technology and computerized office equipment – should be able to benefit from a close working association with people in all cultural fields, and the attitudes, insights, principles and policies that guide their work. Since the transfer of responsibilities was made in 1980, it is our estimation that only a modest beginning has been made in encouraging a meaningful interaction between the arts and the communications wings of the department. It is our hope that a greater emphasis will be placed on the need to realize in organizational, personnel and policy terms the hoped-for benefits that motivated the move in the first place. The 1981-82 annual report of the Communications Research Advisory Board, which advises on the research program of the department, made just such a recommendation, stressing that the availability of appropriate content is critical to the acceptance of the new communications technologies and the two must evolve together.

The very real shortage of "software," the creative output on which this Report centres, presents Canada with an opportunity that may not reappear for decades. In this Report, we are expressing the view that our country is blessed with an abundant potential for creative work that needs to be realized and exploited. Canada has been a world leader in developing communications technologies. These affect our culture in ways that are at the same time frightening and invigorating. What we have not done in Canada is promote the use of this technology by creative people at the same rate as we have developed the hardware.

We in Canada must grasp this opportunity. The product emerging from our communications laboratories in government centres and what have become glamorous "high-tech" industries must be understood and used by individual artists, producers and performing arts companies. We know about the exciting work of our musicians and video artists, supported in many instances by the Canada Council, in seizing on the possibilities of the new technology and producing works of world standard. We would like to see this activity continued. *But we also see a vital, stimulative role for the Department of Communications in the high-technology field, and would encourage development of an arts and technology program within the department. The objectives should be the promotion and funding of research and experimentation, and the provision of access to research results and the hardware itself to artists across the country.*

There exist additional functions within the department in the administration of lottery funds for cultural purposes and the subsidized postal rates for mail of a cultural nature, but these will be addressed, respectively, in Chapter 3, "Marshalling Resources," and Chapter 7, "Writing, Publishing and Reading."

8.   A primary function of the federal department housing the Arts and Culture Branch is to assist in providing the environment in which cultural life may flourish and the cultural agencies may best achieve their purposes. In the course of advising the minister on broad cultural policy directions, departmental officials should pursue this primary function by fostering communication and consultation, providing an accurate knowledge base for cultural activities, and assisting artists and cultural groups to make the fullest use of appropriate technologies.

The Canada Council

The Canada Council will be discussed in many chapters of this Report, since its funding policies and programs play such an important role in different aspects of our cultural life. But precisely because the Council has had such a multifaceted and pervasive influence, it requires a more general discussion here. Not only does the Council's mandate cut across many arts disciplinary lines, it also embraces the primary producer (the central concern of this Report), the individual creative artist. The Council's mandate is therefore a uniquely sensitive and fundamental one, and certain principles about its operations must be understood.

The Council was founded 25 years ago from the time of writing, as a result of a major recommendation of the Massey-Lévesque Commission. Its programs provided support for artists, arts organizations and scholars in the broad fields of the arts, the humanities and the social sciences. In 1978, in line with the government's decision to rationalize funding for research activities, the humanities and social sciences division was split off from the Council and a new agency, the Social Sciences and Humanities Research Council, was formed, leaving the Canada Council to concentrate entirely on support of the arts.

In the past 25 years, the Canada Council has experienced dramatic growth parallel to the growth of the arts themselves. When considering this period in the arts in Canada, it is important to remember that the Council did not *make* the artistic explosion of the period happen. The energy, creativity and talent of artists, as well as what the Massey-Lévesque Report termed the "prevailing hunger" for what they could give, were out there in the land, and much fine work was already being done. But the Council served as a catalyst and an enabler, and in that supporting role it served well.

Perhaps the main reason why the Council did serve well is that from the beginning it consistently sought the advice and guidance of the arts community, and has maintained close contact with that community through its system of juries and panels and through hundreds of individual assessors. In addition, the Council was (and still is) staffed by individuals with a knowledge and understanding of the arts and artists. It has been able to attract many of its staff from among practitioners in the arts, who normally return to their own fields after a stint at the Council. The movement of people between arts production and arts support can only be stimulating and useful to both sides, and we encourage the Council to maintain this practice.

The crucial matter of budget allocations among the various artistic disciplines is a matter for decision by the Council itself, advised by members of the staff. These, in turn, draw on the advice and guidance of the Advisory Arts Panel (composed of practising artists, writers, teachers, artistic directors, arts administrators and others), their contacts in the arts community, and their own experience. The specific granting decisions within each section's programs are also made by the Council, acting on the advice of the staff. Applications for grants are adjudicated by panels or juries of specialists in each discipline or by individual assessors. Final decisions rest with the Council itself, as the organization's supreme governing body.

These carefully worked out decision-making procedures, with their system of checks and balances, are an attempt to ensure that the governing principle in awarding grants remains the excellence of the project or artistic activity. This system derives from, and is central to, the Council's statutory power to make its own program policy and granting decisions, and represents the essence of the arm's-length relationship between the Council and government.

Much was said to us during our public hearings about the merits and failings of the Canada Council's jury system in awarding individual artists' grants. Although there appeared to be among our intervenors substantial majority support for the system, we heard a number of recurring criticisms about the way in which it is administered. It must be acknowledged that most of these criticisms originated in the field of the visual arts (see Chapter 5), although professionals in other disciplines also made suggestions for improvement.

We have concluded that the jury adjudication system can serve the arts and artists as well as, if not better than, any other system of awarding individual artists' grants. It is essential to the fairness and credibility of the process that its integrity be maintained and be seen to be maintained, and to this end we urge the Council to take all reasonable care in its selection of juries. In particular:

- There should be fair and adequate representation of artistic background and philosophy, region, sex and age among members of juries.
- A very large pool of qualified jurors should be drawn upon, representing a wide range of knowledgable people, and membership should be rotated frequently so that no individuals or representatives of specific groups may exercise undue or prolonged influence on jury decisions.

We understand that the Council does attempt to follow these principles. But they are worth stating here because they are so crucial in maintaining the credibility of the system. Juried competitions in which there are a limited number of grants available will inevitably produce more disappointed candidates than successful ones; a certain amount of disillusionment with the system is therefore unavoidable. We feel that the results of jury adjudications will be more widely accepted if Canadians have faith in the integrity of the process and of the people operating it. The Council could therefore do more to explain its adjudication process both to the arts community and to the public.

Closely related to this concern is the need for regular and effective communication and consultation by the Council with the arts and culture community and the public. Given the ability to communicate with increasing ease and efficiency, with electronic tools at hand that can provide a quick and effective flow of information from one part of Canada to the other, we believe that the Council would be wise to forego its longstanding plan to develop its own regional office network. Canada Council officers travel a great deal, as they must, and the jury and advisory units fundamental to the operation of the Council also provide a basis of understanding the needs and issues specific to various parts of the country. Direct contacts between clients and the Council's officers and decision-makers are an essential part of the operation in any case. But in addition to these modes of communication, the Committee encourages the Council itself to undertake periodic public hearings in various parts of the country to strengthen its contacts with its constituency. Furthermore, in our preceding section on the Department of Communications we recommended a greatly strengthened arts and culture component within the department's regional and district office network, and it seems to us that this network could serve the Council effectively, by providing the interested public with the Council's publications and information brochures and by passing on queries to the relevant Council personnel.

Community arts support is another area in which we believe the Council must become more committed and active, extending its responsibilities to nonprofessional arts activities of quality and local or regional importance. We have frequently heard the argument that the Canada Council must not weaken its position on "excellence" as a criterion for arts support, and that a large, differently oriented staff would be required to handle the vast clientele involved in community arts. We have no desire to see the Council's concern for the highest possible standards compromised in any way. At the same time, we cannot see how the Council can continue to give such low priority to community arts activity in theatre, visual arts or music-making at all levels when it devises its policies for particular arts disciplines. In addition, it has been made clear to us that professional artists can develop valuable and productive relationships, to say nothing of sources of revenue, through working with and for such groups. *The Canada Council should therefore build up a carefully prescribed program of assistance to enable community arts organizations to employ arts professionals, with the objective of enhancing the quality of community arts work and public enjoyment of the arts generally.* The elements of the kinds of support activities we have in mind are already in place at the Council in programs such as Explorations, and these should be extended and made more generally applicable.

Clearly an expansion of the Council's activities, such as those we propose in the succeeding chapters of this Report, would require an increase in the Council's annual parliamentary appropriation. Such an increase is required in any case, merely to allow the Council to continue the crucial work that it has been doing. In spite of its record of achievement, the Council has been perceived by the artistic community for the past several years as being in a state of crisis. And if the Council is in crisis, it follows inevitably that the arts in Canada must be in a similar condition. The central problem was summarized for us in the Council's brief to the Committee:

"Today the Council finds itself faced with an increasingly eroded field of clients and potential clients, with the growing expectations of both artists and audiences, with double-digit inflation and an effectively shrinking budget. With the erosion of the spending power of our funds, we have been forced to forego supporting new ventures and new initiatives. Survival, rather than achievement, is becoming the order of the day."

In the realm of the arts, the consequences of such a situation are far more calamitous than a little enforced belt-tightening. In order to flourish, the arts require daring, experimentation, risk. But because of several years of budgetary restraints and even cutbacks at the Council, "support to new companies, to younger artists, to those inventive spirits on the frontiers of art, is simply not possible unless we rob Peter to sponsor Paul," to quote the Council's brief again.

The Council was correct in terming its parliamentary appropriation over the five years 1975-76 to 1980-81 "a sustained diminuendo." The value of the appropriation in real economic terms fell by an average of 2.1 per cent a year. Indeed, the Council estimated that its budget would have required an additional $13.3 million in 1980-81 dollars merely to have kept pace with inflation during that period. The consequences for artists and arts organizations that have been sustained by the Council – theatres, orchestras, dance companies, galleries, publishers – can be imagined, and will be described in the chapters that follow.

The consequences to others are at least as great. When funds are scarce, sustaining the established operations becomes a priority; we dare not lose our arts organizations of quality and experience. As a result, the new, the emerging, the experimental – in fact the future – must wait in the wings until funds are once more available in sufficient quantity to enable their appeals to be considered, too. We cannot deny ourselves that future. Although there are indeed other channels within the federal government offering support to arts programs and cultural activities, only the Canada Council among federal agencies is concerned with sustaining top-level arts organizations and encouraging the emerging or established individual artist. The Council's funds should not be allowed to be eroded to the point where it is no longer able to fulfil its responsibilities to the country as a whole.

9.   The federal government should regard the Canada Council as a primary instrument of support to the arts. Accordingly, it should augment the Council's annual parliamentary appropriation, having regard for the real, as distinct from the nominal, value of the Council's grants and sustaining support and for the consequences that will follow if the real value of that support is allowed to diminish.

Parliamentary appropriations must be of a magnitude that will permit new initiatives, both inside and outside the Council's current areas of support, to be developed and sustained.

The Implications of Federalism

The federal government is not, of course, alone among Canadian governments in concerning itself with the support of culture. Provinces and municipalities have been similarly involved – in the operation of libraries, archives, museums, and in the encouragement of the visual, applied and performing arts, of writing and publishing, and of the newer cultural industries. All provinces have vigorous ministries for culture or the arts and four (Newfoundland, Ontario, Manitoba and Saskatchewan) also have arts councils similar to the Canada Council. The Saskatchewan Arts Board was Canada's first. The provincially based systems of public schooling provide the primary channels for cultural transmission to the young, and provincial and local education authorities give varying degrees of training in and for the arts.

It was not part of the task of this Committee to examine the cultural policies and programs of these other jurisdictions, although in the course of our hearings across the country we were able to meet, either publicly or privately, with many ministers and provincial officials involved. But no examination of federal cultural policy would be complete without giving some attention to the implications of the concurrent activities of the other governments.

In the representations made to us, in briefs and at public hearings, relatively little was said about federal-provincial questions of jurisdiction. The dominant mood, in fact, was one of impatience – amounting at times to exasperation – arising from the sense that pleas of lack of jurisdiction were being used by one or another government to justify inactivity in the face of urgent needs, or that confusion was being caused by the failure of authorities in the various levels of government to consult one another and to harmonize their activities.

The views of this Committee on the role of government in cultural matters have, we believe, important implications for the relationships among governments on such matters in the Canadian federal system. If cultural life is to be autonomous and self-directed, it is important that it not become excessively dependent on one source of support – and especially on one governmental source. For this reason alone we welcome the support of all governments – federal, provincial and municipal – to cultural activity, and would wish, in fact, that all might increase their exertions in this direction.

But there is, we believe, an even more compelling reason why it is both unnecessary and inappropriate to differentiate the roles of the different levels of government with the aim of endowing each or any of them with exclusive powers. What has been said about the need for federal activity in support of culture to be directed to cultural purposes applies with equal force to comparable activities on the part of all other governments. And as long as this imperative is respected by all, there should be little sense of rivalry among them. When jurisdictional conflicts erupt over cultural matters, the inference may be drawn that one or both of the contending parties is bent on using cultural programs for political ends and finds its ambitions thwarted by the other. The effect of this can only be to politicize the support of culture by all governments.

Only in one matter among all the aspects of cultural policy that we have examined do we find concurrent activity unacceptable: namely, in the exercise of regulatory powers, especially over broadcasting. Only if there is a single regulatory authority will it be possible to sustain and expand Canadian production of high quality that will serve the widest possible range of interests and tastes and provide the greatest access by Canadian talent in all parts of the country to its potential audiences. As will be seen in Chapter 10, "Broadcasting," we consider that this need is, if anything, reinforced by the dramatic technological developments, actual and prospective, in the delivery of visual images to Canadian homes.

Regulatory functions of this kind are, however, a special case. In the general support of culture there is ample room – and need – for all levels of government.

Inevitably, the cultural activities of each actor in the federal system will impinge on those of others. In some situations, such as the development of countrywide library and archival systems, and the preservation and public enjoyment of heritage resources generally, there will be elements of interdependence among the various public agencies involved at different levels of government. And as patrons of the contemporary arts, authorities within each jurisdiction are likely, in the very nature of things, to pursue their own distinctive courses – reflected in their ranking of priorities and choices of criteria. Confronted by this multiplicity of public patrons, each applying its own standards and conditions, cultural organizations may well experience a certain confusion and frustration at times.

This is not, however, an argument for the concerting of all public programs in a single countrywide "system" of patronage. The fact that agencies at different levels develop their programs within different cultural perspectives is, in our view, not only necessary but desirable, and we must caution against an undue preoccupation with intergovernmental coordination.

The essential need is for a willingness to consult, coupled with a free flow of information among public authorities within different jurisdictions. It is our clear impression, in fact, that most cultural agencies and offices need little urging in this direction and sense a strong community of interest with their counterparts in other levels of government – and, for that matter, with those in the private sector who are deeply involved in the support of cultural activity. Certainly we have found this to be generally true of the Canada Council, the National Library and the Public Archives, and we would expect the establishment of a Canadian Heritage Council, which we propose in Chapter 4, to improve relationships within the museum community.

As we noted above in the section on the Department of Communications, federal and provincial ministers responsible for cultural affairs, and their respective departmental officials, will continue to be involved in this consultative process. But it follows from our general view of the role of governments in the support of culture that cultural affairs need never be a contentious item in the agendas of federal-provincial ministerial conferences.

3
Marshalling Resources: The Political Economy of Culture

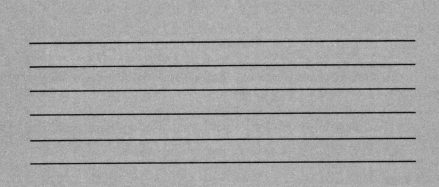

3

Marshalling Resources: The Political Economy of Culture

All cultural pursuits use resources in the broad sense of that term, which embraces not only those goods and services that accountants deal with, but also human talent, knowledge, skills, energy and time. For much of our cultural activity, the principal requirement may be only the leisure time of those taking part – itself a scarce resource, although less scarce than it used to be. Increasingly, however, cultural pursuits require resources that must be paid for: buildings, equipment, supplies, and the efforts of artists, producers and distributors. Wherever the Committee went, we were told – by the artists, producers and distributors, it is true, but also by those who watch and listen and read, or devote their leisure time to more active roles – that the resources available in Canada were inadequate or misdirected or both.

Many of the findings and recommendations throughout this Report have to do, by implication at least, with just such matters. But it seems to us useful to consider in a general way the role of the federal government in influencing the flow of resources to culture. Why does the government intervene? How much can – or should – it do? At what points in the complex sphere of cultural activity should its assistance be brought to bear? And what forms should its intervention take?

It is not at all clear from the national accounts how much of the Gross National Expenditure is devoted to cultural activity. Even the classification of activity under this heading is far from precise. But estimates of total recorded cultural expenditures in Canada (excluding formal education) for the current year range from $7 billion to $9 billion – upwards of $300 for each man, woman and child in the country.

That the federal government is already deeply involved is abundantly clear from the public record. Federal expenditures on cultural activities in 1981-82, according to the official Estimates, totaled some $1.2 billion. This means that direct federal expenditures account for about one-sixth of all the resources devoted to culture. In addition to this, through provisions in the tax laws, the government encourages Canadians and Canadian organizations to make gifts to or investments in cultural undertakings, by offering tax reductions as a partial offset against the amounts given or invested. When governments forego tax revenues by such devices, they must raise compensating sums in other ways; hence the expression "tax expenditures," to indicate that such incentives involve a charge on the public purse and consequently on all taxpayers.

The Case for Public Action

Because the allocation of resources is the stuff of economics, it is scarcely surprising that those who champion government activity in support of culture tend to couch their arguments in economic terms – or, all too often, in what they mistakenly imagine to be economic terms. There is, in fact, a wide measure of agreement among economists on a number of economic justifications for government intervention to increase the flow of resources to cultural activity. But before considering these, it is necessary to dispose of certain fallacies that masquerade as economic arguments and which, despite their invalidity, are so persistent and widespread that they cannot be ignored.

Government, it is said, is justified in increasing the flow of resources to culture in order to create employment, to improve the balance of payments, to enlarge Gross National Expenditure – or even, because of the taxable cash flows generated, as an ingenious way of increasing tax revenues. Since the inescapable inference is never drawn that cultural expenditures should be curtailed when there is full employment or a favourable balance of payments, there is an attractive plausibility to these arguments (although the frequent assertion that a given expenditure will be *exceeded* by the consequent tax yield might be expected to strain the bounds of human credulity). Money spent on culture clearly can create employment; it can result in Canadian goods and services that will displace imported goods and services; and as the money works its way through the economy, it will be reflected in Gross National Expenditure and generate tax revenues. What is overlooked, however, is that when resources are applied in one direction they cannot be applied in others which might have yielded even greater benefits to employment, the balance of payments, and productivity.

In both Chapters 1 and 2, we have emphasized the need for government activities in support of culture to be directed first and foremost to cultural purposes. In the same vein, we must conclude that although employment, economic growth and the balance of payments are inescapably the concern of government, they are most appropriately pursued by such measures as fiscal, monetary and commercial policies, and that whatever effects cultural programs may have on them are necessarily incidental.

The Market, and the Measure of Cultural Benefits

The arguments advanced by economists for government intervention in support of cultural activity all relate to the failure of the market to function properly – the "market" being the shorthand expression for the sum of the multitude of individual transactions which govern both the allocation of resources to the production of goods and services, and the distribution of those goods and services throughout society. In effect, the market works by a matching of supply and demand – a balancing of costs, in terms of the resources employed, against the benefits enjoyed from the resulting goods and services. If the costs of some activity are not fully reflected in the market (and environmental costs are a case in point) too many resources will flow into that activity, and the incomes of producers will be correspondingly inflated. If, on the other hand, the market fails to register the full benefits conferred by an activity, the latter will be denied its proper share of resources and the incomes associated with it will be curtailed. The principal economic justifications for government intervention in support of cultural activity involve market "failures" of the latter sort.

One form of this failure can be readily understood by recognizing the longevity of cultural products, which sets them apart from other human creations. Most wants and needs are met by goods that are produced and consumed within a brief span of years or even days – our food, our clothing, our gadgetry, even most of our structures. Only when we ascribe cultural values to them – as expressions of a pattern of living and thinking characteristic of their own particular time and place – do we take steps to preserve human artifacts of this sort. In this way we make cultural objects of every conceivable product of the human mind and human hands: neolithic weapons, Viking ships, Chippendale chairs or the Great Wall of China. But cultural products have this quality – or at least aspire to it – from the moment of their inception, whether they be a Parthenon or a Taj Mahal, the speculations of the pre-Socratics or the analects of Confucius, Kabuki theatre or the plays of Shakespeare.

The market cannot reflect such lasting benefits. To the writer, the composer, the painter or the scholar, the market presents a demand that reflects, at best, only the benefits to his or her own generation. Yet each generation must not only preserve and pass on all that is significant in its own cultural inheritance, but must also add to that stock new elements of its own creation, for which the demand of its own time may be small but from which large future benefits may flow. In a sense, then, it is the crucial function of the patron of culture – whether a Medici or a Canada Council – to serve as agent on behalf of the future, a surrogate for later generations.

Other instances of failure by the market to reflect the demand for cultural products in its entirety have been identified by economists. There may be uncertainty on the part of many people about whether they will be able to avail themselves of a cultural event. But if there is a widespread desire nonetheless to possess the option of doing so, even at some cost, intervention from beyond the market may be needed to allocate enough resources, reflecting that latent demand, to make the event possible. In other cases the market may fail because the cultural creations in question – like the fountains of Rome or the spires of Oxford – are so freely accessible to any who may find pleasure in them that the market can never recover the cost of their creation from those who benefit. In these circumstances, the market may register little demand – reflecting little of the actual benefits in terms of public satisfaction – and, in the absence of intervention to remedy this fault, will allot too few resources to any such cultural purposes.

As a logical argument for government intervention to increase the flow of resources to cultural activity, the catalogue of market failures is persuasive. But it leaves unanswered at least two important questions. How much is needed to remedy these failures? And where should the additional resources be directed? The market is in fact the only mechanism available for measuring demand in terms that can be translated into quantities of resources, and when the market fails we can only guess at the scale of the remedies required. For the same reason, because the market fails to register benefits and no alternative means of measuring them are available, attempts at cost/benefit analysis are bound to fail. Only a judgment that is both intuitive and prophetic will serve. Comparable difficulties are encountered in deciding which new cultural products will prove of lasting benefit or excite a latent demand, and which will prove abortive or ephemeral. The fate of most cultural creations, whether aesthetic or intellectual, has been quite properly the dustbin of history – or, at best, a kind of cultural compost heap. But there is no calculus or empirical test to tell us where the promise lies. In the end, the economists can tell us only that an act of faith – and judgment – is required.

Cultural Activity as "Merit Goods"
Several other classes of economic arguments in support of government intervention in cultural activity deserve notice, although they may advance us no closer to an appropriate allocation of resources.

The first group of arguments are not, in fact, specific to cultural activity but have a much wider application; these relate to situations in which the domestic market is affected by foreign influences in ways that may require corrective interventions for as long as the effect of those influences persists. One of these is the "infant industries" argument – the notion that the domestic market, although quite capable of supporting a domestic industry, is so preempted by foreign producers enjoying a head start and the economies of a large output that aspiring domestic producers, however efficient, cannot hope unaided to reach a level of output where their prices will fall to levels where the market will sustain them. It is an argument with a long history in every industrially developing country, used to justify tariffs, subsidies and a variety of other protective or preferential measures – which should be temporary in the circumstances urged in justification but tend to outlive those circumstances.

An analogous situation occurs when the foreign intrusion in the domestic market is created or sustained by the actions of governments in other countries designed to foster their own industries. In the special case of "dumping" practices, the argument for protective measures to counter this invasion is widely accepted, on the grounds that the effect of such practices is to distort the allocation of resources, at a real economic cost. But other forms of foreign intervention may, in fact, be benign in economic terms; if the foreign products are essentially identical to the domestic products they displace, their effect may simply be to satisfy the domestic demand at lower cost and permit the reallocation of domestic resources to other purposes. In any event – as in the case of the infant industry argument – it is possible, in theory at least, to apply empirical tests of whether protective measures are justified, although judgment will be needed to settle the kind and degree of intervention appropriate to the circumstances.

It is no accident that the word "culture" does not occur in sketching these arguments, for this class of argument relates essentially to commercial and industrial policy and touches only incidentally the cultural policies and practices of government. Economists do sometimes find in these situations some special justification for the protection of cultural activity at home, but on closer examination it becomes evident that, consciously or unconsciously, they have reached beyond the range of economic processes to ascribe social values – unknown and unknowable in any market, however perfect – to cultural activities and products.

This same resort to social values is the distinguishing characteristic of the final class of justifications frequently offered by economists for government support of cultural activity. In some of these the argument is made in economic terms, without recognizing that it rests, in fact, on a judgment of value quite independent of economic considerations. One such is the often-cited argument focused on differential rates of increase in productivity, associated with William J. Baumol and William G. Bowen. The key to their case is that the arts (specifically the performing arts, in their original presentation of 1966) rely heavily on human effort, which can seldom be displaced by labour-saving technology to increase productivity. As other sectors of the economy experience gains in productivity, wage rates must rise for all, including the cultural sector, and with little or no gain in productivity to offset these increased labour costs, the prices of cultural products must rise. But if demand is sensitive to these price increases – and some studies indicate that it is – cultural activity will lose its audiences and suffer a decline. Rising subsidies are therefore necessary even to sustain a steady level of cultural output.

Discussion of this thesis has concentrated on two questions. It is asked whether, as rising productivity in other sectors raises incomes, demand for cultural products may not keep pace with – or conceivably outstrip – their increases in price. It is also argued that the measurement of productivity applied to the arts may be too restrictive, making too much of the fact that, for example, the performance of a quintet will always require five musicians and neglecting to notice that new technologies such as broadcasting and recordings may, in effect, increase the productivity of the musicians very considerably by enabling them to satisfy new kinds of demand.

What seems to be overlooked, however, is that even if there is little or no gain in productivity, and even if rising prices do depress demand, the case for intervention remains to be made. Economists have, after all, accepted with equanimity the effect of low productivity growth on such activities as domestic service. Certainly they would see in this no evidence of market failure; on the contrary, it is more likely to be seen as the economic universe unfolding as it should. If, then, a decline in the output and consumption of cultural goods is judged to require corrective measures, it can only be because any such decline is deemed to be socially undesirable. If the market has failed, it is not because its reflection of the forces of supply and demand is defective, but rather because supply and demand are judged to be inadequate or inappropriate criteria for the allocation of resources to cultural purposes.

This puts the Baumol-Bowen thesis squarely in the class of arguments based on the concept of "merit goods": the notion of a category of goods and services that deserve to be fostered, in both their production and public enjoyment, irrespective of how the market may measure costs and benefits – simply because they are meritorious. Clearly this concept offers a congenial setting for the view taken by this Committee of the manifest value of cultural activity in releasing the creative potential of a society, and in illuminating and enriching the human condition – celebrating its strengths and exposing its frailties.

In this view, intervention to increase the flow of resources is necessary both to foster the creation of cultural goods of all kinds and to enlarge their accessibility to all members of society in accordance with the preferences of each. Pushed to its limit, it might seem to suggest that, ideally, neither output nor availability should be constrained by market forces – clearly an absurdity in a world of finite resources. But if the claims on resources can only be relative, the justification appears to be no less valid. It may not be enough simply to remedy market failures (to the extent that these can be measured); something more may well be needed in order to achieve that allocation of resources which yields the best balance of benefits to society.

In a sense, the merit goods case and the argument of market failure merge into one another; what distinguishes them is the degree of public awareness. For implicit in the notion of merit goods is that cultural activity confers benefits of which the public, or some significant part of it, is simply unaware: there is, in effect, a failure of information. To the extent that people can be made aware – and the argument can be made that government should sponsor or support efforts at public "consciousness raising," as it has done for physical fitness through the Participaction program – the merits of culture then become benefits which people feel but which remain largely ignored by the market, and we are back to the original problem of market failure.

Mass Markets and Minority Tastes

These arguments for government intervention are of particular relevance to a number of concerns that were recurring themes in representations made to the Committee and in our own deliberations. One of these was the necessity of sustaining a range of cultural activities that accommodates the widest possible variety of interests and preferences. The virtually limitless variability of tastes, coupled with the fact that much cultural activity caters to only small minorities, tends to circumscribe the range of preferences to which the market, left to the interplay of its own forces, will respond. And in the judgment of some economists, this problem is aggravated by the large element of risk or uncertainty associated with the launching of new cultural ventures – a new book or magazine, a new record or film, a new play or musical work, or a new painting or sculpture that breaks away from familiar conventions.

To the extent that these ventures involve substantial investments of resources – as most do, in one form or another – producers will seek ways of reducing the risk. They will make efforts to detect the early success of a new work, concentrating resources (including advertising) on reinforcing that early trend. Successful ventures are exploited in every conceivable way: by producing sequels, through adaptations in other media, by generating "star" status for creators or performers associated with the success. The effect of all such measures, however, is to reduce risk at the price of narrowing the range of interests and preferences served.

For certain kinds of cultural products – those employing industrial patterns of organization for their production and distribution, like films, records and books – uncertainty may be reduced by organizing on a scale large enough to permit the pooling of risks associated with a wide variety of products. If, in fact, the pooling of risks increases the range of preferences served, a case can be made for government policies and programs that will foster the development of enterprises large enough to achieve this result. But even large-scale organizations may prefer to reduce their risks without diversifying their efforts. The more dependent producers are on serving large audiences in order to recover costs or simply to maximize their revenues, the greater will be the tendency to cater only to those tastes that are most widely shared – as film production and commercial television have shown.

In the view of the economist Kenneth Boulding, this concentration on the culture of mass production and mass consumption has potentially disastrous consequences. By his account, the culture of mass appeal – the superculture – is incapable of sustaining itself creatively and relies for its continuing vigour and productivity on the creative and experimental capacity of those kinds of activity that serve minority interests; yet, by its very success, it tends to eclipse and extinguish the activity on which it depends. Whether or not a parasitic relationship of this kind *can* be demonstrated remains to be shown. But regardless of whether any such process of cultural extinction can be proven, the fact can be demonstrated that, historically, those cultural activities that have conferred the most lasting benefits, and which have been seen, in retrospect, to have done most to illuminate their times, have more often than not served only minority interests in their own day. On grounds either of market failure or of diffuse social values, the case for intervention applies with special force to the satisfaction of minority preferences.

Again there will be limits to the degree of intervention, which will remain, of necessity, matters of judgment. Not every minority interest can be served, and no tastes can be met to the point of satiety. But, given the general case for intervention, the problems posed by minority preferences must weigh heavily in deciding where resources should be directed.

Metropolis and Hinterland
The regional aspirations expressed to the Committee throughout the country encounter difficulties comparable to those associated with minority preferences. The difficulties in this case, however, owe less to defects in the working of market forces than to the restricted size of markets served by activities outside the major metropolitan centres. Inevitably, this limits the range of cultural activities that can be supported; a smaller centre or sparsely populated region cannot hope for a resident opera company or for institutions rivalling the Royal Ontario Museum. If, by good luck or good management, adequate physical facilities can be found, a concentrated effort can generate an extraordinary seasonal market of limited duration to support a festival in, for example, Stratford, Charlottetown or the summer theatre movement in Quebec. But a cultural event of this kind, like the interest it attracts (for this is a case of supply creating its own demand) is temporary; its cultural roots in the community, as distinct from its impact on the local economy, remain weak.

The limitations of market size have other, more pervasive effects on cultural activities in regions outside the metropolitan areas. At least since the time of Adam Smith it has been recognized that the degree of specialization in the use of production resources is governed by the size of the market. This affects the pattern of cultural activity in smaller markets in a number of ways. As we reported in our *Summary of Briefs and Hearings*, the submissions received from universities laid particular stress on the cultural role of universities in smaller communities as animators, impresarios, and suppliers of cultural events and services. The clear inference was that the existence within metropolitan centres of richer and more varied cultural services of a specialized nature made it unnecessary, and even inappropriate, for universities in those centres to assume this role to anything like the same degree. By implication, the metropolitan universities should be able to devote themselves more singlemindedly to their own distinctive functions of advanced learning and research – a further manifestation of the greater specialization characteristic of larger markets.

Specialization also expresses itself in professionalism. It is significant that those who urged that there be greater sensitivity to regional needs in federal programs of cultural support also tended to deplore an excessive emphasis on professional activity in the shaping of those programs. We must, in fact, agree that if government intervention is restricted to the support of professional activity, especially in the performing arts and the cultural industries, the beneficiaries of that intervention will be heavily concentrated in the larger centres.

There has, of course, been a striking increase in professional activity throughout the country. But the Committee encountered some evidence that professional performing arts companies in small centres must bear additional costs as a consequence of having to compensate their members for the disadvantages of their location. These include not only the intangible but very real costs of diminished visibility – to audiences, to their peers elsewhere, and through reviews of their work – but also the more direct loss of income from other uses of their professional skills, such as broadcasting or advertising, which are concentrated in the metropolitan areas.

As in the matter of minority preferences, it is a question of judgment how far government should intervene to remedy the disadvantages experienced by regions remote from metropolitan centres. It is sometimes argued that regional interests can be better served by provincial and municipal authorities than by the federal government, and we entirely agree that these are, or should be, matters of particular concern to the provinces and cities affected. But we must recognize, at the same time, that unless account is taken of regional problems in the framing of federal programs, the latter may, in fact, aggravate those problems. The effect of an excessive concentration of resources on professional activity has already been mentioned as one example of how this can occur. Another can be seen in the effects of encouraging private donations to cultural activities by allowing deductions from personal and corporate taxable incomes. Inescapably, government intervention in this manner to increase the flow of resources favours the metropolitan centres, because of the concentration – not only absolute but relative to population as well – of personal and corporate incomes in these centres. Moreover, if the geographic imbalance of such tax expenditures has the further consequence, by stimulating cultural ventures in those centres, of generating a comparable increase in metropolitan claims on government assistance in more direct forms such as Canada Council grants, the resulting distribution of direct support will almost certainly compound the distorting effects of the tax incentives.

Even government efforts to enlarge the flow of cultural products of high quality throughout the country – in such forms as broadcasting networks, traveling exhibits, or the touring of artistic performances – may be seen by regional interests as a preempting of regional markets by metropolitan products. This perception may resemble the way in which foreign intrusions are viewed as a cause for protective measures of government intervention on behalf of national cultural interests as a whole. We recall being told in Yellowknife by spokesmen for the Inuit Tapirisat that, in the eyes of the northern peoples, the threat to their culture from sources outside Canada paled into insignificance beside the threat from our own metropolitan centres.

The fact that certain forms of intervention may produce such side effects in no way weakens the case for intervention – or even for using the instruments in question. It does, however, underscore the need to weigh carefully the full range of consequences of each mode of intervention available to the government, in the light of all the cultural purposes to be served. It also suggests that, just as there is no simple formula for calculating the proper degree of intervention, so too there can be no inner consistency among the methods of intervention employed. Each will entail both costs and benefits – and cultural costs and benefits in particular. Because these will defy precise measurement, the determination of the right mixture, like that of the appropriate sum of resources to be applied, will always be a matter of judgment.

The need for judgment and foresight in the application of resources has been a recurring theme in the foregoing pages. The fact that no mechanisms exist for calculating the degree of intervention required or for identifying with any precision how it should be applied presents a chronic difficulty: whose judgment and foresight is to be trusted? Part of the answer was seen in the preceding chapter, in our emphasis on the autonomous status required by federal agencies which must make such judgments, on the care that must be exercised in choosing their members, and on the importance of the criteria and procedures by which they act. But however well-intentioned and well-informed, no single source of resources can be infallible as judge and prophet. Moreover, an excessive concentration of this function in the hands of a single authority like the federal government, which must pursue many purposes unrelated to the needs of cultural life, magnifies the risks. It is therefore essential that resources should flow to cultural activities from a multiplicity of sources, each guided by its own judgment of needs. And the extent to which this will happen will itself be influenced greatly – if not decisively – by the government's own choice of modes of intervention. For, as will be seen in the following sections, certain of the courses open to the government and its agencies have the effect of stimulating resource flows from a wide variety of sources in the private sector – or from other governments – with an accompanying dispersion of the exercise of judgment.

Modes of Government Intervention

The federal government plays a number of overlapping roles in the cultural life of the country. Through agencies such as the Canadian Broadcasting Corporation, the National Film Board and the National Arts Centre, it is a proprietor of production agencies. In its operation of museums, archives and parks it serves as custodian of our cultural heritage. By a variety of means, including the commissioning of works, the giving of grants and the award of prizes, it plays the part of a patron. It acts as catalyst through tax incentives designed to stimulate private investment and philanthropy. And using its legislative power to prescribe standards and quotas and to define property rights, it serves as regulator.

In all these roles, its actions have the effect of influencing the flow of resources to the cultural sector, or the distribution of resources among regions or cultural preferences, and among the various participants in cultural activity. But each role entails its own characteristic modes of intervention, and for any given problem, the impact of government intervention can vary enormously according to the choice of modes. For example, the government can encourage the publication and sale of Canadian books by paying subsidies to publishers for the production of books chosen by some test of quality; alternatively, as in Ontario's Halfback scheme, described later in this chapter under the heading "Government as Patron," it can apply a subsidy to purchasers of Canadian books. In both cases, there is an intervention in the market to increase the flow of resources – in the first instance by absorbing some part of the cost of book production, and in the second by sharing with the reader the purchase price of his own choice of books. But the consequences of the first course may be very different from those of the second in terms of the kinds of books produced and bought.

The choice of modes of intervention may involve first of all a choice of roles. The latter are not mutually exclusive, and all governments exhibit mixtures of roles in their cultural programs. They do so, however, in varying proportions, and the resulting variety in patterns of intervention among countries is one of the first things to strike an interested observer. Many European countries are heavily involved as proprietors and producers, not only of their broadcasting systems but also of most of their great orchestras and operatic, theatrical and dance companies. In the United States, on the other hand, the national government has relied primarily on the role of catalyst, using its tax laws to encourage private support of artistic production. In Canada the dominant role of the federal government has been that of patron; the European model is found only in such exceptions as the Canadian Broadcasting Corporation, National Film Board and National Arts Centre. Even in these, the political and bureaucratic links to government have been minimized – following the pattern pioneered in the United Kingdom in the British Broadcasting Corporation and the Arts Council of Great Britain – by devolving the responsibility to autonomous bodies.

A number of the representations made to us urged that the federal government enlarge its role as catalyst by increasing the tax incentives offered to private donors on the United States model. The fact that important incentives are already available (on a scale unknown within European countries, although less generous than U.S. provisions) underscores the fact that these varied approaches can be employed simultaneously – as does the growing American resort to direct patronage following the establishment of the National Endowment for the Arts in 1964.

The fact remains, however, that choices do have to be made. Although governments may choose varying combinations of roles, as proprietor, patron or catalyst, it must be recognized that *all* roles involve the diversion of resources to cultural activity at the expense of other public or private uses of those resources. The aggregate cost of all forms of intervention will always be an issue for the political process to settle, whether that intervention takes the form of state ownership of cultural undertakings, or of direct grants and subsidies, or of indirect assistance through tax incentives. The latter question is, of course, not unrelated to the former; the more closely the chosen modes of intervention correspond to the public perception of needs, the greater will be the public acceptance of the tax burdens involved. But it is quite unrealistic to expect the federal government to enlarge its proprietary role in emulation of the European model, or to broaden its tax incentives on the United States pattern, while at the same time assuming that it will continue to be a more open-handed patron of culture than either European or U.S. governments.

There is no ideal mixture of roles for all governments. We cannot say that the European pattern is better than that of the United States, or that either of these is better than the Canadian pattern. The modes of intervention most characteristic of each yield different results – and these differences will be explored in the following sections. But each country has not only its own historic traditions (including national habits of private philanthropy), but also its own pattern of cultural activity and its own sense of its cultural needs. These distinctive characteristics are crucial to its choice of the mixture of roles that it finds most appropriate.

That mixture is not, of course, immutable for any country. Changing circumstances may diminish the efficacy of a traditional role, or create problems that require a shift in emphasis from one role to another. It was, for example, precisely this kind of change that emerged as the central preoccupation in our examination of Canadian broadcasting and dominates discussion in Chapter 10. It became clear to us that the heavy reliance of the past on federal proprietorship of a production organization (the Canadian Broadcasting Corporation), supplemented by a growing resort, especially since the 1960s, to regulatory measures through the Canadian Radio-television and Telecommunications Commission, is ceasing to meet the evolving cultural needs of the country. New circumstances are creating new needs, and new approaches must be found involving a redefinition of goals and a readjustment of roles. The degree of federal intervention required may be even greater than before, but the modes must change.

In considering the relative strengths and weaknesses of the various modes of intervention available, one must bear in mind the justifications for intervention examined in the first part of this chapter. But, above all, the efficacy of each measure must be judged against cultural objectives.

The Government as Proprietor

As noted above, the Government of Canada has seldom ventured into the ownership and operation of undertakings for cultural production. The Canadian Broadcasting Corporation, National Film Board and National Arts Centre are the only noteworthy instances. In fact we found no evidence, in the briefs received or in our public hearings, of a significant desire on the part of Canadians to adopt the European pattern of state-owned orchestras and performing companies.

Even in those few instances in which the government has created its own enterprises, it has not done so out of any wish for direct control of the operations involved. On the contrary, in both the Canadian Broadcasting Corporation and National Arts Centre, it has, from the outset, adopted a form of

organization which shielded the operations from any direct government control; and although the Film Board was denied the same degree of autonomy
(a defect which, as we have pointed out, should be corrected), it has in practice been given comparable freedom in the production undertaken on its own
account – the work on which its reputation has been built.

For our own part, this Committee has espoused the view that the essential task of government in cultural matters is to remove obstacles and enlarge
opportunities, without seeking to direct. Cultural activity must permeate
society, and cannot be delivered by a beneficent state. This view is reflected in
Chapter 1, and its implications are developed in our findings and recommendations in Chapter 2. In effect, we have concluded that, for government-owned
undertakings of this kind, the powers and prerogatives normally associated
with ownership should be delegated to autonomous boards, in relation to
which the role of government itself is properly that of patron rather than
proprietor.

The fact that in broadcasting, film and the performing arts the
government-owned undertakings share the stage with major nongovernment
actors has important implications for the role and direction of the former. It is
reflected, in the relevant chapters that follow, in a consistent emphasis on the
notion that the programs of state-owned undertakings should be so framed as
to complement the offerings already available from other sources, and be
modified where necessary to reflect changes that have occurred in that external environment. It also leads us to urge a much greater reliance on external
production resources for the content of their programs. As will be evident from
our chapters on broadcasting, film and the performing arts, if the government
is to accept the principle of the *complementary* nature of its programs, and
rely more heavily on external creative resources, there will be effects on both
the volume of resources devoted to the government-owned enterprises and
the manner in which those resources are applied. There will also be consequences in the impact of those resources on the level of cultural activity and
on its distribution throughout the country.

Further implications flow from the importance attached to access in
Chapter 1 – not only the accessibility of cultural activity to the public at large,
but also the access of creators and performers to the means of cultural expression. In its broadest sense, accessibility implies not only overcoming barriers
of geography, language and income, but also accommodating the diversity of
tastes and experience that is the reality of Canadian society. This affects not
only the allocation of resources, in terms of the program content of state-
owned undertakings, but also the ways in which those resources are obtained.

The latter question involves two separate issues. One concerns the
sources on which government can draw in directing or stimulating the flow of
public and private resources into cultural activities – general tax revenues,
special earmarked levies, lottery revenues, or private philanthropy. Because
this issue is faced by government in one way or another whether it acts as
proprietor, custodian, patron or catalyst, it will be examined later under the
general heading of "Finding the Resources." But the second issue relates more

directly to the role of proprietor (or, as will be seen, of custodian) and concerns the extent to which a publicly owned cultural undertaking should be required or expected to obtain its resources through its operations.

The issue can be seen in different forms in each of the producing undertakings owned by the federal government. If the National Arts Centre were required to maximize its box office revenues, the result would almost certainly be a program of offerings and a scale of ticket prices that would make the Centre irrelevant to a wide range of tastes and inaccessible to a large element of the population. On the other hand, the total removal of financial barriers by eliminating all admission charges would not only pose very practical problems of accommodation, but would confer on the residents of Ottawa and Hull, at the expense of the Canadian public at large, benefits that were denied to all others. Obviously a reasonable point of balance must be found, bearing some rough measure of comparability with the practices of other producing organizations throughout the country. The fact that such questions as program content and pricing policy are delegated to the organization and its directing board in a sense relieves the government itself of responsibility for striking the balance between government support and box office revenues. But the government, in deciding on the extent of its support must accept, tacitly at least, the judgment of the Centre on that score.

For the National Film Board, from its inception, there was little expectation of earnings. It could have been otherwise. The fact that its products are distributed through channels known to the organization and exhibited to audiences who must assemble for the purpose, would have made it quite possible to require the Board to rely on earnings to finance a substantial part of its operations. However, the central task assigned to the Board was to interpret Canadians to themselves and to the world, and to make its productions freely available to the widest possible audience. If commercial exhibitors chose to use its short subjects – as in the early years they often did – the resulting revenues were a bonus. Feature film production, when it came, might have caused complications, but the pursuit of commercial success never became a requirement, explicit or implicit, of government financing policies.

Not so – regrettably, in the view of this Committee – for the Canadian Broadcasting Corporation. For radio and television broadcasting, until the advent of pay-television, no means existed of recovering costs from the audience based on actual listening or viewing time – since access to material broadcast through the air can be neither controlled nor measured. Consequently, commercial broadcasting developed on the basis of revenues from advertising, which means that broadcasters succeed by delivering audiences to advertisers, and the delivery of programs to listeners and viewers is essentially a means to this end. This has been considered to be the only significant means available to the CBC for obtaining revenues from its operations. The fact that it feels obliged to follow this course – for television, but not for radio – has affected its programming in ways that seem to us (as to others before us) to be irreconcilable with its proper role in the cultural life of the country.

The Government as Custodian

Cultural assets inherited from the past, together with new creations of lasting value, require custodians to ensure their preservation and accessibility. Much of this occurs spontaneously throughout society: families treasure their heirlooms and transmit their genealogies from generation to generation; organizations of all kinds preserve the records of their accomplishments – and even, at times, of their failures. But increasingly, this heritage is seen as a collective good of society for which governments are asked to assume growing responsibilities, requiring the use of ever-larger resources.

In responding to these demands, the federal government encounters a wide choice of modes of intervention, reflecting the entire range of roles examined here. In its grants to museums throughout the country it serves as patron. Acting as catalyst, it stimulates public interest and creates incentives to private efforts at conservation. By regulation, it restrains the export of cultural property and safeguards natural environments, endangered species, and sites and artifacts of historic interest.

But, in addition, the federal government has from earliest times played a proprietary role of a special nature, as custodian – of parks, environmental reserves, wildlife sanctuaries, historic sites, buildings and monuments, of a growing array of museums, art collections, libraries, and archives of documentary material and audio-visual records of all kinds.

As custodian, the government – or the agencies through which it acts – faces the same choices in the allocation of resources among, for example, acquisition, conservation and public access, as do all other custodial institutions. The implications of this are examined more fully in Chapter 4 on "Heritage." In addition, the government faces the same question that it encounters as proprietor of producing organizations: to what extent should custodial institutions obtain their resources from charges levied on the users?

For the greater part, the custodial activities of the federal government have observed the principle that the use of public funds to preserve the cultural heritage requires that what is preserved be made freely accessible to all members of the public. In fact few other governments, in Canada or in other countries, have applied the policy of free access as widely, especially in their museums and art galleries. Only in national parks and historic sites does the federal government apply user charges – at rates that recover only a part of the cost of the amenities and services that must be furnished, and which can have little deterrent effect when seen in the context of transportation and other unavoidable costs that users must bear.

Because the public use of institutions in this category requires attendance in person, admission charges give rise to no administrative difficulties; what is involved, therefore, is a question of pricing policy. Charges can be varied according to classes of users – with special rates or exemptions for children or students, for example – as is the frequent practice among museums. The object of any such pricing policy is, in fact, to strike the most satisfactory balance between, on the one hand, the desire for operating revenues and, on the other, the minimizing of deterrents to public use. For certain custodial institutions, however – and for museums especially – the need to secure revenues from operations may well affect the internal balance of their programs, inflating the allocation of resources to displays at the expense, in particular, of conservation and research.

The innovation of "blockbuster" exhibitions in recent years has, in some cases, provoked charges of a distortion of aims and misapplication of resources, and criticism that the charges levied for admission jeopardize the principle of the widest possible public access. Special events of this kind may, however, be financially attractive to the institutions as a means of cross-subsidization, since net earnings from the special exhibitions permit the museum to enlarge or enrich its regular program of services to the general public.

The Government as Patron

The role of patron, as we use the term here, involves the direct infusion of resources into cultural activity, unaccompanied by any rights of ownership or responsibilities for management. It has become, in fact, the dominant role of the federal government in cultural matters – to the extent that, as noted previously, most of the government-owned institutions engaged in both production and custodianship conduct their operations at arm's length, and the government limits its role in effect to that of patron.

It is also the role embracing the widest range of modes of intervention:

- Purchases and commissions;
- Grants and direct subsidies in a variety of forms and for a variety of purposes;
- Relief from taxes or from the cost of certain public services;
- Loans and loan guarantees;
- The provision of services that facilitate cultural development;
- The awarding of prizes and honours;
- The stimulation of public interest.

The range of choice open to the government and its agencies among these measures is virtually limitless. Moreover, according to how they are applied, the cultural impact can vary greatly.

At one extreme the government can limit its own role to that of paymaster, leaving it to the market to determine how its assistance is to be shared among claimants, and how the benefits are to be spread throughout the chain of activities that link original creation to the ultimate distribution of a cultural product. This, in effect, is what happens in that part of the Canadian Book Publishing Development Program of the Department of Communications which uses publishers' sales volumes as the criterion for the apportionment of subsidies. By the mere fact of injecting additional resources into the sector to which it relates, it undoubtedly increases the volume of activity; in the process it makes more of the product accessible to the consuming public by reducing prices, and may generate more original creation – although this need not necessarily follow. It has the further attraction, from the government's viewpoint, of administrative simplicity, as the criteria of choice are minimized and judgments of relative merit are virtually eliminated; and from the viewpoint of the industry, it involves the least interference in their commercial judgments.

On the other hand, the very neutrality or non-judgmental quality of this kind of measure limits its utility as a means to cultural ends. Given the nature of the market failures which require government intervention, if that intervention is directed by such criteria as sales volumes, which are themselves a reflection of those failures, it may only serve to accentuate the original fault rather than provide a remedy. Intervention in this form may yield some cultural gains, but it is essentially an instrument of industrial rather than of cultural policy.

The cultural impact of such programs can be enhanced by introducing qualifications in the form of criteria that reflect specific cultural goals. In the program of publishing support, for example, the level of assistance can be related to the volume of sales of only certain categories of books. But by subjecting the assistance to qualifying conditions of this sort, its utility as an instrument of industrial policy may be weakened, and the balance of advantage between industrial and cultural goals will be a matter of judgment.

The same is true of some other modes of intervention listed above: when, for example, a cultural sector is relieved of certain costs on a non-discretionary basis this has the same economic effect as a grant. Exemption from taxes of one kind or another (including customs duties), the application to certain material of special postal rates below the general rates applying to other mail, or the provision of free services (including the cultural marketing and promotion organization suggested in Appendix 1 to this chapter) can produce the same effect. The fact that the contribution of such measures to the attainment of cultural goals is limited – and may even be incidental – does not necessarily invalidate them. Their cultural impact, relative to their cost, may be great enough to make them useful adjuncts to a policy of cultural development. We believe this to be true of the proposed marketing and promotion organization. On the other hand, we must question whether the postal rates applying to printed matter yield cultural benefits on a scale justifying the cost borne by the Department of Communications; equivalent or greater benefits might well be achieved at lower cost by other measures better suited to the same cultural objectives.

In the same mode, one must include subsidized loans and loan guarantees, which make short-term and, in some instances, longer-term credit available to enterprises which are otherwise sound business ventures, but which bankers and other lenders judge to be too risky. One advantage of loans and loan guarantees is that they can be available on a continuous basis and more automatically than grants.

Further support in this category might be extended to cultural undertakings in the form of the financial assistance and managerial advisory services of the Federal Business Development Bank. The programs of this institution embrace loans for the acquisition of fixed assets or for working capital, venture capital in the form of equity financing, and a variety of management services. These include Counselling Assistance to Small Enterprises (the CASE program), which makes available advice in most aspects of management from retired business people with experience tailored to the needs of the clients, in addition to a variety of courses, seminars and management clinics for owners and managers. The need of cultural organizations for assistance in all these forms was a recurring theme in representations made to this Committee. From our discussions with senior officers of the Federal Business Development Bank, it is our clear impression that the Bank would welcome the cultural industries among its clientele and would cooperate fully in removing obstacles to their participation in its programs. The most pressing needs would be to develop appropriate knowledge and experience both within the Bank's own staff and among the advisers and councillors on whom it draws in its services, and, for purposes of lending and investment, to find other federal authorities prepared to share the risks associated with certain cultural enterprises.

10.   The Department of Communications, in consultation with the Federal Business Development Bank, should promote the use by cultural enterprises of the financial and managerial services of the Bank and consider, jointly with such cultural agencies as the Canada Council and the Canadian Film Development Corporation, how the needs of the Bank for expertise and risk-sharing in respect of cultural activities might be met.

Another instance in which a market mechanism is used to determine the allocation of resources and their distribution throughout the process of cultural production is the voucher scheme exemplified by the Halfback program devised by Ontario. Under Halfback, lottery tickets which failed to win prizes received a cash value of half their purchase price when applied toward the purchase of a Canadian book or recording, a ticket to a movie, play or concert, or subscription to magazines or performance series. The scheme provided, in effect, a means of injecting resources into cultural activity and of expanding markets and audiences for cultural products, but left the direction of those resources in the hands of consumers. At the same time, it preserved in the hands of the government a crucial steering function, through the power to define – or tag – those products and activities for which the vouchers could be used. As a consequence, the pursuit of cultural objectives can be made central to voucher schemes of this sort; in the opinion of this Committee, they offer significant potential benefits as instruments of cultural policy, which should not be neglected by the federal government.

11.   In view of the distinctive merits of voucher schemes for sub-
      sidizing public attendance at cultural events and purchase of
      cultural products, the federal government and its agencies
      should include such measures in their programs of cultural
      support.

The sharing of philanthropic burdens rather than consumer costs can be
pursued by the use of matching grants – a device more commonly employed
in the United States than in Canada, although they have been used extensively
by provinces in the distribution of lottery funds. In effect, the public authority
agrees to provide funds for purposes which it has designated or approved, in
some stated ratio to funds which have been secured from other sources. The
attraction of this arrangement to the government is that its contribution is
made conditional on the clear demonstration of support for the project by
other donors. The government can vary the stringency of its controls by being
more or less specific in defining the conditions which a project must meet in
order to qualify. And in setting the ratio of its own contribution, it can define
the degree of outside support which it considers appropriate. For the private
donor, it has the advantage of increasing the "leverage" of his donation according to the extent that the government is prepared to match it – a feature that
is shared by certain tax incentives that are examined in the next section.

In effect, matching grants offer a positive incentive to private philanthropy. They enable community interest and enthusiasm, to the extent that
these are reflected in the pattern of private giving, to influence the use of
public resources. Given our conviction, expressed in Chapter 2, that cultural
activity has its own role and purposes in society, clearly distinguishable from
those of government itself, this mode of intervention has obvious attractions;
by enlarging the scope for private initiatives, it inhibits, in equal measure, any
tendency on the part of government to intervene in cultural matters for inappropriate ends. It may also provide a way of sharing burdens – and diffusing
powers of control – among different levels of government. In short, it encourages the infusion of resources into cultural activity from a multiplicity of sources
– and thereby enhances the diversity and autonomy of cultural life.

It must be recognized, however, that matching grants have their limitations. One potential weakness follows from the fact that resources flowing
into cultural activity, from all sources, are characterized by varying degrees
of uncertainty or unreliability. To the extent that these flows are made dependent on one another, that element of uncertainty – which is a constant
problem for all cultural undertakings – may be aggravated. *In the opinion of
this Committee, the federal government cannot guarantee the stability of
the total resources available, and should not be expected to do so. But its
own interventions should themselves be characterized by a high degree of
reliability,* and the contingent nature of matching grants works against this
aim.

This element of contingency also poses difficulties for the government itself, by tending to create an open-ended commitment. The government may, of course, avoid this problem by setting a strict limit on the total resources it is prepared to commit. But introducing an element of uncertainty into its offer of matching support may well weaken the incentive effect of that offer – to say nothing of the resentment it may generate among outside donors who contribute to a project in the expectation of matching gifts, only to be told that the money has run out.

A further defect of matching grants is that they work to the advantage of those undertakings that enjoy the greatest access to private funding. Use of this device therefore tends to skew the distribution of public funds in favour of the interests and cultural preferences of the more affluent sectors of society, and to yield an inequitable concentration of benefits to the larger urban centres. Quite apart from any objections to this regressive effect on grounds of social policy, it is no less objectionable as a matter of cultural policy for its relative neglect of the cultural interests of less affluent groups or regions.

In brief, matching grants are not a panacea. But as part of a broad spectrum of instruments, they have a useful role to play, as a means of encouraging cultural initiatives and resource flows from a multiplicity of sources throughout society. They lend themselves particularly to community-based capital projects or special events; they may not, on the other hand, afford a satisfactory means of providing sustained operating support, although they have been used in the United States for a significant part of the sustaining support given by government to public broadcasting.

In Canada, discretionary grants play a relatively larger part in the allocation of resources by the federal government and its agencies; virtually all the programs of the Canada Council involve measures of this kind. The dominant characteristic of such grants is the high degree of control available to the granting authority. Not only does it retain full control over the definition of objectives and criteria; it can also subject each request for assistance to a test of cultural merit of its own choosing. Obviously this allows resources to be applied in a highly selective manner, with the possibility of achieving maximum cultural benefit. By the same token, however, it carries with it the greatest possibility of manipulation by the granting authority, including the greatest risk that cultural purposes will be subordinated to other ends. Hence the need, on which such stress was laid in the preceding chapter, for insulation from political control of objectives and criteria. Moreover, the need for sensitivity to a wide diversity of attitudes and preferences requires the utmost care in the definition of eligibility, the framing of selection procedures and the choice of judges and advisers.

How much direction a granting agency may choose to exercise can vary widely. In making grants to performing arts organizations, for example, it may content itself with general judgments of quality, leaving the organization unfettered in deciding the content of its program. If, on the other hand, the agency wishes to influence the content of the programs it supports – in order, say, to promote the inclusion of works by Canadian composers, playwrights or choreographers – the criteria by which its support is determined may be broadened to include the particular goals it wishes to pursue. However, this approach may leave the performing company in some doubt or confusion as to the probable effect of alternative programming choices on the size of its grant. To avoid this difficulty, several alternatives are available. The granting agency may require that programs include a prescribed quota of certain kinds of content as a condition of support. Alternatively, it can offer a base level of support unqualified by program requirements, with additional sums being available for content that it wishes to encourage. Because the balance between the basic support and the supplementary incentive is controllable, the use of incentives can be made less coercive (or less painfully so) than quotas. *To be effective, however, the conditions attached to incentive grants must be clearly stated in advance.*

The use of grants also involves choosing the point at which resources might best be introduced into the chain of cultural activity linking original creation and public enjoyment. For example, the objective of encouraging original Canadian creation – to which this Committee attaches the highest importance – can be served by a variety of approaches. Grants to performing arts companies, with appropriate incentive elements, can have this effect; in this case the granting agency leaves to the companies – or at most shares with them – the selection of writers, composers or choreographers. Special grants to performing companies for the commissioning of works or the financing of resident creative artists will produce much the same result. Alternatively, grants may be made directly to the artists themselves, which may offer the advantage of extending the opportunity to a greater number, but gives less assurance that the resulting works will be performed. Similarly, support for the training and professional development of both creative and performing artists can be given to the aspiring artists directly, or to training institutions, or in the form of grants to performing companies for apprenticeship programs. Somewhat comparable choices between grants to publishers and grants to writers will be seen in Chapter 7. It must be emphasized that these alternatives are not mutually exclusive; rather, the aim must be to strike the most productive balance among them.

Among the proposals made to the Committee as possible remedies for the inadequate – even derisory – returns to artists in Canada were a number focused on tax treatment, many of them reflecting findings and recommendations of the 1978 Report prepared by Russell Disney for the Secretary of State on "Federal Tax Issues of Concern to the Arts Community in Canada." Some of these, dealing with matters such as the treatment of artists' costs (and whether or in what circumstances artists should be considered as employees or self-employed), the valuation of works donated by artists to public institutions, and the income-averaging tax provisions available, sought little more than equitable treatment in comparison with other classes of taxpayers. Although such proposals may appear to the Department of Finance to require departures from standard practices, to the extent that they involve nothing more than simple equity they can scarcely be construed as special pleading, and this Committee supports them unreservedly.

12. Tax provisions respecting the employment status of artists and such matters as the calculation of their costs against income, the valuation of works given for public use and enjoyment, and their entitlement to income averaging must afford equitable treatment in comparison with those applicable to other classes of taxpayers.

Other suggestions went farther, urging in effect a special tax treatment for artists – in one case proposing a tax exemption for earnings of less than $20,000 a year derived from artistic creation. A number of submissions referred to the practice of the Republic of Ireland in granting tax exemptions of this sort. Quite apart, however, from questions of social justice raised by the conferring of a special tax status on artists, such proposals seem to us to be of questionable value as a means of improving the rewards to artists. The problem, after all, is not one of excessive tax burdens, but rather of inadequate incomes. Tax concessions of this kind benefit chiefly those who have least need of them.

The object, it seems to us, must always be to attack the root causes of the inadequate flow of resources to artistic creation or to cultural activity generally. Where specific problems can be identified – such as inadequate copyright laws, or the consequences of such new, widely available technologies as photocopying or home taping – appropriate specific remedies may suggest themselves; several of these will be found in the chapters that follow. But to the extent that more general problems of market failure are involved along the lines examined in the first part of this chapter, more general and indirect measures must be adopted to divert resources to the cultural life of the country – resorting wherever possible to those modes of intervention that encourage greatest use of the creative potential of Canadians.

To meet the problem of market failure stemming from lack of information – of public awareness of cultural benefits – nothing less than widely diffused programs of education and animation may be needed. This is a relatively underdeveloped instrument in the repertoire of Canadian governments. Indeed, the idea of official action to stimulate public demand for and appreciation of cultural products, however broadly conceived, may arouse fear of heavy-handed taste-making. The concentration of patronage powers in the hands of the state may well be acceptable to the tax-paying public only if there is clear evidence that the application of public resources to culture is sensitive to the public's own pattern of interests and preferences, neither serving the tastes of some elements to the neglect of others, nor seeking to generate uniformity of taste. But as long as the need for diversity is accepted as a governing principle, public interest can be stimulated by fostering the

widest possible exposure to and participation in cultural activity of high quality. In the long run, this may be the main challenge for an effective policy of
public intervention in culture, and the best guarantee that the resources
applied will be commensurate with the public benefits.

It is with this goal in view that we propose, in Appendix 1 to this
chapter, a marketing and promotion organization that would assist those
engaged in cultural undertakings to stimulate public interest in and demand
for their activities. Because the organization would be essentially an enabling
device – encouraging and assisting the efforts of those directly engaged in
cultural pursuits – and would be directed by a broadly based board representative of the interests it serves, the role of the government itself would be that
of disinterested but benevolent patron. In this way the pitfalls of partiality,
and the public suspicions to which these give rise, may be avoided.

The Government as Catalyst
As may be apparent from the foregoing section, the role of patron merges im-
perceptibly into that of catalyst. The principal characteristic of modes of intervention considered under this heading is that they do not involve direct
disbursements of public funds, relying instead on the use of tax incentives.
And, as for matching grants, the primary object of such incentives is to encourage private initiatives for the support of cultural activities.

A number of representations made to the Committee urged a greater
use of tax incentives, and changes in the way they are applied. Three aspects
of existing income tax law attracted particular attention:

•   the treatment of charitable gifts and donations as deductions from
     income rather than as an offset to tax;
•   the application of capital gains tax to securities and properties
     donated to registered charities;
•   the standard $100 deduction allowed in lieu of an itemized claim for
     charitable donations (and medical expenses) supported by receipts.

The first point at issue concerns the tax law provision that permits as a
deduction from taxable income, gifts made to registered charities, including
cultural organizations, not exceeding 20 per cent of the taxpayer's net income. It was pointed out to the Committee that, as an incentive to private
philanthropy, the effectiveness of this provision depends on the taxpayer's
marginal tax rate, which increases with the size of the taxable income. For
larger incomes this yields a tax benefit of up to half the charitable donations,
but for smaller incomes the benefit may be as little as 10 per cent. The effect
is not only to discourage a broadly based pattern of private philanthropy
(aggravated, as will be seen, by the $100 standard deduction), but also to
concentrate control over the application of public resources, in the form of
foregone taxes, in the hands of the more affluent taxpayers. This is con-
trasted with the tax treatment of contributions to federal political parties for

which the taxpayer is granted, instead of a deduction from income, a reduction of the tax itself on a sliding scale designed to encourage smaller contributions without regard to the level of income.

The second complaint concerns the fact that, although gifts of assets (such as buildings, works of art or securities) are valued as deductions from income at their worth at the time of the gift, the resulting tax benefit is substantially reduced by the requirement that any increase in value that occurred while the assets were owned by the donor be taxed as a capital gain. It is argued that, because the full benefit of the capital gain is being passed to the charitable organization, the donor should not be taxed; and it was pointed out that the law in the United States imposes no such tax on philanthropy of this kind, which may account for the greater propensity of well-to-do Americans to make large gifts and bequests for cultural and other charitable purposes.

What is at issue here is not whether there should be an incentive but rather the extent of that incentive. Under the existing provisions of Canadian tax law, the tax benefit derived from a gift of assets represents the marginal rate of tax applied to the full market value of those assets, but that benefit is in effect reduced by the liability for tax, at the same rate, on half the value of the capital gains component of the market price. There is still a substantial net benefit, and although exemption from capital gains tax would increase the incentive to private philanthropy of this kind, it remains a question of fiscal rather than cultural policy whether the additional tax expenditure is acceptable. There will be a special problem associated with gifts of such a size that the tax owed on capital gains exceeds the tax benefit available as a reduction in the first year. To encourage such gifts, it would be necessary to spread the benefits over a period of years. However, according to the terms of the November 1981 federal budget, donations in one fiscal year can be carried over and charged against income over an additional five years. This would in effect permit the capital gains liabilities to be averaged over six years.

The third target of representations to the Committee – the standard $100 deduction – raises a number of questions. The Tax Reform Committee of the National Voluntary Organizations argues that for the vast majority of taxpayers – who use this deduction in place of a claim supported by receipts for donations – the deduction provides no incentive to philanthropy; coupled with the use of a deduction from taxable income rather than a tax credit, as noted above, it may even discourage charitable giving by taxpayers in the lower income brackets. The Tax Reform Committee therefore proposes abandonment of the standard deduction, and the application of a tax credit amounting to 50 per cent of donations for which receipts can be shown. It is claimed that the effect of the standard deduction is to cost the government $250 million annually in tax reductions, against which there has been little compensating diversion of resources to charitable purposes. If a tax-credit arrangement were so designed that the cost to the government in foregone revenues remained the same, the resulting increase in charitable giving could be substantial.

One difficulty associated with the use of tax incentives is the degree of uncertainty about their effectiveness. If the net cost to all donors of making a gift is uniform, is the propensity to give uniform for all income levels? If that cost is reduced by increasing the tax benefit, will the volume of charitable giving increase proportionately, or by a greater or lesser amount? Moreover, because the tax law applies to charitable gifts for a wide range of purposes, including the educational, medical, welfare and recreational as well as the cultural, it is necessary to ask whether the incentive effects are the same for all categories of charities.

The answers to these questions are by no means clear, and the information available in Canada is sparse. However, studies in the United States, although based on imperfect data, give some indication of the probable answers: first, the incentive effects of any given rate of tax benefit are almost certainly greater as the income level rises; second, the effect on charitable donations of changes in the rate of tax incentives also seems to increase as the income level rises; and third, both of these phenomena appear to be more marked in relation to donations to cultural activities than to most other categories of charitable gifts. By implication, the incentive effect of any given sum of tax expenditures (that is, of total taxes foregone) will be greatest, and especially for private giving to cultural activities, if the tax benefits are directed to the higher tax brackets.

This is clearly objectionable as a principle of tax expenditures in support of culture, on grounds of cultural no less than social policy – for the reasons already identified in the examination of matching grants. It is our view that government action by way of tax incentives must promote private interest in and support of culture on a broad social basis, and the rates of tax benefit should therefore be at least as great for lower as for higher levels of income. For this reason we find merit in the proposal for the elimination of the $100 standard deduction and the substitution of a tax credit in its place.

For lack of reliable estimates of the cost of alternative rates of tax benefit, this Committee must stop short of a recommendation. *However, we urge consideration of an approach that would grant a tax credit of a fixed percentage of charitable donations for which receipts were submitted, up to a total credit of $100; for donations in excess of those required for the maximum tax credit, the existing practice of permitting deductions from taxable income would continue, with the limitation that the effective rate of benefit at the highest tax level should not exceed the rate governing the initial tax credit.*

By way of illustration, should the initial rate of tax credit be 50 per cent, it would apply to all donations of $200 or less; donations in excess of $200 could be claimed, as they now are, as deductions in computing taxable income, the maximum rate of tax also being 50 per cent. The rate of tax credit could be reduced, however, with modifications to the provision for additional deductions from taxable income, in order to bring the maximum rate of benefit into line, should the total cost to the public treasury of allowing the 50 per cent ratio be found to be unacceptably high.

A change on these lines would obviously apply to personal income tax only. For corporate gifts to registered charities, the existing tax treatment – which permits the deduction of charitable donations to a limit of 20 per cent of net income – need not be changed. The record of corporate philanthropy in Canada suggests that business organizations in this country are relatively unaffected by incentives of this sort. In 1978 only 8.5 per cent of Canadian corporations with taxable incomes reported donations to charitable purposes, and in the following year this proportion fell below 8 per cent. Although the reported donations amounted to sizable sums ($144 million and $171 million in the two successive years) they represented, in fact, only one-half of 1 per cent of total net income declared for tax purposes in each of those years – a far cry from the 20 per cent of income permitted by law. And of particular interest in the context of cultural policy is the fact that donations to the arts formed the smallest part of corporate giving – being exceeded by support for welfare, education, community projects, health and religion – and accounted for less than 5 per cent of the total, or one-fortieth of 1 per cent of pre-tax income. In the light of this record, it is doubtful that anything less than a tax benefit equal to the full amount of charitable donations – the effect of which would be to shift the entire burden of corporate giving to the general revenues of government – would significantly enlarge corporate philanthropy to cultural activities. *We can only hope that the efforts of business organizations which concern themselves with such matters will succeed in stimulating an increased flow of resources into the cultural sector.*

Tax provisions also influence the channeling of personal and corporate wealth to cultural purposes through the endowment of charitable foundations. This kind of philanthropic institution, which has been so prominent in the funding of cultural development in the United States, has not developed to the same extent in Canada – not only because there have been fewer large concentrations of wealth in this country but also because our tax laws have provided less incentive for such concentrations to be dedicated to charitable purposes in this manner. The history of private foundations, in both countries, has unfortunately been marred by instances of their misuse, necessitating the institution of legislative and administrative controls on their operations. But the need to regulate their activities in no way diminishes the value of foundations as independent sources of support for cultural activities. *In view of the importance we attach to encouraging the flow of resources to cultural activity from a multiplicity of sources, tax incentives for the endowment of foundations, with appropriate safeguards, clearly serve the public interest.*

The use of tax incentives is not limited to the stimulation of private donations. In some circumstances they can also be used to divert resources to cultural purposes in the form of private investments. One use of this device was reflected in the federal budget of November 1981, in the provision that increased the incentive (or, strictly speaking, removed the pre-existing disincentive) to restore and rehabilitate buildings of historic significance rather than demolish them to make way for new structures. The most striking example, however, is the tax shelter created in 1974 by granting a 100 per cent Capital Cost Allowance to investors in films meeting specified requirements of Canadian content. Because of the remarkable surge in investment in the years immediately following its adoption, this provision has attracted a great deal of attention – and of envious attention on the part of other cultural industries and of the producers of sound recordings in particular. Canadian experience with this method of stimulating the flow of resources to cultural activity is confined to its application to investment in films, and our appraisal of its effects – both industrial and cultural – will be found in Chapter 9. As will be seen, it is our conclusion that tax-shelter provisions of this kind can serve cultural purposes in a limited way if the qualifying conditions are defined with care. But their principal contribution is to industrial development, and for maximum effectiveness on this score the qualifying conditions must be kept to a minimum.

The Government as Regulator
All the modes of intervention examined to this point rely on the capacity of the government to command vast resources and to direct them to purposes deemed to serve the public interest. Even when the government acts as catalyst, using tax measures to influence the use of private resources, its effectiveness depends on the incentive effect of the tax expenditures involved, which themselves represent the application of public resources in another form. But behind all the actions of government, however benign their appearance, lies the power of the state to make laws and to compel their observance. And some of the approaches available to government in influencing the flow of resources to cultural activity rest squarely on this power to make and enforce rules that define the rights and obligations governing transactions among members of society. Interventions in this category rely for their sanction on the threat of punishment rather than the promise of reward.

The most obvious example of this is found in the regulatory powers of the Canadian Radio-television and Telecommunications Commission and the use of those powers to prescribe Canadian content quotas for broadcasters. The beneficial impact of these regulations on the production and sales of the Canadian recording industry makes it clear that such regulatory measures can have significant economic effects of some cultural importance. Not surprisingly, this success has strengthened the interest of other Canadian producers of cultural products in the wider application and stricter enforcement of quotas in other segments of the process by which creators, performers and producers reach Canadian audiences.

From the point of view of the government, quotas have the attraction of being relatively cost-free. Against this, however, must be set the fact that, by restricting the freedom of action of those to whom the quotas apply and, in some circumstances, the freedom of choice of the consumers of cultural products (or their own perception of this), a heavy reliance on quotas can generate public resistance and resentment. To the extent that quotas impose higher costs without at the same time providing resources to compensate, they may also reduce public access to the enjoyment of cultural products. The record of broadcasting quotas further suggests that, because it is left to the market to provide the resources needed for compliance, the use of quotas alone – at least in the manner in which they have been applied – is of very limited use in stimulating Canadian activity that serves minority preferences.

For all these reasons, we have concluded that although Canadian content quotas, used by themselves, can serve in some circumstances to alter the allocation of resources and in the process to direct a larger share to Canadian creators, performers and producers, they do little or nothing to provide additional resources to the cultural sector as a whole. In order to attain coherent cultural policy goals, and to remedy the kinds of market failure identified at the beginning of this chapter, regulatory action in the form of quotas must, as a general rule, be accompanied by more positive measures to increase the resources available to cultural activity in Canada.

A very different example of the rule-making role of government which relates especially to culture is the law of copyright. By defining creators' proprietary rights in their creations and prescribing penalties for the unauthorized use of those works, copyright establishes the *minimum* conditions for a fair return to them for the use and enjoyment of their creations by others. Creators' ability to profit from the rights created by copyright law is, of course, dependent on the public's interest in their products, expressed as market demand. The law itself cannot, for example, compensate creators themselves for benefits to later generations – which was identified as one of the manifestations of market failure characteristic of cultural goods. Nor is it the best remedy for breaches of their rights in circumstances that make those rights unenforceable. Nevertheless, copyright remains one essential means by which government can influence the flow of resources to and within the cultural sphere, in the interests of ensuring that creators are rewarded for their efforts. In addition, copyright also simplifies transactions between all parties dealing with cultural products.

Because of the widespread dissatisfaction with the existing copyright law of Canada, which the Committee encountered in almost every sector of cultural life, we point to some general principles that should, in our view, be decisive in the copyright law revision that is now so belatedly in progress. This statement will be found in Appendix 2 at the end of this chapter.

Finding the Resources
As we have noted at several points, when the government acts to increase the flow of resources into cultural activity, those resources must be diverted from some other purpose; they cannot be conjured into existence by fiat. Where the government is to find the means of assisting culture is essentially a question of fiscal rather than cultural policy. But a number of the representations received by the Committee proposed measures not only for applying resources, but also for obtaining them. Our consideration of the marshalling of resources requires some examination of these proposals and of their implications.

It is, of course, a basic principle of public finance in the parliamentary tradition that the raising of money and the spending of it are kept separate. As a general rule, all revenues raised by authority of Parliament are pooled in the Consolidated Revenue Fund, and all authorized expenditures are paid from these general revenues. Expenditures for cultural purposes, almost without exception, have been dealt with in this way. Even the so-called tax expenditures used as incentives to private philanthropy and investment, because they involve the foregoing of taxes which would otherwise have flowed into the Consolidated Revenue Fund, constitute a charge against general revenues.

The proposals made to this Committee all involve departures from this normal practice by the use of earmarked revenues: funds from a specified source which are expressly dedicated to a specified use. Most of these suggestions were aimed at increasing the flow of resources into television production and are noted in the concluding section of Chapter 10 on "Broadcasting." We had also to consider a proposal, modeled on British practice, for creating a film production fund by a special levy on attendance at motion picture theatres. Other suggestions involved the earmarking of lottery revenues for particular or general cultural uses.

Governments have, in fact, found the device of earmarked revenues useful from time to time for certain purposes. It will be recalled that the Canadian Broadcasting Corporation, for some years after its creation, was financed out of the proceeds of the licensing of radio receivers; and in the early years of television, an earmarked excise tax on television receiving equipment was employed.

The attractions of earmarked revenues to those proposing them are readily appreciated. Above all, they may seem to offer greater security of revenues by eliminating the uncertainties involved in dependence on annual parliamentary appropriations and the lapsing of unspent balances at the end of each fiscal year. In addition, because the activities to which the funds are dedicated will be exempted from much of the governmental and parliamentary scrutiny associated with the appropriation and expenditure control process, earmarked revenues may be viewed as strengthening the autonomy of those operations. Their popularity may also reflect a general tendency, common to all sectors of society, to claim a special entitlement to revenues resulting from charges levied on the affairs of their respective sectors.

There may be implicit in these proposals an anxiety about the strength or reliability of the government's awareness of, or sympathy to, the needs of the cultural sector for public resources – the fear that, in the competition for annual appropriations, their claims may be shouldered aside by others. The proliferation of requests for earmarked sources of revenue may also be, in a sense, a sign of the times – a reaction to the persistent and growing difficulty encountered by all governments in satisfying the demands with which they are bombarded from all sides.

Even from the viewpoint of a government, earmarked levies may be attractive in special circumstances. It may be easier to exploit a previously untapped source of potential revenue by dedicating a new levy to a specified use of sufficient popular appeal to outweigh the resistance to the levy itself. In the ideal situation the revenues will be applied to the benefit of a majority of those who pay the cost. (The ultimate is the Ontario government's Halfback scheme, in which all who have contributed have done so voluntarily, and all contributors can benefit.)

As a general rule, however, the idea underlying earmarked revenues is incompatible with the principles of public finance in a parliamentary system. In the United States, where the separation of powers sets the branches of government apart from one another and fosters a sometimes defiant independence in their behaviour towards each other, legislatures may find in earmarked taxes, paid into special accounts for purposes delimited by statute, a useful device for restraining fiscal manipulations by the executive branch that might frustrate legislative wishes. In Canada, however, no minister of finance (or provincial treasurer) can ever be persuaded that particular sources of revenue authorized by the legislature are somehow beyond the range of the government's fiscal and expenditure policies. The consequence is that any independence and security of revenue sources that an earmarked levy may seem to confer on the activities to which it is dedicated is more apparent than real. In the last analysis – as we have recognized in Chapter 2 – the government, with parliamentary sanction, will determine not only the total allocation of resources to cultural purposes but also the manner in which they will be shared among the principal programs that serve those purposes. And in doing so, the government will not limit its view to the annual appropriations approved by Parliament, but will take account of the total flow of public resources, including earmarked levies and lottery funds.

In the opinion of this Committee, a good case can be made for earmarked revenues only in special circumstances. One such exception occurs when a specific problem can be addressed by the application of funds raised by a levy on activities that can be identified as the cause of the problem. An example of this can be found in our suggestion in Chapter 8 that the problems created by home taping for Canadian record production (and for all the creative artists, performers and others involved in the production and distribution of sound and video recordings), be met by a surcharge on blank tapes, the proceeds of which can be used to subsidize the purchase of such Canadian recordings. The fact that the utility of an arrangement of this kind depends on the circumstances of each particular case is illustrated by considering the comparable problem created in respect of books and periodicals by photocopying and library borrowing rights. In these instances, earmarked revenues will not serve, partly because of the impossibility of devising an appropriate levy and partly – in the case of library borrowing – because of the deeply entrenched tradition of free access to public libraries. Whatever remedy is developed must rely on the application of general public revenues, as will be recommended in Chapter 7.

An exception of wider applicability may be encountered where those who pay the levy are identical with those who benefit from its earmarked use.

The proposal concerning sound recordings, referred to above, also meets this case as the application of the special fund would be governed by the use of vouchers issued to those who paid the levy. In a less precise way, this was also the justification for the financing of the CBC from licence revenues during its first two decades when it was the only source of network broadcasting throughout Canada. It was, in fact, a form of "user pay" appropriate to a situation in which payment for use could not be obtained through the mechanisms of the market, but all owners of radios could reasonably be assumed to be users and therefore beneficiaries of the services financed from their licence fees.

Proponents of an earmarked tax on cable subscribers to create a fund for new Canadian production, or advocates of "universal" pay-television (which amounts, in essence, to the same thing), draw on a similar justification for their proposal. In our view, the circumstances are quite different, and as a consequence the justification is questionable. It is, after all, the distinguishing mark of pay-television (and of cable services generally) that it exploits the new possibility of metering use by viewers and charging users accordingly or, alternatively, of requiring those who wish to subscribe to pay for its availability. The weakness of this approach, which gives rise to the proposals for non-discretionary charges, is that it may offer little to satisfy minority preferences. This Committee is entirely sympathetic to the objective of serving minority interests, and of fostering the greatest possible diversity in cultural activity. But when, as in this proposal, there is no close correlation between the distribution of costs and the distribution of benefits, the scheme becomes essentially one of cross-subsidization – that is, the measures employed by one group in pursuit of their interests are taxed in order to serve the different interests of some other group. In this situation, the case for earmarked revenues breaks down. Cross-subsidization is, on the other hand, the very essence of government expenditure out of general revenues, of which the underlying principle is that money raised according to ability to pay is used to provide services according to need.

Our preference for the use of general revenues is reinforced by the recognition of certain defects inherent in earmarked revenues. Resources that are provided in this manner will tend to represent, not a judgment of need but rather whatever happens to be the yield of the earmarked revenue source. Initially there may be a correlation between the need and the yield, but with the passage of time that correlation may diminish rapidly. In place of the supposed security of resources there may in fact be only inflexibility on the one hand or instability on the other – as has been characteristic of lottery revenues.

Dedicating a revenue source to one particular use also tends to isolate that activity, not only from the processes of government expenditure control generally, but also from any process for the balancing of resource allocations to cultural purposes in particular. In our own deliberations, conducted over a period of persistent recession, we have become increasingly conscious of the difficult but inescapable necessity of assigning priorities to the diverse and urgent claims for the public support of cultural activity. To endow any one cultural agency or program with its own source of income, to which it has an exclusive and unqualified right, seems to us to fly in the face of this necessity.

13.   Public funds for the support of cultural activity should as a general rule. be financed from general revenues. The earmarking of revenues from a specified source for a specified use should be employed only when there is a close correlation between the incidence of the financial burdens imposed and the distribution of benefits, and its adoption as a means of cross-subsidization should be avoided.

As we recognized in Chapter 2, the allocation of public resources to cultural activities generally, and among the various major programs competing for those resources, can only be decided by ministers guided by the advice of those entrusted with the direction of those programs, and by the workings of the political process itself. Looking back over the past 30 years, we must conclude that until the mid-1970s the government's sensitivity to cultural needs and the importance it assigned to those needs in its allocation of resources were on the whole commendable. If there has been uncertainty and hesitancy in recent years we would rather attribute this to the novelty and complexity of the problems that emerged in those years – which have dominated our own proceedings – than to any slackening of the government's interest in or commitment to cultural life. If we are right in this, the record of the past should dispel any fears that culture will be treated as a residual item. We are confident, instead, that in the allocation of the resources at its disposal the federal government will respond to the needs and dynamism of the arts and culture of the country and give them the increased attention and funds which we claim they deserve.

Appendix 1

A Marketing and Promotion Organization

If we are to increase public awareness of the benefits of cultural activity and to promote greater enjoyment of it, Canadian artists and their work must be publicized – and marketed – more effectively than they have been in the past. Success in these efforts will stimulate demand for and consumption of the cultural output of the country. In the process, public recognition of our artists will be expanded and their financial rewards improved.

We do not see this task of marketing and promoting the arts as a direct responsibility of the government; experience and observation suggest that governments and government agencies are not the best promoters. Its encouragement and material support should, however, find a place in federal cultural policy. And the fact that, for whatever reasons, the private interests that would reap the most direct benefits have failed to develop effective mechanisms on their own initiative indicates to us that the federal government should take the lead. We therefore recommend the establishment of a marketing and promotion organization.

It is important in our view that the proposed marketing and promotion organization should look on itself primarily as an enabling body, one that encourages things to happen. The organization should not itself sell or distribute Canadian cultural products, but should seek to increase public awareness of their importance and to devise ways of enlarging their markets.

14. The federal government should assume a leading role in fostering the creation of a nongovernment organization designed primarily to devise initiatives and provide impetus in the marketing and promotion of Canadian arts.

After the initial impetus of the organization has been achieved, the role of the federal government – and of provincial and municipal governments if they participate as we would hope – would consist exclusively of providing sustaining funds. The organization's policies would be the responsibility of a board made up of members of the business and arts communities and the consuming public. It would pursue activities such as those indicated below, and since these would not be profitable in a commercial sense, the organization would need public funds. Should some specialized activities prove to be profitable, it is possible to imagine the investment of private funds. Such an organization would also, we hope, attract funds, expertise and other resources from private and corporate donors.

There can be no doubt that one of the important marketing and promotion activities of the proposed organization would be advertising. This is a widely used instrument for the dissemination of information about products of all kinds and should be used aggressively, as has often been done in the past by performing arts companies, museums, and the cultural industries. The preparation of advertising material, the purchase of space and time for its diffusion, the building up of expertise about the use of advertising would naturally fall within the mandate of the body we are proposing. So, too, would be the acquisition of free space and time in print and broadcasting outlets, and their redistribution to various members of the arts consituency.

A close working relationship with the producers of cultural and artistic products in both large and small communities would be essential. Some communities might need to be persuaded, others reminded, that life in their area would be improved through increased cultural activity. Elsewhere, groups and individuals might have to be assured, as one of our Committee members put it, "that a box of crayons is as important as a football" when it comes to allocating time and money. It would therefore be a primary objective of the organization to encourage involvement and participation in creative experiences.

Promotion implies selection; it is not possible to promote everything at the same time, although it may be possible to promote almost everything over time. The selection process is a difficult one which entails the exercise of discretion and judgment and, therefore, from many points of view, the making of "mistakes." It is for this reason in particular that governments, which are pressed to promote everyone equally, are poor promoters. But that is not the only conclusion that one should draw from the foregoing. If the artistic community is not tolerant and cooperative – if it cannot appreciate that the benefits from promotion activity accrue over time to the whole of the community – the marketing and promotion organization we are proposing will not be able to function efficiently.

The art of spending money successfully requires careful balancing of alternatives and therefore much information about the properties of each alternative. This is why, in the markets for everyday products, so much money and effort on the part of businesses goes into the building of goodwill, brand names and trademarks. The world of arts and culture is no different. In a way the dilemma of buyers is greater there, since the products offered are never the same. Choosing a book, a play, a film, a record, a concert requires a lot of information. In the same way that buyers of everyday goods and services – peas, shoes or tennis balls – economize on information by responding to goodwill, brand names and trademarks, so do buyers of artistic and cultural products economize on information by a reliance on "stars," which can be performing arts companies as well as individuals.

If this marketing and promotion organization is to be successful, one of its goals will be to promote stars. Stars not only help buyers to choose but also serve to highlight various kinds of excellence. They should be recognizable not only among rock musicians and film actors, but also among composers, choreographers, painters, writers, performing arts companies – the best we have to offer in all fields.

Building and promoting stars is costly and risky; it is very selective and will require the full cooperation of the artistic community. The benefits of stardom do not accrue exclusively to the stars; all of the arts world benefits.

Marketing and promotion imply a detailed knowledge of the field in which the product or event is to be sold. A special kind of knowledge is indicated and a special kind of expertise called for. The proposed organization would therefore be expected to engage in market research and to call on the services of market research experts when developing advertising campaigns, deciding on the promotion of stars and choosing which products to promote through methods such as voucher schemes.

All artistic and cultural products reach buyers through distribution networks, at least if we do not give too narrow a meaning to that expression. Throughout our hearings and in the briefs we have received, many specific distribution problems have been brought to our attention. Some appeared to us, at least in the first instance, as possibly in restraint of trade and therefore against the law of the land; others reflected a lack of information or some other impediment. One of the tasks of the organization we are proposing would be to investigate these distribution barriers in arts and culture and to undertake appropriate action to have them removed.

The range of activities open to such a marketing and promotion organization would be limited only by its imagination and knowledge of the cultural world, and would grow with experience. These activities might encompass such diverse operations as the promotion of film and book clubs, the development in cooperation with performing arts companies of schemes for the "optimal" pricing of seats to attract different potential audiences, or fostering the use of Canadian visual and applied artworks for book and record jackets. It might also be expected, for example, that one of its first undertakings would be to devise and promote a voucher scheme on a national basis. Certain activities – such as the voucher scheme – would call for the cooperation of governments. All of its work would require close relations with organizations involved in international and domestic touring, in record, book and film sales, and in television and radio.

The essence of the role of this marketing and promotion organization we are proposing would be to bring together the art and its buyer, the event and its spectators, the creative work and its audience. This we describe as one of the fundamental elements of cultural policy and crucial to its success. It is therefore vital that we acknowledge the importance of marketing and promotion services, devise ways of improving them, learn more about them and hone techniques to make the best use of them.

Appendix 2

Copyright

Although much of the discussion in the earlier part of this chapter dealt with market failures, copyright legislation is an instrument aimed at improving market efficiency. In addition, throughout our public hearings, this Committee was told repeatedly and forcefully that copyright protection is fundamental to the interests of creative artists. Authors, composers, visual and applied artists of all kinds, filmmakers, choreographers, photographers, architects and all other creators see in copyright law a means of protecting their professional integrity and that of their works. It also acts as a means of providing proper recompense for use by the public of their creations. For the public, copyright legislation provides assured access in a clearly understood and manageable way to the world's creations in return for reasonable payment to owners of the works. A good copyright law should therefore make it clear that those who create works (let us call them "authors" while we refer at the same time to composers, painters, choreographers, filmmakers, photographers and the others who create intellectual properties) have control over their works and are entitled to a fair return for those works commensurate with the use made of them by the public.

At the same time, nobody should be under the delusion that copyright legislation, by itself, will solve either the economic or social problems of all authors. Copyright legislation serves best those authors whose works appeal to large segments of the public, wherever in the world they may be. It cannot solve the social and economic problems of those authors whose works, although they may have great aesthetic or academic value, will earn very little because they appeal to relatively small numbers of users. The value to a society of its poets, composers of classical music, writers of essays, historians, philosophers and their like must be measured and paid for through means found outside the realm of copyright.

Canada's Copyright Act, enacted in 1924, was based on a British model of even earlier vintage. It has long been clear that the law is out of date and has been left behind by technological and social changes. The inability to arrive at acceptable revisions, even after years of effort, is shocking. This Committee can only applaud recent efforts that promise a set of proposed revisions to the Copyright Act for presentation to Parliament. Even as this Committee has been developing this Report, two government task forces and an interdepartmental committee have been considering those revisions. One group was organized by the Department of Consumer and Corporate Affairs, which is responsible for the administration of the present Copyright Act, and the other by the Department of Communications, through which most of the cultural agencies report. We sincerely hope that, this effort will result in real achievement within the projected timetable and that the government will be able to offer to the patient cultural community and to the Canadian public a revised Act that is both effective and appropriate to the times.

Because of that review, which we believe is coming to imminent fruition, we offer here only some general views, instead of specific recommendations.

We hope that the revised Act will apply its own principles in an equitable way to all creators in all disciplines, removing instances of differentiation and discrimination. It should also be flexible enough to admit new forms of creative expression using new media, which may emerge in the future and to which similar protections should be made applicable.

We further expect that the new Act will reaffirm and strengthen the concept that authors of artistic and intellectual works are the owners of their creations. Advances in technology and delivery systems should not weaken that fundamental right. Any rights that the author, as the owner, may choose to assign to others should be divisible by use, time, geography, medium, language and in many other ways. Limitations on the authors' control over their works should be applied with caution and sensitivity. Thus, although "fair use" and reasonable access by the public are necessary intrusions into the rights of the owners and should be acknowledged, fair returns to them must be considered at the same time.

Such an attitude would tend to remove many of the exemptions from infringement now found in the Copyright Act. There is no reason why authors should be asked to provide special subsidies to agricultural fairs, juke-box operators and religious institutions. The release of rights, whether or not in return for payment, to churches or schools should be the prerogative of the copyright owner; control over such decisions should not be removed by law. By the same token, the use of compulsory licensing as a means of assuring access should be employed, if at all, only when that device is considered to be absolutely necessary and should always assure adequate payments to the copyright owners for such usages. Fees that are set by regulation, when that proves to be essential, should be fair and should be open to periodic review, avoiding situations such as now pertain where a fee set in 1924 is made to apply in the 1980s.

It can be anticipated that new collectives of authors will emerge, to administer rights and benefits more effectively through joint action. The affairs of such organizations should be conducted by their Canadian membership and directed exclusively to the protection and administration of the copyright interests of their members. With increased activity by collectives, there would be an important role for a strong copyright tribunal to supervise collectives, set fees, handle appeals and deal with a wide range of related issues. One other important function of such a tribunal could be the supervision of a periodic review, perhaps every 10 years, of the terms of the Copyright Act.

This Committee, then, is in complete agreement with the general idea that creators should be compensated for uses by the public of their works. In the specific case of payment for public use to writers, a Canada Council plan for compensatory grants is discussed in some detail in Chapter 7, where we also describe an alternative plan. We want to see the introduction of some such plan without delay. In the long run, however, we believe that copyright law procedures would have the advantage of enshrining the rights in question and generalizing their application. In some circumstances a serious outflow of funds to foreign authors might result. Under the right kind of copyright legislation, authors' collectives could administer the rights in question, protecting the interests of their members in such a way that assignment of rights to foreign authors would be accepted only if their own country offered reciprocal arrangements.

Home recording and photocopying are both technical infringements of copyright under the 1924 Act. Although such practices are not condoned in law, they are common and not practically preventable. They clearly constitute a use of authors' work, yet no payment is made to the copyright owners. Some countries have established taxes or levies on reproducing machines or materials, but no workable ways have yet been found to compensate specific owners for the copying of specific works. Payments resulting from the levies have been distributed either to authors' general pension funds and other benefit programs, or to collectives of owners for distribution to their members through measures of their devising.

It has been proposed that such copying practices be exempt from infringement under the revised Act through clauses describing "fair use" and that some form of levy might be introduced at a later date. In line with our general principles, we hope that the revised Act would see that authors are fairly treated with respect to all uses made by the public of their creative output.

Future technology will undoubtedly continue to produce devices that will win wide public acceptance and that might tend to weaken further the position and interests of authors. If copyright laws cannot adequately protect those rights and interests, direct government programs should do so. Current penalties designed to cope with infringements of copyright clearly fail to discourage piracy and other forms of theft. We deal further with this matter in Chapter 8, "Sound Recording."

As for what are called "moral rights," we take the general position that the integrity of authors and of their works should be protected and that they should be able to prevent distortion and mutilation of their works. Visual artists should have control over the use of their names, some measure of control over distribution and other pertinent moral rights. Such rights should persist for the whole term of the copyright, and that term should be the lifetime of the creator plus 50 years. As we have said, all such rights should apply equally to all creators including photographers, choreographers, designers and others. Visual artists have a related, special concern for "droit de suite," or control over their works after they have passed out of their hands, including the right to share in the proceeds of successive sales of their works. Without reciprocal arrangements with other countries, any such scheme would be, to say the least, imperfect. It would not serve our artists well if Canada were to act alone in this regard, without coordinating its efforts with those of other countries. Canada should act in concert with other countries to establish a common international regime for "droit de suite."

We are also concerned about many other areas where copyright law is of great importance: in broadcasts, performances, cable rediffusion, satellite transmissions, computer programs. The Committee hopes that the general principles discussed above will govern the decisions made by the federal government in these cases. We repeat our conviction that it is in everyone's interest to guarantee and protect the basic rights of creators to the ownership and control of their works, and to provide proper compensation to them for the use of their works by others.

4
Heritage

_____

_____

_____

_____

_____

_____

4

Heritage

In April 1949, the Privy Council of Canada set in motion the work of the Royal Commission on National Development in the Arts, Letters and Sciences, referred to in this Report as the Massey-Lévesque Commission. The order-in-council stated as a first principle that "the Canadian people should know as much as possible about their country, its history and traditions, and about their national life and common achievements." There is still no better justification for the many varied activities and institutions now devoted to the preservation of Canada's national heritage.

Our heritage begins with the land itself and its many natural wonders. It encompasses prehistoric remains and the traditions of the Indian and Inuit peoples. Our national heritage is made up of the tangible and the intangible. It includes folk tales and family histories, paintings and prime ministers' papers, old houses and old stones. It is present in the countryside and in the urban centres of our country, in public museums and private collections. Our heritage inspires, enlightens and enriches contemporary Canadian experience.

The preservation of these irreplaceable heritage resources has been assumed by heritage institutions sponsored by all levels of government, as well as by private corporations and citizens. Museums, art galleries, archives, historic buildings and sites, and specialized public and private collections are all custodians of heritage resources.

At the federal level there has always been some recognition of the importance of what we now refer to as heritage. In 1867 Canada already possessed a significant architectural and engineering heritage, as well as archival and library materials in all the existing provinces. Canadians and visitors to Canada in Victorian times were fascinated by our natural heritage and left a legacy of writing and painting inspired by it. From the first, a few farsighted federal officials managed with very limited funds to create the foundations of our national heritage collections. There were, for instance, Sir William Edward Logan and G.M. Dawson of the Geological Survey which preceded the former National Museum of Canada; Marius Barbeau and Diamond Jenness of what became the National Museum of Man; John Macoun of what was eventually called the National Museum of Natural Sciences; Eric Brown, H.O. McCurry and Kathleen Fenwick at the National Gallery of Canada; Arthur Doughty and W. Kaye Lamb at the Public Archives of Canada, to name only a few.

In spite of the prodigious contribution of these individuals and others who worked with them, federal involvement in the heritage field, until the formulation of the National Museum Policy in 1972, could be characterized as negligible commitment rather than wilful neglect. The Centennial celebrations in 1967 marked a change in both public and government attitude toward our national heritage. Canadians are now more aware and concerned about their heritage than ever before. This is reflected in the astounding growth of custodial institutions and historic sites and parks, and the numbers of visitors they receive. The Canadian Museums Association told us that "the 1,600 custodial agencies in Canada serve an estimated audience of 40 million visitors annually."

Canadians have shared in the increasing international interest and concern for the preservation of heritage since 1976 by recognizing the International Convention for the Protection of World Cultural and Natural Heritage. The World Heritage List established and monitored by the World Heritage Committee of the United Nations Educational, Scientific and Cultural Organization (Unesco), which includes world renowned treasures such as the pyramids of Egypt and Mont-Saint-Michel, now includes seven Canadian natural and cultural sites.

The growing public interest in and support for heritage activities in Canada was recognized in the increased funding provided for heritage programs through the National Museums of Canada, the Canada Council and the Heritage Canada Foundation. Without this support, many heritage activities would not have been undertaken and much of the riches of our heritage would not have been disseminated across Canada and overseas. Heritage is inevitably a growth area, by its very nature always expanding and seldom contracting, yet since 1976 there has been no increase in the real value of funds allocated to the National Museums of Canada or to the Canada Council, while the Heritage Canada Foundation has seen its endowment diminish. Heritage institutions in Canada are currently unable to conserve, catalogue or adequately display the material they now possess. How then can they be expected to enlarge their collections significantly or undertake new activities?

The consequences of the current situation for Canadian culture should not be underestimated and are a matter of grave concern to this Committee. It must be recognized that our past is too precious to lose because of inadequate funding. Heritage is irreplaceable; it cannot be ignored or neglected for years and then retrieved; it needs constant preservation. We direct the attention of governments at all levels to what one brief described as "the *totality* of our inescapable heritage responsibilities." *We urge governments to make a substantial commitment at once to the preservation of our heritage, to recognize its unique nature, and the need to maintain this priceless inheritance for ourselves and for generations to come.*

There must also be a renewed commitment to effective management of heritage interests by existing custodial institutions. We agree with the National Museums of Canada, the federal agency which deals with many heritage concerns, that, in future, these institutions

"may have to accept limitations on growth and place much greater emphasis on cooperative ventures, including not only shared sponsorship of exhibitions and other programme activities, already fairly common, but shared conservation, storage and research facilities and joint stewardship of collections as well."

Technological advances over the next 20 years undoubtedly will have an impact on the management of our heritage resources. Even though in recent years great advances have been made in techniques for preservation and conservation, it is still necessary, because of Canada's distinctive problems of distance and climatic extremes, to discover better and cheaper ways to protect, accommodate, distribute and display the tangible evidence of our past. Great technological changes in information disposal systems have also occurred over this same period, yet access to heritage material has not become proportionately any easier. Even so, no information retrieval system, however efficient, could ever be an adequate substitute for the exhilarating experience of actually viewing at first hand a unique object, specimen, work of art or building of historic interest.

These considerations, and the more detailed ones which follow, have led us to several conclusions about various aspects of our national heritage, its due recognition and its preservation. We have, however, two central recommendations which are interdependent and reinforcing, and which underlie many others and so should be stated at once, leaving specific observations to emerge in context.

To give adequate expression to the importance we attach to heritage as a distinct and vital component of Canadian culture, we propose the establishment of the Canadian Heritage Council, a new independent agency with broad national objectives. Further, because we also attach special importance to federal heritage institutions in the National Capital Region, we propose that the Board of Trustees of the National Museums of Canada devote itself entirely to the supervision of the existing four national museums, together with any future museums or galleries located there or elsewhere in Canada which may be created in response to other recommendations in this Report.

15.   The Government of Canada should establish an arm's-
       length agency to be known as the Canadian Heritage
       Council, to be a visible champion of heritage interests in
       Canada, recognizing the importance and particular
       characteristics of those interests, to promote heritage arts
       and sciences and to support heritage institutions.

16. The National Museums of Canada, guided by its Board of
     Trustees, should retain supervisory responsibility for the
     four existing and any proposed federal heritage custodial
     institutions in the National Capital Region or elsewhere. It
     should, however, relinquish to the proposed Canadian
     Heritage Council responsibility for the various categories of
     grants and assistance now given to nonprofit museums
     throughout Canada under the Museum Assistance Program-
     mes, for the continuation of the National Inventory of the
     cultural heritage, and for the Canadian Conservation In-
     stitute – all of which are at present administered and fund-
     ed by the National Museums of Canada as part of the
     National Programmes.

Current Problems in Heritage

Effective resolution of the problems experienced today by heritage institutions and disciplines will greatly affect the management of heritage resources
in the future. These problems have arisen in organizations involved with
movable heritage, such as archives and museums, as well as in institutions
concerned with fixed heritage, such as natural sites and the built environment. The provision of additional funding is obviously a basic need but it is
not by any means the only solution to the difficulties evident in various aspects of heritage – recognition, acquisition, conservation and dissemination.

Recognition of Heritage Value
Problems in the identification of heritage material worthy of preservation
arise mainly in relation to fixed heritage, especially historical and archaeological sites and materials found on them. Parks Canada, through its
National Historic Parks and Sites Branch, is the federal agency which has an
important cultural responsibility in the identification, protection and preservation of many of Canada's significant in situ historic, architectural and archaeological resources. The Parks Canada brief drew our attention to a difficulty which will require legislative action to resolve.

The Minister of the Environment, to whom Parks Canada is responsible,
may designate a site as being of national significance under the present
Historic Sites and Monuments Act, but unless the Crown acquires the site
there is no way of ensuring it will remain unaltered. The Parks Canada brief
pointed out that federal designation, unlike provincial designation which in
almost every case imposes legal restrictions on the future use of the property,
"places no restrictions, other than moral ones, on the disposition of property
in private hands or property held by other levels of government." The essential purpose of the recognition of the heritage value of a site is frequently
thwarted by formal federal designation and, distressingly, such designation

has often led to theft or vandalism. Parks Canada has been forced to designate secretly, but not mark officially, certain potentially vulnerable sites.

The Department of the Environment now has the authority to prevent the destruction of Canada's natural heritage through the duly authorized Environment Assessment and Review Process. A similar process should now be established in law to give protection to designated historic and archaeological sites from unconsidered alteration or destruction. The Committee supports the view expressed by Parks Canada and recommends that:

17. Existing federal legislation relating to the designation of historic sites should be strengthened to compel heritage impact studies to be carried out and reviewed before any such site is sold, developed or in any way altered from its present use.

More effective legislation is, in our view, also required to protect heritage resources in the Northwest Territories. In this case the resources are virtually all located on Crown land and their protection is therefore clearly a federal responsibility. Unfortunately, as we were told by the Director of the Prince of Wales Northern Heritage Centre, neither the federal nor the territorial governments have assumed this responsibility, with the result that these "priceless, nonrenewable resources are being disturbed and destroyed at an alarming rate."

Minimal protection is now provided by the Northwest Territories Archaeological Sites Regulations (under the Northwest Territories Act). These regulations are outdated, ineffective and offensive to the residents of the North. They require that all specimens found in the Northwest Territories be deposited with the Archaeological Survey of Canada in Ottawa. While this prevents private interests from assuming ownership of important heritage material, it effectively prevents this material from being exhibited in context. This deprives Canadians who live in the North of opportunities to see objects which are part of their own heritage in the region in which they were found.

18. The Department of Indian and Northern Affairs, as the federal department which administers the Northwest Territories, should review the existing Northwest Territories Archaeological Sites Regulations with the Archaeological Survey of Canada and the National Historic Parks and Sites Branch. It should proceed at once to develop a comprehensive heritage preservation act which clearly states the responsibilities and obligations of government, industry, special interest groups and individuals for the prehistoric and historic archaeological resources of the Northwest Territories, and gives recognition to the interests of Canadians in the Northwest Territories to retain such materials in the context in which they were found whenever possible.

Throughout Canada much greater recognition of the value of our "built heritage" could also be given by federal authorities. The Department of Public Works has on its inventory of buildings owned by the Crown many structures dating from 1867 and earlier. Federal public buildings often shaped the towns that grew up around them. Parks Canada and the Department of National Defence have control of other historic federal properties. Officials of the Department of Public Works, appearing on March 10, 1981, before the Senate Committee on National Finance, gave assurances that new criteria were being developed for a policy on heritage buildings. The Department of Public Works has for some time required that proposals submitted to it for construction or land use projects include an assessment of their possible impact on existing heritage properties. Recycling a heritage building to meet contemporary building code and client requirements admittedly presents difficulties, but such a solution, in our view, should always be the first consideration. Both Public Works and the Heritage Canada Foundation have found by experience that adaptive re-use of a heritage building can be an economically competitive solution, with the important additional gain that an architecturally and historically significant structure is preserved in its original context.

Our concern for recognition of our built heritage has a special application in the National Capital Region. The nation's capital should be a showplace for our accomplishments, a place in which we have pride, a symbol of our rich and varied past and present. Its buildings should tell both Canadians and visitors how we view ourselves and how we value our achievements. The National Capital Commission and the Department of Public Works are to be commended for the care taken to preserve the parliamentary precinct and the heritage context of Sussex Drive, and for the imaginative use of the historic Rideau Canal, to cite some examples.

Federal departments with construction responsibilities have shown some sensitivity to the value of the built heritage, recycling, reconstructing and restoring large and small properties in Ottawa and elsewhere, but many buildings have also been lost.

It is the view of this Committee that the federal government must actively demonstrate that it puts a high priority on the preservation and use of the heritage properties under direct federal control, so that Canada's built heritage receives from others the recognition, protection and preservation required to ensure that Canadians never lose their sense of place and continuity with their past.

Collection

We consider it relevant to heritage policy to make some observations about the balance between Canadian and non-Canadian content in our national heritage collections. The work of creative artists from many countries has always been collected by Canadian galleries, while many Canadian museums have specialized collections from around the world. It is appropriate that

Canadians should have the opportunity to become familiar with the accomplishments of other countries. In this connection, the Royal Ontario Museum quoted to us the wise comment by Northrop Frye that "It is only when we have made the effort to understand other ways of life that we can come to see our own as a specific culture too."

Pride of place in Canadian heritage institutions should, however, always be reserved for the works of our own creative artists of the past and present. This is not at present evident in major collections other than those of the four federal museums. Unhappily some aspects of Canadian creative endeavour are underrepresented or entirely missing in the present collections of both federal and non-federal institutions. These areas include Native art and archival material, the applied arts (including unique crafts and industrial design), films and photographs, radio and television tapes, and often the most innovative and experimental contemporary creation. Many of these omissions can only be amended by the creation of entirely new collections within a new custodial institution which we propose in Chapter 5.

In this general discussion of current problems in heritage, certainly the most serious problem in the collection aspect concerns Native peoples' art and archival material. We have previously indicated that, in our view, the peoples of Indian and Inuit ancestry must have a special place in Canadian cultural policy. It is therefore distressing to find that, of the national museums, only the National Museum of Man systematically collects Native art and artifacts and even that museum has only recently given some emphasis to contemporary creation. The National Gallery of Canada neither collects nor displays the work of Indian or Inuit artists. Many works by these artists have for years been successfully shown in other countries where they are now sought by collectors. Two extensive and important collections of Indian and Inuit art, assembled by the Department of Indian and Northern Affairs, have never been shown to the public or even systematically organized until recently.

Federal collections of historical records of the Indian, Inuit and Métis peoples should also be strengthened and made more accessible. The history of these peoples is almost entirely an oral tradition. Unfortunately, to quote from the brief presented by the Inuit Cultural Institute, "this body of information is not being retrieved and disseminated fast enough. That is a disastrous loss to Canadian scholarship in general, and Inuit culture in particular." This could also be said, with truth, of the loss to Indian and Métis cultures as well.

On a happier note, Canadian collections of heritage materials have been greatly assisted by the creation of the Canadian Cultural Property Export Review Board, a quasi-judicial body established in 1977 under the terms of the Cultural Property Export and Import Act. The objective of that legislation was to provide means to ensure that the best examples of Canada's heritage in movable cultural property are kept in the country. The Act authorized three ways to achieve this objective: export controls, tax incentives to encourage donations or sales of private collections to designated public institutions, and grants or loans to help designated institutions buy objects which are stopped at the border by the control system or to repatriate cultural property of heritage value (and deemed significant to Canada) which is offered for sale often outside Canada.

To give an idea of the increasingly successful application of this legislation, it is interesting to note that in 1980-81 the Review Board issued 279 cultural property income tax certificates. These certificates establish an acceptable fair market value of proposed sales or donations. As a result nearly $15.5 million worth of cultural property was transferred to designated collecting institutions and public authorities, of which almost $13.5 million was in donations. During the first five years of the program, acquisition grants to designated non-federal institutions in every province totaled nearly $1.2 million, while federal collecting agencies received $2.5 million. Grants are given to supplement funds provided by institutions from their own varied resources to meet the purchase price of a desired property.

The Review Board has consistently drawn attention to certain difficulties it has experienced under the present statutory arrangements. In each instance the changes the Review Board desires are, in our view, not only compatible with the original purpose of the legislation, but would also benefit both artists and institutions. We wish to comment here on those which most directly affect the collection of heritage properties in Canada.

The Review Board has queried the method and level of funding for the grants which the enabling legislation authorizes it to give. The amount allocated for this purpose each year has, in the opinion of the Review Board, never been large enough to ensure that it could meet the costs of a major emergency purchase of heritage property, nor does it now reflect the realities of the international art market or the reduction in the purchasing power of the Canadian dollar. Furthermore, the unspent balance of this allocation cannot be carried over to the next fiscal year. This jeopardizes the often protracted and delicate purchase negotiations. In both cases this is an unnecessarily restrictive arrangement which should be altered at the first opportunity to recognize the uncertainties inherent in the art and heritage properties markets.

19.   The annual sum appropriated for grants made by the Canadian Cultural Property Export Review Board should properly reflect the unpredictable and high prices of the international art market. Unspent balances from this appropriation should be carried forward to succeeding fiscal years and the Cultural Property Export and Import Act should be amended to provide authority to do this.

The Review Board has, we believe, fulfilled its functions well. The members of the Board are appointed by the Governor in Council on the recommendation of the Minister of Communications, and its administrative services are provided by the Department of Communications. These arrangements cause the Committee some misgivings. Because of the nature of its duties, the Review Board must be free of the merest hint of political influence. The composition of the Board is crucial to the effective operation of the program, and Board members must command professional respect earned by their expertise. Recommendations made by the minister should, in our view, always be based on consultations with the various heritage disciplines directly affected by the Board's activities. The Review Board and its support staff should also be removed from their present direct departmental situation. Although the duties of the Board are important, they are relatively narrow in scope and do not justify a completely independent status. We consider that the Canadian Heritage Council we have recommended as the principal agency for heritage activities would provide the appropriate administrative framework within which the Review Board could work independently, in the way that the Canadian Commission for Unesco now works within the administrative framework of the Canada Council.

20.   The Canadian Cultural Property Export Review Board
       should, while retaining its independent status, be
       associated for administrative purposes with the proposed
       Canadian Heritage Council.

Conservation

Conservation is the fundamental activity in the heritage field. Without conservation our heritage will disintegrate and eventually disappear; without conservation the objects and ideas which link us to our past will vanish, never to be retrieved. The present situation is very grave. Canadian custodial institutions lose more of our heritage every year through deterioration and lack of conservation than they gain through acquisitions. Archivists, for example, often find that 20th century documents are on poor quality paper which quickly disintegrates, making imperative the need to find new ways to conserve these irreplaceable records. Heritage groups protest the destruction of a number of historically significant buildings every year. Curators of scientific specimens and artifacts and of works of art, both ancient and modern, are today fighting a losing battle even to keep in existence the objects they now possess.

The four national museums and the National Historic Parks and Sites Branch have always had the capacity to carry out some conservation of their own collections. This individual federal conservation activity was extended by the opening of the Canadian Conservation Institute in December 1976 as one of the constituents of the National Programmes of the National Museums of Canada. The Institute treats artifacts in collections in museums and galleries throughout Canada on a regular and emergency basis from its laboratories in Ottawa and on site through its mobile conservation units. It has a small internship program to provide on-the-job training in conservation techniques and conducts some research into conservation methods and problems. Results of these research activities are published in technical bulletins. The demand for the conservation services available from the Institute has been so great, however, that essential development of its research and education activities has been delayed.

This important service was initially also provided in regional conservation centres, which were closed in 1978 when government budgetary restrictions reduced the annual appropriation to the National Museums of Canada. The closure of these regional centres has further increased the conservation workload of the Canadian Conservation Institute in Ottawa. This is far from ideal. Conservation work should always be done as close as possible to the collecting institution. Major museums in all parts of the country should have their own in-house conservation facilities where the results of the research into new techniques carried out by the Institute might be applied and where smaller regional museums could be assisted with their conservation problems.

It is heartening to note that some provinces now have mobile and other conservation units offering a necessarily limited service to local collections which need basic conservation assistance. The Canadian Conservation Institute, however, has a national role to play in basic preventive conservation training and particularly in research to find new conservation techniques. The preservation of contemporary documents on wood pulp paper is an important example of the need for research in this field. The work of the Institute should be for the benefit of all the heritage institutions of Canada. As such it would, we believe, be more appropriately associated with the proposed Canadian Heritage Council. This change would serve in part to emphasize the primary research function of the Institute and its role as a national resource during an emergency rescue operation for heritage materials.

21.   In recognition of the fact that conservation is a vital national aspect of heritage, the proposed Canadian Heritage Council should give special consideration to requests for grants which will ensure that every region of Canada has access to regional conservation facilities. The Canadian Conservation Institute should report directly to the Canadian Heritage Council and receive its funding from appropriations made to the Canadian Heritage Council. The Canadian Conservation Institute should give priority to research into new conservation techniques, the results of which it should share with all Canadian heritage institutions.

Research
Lack of research, like lack of conservation, jeopardizes the whole heritage field. Without research, it is impossible to identify what should be preserved,

how it should be kept and the ways in which this knowledge can be made accessible. Yet research, the least visible activity in the heritage process, is usually the last to be funded and the first to be cut. Everywhere in Canada we met representatives of heritage institutions who emphasized the neglect of long-term concentrated research based on actual collections. There is also an acute need for published material based on the Canadian heritage experience for use in training curators, conservators and educators. Research publications on how Canadian geographic and climatic conditions affect preservation and conservation would, for example, be extremely useful. It was put to us that because research is the basis for all heritage programs of exhibition, publication and interpretation, it requires sustained support.

Research based on collections can only be undertaken effectively if collections are well managed. Appropriate accessing, identification and cataloguing leading to comprehensive inventory control must be carried out with precision. If these processes are not in place, collections are not accessible and are therefore virtually useless. We were told that there is a pressing need for inventories of archaeological material and historic buildings. Federal institutions, including the Public Archives of Canada and the four national museums, urgently need to improve their collections management. Other custodial institutions across the country have benefited, to a certain extent, from funds available for registration upgrading through the National Museums of Canada's Museum Assistance Programmes. Nonetheless, it is fair to say that virtually every heritage institution could and should adopt new, improved methods for collections management and uniform methods using current technology, which are relatively simple to process and financially more efficient over the long term.

The need to have easily accessible information about the content of collections and of existing heritage buildings to facilitate research and collections management prompted two federal agencies to set up inventory programs early in the 1970s. The Canadian Inventory of Historic Buildings was begun in 1970 by the National Historic Parks and Sites Branch. It is a computerized program to survey, analyze and classify existing old buildings which may be worthy of preservation. Much valuable data has already been accumulated in this inventory. Exteriors of about 200,000 buildings have been surveyed and their features indexed. The interiors will also be surveyed, and approximately 1,800 have been completed.

In 1972 the National Museums of Canada, as part of its National Museum Policy, began a National Inventory program to compile a computer-based inventory of all the public, scientific and cultural museum collections in Canada. In its first eight years expenditures on this program have totaled about $7.5 million. The Secretary General of the National Museums of Canada told a parliamentary committee in February 1982 that the original purpose of the inventory had been to provide the museum community with an information bank which could be used for research, exhibitions and educational purposes. However, with increased emphasis on more efficient collections management by the Auditor General and the central agencies, the inventory has also been made into a more effective tool for planning and control of acquisitions. The National Inventory will ultimately give access to information on an estimated 34 million objects in Canadian collections, including those in museums, university collections and collections of government departments. Of these, about nine million objects are in the care of museums, 1.5 million in the National Museums of Canada. There are 150 participating institutions in this inventory project.

There have been problems with both the mechanical and factual aspects of the creation of the National Inventory. To begin with, there was no clear conception of the scope of the collections to be included because participating museums across the country had no idea themselves of what they had in their custody. By February 1982, the Secretary General of the National Museums could report that 42 per cent of items given high priority by the museum community had been inventoried, or in other terms, 37 per cent of the man-made objects. He estimated that within five years all nine million objects in the 150 participating museums will have been entered. The cost of completing the project is estimated to be $2.7 million, but researchers in the participating museums will then have access, through widely available computer terminals, to this extraordinary information base.

Both the Canadian Inventory of Historic Buildings and the National Inventory program should be completed with all possible dispatch. They are of enormous potential benefit to all heritage activity in Canada. As basic information resources which will require sustained support, both national programs should be transferred from their present departmental jurisdictions and placed under the administration of the proposed Canadian Heritage Council.

22.   The National Inventory program and the Canadian Inventory of Historic Buildings should be completed as soon as possible to facilitate collections management, exhibition planning, research and education activities based on heritage collections throughout Canada. The proposed Canadian Heritage Council should assume continuing responsibility for the National Inventory program and the Canadian Inventory of Historic Buildings.

Display and Dissemination

Display and dissemination are the ultimate goals of collection and conservation. A justification for retaining the works of the past is that they will be seen and will be available for interpretation and reinterpretation. Since the establishment of the National Museum Policy in 1972, the National Museums of Canada has been active in facilitating and promoting the dissemination of movable cultural heritage to museums in all parts of Canada and abroad, through a group of five programs which are collectively called the National Programmes: the Museum Assistance Programmes, the Canadian Conservation Institute, the National Inventory, Mobile Exhibits and the International Programme.

As recommended above, the Canadian Conservation Institute and the National Inventory should, we believe, be transferred to the proposed Canadian Heritage Council. As we see its future role, the Canadian Heritage Council should be primarily concerned with grants to increase access to and knowledge about heritage. It follows then that the Museum Assistance Programmes should also become a responsibility of the proposed Canadian Heritage Council.

The Mobile Exhibits program circulates heritage materials from the national collections throughout Canada in three theme-coordinated caravans called Canada North, Atlantic Canada and Canada West. Over two million Canadians have visited these caravan museum exhibits since they began circulating. The earlier Discovery Train which had a similar purpose has now been dismantled. This extension activity of the National Museums should remain with that organization, but other methods of dissemination including travel grants to individuals, publications and films might be fostered by the Canadian Heritage Council.

Access to our nonmovable culture – such as heritage buildings and natural sites – is, at present, provided by the National Historic Parks and Sites Branch and through the work of the Heritage Canada Foundation. The former is discussed elsewhere in this chapter. The Heritage Canada Foundation was established in 1973 and endowed by the federal government to act as an independent, nonprofit organization "to encourage the preservation and demonstration of the nationally significant historical, architectural, natural and scenic heritage of Canada." The Heritage Canada Foundation concentrates its energies on the preservation of the built environment and to this end has purchased buildings, encouraged the training of architects and artisans in the skilled work of restoration of heritage buildings, provided advisory services and conducted research.

The Heritage Canada Foundation, during its short life, has achieved notable success in restoring, preserving and therefore assuring to present and future generations access not only to individual buildings of historic interest but also to entire streets or areas of heritage significance. However, the effectiveness of this foundation is being reduced by the decreasing value of its endowment. The Heritage Canada Foundation must continue to be independent but should receive support from the proposed Canadian Heritage Council, not only in the form of additional funding for its restoration activities but also for its training and advisory services.

Access by inhabitants of the North to their own art and artifacts presents special problems, and these were raised with us by many groups during our hearings. The federal government has clear responsibility for artifacts in the Northwest Territories and the Yukon. Despite the efforts of the only territorial custodial institution having staff and facilities, the Prince of Wales Northern Heritage Centre in Yellowknife, much of the cultural material of Canada's north country is either ignored or shipped south. As mentioned above, under the Northwest Territories Archaeological Site Regulations all specimens found in the Northwest Territories are deposited at the Archaeological Survey of Canada, in Ottawa. Specimens found in the Yukon have been shipped south because no environmentally secure storage has been provided for them there. This, in effect, denies the inhabitants of those regions access to their own past.

This is no longer acceptable. Northern Canadians are proud of their heritage and want to see it displayed in their own communities. *Environmentally secure display centres should now be opened in various places in the North, so that art and artifacts can be seen in context by the local inhabitants and visitors, and so that traveling exhibitions of artifacts taken from the North, now held in Ottawa and elsewhere, can be returned for placement or circulation in the originating communities.*

Over the past 10 years, the National Museum Policy, with its emphasis on democratization and decentralization, successfully increased the number of heritage facilities and encouraged public interest. However, in doing so, it has caused the basic heritage activities of collection and conservation to be seriously neglected and minimally funded. As a result, some of our unique collections are now in jeopardy. It is desirable that public access to heritage materials not only continue but increase. Nonetheless, it must be recognized that the basic support activities of collection, conservation and research are essential to sustaining public interest and are equally deserving of financial support.

Curators responsible for heritage materials must constantly be aware of the audience likely to view the exhibitions and displays they arrange. Viewers are not all alike. Their interests, aspirations and sensitivities differ widely from region to region. It is entirely reasonable that institutions in each region should develop collections and exhibitions which reflect the distinctive characteristics of that region. We fully agree, for instance, with the contention of the Inuit Cultural Institute that it is counterproductive to attempt to impose "southern" notions of cultural development on the North. It was apparent to us from our countrywide discussions with those involved in heritage activities that the National Museums of Canada, in pursuing the objectives of the National Programmes, has not always been as sensitive as it could have been to provincial and regional priorities, interests and standards, and has sometimes acted in a directive rather than a reactive way toward the non-national museums.

Federal support must also be made available for the dissemination of non-Canadian material. It, too, is part of our past. Access to the culture of other countries by purchasing works for Canadian collections is an expensive proposition. So, too, is the borrowing of objects from other countries for international exhibitions; the borrower must not only pay the transportation costs

to Canada, but also the extremely costly mandatory insurance on these objects. Many countries have adopted indemnity legislation which enables
them to underwrite the costs of such insurance. The Art Gallery of Ontario
presented the case for a similar Canadian indemnification plan which, it was
estimated, could save Canadian cultural institutions about $1 million annually
in insurance premiums.

A formula to share risks associated with insuring exhibitions was
adopted in principle in May 1982 in Regina, by federal-provincial ministers
responsible for culture and historical resources. It is encouraging that the
basis for agreement on how to solve this burdensome, recurring problem has
been established.

One other aspect of dissemination must not be overlooked. Until now
heritage materials have been disseminated by a few traditional methods and
except for the use of computer-stored information in the National Inventory
and the planned computerized bibliographic network of the National Library,
newer communication systems have been virtually ignored. In future,
heritage institutions will undoubtedly take more advantage of the opportunities to display their collections to larger audiences provided by television
and to increase the exchange of information by the use of videotex systems
such as Telidon and other information retrieval and display technologies.

23.   The proposed Canadian Heritage Council should encourage
       and support the dissemination of heritage materials
       throughout Canada, and in order to do so should assume
       from the National Museums of Canada direct responsibility
       for grants now given under the Museum Assistance Pro-
       grammes. To facilitate access to nonmovable heritage, the
       proposed Canadian Heritage Council should cooperate with
       the National Historic Parks and Sites Branch of Parks
       Canada, and with the Heritage Canada Foundation, and
       should assist activities of the Heritage Canada Foundation
       financially if requested.

Staffing and Training
Many intervenors told us about another problem endemic in the heritage
field, the lack of qualified staff. There are very few fully qualified curators and
museum administrators in Canada because, until recently, no qualifying
courses were available here. The graduate degree program in museology at
the University of Toronto and the Royal Ontario Museum began in the late
1960s. When the Canadian Conservation Institute was set up in 1976, there
were not enough trained experts anywhere in Canada to staff it adequately.
Competition for the limited qualified personnel has existed among heritage
agencies for years.

Since 1972, when federal training grants to colleges and universities
became available through the National Programmes of the National Museums

of Canada, a number of colleges and universities have offered courses designed to prepare students for professional careers in various aspects of museum
operations. These include a museum technicians' course developed by Algon-
quin College in Ottawa and the conservation course given by Queen's University in Kingston. Even so, many students must still leave Canada to receive
advanced training.

In many of the specialized areas of heritage, "learning-on-the-job" is virtually the only form of training possible. For instance, there was in all of
Canada no formal diploma training program in archival science until 1981
when the University of British Columbia introduced such a program. There
must be more initiatives of this kind in other branches of the heritage field. A
steady infusion of well-qualified professional custodians will increasingly be
required for the successful management and development not only of Canadian archives but of other heritage resources as well.

24.   The proposed Canadian Heritage Council should support
       initiatives to develop training programs in professional
       heritage management.

Volunteers and Service Organizations

National service organizations in the heritage field take a special interest in
maintaining and developing professional standards in training and performance. At present, grants to such organizations are quite haphazard, some
receiving assistance and others not. We suggest certain criteria for the funding of such bodies in our discussion in Chapter 2 of the respective functions
of the Department of Communications and of the cultural agencies. The
operation of national service associations in Canada is expensive, given the
distances to be traveled to meetings and the bilingual character of their
publications and discussions. These factors should be considered by the proposed Canadian Heritage Council when the criteria for grants to national
organizations – such as the Canadian Museums Association or the Canadian
Archaeological Association – are established.

We have received many comments about the important contribution
made by volunteers who perform essential services in heritage institutions
which would not otherwise be provided. Unfortunately, many institutions
have recently noted that the number of volunteers active in this work has
decreased. And this has happened at a time when museums need more staff
to cope with the increased use of their facilities but have less money to acquire such staff.

The degree of dependence on volunteers by heritage institutions can be
judged by the results of a recent survey conducted by the British Columbia
Museums Association which showed that over 68 per cent of the staff of the
British Columbia Museums was voluntary. Clearly these essential, committed
volunteers must be adequately trained. But there are difficulties. We were

reminded by the Chairman of the Board of the Restigouche Gallery that many of the dedicated people who have made things happen in their community are often not able to finance trips to the seminars, workshops and conferences that have been arranged to help them enlarge their skills. We therefore make the following recommendation on behalf of volunteer staff in heritage institutions, suggesting that training assistance must be provided for these essential services through existing or proposed federal funding programs.

25.   Encouraging volunteers in heritage organizations by offering them special training is money well spent, and grants for the purpose of training volunteers should now be made through the Museum Assistance Programmes of the National Museums of Canada and, ultimately, by the proposed Canadian Heritage Council. In addition, recognized national heritage service associations should be eligible for financial assistance toward the cost of annual meetings and publications.

Accommodation for Heritage Collections
The improvements in the accommodation of heritage institutions during the past 30 years have been outstanding. These changes are due to a very large extent to the substantial support given for this purpose by the National Museums of Canada and the Departments of the Secretary of State and Communications. The National Museums brief stated that "135 museums and art galleries have received federal grants for new or renovated facilities, better equipment and more sophisticated environmental controls." Provincial governments and private donors have also contributed heavily to the cost of building new heritage facilities and upgrading old ones. Today, most provinces have efficient facilities for the preservation and display of their collections.

It is unfortunate that federal institutions have not benefited nearly as much during this period, with the single exception of the now inadequate building shared by the Public Archives of Canada and the National Library. The February 1982 decision to provide $185 million for the construction of facilities for the National Gallery of Canada and the National Museum of Man goes some distance toward meeting the desperate need for safe and adequate display and storage of these important national collections.

The Board of Trustees of the National Museums of Canada has for some time strongly urged the central agencies, the Treasury Board of Canada and the Privy Council Office, to provide funds for new accommodation for national museums. It has been stated that the process of designing and building the new quarters for the National Gallery of Canada and the National Museum of Man will take five years. It is imperative that construction plans for these buildings be developed and brought to fruition with all possible speed.

We would be delinquent, however, if we did not also draw attention to the crowded conditions of the Public Archives of Canada and the National Library, as well as the detrimental and unsuitable locations in which the National Museum of Natural Sciences and the National Museum of Science and Technology now operate. If we wait until the recently authorized federal museum buildings are completed before the next ones are even considered, the provision of proper accommodation for our immediate and pressing heritage needs alone will take at least 25 years, while future technological advances, particularly in preservation and conservation, will undoubtedly necessitate structural changes in existing buildings. We must not dismiss accommodation as a concern simply because heritage institutions in many parts of Canada are housed today better than they were before.

26.   Suitable buildings should be provided for the National
      Museum of Science and Technology, the National Museum
      of Natural Sciences, the Public Archives of Canada and the
      National Library of Canada as soon as possible, in line with
      the accommodation priorities established by these institu-
      tions for the heritage collections for which they are
      responsible.

Funding

Inadequate funding is the root cause of many of the current problems in heritage already discussed. It is our firm conviction, and therefore worth repeating, that heritage is both perishable and irreplaceable; it cannot be put in limbo for lack of money and later retrieved unimpaired.

Funding for heritage activities now comes from many sources. We found general support for the principle of multiple sources of funding among non-federal heritage institutions which recognize the desirability of seeking support from federal, provincial and municipal levels of government, as well as from benefactors outside government. Multiple-source funding gives these non-federal institutions a measure of protection from the disappointments which can occur if dependence is placed on a single source of funds.

Representatives of the smaller museums and galleries outside the major cities told us in some detail about the extra costs they incur by virtue of their size and location. It is simply much more expensive for small institutions to initiate, receive and circulate exhibitions because services such as packing and shipping and similar unavoidable support requirements are not readily available. These extra costs have evidently not been considered in determining the size of the grants smaller institutions receive. There is much good sense in the proposal made by the Saint Mary's University Art Gallery that "a policy of equalization be implemented rather than the present practice of 'the richer you are, the more funding you get'."

This problem is particularly acute for the National Exhibition Centres, which are located in smaller communities across Canada. These centres, mostly established since 1972 with encouragement and capital grants from the National Museums, were never intended to become full-fledged collecting museums, but rather to be environmentally secure places capable of receiving traveling exhibitions. It was also expected that they would enjoy sufficient community support to cover basic operating costs.

Unfortunately, neither expectation has been met. The larger museums – that is, the four national museums and the 21 designated Associate Museums – have been unable to produce the numerous, inexpensive exhibits the centres expected to receive. The National Exhibition Centres have been obliged to create their own exhibitions and programs to fill the gaps. Furthermore, community funding has not been sufficient to permit them to stay open without federal assistance for core funding. The National Museums of Canada recognizes that in the future the needs of these centres, like those of the Associate Museums, can only increase. If the principle is accepted that our heritage should be available to everyone, it is necessary to equalize funding to allow smaller institutions to mount exhibitions and programs that will attract support from the communities where they are located.

27.   There should be increased federal assistance to smaller heritage institutions, including the National Exhibition Centres. Other levels of government, interested individuals and corporate sponsors should consider commensurate increases in support.

International Heritage Activities

In 1975 the National Museums of Canada set up an International Programme to promote interest in international museum activities, and to coordinate international exhibitions coming to Canada and other international exchanges in the heritage field. This program has been associated with a number of notable exhibitions made available to museums in all parts of Canada. Officials responsible for the International Programme in the National Museums work closely with the Bureau of International Cultural Relations in the Department of External Affairs and take part in the advisory committee of that department on international cultural affairs.

The International Programme is the second of the five components of the National Programmes which, in our view, should not be transferred to the supervision of the proposed Canadian Heritage Council. As a result of our review of international cultural relations, which can be found in Chapter 11, we recommend the creation of a new international cultural agency. The National Museums' International Programme should become a part of that new agency when it is formed. The Canadian Heritage Council would, however, be a source of counsel on heritage matters as they relate to international activities and could be expected to give grants to help bring international exhibitions to Canadian museums.

The National Historic Parks and Sites Branch coordinates Canada's participation in international heritage activities organized by the Paris-based headquarters of Unesco, and gives an annual grant for that purpose which is largely concerned with natural heritage. We consider it appropriate that this heritage activity should also be assumed by the proposed Canadian International Cultural Relations Agency in cooperation with the National Historic Parks and Sites Branch as required.

Federal Heritage Activities

The federal government is heavily involved with heritage. Not only is it directly responsible for nonrenewable resources owned by the Crown, but it is also responsible for the preservation and availability of existing national collections. In addition, the federal government has given substantial funding or program assistance to a wide variety of non-federal heritage organizations in all parts of the country.

The all-encompassing nature of heritage is reflected in the number of federal departments and agencies with responsibilities or interests in this field. At least 52 federal organizations have a heritage role. While the principal responsibilities are divided among Environment Canada and the Department of Communications and its related agencies, particularly the National Museums of Canada, there is extensive activity in other federal departments and organizations as well. At least 12 organizations maintain collections for exhibition. Besides the museums within the National Museums of Canada, these include the Canada Council, the Department of External Affairs, the National Film Board, the Canada Post Corporation and the Bank of Canada. Scientific research collections are maintained by departments such as Agriculture and Environment, as well as the Department of Energy, Mines and Resources.

At least 14 federal bodies are involved in funding or program assistance for heritage purposes. These include the Canada Council, the National Capital Commission and the Departments of Communications, and Indian and Northern Affairs. In addition, many of these federal agencies either manage historic buildings or devote resources to their restoration and to giving the public access to them.

Despite the number of federal organizations involved, federal activity in support of heritage concerns has often been covert, uncoordinated and dispersed. This lack of real commitment does grave injustice to the importance of our heritage. The federal agencies and departments with prime responsibility in this area must not only adopt realistic heritage policies but also implement these policies in the most effective possible way. In this connection, we have some comments to make on past policy, and some suggestions to offer for the future.

The National Museums of Canada

One of the principal federal bodies concerned with heritage is the National Museums of Canada. This Crown corporation was established in 1968 to be responsible for and provide services to the four national museums – the National Gallery of Canada, the National Museum of Man, the National Museum of Natural Sciences, and the National Museum of Science and Technology. The Canadian War Museum became a division of the National Museum of Man, and the National Aeronautical Collection was incorporated into the National Museum of Science and Technology. The purposes of the corporation, as stated in the enabling Act, are "to demonstrate the products of nature and works of man, with special but not exclusive reference to Canada, so as to promote interest therein throughout Canada and to disseminate knowledge thereof."

In 1972 a National Museum Policy was announced and funds were made available for improved assistance and services to museums generally, including non-federal institutions. As a result, a network of 21 Associate Museums was organized and 25 National Exhibition Centres were established; the Canadian Conservation Institute and the National Inventory were created; training programs were developed and an Emergency Purchase Fund was authorized to cope with costs of unforeseen acquisitions. Since 1974, the National Museums of Canada has been divided for administrative purposes into six operational units: each of the four national museums, the Corporate Secretariat and Services, and the National Programmes.

In examining the effectiveness of this important Crown corporation, it is helpful to look at the reasons for its formation. In the 1960s, it became clear that new legislation was needed for all the national museums. Two bills were prepared, one for the National Gallery of Canada and one for the three other national museums. The two draft bills were virtually identical since they dealt with the basic functions of a museum which are the same regardless of the character of the collections. The bills emphasized function rather than discipline; they were concerned, in the main, with management authority, financial and other controls rather than with aesthetic or disciplinary considerations. It was evidently assumed that if the three museums, each having quite different collections, could be joined together, a fourth, the National Gallery of Canada, could be added with equal validity.

The amalgamation of the four national heritage institutions was to bring about the use of common administrative and financial services, making it possible to pool scarce resources and avoid duplication. These centralized services, in short, were to reduce the burden of housekeeping for the four museums and to provide more cost-efficient services. Furthermore, to those sponsoring the legislation, combining four separate institutions was thought to be more desirable since the resulting single museum corporation was likely to be more forceful in its dealings with the central agencies.

The individual museums were to retain their separate and specific identities. The legislation confirmed that each museum had the status of a

separate cultural body, the corporate framework being solely for administrative purposes. The directors of the individual museums were given
direct reporting responsibility to the Board of Trustees. Directors retained
overriding responsibility for the management of their respective museums,
including the full exercise of professional judgment, while the newly created
position of Secretary General of the corporation was given responsibility for
the coordination of the day-to-day activities of the corporation, particularly its
common services.

This important and subtle balance between the role of the directors on
the one hand and the role of the Secretary General on the other was altered
by the addition of the National Programmes to the corporation in 1974 as
part of implementation of the 1972 National Museum Policy. This addition
modified the corporation's original role considerably. It was no longer simply
an organizational and service umbrella for the national museums; it was now
also a well-funded federal cultural agency instigating national programs and
providing national services.

The National Programmes, set up as a new section of the corporation,
became the responsibility of the Secretary General who was recognized by
the central agencies, for accountability reasons, as the chief executive officer,
a title not explicitly authorized by the Act of incorporation but subsequently
recognized in the bylaws. Thus, between 1968 and 1974, the role and
organization of the National Museums of Canada changed considerably and
in such a way that the original intent – the operation of four federal
museums in Ottawa – was subsumed under a larger national policy.

The original reasons for placing the four national museums in a single
organization – reduction of administrative costs by amalgamating common
services, more autonomy under a Crown corporation than in a department
and increased clout with the central agencies of the government – on balance
still seem reasonable to us. The addition of the National Programmes to the
structure of the corporation as originally established was, however, in our
view, ill-conceived. As well as causing new problems, this change seems to
have exacerbated continuing problems implicit in the administrative arrangements made by the 1968 Museums Act.

At present the National Museums of Canada functions as a Schedule B
Departmental corporation under the Financial Administration Act, the Public
Service Employment Act, and the Public Service Staff Relations Act. Hence it
is subject to the same controls imposed on departments of government. For
the corporation, these include the requirement that ministerial approval be
sought for acquisitions costing more than $200,000 and Treasury Board ap-
proval for purchases exceeding $1 million; that parliamentary appropriations
for acquisitions lapse at the end of each fiscal year; and that the Public Service Commission recruit all employees, except the directors of the four
museums and the Secretary General. In recent years, under pressure from the
Comptroller General and the Auditor General to make Crown corporations
more accountable, the central agencies have increasingly encroached on the
independence of the National Museums' Board of Trustees. This, in our view,

is regrettable. As previously stated in Chapter 2, under the headings "Policy Direction" and "Administrative Controls," the Board of Trustees of the National Museums of Canada, like the boards of arm's-length agencies, would be a more effective manager if it had more independence from ministerial direction and bureaucratic interference in specific areas.

Several specific factors affecting the independent functioning of the National Museums deserve special comment. The first concerns acquisition decisions. Acquisitions are obviously vital to the establishment and maintenance of heritage collections. They involve highly sensitive decisions of an aesthetic, historic and professional nature. It is important that these decisions be made with integrity and impartiality, without undue influence, and in accordance with the highest professional standards. It is clear, therefore, that all acquisitions, at whatever price, should be made on the recommendation of the director of the museum concerned and with the authority of the board.

Secondly, the National Museums of Canada used to have a purchase account at its disposal. This was a special account in which acquisition funds left unspent at the end of a fiscal year could be carried forward for future use. Although a transition arrangement is in effect for two years, this account was effectively eliminated by the Adjustment of Accounts Act in 1980, when all similar non-lapsing accounts were set aside, again as a way of tightening controls on expenditures and commitments for future expenditures. The acquisition of heritage material is very difficult to plan for in advance. It is impossible to predict when a desired acquisition may come to the market and equally impossible to ascertain the length of time needed for purchase negotiations. While appreciating the motives for the Adjustment of Accounts Act, this Committee believes that the abolition of the non-lapsing account for acquisitions was an unwise decision which severely curtails the independence and the exercise of professional competence by the National Museums.

And thirdly, the present complete integration of all of the corporation's employees, including, of course, those working in the four national museums, into the mainline public service, is not always in the best interest of the museums. The museum profession requires highly specialized professional and technical personnel. More flexible terms and conditions of employment, including part-time employment, internships and secondments from other museums, academic and research institutions, would increase the effectiveness of the operation. Such flexible arrangements could be explored with the Public Service Commission which has mechanisms to meet many of these personnel problems. This staffing problem affects other cultural agencies as well, a point discussed in more detail in Chapter 2.

These then were the considerations which led us to the second of our major recommendations about the future direction of heritage policy – that the National Museums of Canada concentrate on running the existing or proposed national heritage institutions in the National Capital Region or elsewhere, but relinquish to the proposed Canadian Heritage Council responsibility for three components of the National Programmes – the Museum Assistance Programmes, the National Inventory and the Canadian Conservation Institute.

28. The Board of Trustees of the National Museums of Canada should be given full responsibility for the operation of existing and future national heritage institutions in the National Capital Region or elsewhere, for staffing those institutions and for negotiating acquisitions for its various collections from a non-lapsing account to which annual appropriations for this purpose are made.

Other Federal Heritage Activities

We have already described the workings of two other agencies which exist because of sponsorship and funding by the federal government but which are fundamentally independent. These are the Canadian Cultural Property Export Review Board and the Heritage Canada Foundation. Another independent agency is the Art Bank of the Canada Council. In many respects the Art Bank acts very much like a museum in that it collects and preserves art objects and displays its holdings. The Art Bank is discussed in Chapter 5.

Many other federal government departments have collections and some have museums. But, as no authorized guidelines are applicable to all federal museum activities, they do not have to meet the standards the federal government demands of non-federal museums supported by grants from the National Museums of Canada. Consequently, accommodation and display of collections, conservation practices, research and public accessibility vary greatly from department to department. Administration of these other federal collections is haphazard, depending on the interest and knowledge of a few individuals whose professional training may have been in disciplines remote from heritage preservation, working in departments whose policies are directed toward concerns other than heritage.

While the location of these other federal collections within agencies whose priorities are not primarily museological could cause some problems, it is not necessarily advisable to alter the present arrangements. Many collections form an integral part of the workings of their parent organizations and could not sensibly be separated from them. For example, to remove existing collections of technically heritage items from the Cape Breton Development Corporation, from Rideau Hall or from Agriculture Canada would work against the original reason for the creation of such collections and would render them virtually useless. However, some federal collections, including those of the National Historic Parks and Sites Branch of the Department of the Environment, the Public Archives of Canada, and the National Library, are comparable to those in the national museums. These essentially heritage activities were also reviewed by the Committee.

National Historic Parks and Sites

The National Historic Parks and Sites Branch of Environment Canada controls and administers 23 national parks and 54 national historic parks and major sites. Under the authority of the Historic Sites and Monuments Act, 1953, the minister responsible can mark or commemorate historic places, establish historic museums, acquire historic places, and provide for their administration, preservation and maintenance. The minister receives advice on these matters from the Historic Sites and Monuments Board which was first established in 1919.

The National Historic Parks and Sites Branch is clearly engaged in museological activities, in research, and in the collection, preservation and display of heritage material. There is some competition for staff and acquisitions between this branch of the Department of the Environment and the National Museums of Canada, and coordination and cooperation in these matters is limited. Each agency has its own conservation laboratory and both are located in Ottawa. Together they employ four-fifths of all the conservators in the country, but classifications and rates of pay are not uniform for jobs which require similar or identical qualifications. It seems clear that the purposes and broad methodologies of the Historic Parks and Sites Branch and the National Museums of Canada are very similar. Ideally they should be more closely associated administratively and operationally. This would help to underline the breadth of Canada's heritage, and would emphasize the fact that heritage as a national concern includes not simply objects in a museum but also natural sites and historic buildings. We do not wish to give this suggestion the force of a formal recommendation and we realize that there are reasonable arguments to be made in defence of the present departmental arrangements, but this proposal certainly merits future consideration.

Public Archives of Canada
The importance of preserving public records was recognized by the first federal Parliament which approved a grant for this purpose in 1872. A full-time Dominion Archivist was appointed in 1898 and the basic definition of the responsibilities of this office and the nature of archival material to be preserved was set out first in formal legislation in 1912. This Act assigned to the Dominion Archivist custody and control of "public records, documents and other historical material of every kind, nature and description." The Public Archives Act has not been significantly altered since.

The Public Archives of Canada is effectively a department on its own. The Dominion Archivist has the rank of a deputy minister, and reports to the Minister of Communications about Public Archives activities. In addition, the Public Records Order of 1966 assigned to the Dominion Archivist control and management of public records, which were further defined as "correspondence, memoranda or other papers, books, maps, plans, photographs, films, microfilms, sound recordings, tapes, computer cards, or other documentary material, regardless of physical form or characteristics" originating in departments of the federal government. In this capacity the Dominion Archivist is responsible directly to the Treasury Board. A Records Management Branch conducts this administrative function, and the Central Microfilm Unit provides microfilming services to government departments at cost.

To carry out its heritage activities the Public Archives is now organized into eight divisions, each one devoted to a particular archival medium: films, television and sound recordings; pictures, medals and seals; photographs; maps and architectural records; machine readable records; federal textual records; private manuscript documents and documents from other countries; and a library. In addition, the Archives has been given certain curatorial responsibilities. It looks after all portraits on display in the Parliament Buildings and, under the terms of the Laurier House Act which incorporated the terms of the bequest by William Lyon Mackenzie King, the Dominion Archivist has charge of Laurier House and its contents, which now also includes memorabilia of Lester B. Pearson.

Since 1912, then, the Public Archives of Canada has freely interpreted the single unrevised statement of its mandate to collect and preserve "other historical material of every kind, nature and description" as authority for its contemporary activities. These activities should now be more authoritatively defined in a complete revision of the Public Archives of Canada Act, which would not only reflect the scope of its current archival collections and the methods of their preservation but also give statutory authority for the records management duties the Archives performs by virtue of the 1966 order-in-council and clarify its curatorial responsibilities.

The Public Archives is a vital heritage custodial institution, similar in purpose to museums in the National Museums of Canada. The importance of archives was admirably delineated in the Public Archives brief to this Committee:

"If the archives of a nation, a government or an organization are not preserved, then the history of that nation, government or organization will be forgotten, and the price which a people pay for the loss of their history is a misunderstanding of their roots, a confusion in their identity and the misinterpretation or misrepresentation of the nature of their country."

Archival activity in Canada has been reviewed in depth by two inquiries in the last 10 years, first by the Commission on Canadian Studies which dealt with archives in that context in its report, *To Know Ourselves*, released in 1976, and later by the Consultative Group on Canadian Archives which reported to the Social Sciences and Humanities Research Council in 1980. Both these reports engendered a widespread response from government and nongovernment archives individually and collectively through their professional associations. Discussions have emphasized changes which should be reflected in a new Public Archives Act, which has been in preparation for some time.

The Public Archives of Canada is the largest in the country in terms of holdings and size of staff, but it is part of a nationwide archival community which includes provincial, municipal, business and private institutional archives. This extended archival network developed because it was recognized that archives can "document the public, corporate, communal, cultural, commercial, intellectual, and private lives of Canadians.... Archives are a heritage for all Canadians for all time," to quote a past president of the Association of Canadian Archivists.

The growth in numbers of archival holdings, and the increased awareness not only of their heritage value but also of the imperative need for their preservation, suggest to us that the Public Archives should include the archival community in Canada in discussions about the new legislation which may also affect them. The two commissions of inquiry and the Association of Canadian Archivists proposed variations on the idea that a revised Public Archives Act should provide for the coordination of archival planning throughout the country, in order to make more efficient use of our total archival resources.

The consultative group of the Social Sciences and Humanities Research Council, headed by Ian E. Wilson, Saskatchewan Provincial Archivist, initiated the discussion of this idea. It recommended that the Public Archives of Canada establish an extension branch to minister to the entire archival system on the basis of policies and priorities recommended by a National Archival Advisory Committee. This proposal has not been viewed as an appropriate solution by either the Public Archives itself or by the Association of Canadian Archivists. The latter organization put forward an alternative in its published response to the Wilson report and in its brief and discussions with this Committee. We fully support the proposal of the Association that a National Archival Records Commission be established to act as an independent funding and coordinating agency, through which the programs, studies and recommendations for a national "cooperating system of archives" could be instituted. On the basis of the submissions made to us, it is clear that this proposal accurately reflects the considered judgment of the entire archival community.

Funding for Canadian archives has never been generous. Even so there seems to be a consensus in the Canadian archival community that money is not the only solution to current problems. We were told that there is a "much greater need to identify major problems in the archival landscape and to develop priorities that will lead to their solutions." This will be the job of the National Archival Records Commission. The Commission will ultimately be expected to make grants for such priorities as capital projects, archival training programs and publications, research in conservation techniques for collections, and standards and building codes for new archival institutions.

The National Archival Records Commission should be created without delay. The need for it is clear. We consider that the Commission, while retaining its independence, should be administratively associated with the Canadian Heritage Council. Its national objectives are consistent with the role in the promotion of heritage interests nationally which we propose for the Canadian Heritage Council, and the separation of the wider interests of the Commission from the ongoing activities of the Public Archives of Canada would be emphasized by such an arrangement. The Commission would then bear the same relationship to the Canadian Heritage Council as that previously recommended for the Canadian Cultural Property Export Review Board. Through direct or indirect representation on the Commission, archivists caring for provincial, corporate and Public Archives collections will be able to set standards for the effective preservation of historical records and ensure their future use.

29.   The Public Archives Act should be revised, following consultations with provincial and private sector archivists, to reflect national needs of archival institutions throughout Canada.

30.   A National Archival Records Commission, to be responsible for the coordination and encouragement of programs devoted to the preservation and use of historical records in the care of archives throughout Canada, should be established as an independent body associated with the Canadian Heritage Council for administrative purposes. The cost of carrying out the national objectives of the National Archival Records Commission should be included in parliamentary appropriations provided for the Canadian Heritage Council.

We have considered some of the specific future needs of the Public Archives of Canada and are entirely sympathetic to the view that the Archives and the National Library, which at present share one building, should have separate but closely connected accommodation. The present building was designed in the late 1950s but completed only in 1966, when the combined full-time staff of the two institutions was just under 450. It is already too small. In 1982-83 the authorized combined establishment totals nearly 1,300 and some units of the National Library are located elsewhere. In addition, the collections of both institutions have grown enormously in the past 15 years and will continue to do so. Indeed, the recommendations of this Committee, which propose the transfer to the Public Archives of the National Film Board film archives and the Canadian Broadcasting Corporation sound and video archives, would increase the space requirements of the Archives considerably. However, the arrangement which provides common services to both institutions is sensible and should continue, since this is evidently acceptable to the Treasury Board as well as to the Public Archives and the National Library.

In pursuit of their individual responsibilities, the Public Archives and the National Library have created certain overlapping areas in their respective collections. Clarification and direction are needed about which of the institutions is primarily responsible for collections of music, maps and literary papers, in particular. We urge the Minister of Communications to resolve the conflicting and disruptive claims about these collections without delay.

The National Library of Canada

The National Library, a federal heritage institution, was formally set up in 1953 as a prompt response by the federal government to an urgent recommendation in the Massey-Lévesque Report. It is responsible for the collection of "library matter of every kind, nature and description... published by a publisher" relating to Canada. Canadian publishers are required to deposit copies of their books with the Library. Various services are provided to the government and people of Canada, including the compilation and maintenance of a national union catalogue of the holdings of major Canadian libraries and the preparation and publication of *Canadiana*, a national bibliography of books by, about or of interest to Canadians or produced here. The Canadian Library Association summarized the function of the National Library for us: "The National Library is, essentially, a library for libraries and its current budget of $17 million represents, for all intents and purposes, indirect aid to libraries by way of services rendered."

In its relatively short existence the National Library has accumulated about three million volumes. It has a number of specialized unique holdings, notably its collection of Canadian newspapers, official publications, music, theses and rare Canadian books and manuscripts. It promotes Canadian books abroad in small exhibitions and by participation in book fairs and cultural exchanges. International scholars as well as Canadians benefit from the availability of National Library bibliographic materials through computer access and microfilm.

The National Library, like the Public Archives, is for most purposes a department of government, and the National Librarian also reports to the Minister of Communications. The National Librarian is assisted in the development of library policies and plans by the National Library Advisory Board, which includes representatives of relevant federal agencies and outside interests including at least five professional librarians.

The composition of the National Library Advisory Board has been considered by the Canadian Library Association. In the Association's formal response to the paper on the future role and priorities of the Library, it recommended that the National Library Advisory Board be reconstituted to "serve as a useful body for monitoring developments in the National Library and information network." The Canadian Library Association suggested that the Advisory Board should closely represent the nongovernmental consumers of National Library services and the learned and professional societies. This valid concern was expressed by an Association which has 4,072 individual members and 964 institutional members representing libraries of all kinds and sizes in Canada. The suggestions it makes deserve close consideration, and we support them.

In December 1979, the National Library released a public report to its minister about the future of the National Library based on an intensive review process. In it the National Library made a major proposal for the establishment of a national decentralized bibliographic and communications network to link the existing bibliographic databases of libraries across Canada, thus improving both information about the availability of books and access to them by library users. By the fall of 1981, the cabinet approved a pilot study on the implementation of the bibliographic network. The leadership of the National Library in this network approach to sharing library resources is uncontested. The brief from the National Librarian told us that four task force groups "consisting of experts from all parts of Canada" have been appointed to help the National Library develop various detailed aspects of the proposal. The National Library Advisory Board has also appointed two committees to participate directly in planning the bibliographic and resource-sharing network.

While not officially represented in this consultative process, the point of view expressed by the Canadian Library Association on most fundamental questions relating to the development of the bibliographic network has been taken into consideration through formal and informal representations. This broad consultation should ensure that the National Library proposals are translated into truly cooperative and acceptable library procedures relevant to the needs of library users. The National Library is obviously alert to the rapid, ever-changing refinements to the data systems which can make our printed heritage more accessible to all Canadians and to interested persons in other countries.

Postgraduate training is more generally available for librarians than it is for archival and museum management. However, the National Library reminded us that the extremely fragile nature of the heritage material for which it is responsible calls for specialized care. "The most significant problem in implementing any sort of a national preservation program in Canada is the dearth of trained conservators and binders in the country." Here surely is an opportunity for the community colleges of Canada to train young Canadians for a specialized, rewarding and uncrowded profession. There is a further urgent need for research in paper chemistry and other preservation methods for application in libraries as in the archives and museums.

Canadian Institute for Historical Microreproductions
The crucial task of preserving printed heritage material is also being undertaken on microfilm. In 1979 with funding for an initial five-year period, first from the Canada Council, then from the Social Sciences and Humanities Research Council, the Canadian Institute for Historical Microreproductions was set up as an independent, nonprofit corporation. Its objectives are to improve access to and ensure preservation of Canadiana printed before 1900 located in Canada and elsewhere.

The National Library has cooperated fully with the Institute and benefits directly from its work through receipt of the master copies of its microfilms. The Canadian Institute for Historical Microreproductions could in future form the nucleus of a national preservation program coordinated by the Canadian Heritage Council. The Institute is performing a vital conservation job which will benefit Canadian and foreign researchers for years to come. It should continue to receive federal assistance to fulfil its patently important objectives.

New Heritage Institutions

We have already commented about those areas of Canadian creative endeavour or of special heritage value which are underrepresented in existing Canadian collections. Some of these will require the development of an entirely new institution. For example, there has been a rich blossoming of visual and applied arts in Canada over the last 30 years, but at the national level only the Art Bank of the Canada Council has been able to respond to this interest in any sustained way. The existing national museums, with their very broad mandates, have been unable to devote necessary and adequate space, time and money to these creations of our contemporary heritage.

Like a number of other countries, Canada should have an institution capable of demonstrating to ourselves and the world at large the richness, variety and vitality of our present-day visual and applied arts. A further discussion and our recommendations on this matter appear in Chapter 5.

While the National Museum of Man has collections of an historical nature, it is not primarily a history museum. There are many missing elements, and we wish to draw attention to one of them in particular. Canada is geographically defined by three oceans and boasts that it stretches from sea to sea, yet we have no federal maritime museums to display our nautical heritage or to document the livelihood Canadians have for many generations derived from the sea.

There are other needs in the natural heritage field which will also require new institutions or new administrative arrangements. Canada still does not have the national aquaria, arboreta or zoological and botanical gardens urged by the Massey-Lévesque Commission. In fact, the conservation, documentation and exhibition of Canada's "natural" past are still beset by countless problems.

Some of these problems stem from too narrow an understanding of what constitutes our heritage. Too often we have restricted our definition to those things which people have made. The federal government has tended to separate the natural from the man-made, so that an institution specializing in the preservation, research and display of the natural habitat, such as a park or botanical garden, has not been considered a museum or a custodial institution, and has received different treatment. The most extreme case, as noted above, is the administrative separation of historic and natural parks from the national museums. Our national heritage does include the works of nature, and despite an evident preoccupation with our man-made heritage, we must have access to this vital natural component of our lives.

The heritage significance of heraldry, the study of armorial insignia, was put before us in a brief from the Heraldry Society of Canada. All levels of government, institutions of all kinds and individuals in Canada have petition-ed for and received grants of arms from authorities overseas which include emblematic references to the historical traditions, geographical position and community aspirations of the bearer and which, therefore, have become distinctively Canadian in motif. We were told that "Canadian heraldry is now a living reality, in daily use across the land," yet Canada is not yet autono-mous in heraldry.

The Committee agrees that it is consistent with this Canadian heraldic tradition that the authority which grants permission to use these emblems, officially registers them and later regulates their use, should be located in Canada, independent of, but cooperating with, heraldic authorities in other countries.

Canadian artists should be employed to prepare the unique and ap-propriate designs for the arms, flags, badges and insignia to be authorized by a Canadian Heraldic Authority. Such an authority would in all likelihood be self-sustaining; it might be suitably associated for administrative purposes with the Chancellery of Canadian Orders and Decorations of the office of the Governor General.

31.   In addition to establishing a Canadian Heritage Council (Recommendation 15) the federal government should give consideration to setting up other federal heritage institu-tions such as maritime museums, a national aquarium, arboretum, zoological garden and botanical garden. The proposed Canadian Heritage Council should be called upon to give advice about the establishment of these long-awaited heritage institutions.

A Canadian Heritage Council

At the beginning of this chapter we recommended that there be established a visible champion of heritage interests in Canada. This is the single most im-portant recommendation we have to make about the future management of Canada's national heritage.

Federal heritage policy extends beyond the activities of federal custodial institutions. The 1972 National Museum Policy of democratization and decentralization emphasized the necessity for national programs and services throughout Canada. That this support to the nonprofit Canadian museums and collections has been very helpful is clearly evident. Not only have these custodial institutions been able to improve their conservation and display techniques, but they have also been able to expand their services. Furthermore, the federal initiative encouraged similar provincial actions and ensured that our national heritage has received more public attention than ever before.

Yet these creative and innovative federal programs have also demon-strated all too clearly how much more remains to be done. As the National Museums of Canada candidly admits, many of its projected programs were ahead of their time, founded as they were on an overly optimistic assessment of the capacity of Canadian museums to make full use of them. Slowly the corporation has been forced to recognize that even our largest and richest museums urgently need support simply to maintain a minimum standard of care for their collections. In many instances heritage research, collection and preservation activities are not being carried out simply for lack of funds.

While this Committee believes that additional funds are certainly necessary to rectify this situation, we are also convinced that another part of the problem is one of attitude. As we said earlier, heritage matters are too often simply forgotten. They have no profile. Often they are not even iden-tified for what they are, nor is their significance made clear. The National Museums of Canada, within its powers, has tried to promote such recogni-tion but it was abundantly evident to us that there must be a new initiative to give wider recognition to the importance of our heritage.

At the same time, there is also a need for a separation of functions within the corporation and a need to correct what has, essentially, amounted to a conflict of interest caused by the present administrative arrangements which attempt to combine the four national museums with the National Programmes.

To address this problem we have recommended that the operational section of the corporation – that is, the four national museums and the Mobile Exhibits – be separated from the national service activities, the Museum Assistance Programmes, the National Inventory and the Canadian Conservation Institute. However, these components of the National Program-mes are of vital importance. It is natural, appropriate and correct that they become the core functions of the proposed Canadian Heritage Council and we have earlier shown how they might operate within that organization.

We see the Canadian Heritage Council as an agency with a broad man-date, unencumbered by operating functions, and serving as a focal point for a renewed federal effort to provide the Canadian people with the maximum op-portunities for the understanding and enjoyment of the Canadian heritage. In addition to those elements of the National Programmes transferred from the National Museums of Canada, it should encourage training and assist volun-tary heritage associations. The Council, although not having operating func-tions, would nevertheless be actively involved in promoting and encouraging institutions and individuals to collect, conserve, research and display heritage materials.

The exact structure of the new Canadian Heritage Council will be deter-mined by others. The Council will inevitably be called on to make many ob-jective decisions on standards of quality and other sensitive matters in the course of its duties. We consider the Canadian Heritage Council should therefore be an incorporated agency and should be given the appropriate ad-ministrative independence to carry out its responsibilities.

32.   The proposed Canadian Heritage Council should be given
       independent authority for staffing and be otherwise con-
       stituted to be able to operate with the maximum
       autonomy feasible for an arm's-length agency.

The Canadian Heritage Council as an Intermediary

The nature of heritage is such that many government departments not only
will, but should, maintain activities in this field. It does not seem practical or
desirable to unite all such activities in one institution, for heritage interests
are often very closely tied to particular organizations – the collection of Canadian coins with the Bank of Canada, or the Postal Museum with Canada Post,
for example. However, communication about heritage activities among
departments and agencies is vital, if only to avoid duplications or omissions.
Furthermore, a central repository of information on heritage activities would
be most useful.

We frequently heard of the need for more and improved consultation
among various levels of government. The director of the Norman Mackenzie
Art Gallery in Regina maintained that continued lack of federal-provincial consultation in establishing various guidelines, funding programs and grant
criteria, and lack of federal-provincial consultation with the custodial institutions, often leaves those institutions falling between the boards, unable to
meet the expectations of one funding agency because of the stance of
another.

While many heritage bodies are anxious to obtain a greater proportion
of their funding from individual and corporate donors, there is considerable
uncertainty about how or whether this can be done. At the same time,
private donors might be more willing to contribute to heritage activities if
they could obtain more information about aspects which interest them.

33.   The proposed Canadian Heritage Council should promote
       liaison among various federal departments and agencies
       involved in heritage, among all levels of government and
       between government and the private sector.

The Central Position of Heritage in Cultural Policies

Our heritage, our past, is also part of our present. Without widespread
knowledge of what has gone before, without the transmission of knowledge
from one generation to another, contemporary creation would be rootless. In
this chapter we have called for a change in the general direction of federal
policy in heritage matters and have recommended the major organizational
changes needed to bring about this result. We believe these changes to be
realistic ones likely to have a positive effect.

To summarize our previous recommendations about the responsibilities of the Canadian Heritage Council as we envisage them, it should

- provide assistance to non-federal galleries, museums, archives and parks;
- encourage and sustain conservation, research and inventory programs;
- assist the Heritage Canada Foundation and other deserving national heritage associations;
- offer administrative and financial support for the operation of the Canadian Cultural Property Export Review Board and the proposed National Archival Records Commission.
- promote liaison among government and nongovernment bodies concerned with our national heritage; and
- stimulate and operate programs designed to increase interest in heritage resources in order to heighten and widen their enjoyment by the public.

But structural change is only part, perhaps only a small part, of what is needed if Canadians are to have the opportunity to truly appreciate their own patrimony. What is needed most of all is a change of attitude on the part of governments, a new recognition of the central place that heritage must have in cultural policy. The new structures and institutions we have recommended can themselves play a major part in achieving this.

As one of our intervenors succinctly put it, our heritage collections are "among the principal deposits of whatever we know, the sources of all our judgments, of our intellectual and spiritual vitality and our ability to adapt and renew." When these truths are fully understood and acted upon by governments at all levels, heritage policy will have the best of foundations.

5
Contemporary Visual and Applied Arts

5

Contemporary Visual and Applied Arts

This chapter embraces both visual and applied arts – in the former, painting, drawing, sculpture, printmaking, photography and such newer forms as conceptual, computer and performance art; and in the latter, crafts, graphic, interior and industrial design, architecture and urban and landscape design.

It is customary to separate visual creative work into these two categories. Certainly the distinction has been embedded in government thinking, since policies or programs for visual artists are usually separated from those for applied artists. The Committee is aware that there is overlap between the two categories and that no listing of activity under any one of the headings is finite, complete or constant. We therefore begin by discussing some broad issues which the visual and applied arts share with each other before proceeding to separate issues and our recommendations for federal government policy.

The visual and applied arts provide a striking example of the pervasive influence that artists have on the quality of our daily lives. Most of us are familiar with the impact that an admired painting, print or sculpture makes on our enjoyment of a living or working space. In the same way, the skill and sensitivity which the designers of our homes, offices, shops, parks, furniture, glassware and cutlery can express also affect our response to our environment. Throughout our lives it is possible to stimulate, awaken and educate our aesthetic appreciation of our surroundings. Our broad contention as a Committee is that a public concerned about the quality of the physical environment will be more likely to foster artistic and intellectual activity of all kinds. Visual and applied artists can play a leading role in this process but to do so entails lowering barriers between visual and applied artists and the public. It also entails, to some extent, lowering barriers which exist between visual artists and applied artists themselves – for example, between painters and graphic designers, sculptors and architects, printmakers and craftsworkers. In pursuing this goal, society can look to government for specific kinds of support and encouragement.

Providing the Environment
Government interacts with the various arts disciplines and cultural industries in a variety of ways. In some instances, such as the performing arts, support comes in the form of direct subsidies to companies to defray their annual operating costs. In film, in addition to appropriations to film agencies, government assistance takes the form of tax expenditures related to investment in particular projects. In broadcasting, the federal government exercises a regulatory role governing the conditions under which the whole industry operates. In the visual and applied arts, government involvement takes numerous, different forms at virtually every level of activity. Sometimes these interventions are complementary, and sometimes they overlap or even contradict each other. Without a doubt government possesses a profound ability to improve, influence and provide an environment in which creative work in the visual and applied arts is encouraged and made accessible to the public. The array of instruments available for government in supporting the visual and applied arts include the following:

- Assisting individual creativity through grants, copyright legislation, tax legislation, artist-in-residence programs, artist-run centres, and national or regional service organizations for artists;
- Obtaining both sales and display of artists' work through government purchases and government commissions;
- Inducing private purchases and commissions through marketing schemes and fiscal measures for collectors;
- Assisting public appreciation of the visual and applied arts through the collections and exhibitions of public galleries, through marketing schemes, community arts, critical writing and publication, and education;
- Assisting in artists' training.

In Canada, many of these government programs for visual and applied artists are already in place. Some of them work well; others do not. Certainly there is much more that can and ought to be done by government.

The Contemporary Visual Arts

Contemporary Canadian visual art is building a worldwide reputation for innovation, variety and excellence. When the Massey-Lévesque Report was written in 1951, Canada's international reputation in the visual arts rested primarily on painting. Artists such as Emily Carr, Maurice Cullen, Marc-Aurèle Fortin, Clarence Gagnon, David Milne, James Wilson Morrice, Tom Thomson, the Group of Seven and the "war artists," who were commissioned by the Canadian government to interpret the drama and tragedy of the Second

World War, were becoming known throughout Canada and abroad. In the years following the Massey-Lévesque Report, outstanding new painters have continued the tradition of Canadian painting. The surrealists and Automatistes in Montreal and groups like Painters Eleven in Toronto and the Regina Five have all exercised considerable influence on the contemporary Canadian art scene.

During the 1960s, visual art in Canada became more diversified, less dominated by the medium of painting. Sculpture and printmaking became increasingly important; photography established itself as a major art form; new work began in video, conceptual, computer and performance art. Today some of our visual artists, in both the traditional and innovative forms, are of international calibre and participate in major exhibitions in the world's art capitals.

There has been a parallel growth in the development of structures and institutions to support the visual arts. In the 1950s there were only two visual arts periodicals, *Canadian Art* (now *artscanada*) and *Arts et pensée* (now *Vie des arts*); today there are at least 15, each with its own editorial approach and artistic philosophy. There is an increase in the number of visual arts departments at the post-secondary education level. There are public and commercial art galleries all across the country. Funding bodies – federal, provincial, municipal and private – supporting the visual arts have all been established.

Thus, thanks to the creativity of our artists, the response of a growing audience, and the presence of necessary support structures, the visual arts field has experienced dynamic growth since the 1950s. However, as many intervenors told us during the public hearings phase of our work, difficulties remain in the relationship between our contemporary visual artists and the Canadian public. Although Canada's visual artists have produced fine works which have become known abroad, far too few of these are known to Canadians. It seems to us self-evident that a concerted effort is required to ameliorate this unhappy state of affairs. As a Toronto art dealer told us, "contemporary art is often both difficult and demanding; and unfortunately the general public may often find its meaning, let alone its significance, next to incomprehensible." Indeed, it would be unrealistic and probably undesirable, given the critical function of the arts, to expect universal admiration. But the consequence of the present gulf in understanding is a regrettable loss of public appreciation for the achievements of our artists.

To narrow this gulf, a long-term combined effort of reaching out to the public is required on the part of artists and their intermediaries – the public and private galleries, the education system, the art historians and art critics. This effort is one in which the federal government must invest more resources on behalf of the Canadian people. The remainder of this section on contemporary visual art is therefore devoted to a discussion about strengthening links between artists and the public.

Public Purchasing and Exhibition

Like many Western industrialized countries in the last 20 years, Canada has witnessed a major expansion of the market for contemporary art. To a greater extent than ever before, private individuals and corporations have begun to purchase art for pleasure or investment, or both. And as Canadians have become more aware of Canadian art, its vibrancy and variety of style, the market for contemporary Canadian art has also expanded.

The visual arts marketplace has two components – private and public. Public art-purchasing bodies make an important contribution in the art market for both the artist and the private gallery from which work is often bought. Moreover, when work is purchased by a public gallery or other government body, it will be more likely to become available for public viewing. Key roles in the purchasing and exhibition of contemporary Canadian art can be played by federal, provincial and municipal governments.

Canada now has about 140 public galleries and museums which collect, conserve and exhibit contemporary Canadian art. These include university galleries, galleries owned by municipalities large and small, National Exhibition Centres associated with the National Museums of Canada, as well as major provincial institutions. Attendance at exhibitions is high. According to the Council for Business and the Arts in Canada, attendance at the 32 major public galleries across Canada in 1981-82 totaled some 4.6 million. Gallery publications, catalogues and reproductions have a significant buying public which could be enlarged even further. Gallery education and extension services further contribute to public awareness and appreciation of contemporary art. Many other organizations, including community arts and cultural centres, also exhibit contemporary art. Such a substantial infrastructure requires a considerable investment of public and private resources.

Public gallery funds generally come from all three levels of government and from private sources. Federal support for the specific purpose of funding exhibitions of contemporary Canadian art comes mainly from the Canada Council: in 1981 the Canada Council provided about $2 million for this purpose, over and above its grants to artist-run centres. The National Museums' exhibition assistance program also helps with traveling exhibits and research.

Because of recent budget constraints, established institutions have tended to instal prestigious international exhibitions of popular periods in foreign art in order to attract larger numbers of visitors. This practice is not without its detractors, who argue that more public space, not less, should be devoted to Canadian art. We recognize the undeniable importance and value of exhibitions of art from other countries, indeed of artistic exchanges of all kinds between nations. Moreover, we do not believe that the federal government or its agencies should attempt to direct gallery programming through the imposition of content quotas. However, we do recommend that:

34.   The federal government, through its cultural agencies, should increase the funds available to public art galleries for the purpose of exhibiting contemporary Canadian art.

Certain federal departments have been buying Canadian art for some time. With the establishment in 1972 of the Canada Council Art Bank, the direct purchase of art by the federal government soared. The Art Bank was praised by many of those who came before our Committee and has been a model for similar initiatives by other countries and jurisdictions. Its operations are fairly simple: it buys works of art from living Canadian artists and rents them to federal departments and agencies, as well as to provincial and municipal governments and not-for-profit organizations. Under a modest purchase-assistance program, it also provides matching funds to public galleries for the acquisition of contemporary Canadian art. The Art Bank has also assumed a number of museological functions. From time to time it mounts traveling exhibitions and it has established a small gallery with limited public viewing hours. Between 1972 and 1981, the Art Bank spent well over $6.4 million on some 10,000 works by more than 1,000 artists. These works included 5,000 prints, 2,800 works on paper (such as photographs and drawings), 1,500 paintings and over 700 sculptures.

We commend the Canada Council Art Bank as a body whose program is consistent with the principles we would see embodied in a federal policy for the visual arts. But it is difficult to assess how successful the Art Bank has been in influencing the public to buy or even to appreciate contemporary Canadian art. Because the federal government is the Art Bank's main client, most of the collection can be seen only in the National Capital Region and usually only in government offices. On the other hand, the Art Bank does not appear to have harmed the commercial gallery system, as was feared initially, since most of its purchases are made through dealers. The Art Bank's purchase scheme for public galleries is beneficial; it should be expanded as the allocation of Canada Council funds permits. We also favour some rationalization of the Art Bank's museological activities and its jury composition and selection procedures. During our public hearings we heard many concerns expressed about these latter operations in particular, which we discuss under the Canada Council heading later in this chapter.

In 1964 the federal government decided that the Department of Public Works, under its Fine Arts Program, should allocate 1 per cent of the federal building construction budget to commission art for government buildings. Until the Fine Arts Program (called the "1% program") was suspended indefinitely in 1978, 235 works of art costing $3.7 million had been incorporated into government structures. If considered over the 14-year life of the program, the figure is not large. Yet when the program was suspended, the reason given was overall cutbacks in government spending. There were other difficulties with the program. Some of the artwork was highly criticized by the public, often because the work was not integrated with the building and its surroundings or understood by the local community. We shall have more to say about this program and the use of works of art in federal government buildings later in this chapter under the heading "The Federal Government as Client."

For over 100 years, the National Gallery of Canada has collected Canadian art. Nonetheless, for many Canadians and for the members of this Committee, the National Gallery's collection and efforts on behalf of contemporary Canadian art have been disappointing. Thirty years ago, the Massey-Lévesque Commission wrote that the National Gallery's problems were serious, and many of those who made submissions to our Committee just last year argued that government neglect of the National Gallery has continued. In recent years purchase funds for the Gallery's contemporary collection have dwindled. The Gallery has been prevented from being a national showcase and champion of Canadian art because of the low priority and inadequate resources provided by successive federal governments. The unintended result of this continuing federal indifference is that the right of present and future generations of Canadians, and people of other countries, to know our visual arts is seriously compromised. Some would say it approaches a national shame.

Other collections of contemporary Canadian art within the federal government are in the possession of the Department of Indian and Northern Affairs, the Department of External Affairs and the Department of Transport. These, too, are all valuable collections and warrant a more concerted effort to make them accessible to a wider public.

Difficulties of the magnitude we have been describing in federal policy towards the contemporary visual arts persuade us that a wholly new attitude and approach are required on the part of the federal government. Although we are delighted that the present government has committed itself to building a new National Gallery in Ottawa, we believe strongly that a separate and parallel commitment must be made to the contemporary visual arts. Because the National Gallery is responsible for maintaining and collecting art from many different historical periods, contemporary art will continue to receive emphasis and attention as only one part of the Gallery's collection. The Gallery will continue to bear a broad responsibility for the arts of the past. We therefore recommend that:

35.   **The Government of Canada should establish a Contemporary Arts Centre, with the same status as its four national museums, dedicated exclusively to the collection, exhibition, touring, promotion and development of contemporary visual art in Canada.**

Contemporary arts centres or galleries exist in many countries, an indication of the vitality and social importance of visual art in the 20th century. The Contemporary Arts Centre we propose would work with all related visual arts institutions in Canada, complementing and strengthening the efforts of all to make visual art a more vital presence in our lives.

It is essential that the Centre's collections and exhibitions include all areas of contemporary creativity, whether in traditional forms of painting, sculpture and works on paper, minimal or process artwork, conceptual or performance art, or new work in photography and in the applied arts of crafts, design and architecture. Appropriate federal collections of contemporary Canadian art would become part of its collection. For example, incorporating into the Centre's collection the National Collection of Contemporary Indian Art gathered by the National Museum of Man would remove the unfortunate and unnecessary connotation that works of contemporary Native art are understood best as artifacts and, somehow, are neither contemporary nor art. The Centre could also incorporate into its collection certain parts of the Canada Council Art Bank collection not required for rental purposes as well as that of the National Film Board's Still Photo Division and the National Capital Commission's sculpture installations. Above all, the Centre would pursue a vigorous program of buying outstanding contemporary works. This art would be primarily Canadian, but because visual artists today work within an international context, non-Canadian works should be sought out as well.

The Contemporary Arts Centre would be far more than a static collection of art housed in a single location. It would be a dynamic source for disseminating and promoting the work of Canada's leading contemporary artists. The Centre would conduct a lively touring program whose exhibitions would be adventurous and far-ranging.

In its development assistance role, the Centre would organize and fund exchanges of art and artists between different regions of Canada and between Canada and other countries. The Centre would work in cooperation with the network of artist-run centres across the country. There would be research and publication activities and a substantial distribution program of reproductions on paper and slides to teachers, artists, critics and the general public.

Artists' Centres

One of the outstanding visual arts activities in the last 10 years has been the development of a network of some 35 centres, originally called "parallel galleries" or "alternate spaces," run by artists themselves. These centres are small, flexible organizations which concentrate on exhibiting the work of innovative and experimental artists and those who have not yet established a reputation. They sponsor productions and exhibitions in all forms of contemporary visual art: media art (such as video and audio art), experimental film, artists' books and periodicals and performance art. The application of new technologies has been of particular interest to them. What distinguishes these galleries from the more established institutions (many of which also have diverse programming) is the fact that they are managed, for the most part, by artists and that their top priority is to serve the contemporary arts community and the practising artist. One might add that they are also characterized by poverty: they attract little or no corporate or private funding and they must rely on the support of government bodies, primarily the Canada Council. With two or three notable exceptions, provincial funding has been meagre. Although much of their programming does not have wide public appeal, their umbrella organization, the Association of National Non-Profit Artists' Centres, estimates that their total audience for 1980 was 280,000.

Experimentation is essential to any art form and the contribution of artists' centres in this field has been significant. In fact, much of the international recognition enjoyed by Canadian video and performance artists is due to their efforts. The centres have also played a part in promoting public awareness of contemporary art.

This Committee believes that it is important to maintain this means of linking the work of our experimental artists with the public. We are concerned, however, about the precariously small financial base on which these centres must build their programs. Total dependence on government support is one answer, but we hope other appropriate solutions to the funding problem will be found.

Private Galleries and Collectors

Although accurate figures about the Canadian art market are not available, the growth in the number of commercial art galleries provides evidence that there has been an important increase in the ranks of private collectors in recent years. Each of Canada's large urban centres now supports 20 or more private galleries devoted to visual art. As a whole there are approximately 350 private galleries throughout the country – three times more than 20 years ago. Clients include individual, institutional and corporate collectors. Another trend of recent years has been the decision by large and medium-sized corporations to invest in the visual arts, both contemporary and historical, both Canadian and non-Canadian.

Until recently, corporate collecting was encouraged by a tax depreciation allowance which permitted such purchases to be written off against taxable income at the rate of 20 per cent a year. The November 1981 federal budget removed the tax depreciation allowance, rightly noting that antiques and visual art possessions do not generally depreciate in value. Removing the depreciation allowance also closed a loophole in the government's tax laws by which some corporations sold artwork from the corporate collection to executives at a nominal cost after the artwork had been fully depreciated. The November 1981 federal budget did permit a depreciation allowance for only the first purchase of visual art by living Canadian artists, presumably to protect the market for such work. But the budget had an unforeseen effect. Many corporations cut off their purchases of works of art, including Canadian works that represented both first and subsequent sales of an artist's work. The loss of corporate clients, who often bought not the first-sale work of artists but the second-sale or resale work, also affected the artists' ability to establish their pricing of future works. This has also adversely affected the ability of many galleries to make profits, which in turn makes possible their

promotion of new talent and their capacity to undertake risky and experimental exhibitions. Of greater concern to us, however, is that many Canadian artists have been hurt by the lowering of the demand for their works.

Purchase of art by corporations is an important element in the art
market. Major corporate collections of Canadian art have been assembled in
the past two decades from which all have benefited : the artists, the galleries,
the corporations which have enhanced their premises, and the public, which
has often been able to see such collections when they have been exhibited.

The Department of Finance should find other ways of eliminating the
loopholes which have properly concerned them and which have allowed
some executives to purchase artworks at fictitious prices by, for example, requiring that the fair market value of the works so purchased be used in
calculating income taxes. Devices of that kind would permit the reinstatement of helpful depreciation allowances for the purchase of artworks.

36.   The federal government should stimulate private demand
      for contemporary Canadian visual art through incentives to
      purchase and should apply special depreciation allowances
      to purchases of works of art by any Canadian artist, not
      just living Canadian artists, and to all transactions involving
      these works, not just initial purchases.

Commercial galleries play a vital role as intermediaries between artists
and collectors. They do not merely offer artwork for sale, they promote and
encourage the careers of individual artists and expand the artist's potential
audience and market. It is difficult to know whether an artist receives more
satisfaction from selling work to a public or to a private collector. Certainly
there is a particular kind of recognition when a private collector begins to invest money in an artist's work, especially if the artist's reputation is just
emerging. Private demand for a visual artist's work also may exert influence
on public demand. Many privately held works do find their way eventually to
the public through exhibitions and donations to public galleries.

During our public hearings, we heard from private art dealers about
their difficulties in representing contemporary Canadian visual artists. We
were told that Canada's geography makes shipping costs prohibitive and
limits interregional and international exchanges. We were also told that the
Canadian public is exposed daily to mass-produced "art" objects offered as
original artwork or as sound investments, when they actually have very
limited aesthetic or economic value. An unregulated visual art market means
that consumers, artists and serious dealers have very little protection against
competition from the ersatz or misrepresented product. This is a particular
problem in the once-flourishing market for original prints. All these factors,
exacerbated by difficult economic circumstances at the time of writing,
threaten artistic production and consumption by creating an unstable
market environment in which private galleries must operate.

We believe that the federal government should remove its recently imposed 9 per cent sales tax on original prints produced in Canada. The Excise Tax Act, which applies to manufactured objects, includes in that category original art prints. Some prints are indeed manufactured and should be taxed under this law, but there are acknowledged ways of distinguishing between these and handmade prints. Handmade prints should be exempted. These are prints produced directly by Canadian artists in their studios or by a printshop under the direct supervision of the artist, in relatively limited editions of perhaps no more than 125. Some form of standardized print labeling would also help retailers and consumers to distinguish among the different types of prints and would provide an important service to enthusiastic collectors.

With perhaps a few exceptions, neither the Canada Council nor the Department of Industry, Trade and Commerce have supported private galleries in the marketing of works of art. The Canada Council tends to consider such galleries too commercially oriented to be eligible for its programs, even when the galleries are involved in the distribution of contemporary Canadian art. The Department of Industry, Trade and Commerce, on the other hand, tends to deem galleries too risky, their terms of trade too precarious and their margin of profit too small, to be of interest. Commercial galleries do not qualify as other businesses do for export assistance. It is scarcely surprising, therefore, that although commercial galleries regularly present work by foreign visual artists, they are seldom able to promote Canadian visual artists abroad.

Some private galleries have, nevertheless, made an important contribution to the advancement of contemporary Canadian visual art. It is certain that, given a reasonable degree of financial assistance, they could do considerably more. We believe the federal government should provide financial support to commercial visual arts galleries on the same principle that it supports, for example, commercial book publishing through the Canada Council and the Department of Communications – namely, that the intermediaries (publisher or gallery) must themselves be healthy financially if either writer or artist and, for that matter, the public, are to benefit.

Federal assistance, in our view, should not be given for the existing operating costs of private galleries. It should be given for special expenditures related to the promotion and marketing of contemporary Canadian visual art, exhibition of gallery artists (including new and emerging artists) in other regions of Canada and abroad, exchanges between galleries, and participation in commercial art fairs and international expositions.

The implementation of such programs, including their terms of reference, objectives and strategy, would require the collaboration of two organizations whose creation we recommend – the nongovernment marketing and promotion organization proposed in Chapter 3 and the Contemporary Arts Centre proposed earlier in this chapter. The first of these would be a repository of marketing expertise, charged not only with the task of heightening public awareness of the contemporary arts in Canada, but also with devising marketing schemes in concert with the private sector. The second of these, the Contemporary Arts Centre, would mount its own visual arts promotion activities in coordination with the activities of private galleries. Another agency playing a pivotal role in this connection would be the Canadian International Cultural Relations Agency proposed in Chapter 11. A particular responsibility of this body would be to assist private dealers in securing more exposure for Canadian artists in foreign galleries, public and private. Although the Canadian government cultural centres in Paris, Brussels and London and the 49th Parallel Gallery in New York (established by the Canadian consulate) are valuable showcases for Canadian art, it is also important to hold exhibitions in independent institutions. Foreign critics, curators and investors are often wary of "official" exhibitions.

Public Information and Education
Before an individual sets foot in an art gallery or makes a first purchase of an artwork, a process of awareness has already taken place which shapes some of that person's perceptions and expectations of the visual arts. Contributing to individual awareness are the communications media and the education system. Newspapers, magazines, film, radio and television are influential intermediaries between artists and the general public. The National Film Board, for example, has produced documentaries about Canadian visual art, and magazines such as *Maclean's*, *Perspectives*, *L'actualité* and *Saturday Night* provide valuable coverage on occasion. However, the journalistic coverage of visual arts activity is simply not adequate in most parts of the country. A few critics on major daily newspapers provide excellent service for their readers and for the visual arts, but many more Canadian newspapers do not assign anyone at all to a specialized visual arts beat. Private radio and television are especially negligent in this regard; English and French CBC radio and provincial educational television do much better. Deep disappointment was expressed to us in the coverage provided by CBC television. Apart from an occasional documentary, very little CBC television programming deals with the visual arts. *Television is seen as having a particular responsibility in this area because television is an emphatically visual medium.*

Our particular concern is with the 15 or so specialized periodicals in the visual arts ranging from *Vie des arts* and *artscanada* to *Photocommuniqué* and *Artswest.* These publications have a central importance in their field as forums for discussion and debate about the work of our visual artists. In Chapter 7, "Writing, Publishing and Reading," we state that periodicals should be given a higher priority within federal publishing policy. Although visual arts magazines would benefit greatly from the new measures we propose, specialized magazines cannot appear frequently enough to provide full coverage of current events in Canadian visual art. A more desirable state of affairs would be one in which the mass communications media would provide current events coverage for art. This would free visual arts periodicals to concentrate on providing a critical assessment of Canadian art and documenting its international context.

Art books are also a major contributor to public understanding and appreciation. Authors frequently experience difficulty in obtaining public funding for the research and writing of such books, particularly if they are intended for the general public. Manuscripts of this kind cannot be neatly classified within existing grant programs for either scholars or artists. We hope the modification we propose in Chapter 7 for the Canada Council's grant programs for writers, which would place nonfiction writers on the same footing as writers of works of fiction, will help to remedy this shortcoming.

The importance of introducing schoolchildren to visual art in a lively and imaginative manner must be emphasized. Many intervenors before our Committee were extremely frank about art education programs in our schools and viewed them as pitifully inadequate, focusing as they do on teaching the techniques of art production rather than on expanding the imaginations of our young people. We commend to provincial authorities, who are responsible for primary and secondary school education, the merits of such valuable programs as artists-in-the-schools and visits to artists' studios. The programs of federal cultural agencies can also contribute to art education in various ways. They can, for example, support books and magazines which introduce the visual arts into schools. They can fund the production and distribution of visual art education materials, and support traveling exhibitions of art. We urge federal policy-makers to remain sensitive to all the educational benefits which may accrue from their cultural programs.

The Well-Being of Visual and Applied Artists

Few visual artists in Canada can live by the sale of their work alone. The same can be said of applied artists, especially those working in crafts areas or as freelance graphic artists and designers. A Department of Communications study, which excluded fine crafts and photography and was based on 1978 information, showed that most full-time, independent professional artists in the visual arts field earn a gross income from their art of only $6,000 to $10,000 annually. The situation is even more critical for women artists, who constitute about one-third of the artists in the visual arts field. Half of the women artists surveyed in 1978 reported earnings from their art to be less than $2,200. Once production expenses are deducted, the net revenues from an artist's earnings sink even lower. The income of many if not most of these artists classifies them as highly specialized working poor. A study carried out in 1980 for Canadian Artists' Representation (Ontario) gives a vivid financial picture of the visual artist: low earnings that increase by only 6 per cent a year, production costs that increase by 20 per cent every year, high insurance rates and great vulnerability to economic fluctuations – not to mention a lack of pension, workmen's compensation and paid holidays. The same bleak facts hold for many applied artists. A 1978 survey by the Canadian Crafts Council reported an annual income of only $8,600 for full-time craftsworkers.

Not surprisingly, then, the financial well-being of artists was one of the issues most often raised during our public hearings. We do not consider this special pleading. It is true that artists choose their profession freely without much expectation of a large income. It is also true that they have other rewards, such as the satisfaction of expressing themselves and communicating their values. Yet it is unfair for society to expect artists to subsidize the making of art with underpaid labour. We believe that less art, and less good art, is produced when artists lack financial compensation. And we are all the poorer for it.

There is no simple solution to this problem. Government cannot simply provide each recognized artist with a salary or an enormous tax deduction. Such steps would be inequitable unless they were extended to all other disadvantaged groups in society. However, government can and must pursue attempts to improve the professional climate for visual and applied artists. Grants to buy time for creation, reform in the copyright law and tax laws, more residencies, more assistance with training, and more support and recognition for community arts groups and national service organizations are some of the specific measures which can be taken by government to ease the economic restrictions hindering the making of art.

Copyright

Copyright legislation, which we discuss in more general terms in Chapter 3, provides the means for visual and applied artists to protect their professional integrity and the integrity of their work and to be recompensed for the use of their creations by the public. Although copyright law now confers controlling rights on the owners of works of "artistic craftsmanship," the extent of actual protection afforded the visual and applied artist is unclear, as is the distinction between works subject to copyright and those entitled to industrial design protection. *Of special concern are the many "moral" rights of visual and applied artists – the attribution of artwork, control over use of an artist's name, and prevention of distortion and mutilation of an artist's work. Moral rights belong to the artist, the creator. They cannot be reassigned to owners of artwork, and changes in the Copyright Act should also extend protection to forms of creative expression which, like video, use new media.*

Composers, authors and playwrights have an interest in producing many copies of their work. Not so the visual artist and, in some cases, not so the applied artist. For example, graphic artists and photographers who, as contract freelancers, sell their work to advertising firms or publishing houses seldom retain control over subsequent use of it. Certainly the maker of one-of-a-kind craftswork does not look kindly on another's copy of that work. As a Canadian Artists' Representation publication puts it: "the existence of a copy more likely than not represents an illegal act." Visual artists and applied artists have no inherent "rights" to collect fees for use in magazines, publications, slides or films, unless they have negotiated and contracted those fees in advance. Persons who reproduce the visual artwork of another often do so under the impression that such actions are justified because they provide exposure for artists. *We urge all artists and their associations to monitor the area of artwork reproduction in order to obtain proper controls and compensation for the use of works of art.*

Because it is important to acknowledge the principle that artists should be properly recompensed for the public exhibition of their work, whether or not they still own the work, *we also strongly favour exhibition rights for living Canadian visual artists.* We are pleased that the 70 or so galleries, museums and artists' centres receiving Canada Council funds to defray the costs of exhibiting work by contemporary Canadian artists must pay exhibition fees under the conditions of the grant. Some provinces such as Ontario also have this funding requirement, and many university galleries, whether or not funded by the Council, also pay fees. We believe that the collecting and distributing of funds for public exhibition of works of art would justify the establishment of a mechanism operating on behalf of all Canadian artists and controlled by them.

Taxation

The capability of the income tax system to support artistic activity by the self-employed has certain limitations, as we have pointed out in Chapter 3. We believe that the few artists who have large incomes should be taxed according to the same regulations as any other citizen, and that grants to artists should continue to be considered as taxable income. However, some aspects of the current tax laws and regulations should be changed.

We are concerned about the tax laws applicable to artists who make charitable donations of their works. A collector – or the estate of a collector – can turn over an artwork to a designated institution and receive an exemption of 100 per cent of its value, to be deducted from taxable income. But a visual or applied artist can only claim the cost of material that went into the work because the Department of National Revenue considers the artist to be giving inventory and business income, while it considers collectors to be giving capital. *The taxation system should be adjusted so that visual and applied artists will receive equitable treatment in comparison with other taxpayers for the charitable donation of artwork (see Recommendation 12).*

Many materials and specialized tools have to be imported by Canadian artists, and import duties must be paid even if such materials are not manufactured in Canada and there is no competing Canadian supplier to be protected. We favour the removal of customs duties from imported artists' materials, and also the removal of federal sales tax on all artists' materials, as has been done for sculpting materials. For crafts materials, one solution proposed to us calls for the introduction of a class of sales tax licence to crafts professionals who hold provincial business licences. It was also suggested to us that wholesalers should be allowed to hold crafts materials tax free because most crafts professionals do not buy directly from manufacturers. These suggestions can be readily adapted to meet the needs of other visual and applied artists, too.

Financing

Professionals in the applied and visual arts are not only artists; frequently they are also the managers of small businesses, and may be the sole employee of that business. Applied and visual artists need more business training. Even if they have acquired business acumen, they often experience difficulty in obtaining financing to start up or expand their businesses. The artist's primary collateral may be talent alone. Studies cited to us by the Nova Scotia Designer Craftsmen show that 90 per cent of the crafts professionals receiving development assistance through the Nova Scotia Rural Industries Program are still in operation on a sound financial basis after six or seven years. The Committee does not know of similar studies for other areas of the visual and applied arts.

The federal government, through the Federal Business Development Bank, has programs for loans, venture capital and advisory seminars. Although these could be helpful to artists, the Bank's programs are usually not oriented towards the particular problems of a one-person business. *We believe that national service organizations of visual and applied artists have an important role to play in connecting their members to federal government services and in assisting the Federal Business Development Bank to adapt its policies to the needs of artists.*

Marketing

Many applied artists, especially those in crafts, have difficulty marketing their products. Visual artists usually turn to private galleries for marketing once they have established a portfolio and exhibition record. There are far fewer private galleries marketing crafts. As a result, the public often finds craftswork for sale at fairs, through crafts cooperatives and in small gift shops. Although fairs and cooperatives provide the public with an opportunity to see and purchase fine craftswork and enable crafts professionals to see the work of fellow professionals, they tend to be regional in nature – clearly a limitation on selling and viewing products.

We urge governments to explore ways to assist crafts cooperatives and other artist-run cooperatives to open up potential markets outside their immediate areas. More government sponsorship of traveling crafts exhibitions is needed.

Labeling

Many of the materials used in visual and applied arts production are hazardous to health, yet there are no complete labeling requirements for such materials. There is a clear necessity to require the identification of hazardous contents. There are also other problems, we discovered, which arise directly from a lack of material labeling requirements. It is difficult to maintain quality control for production runs when the composition of materials used may vary from one purchase to the next. Another problem arises in exporting products to another country if the materials used in the work cannot be specifically identified. And restoration and conservation are made much more difficult when the material of which the artwork is composed is not known.

The Canadian Crafts Council has established a hazardous materials advisory committee to Health and Welfare Canada. In its initial work, the committee has prepared information sheets for studios and has initiated investigations of possible hazards. The committee's goal is to gather enough information so that the Department of Consumer and Corporate Affairs will be able to establish better labeling requirements. Canadian Artists' Representation has also been involved in tracing hazardous arts materials and alerting artists to their use. *The Committee urges that the federal government establish and implement adequate labeling requirements on arts materials.*

Training in the Visual and Applied Arts

The institutions providing training in the visual and applied arts are as varied as the field itself. The professional architect, landscape architect and urban planner qualify to practise their disciplines through university degree courses. Interior, industrial and graphic designers may also study in universities or colleges of design. Crafts professionals may be self-taught, or may learn through apprenticeship to master craftsworkers, or may spend a few months or several years at a technical school, community college or university. Many briefs and interventions called attention to the need for more consultation among professional artists' organizations and educational institutions to establish standards.

Although training in the visual arts was once the province of art schools and artists' academies, some Canadian universities have also shown leadership in this field. A few universities maintain fine arts departments which employ professional artists. But in spite of these university initiatives, art schools outside the university structure in many provinces continue to play a vital and productive role in training visual artists. Although standards vary from institution to institution, community colleges and CEGEPs also offer courses and diplomas in the visual and applied arts.

Despite the provincial governments' current restrictions on educational spending, we yet express the hope that the importance of training for visual and applied artists will continue to be recognized, not only in the artists' own disciplines but also in the vital area of business management.

Apprenticeship to a master craftsworker is traditionally an important way for craftsworkers to develop their creative talent. Unfortunately, the time a master devotes to teaching and training an apprentice is time taken away from the master's own art. And when training is completed, the apprentice usually leaves the master to set up independent production.

We have come to believe that measures must be taken to ensure the training of young crafts professionals and that there should be incentives to master craftsworkers to enable them to take on apprentices without a loss of income. This concept would also be important where applicable to other visual and applied artists, such as printmakers, photographers and sculptors.

Residencies

One of the most imaginative and socially valuable ways of providing income for visual and applied artists has been the artist-in-residence programs established by all levels of government. These residencies, enabling an artist to set up a studio in a university, community college, school, or a community outside a major urban centre, have many advantages. In addition to providing income, residencies allow artists to continue producing art while interacting with schoolchildren, post-secondary students or members of the general public. Residencies operate on a cost-sharing basis: a funding body offers a stipend and the host organization provides facilities. They are relatively inexpensive, and their effectiveness in bridging the gap between visual and applied artists and the public can be substantial.

There are a good number of visual and applied arts residencies in Canada; nearly 100 were funded in Ontario alone during 1981. We think there should be many more and that they should be extended to large corporations and industries. For instance, Canada has a number of artists who have acknowledged expertise in computer science and who are actively experimenting with marriages between art and the new technologies. These visual artists could make a significant contribution to the development of innovative software while expanding the uses of new technology if they were in residence at "high-tech" companies or colleges. Furthermore, for applied artists of any sort, opportunities to work on projects established in consultation with industry would permit exploration of areas of production not possible in schools and community centres. At present there are few such opportunities.

Community Arts Centres

In small towns and cities alike, many Canadians experience their first exposure to the visual and applied arts, either as participant or viewer, in community arts centres. There are hundreds of such centres across the country, and their contribution to the visual and applied arts is substantial. Combined municipal and provincial support usually pays part of their overheads, but they also receive federal funding occasionally. All operate on the dedicated and enthusiastic labour of volunteers, who organize classes as well as exhibitions, sometimes in conjunction with the adult education departments of local schoolboards. Indications are that over the next decade this type of rich community activity will continue to flourish.

What should federal policy be in this area? We believe that each level of government has a role to play in supporting the various orders of artistic activity and that the concept of multiple sources of funding is a healthy one. *Thus, the federal government should assume its part in fostering community activity in the visual and applied arts.* Indeed, different programs in the Department of the Secretary of State already respond, partially at least, to the arts at the community level, and in Chapter 2 we suggest that the Canada Council increase its efforts in this area. This federal presence, we must add, should not be overwhelming but should have a fairly narrow focus, such as providing funds for the services of visual and applied arts professionals. This is also an area in which collaboration among the various levels of government is clearly indicated, with the federal role being well defined but secondary within priorities set by the communities themselves.

Service Organizations

Service organizations have an important place in promoting the interests of Canada's visual and applied artists. These organizations attempt to create greater public awareness of the visual and applied arts and are effective in bringing together artists from various regions. Some are active in professional development activities; others provide recognition in the form of awards and prizes.

As we stated in Chapter 2 concerning federal support for service organizations in the arts, federal agencies and departments responsible for assisting specific disciplines are usually in the best position to judge the usefulness and effectiveness of organizations claiming to represent the interests of artists in those disciplines. Undeniably, there is a direct connection between the ability of a service organization to support a small but full-time secretariat and its efficiency. It is not surprising, therefore, that funds for staffing rank very high in the list of service organization demands on government funds. Even with staff help, service organizations rely heavily on volunteer labour.

A special word must be said about service organizations which deal with arts education – such as the Canadian Society for Education through Art. As the mandates of the federal cultural agencies do not include responsibility specifically for education, we suggest that these particular service organizations might fall within the purview of the Department of the Secretary of State, which provides various types of assistance to educational activity at the national level and to voluntary action groups.

In continuing the allocation of funds to service organizations, we suggest that funding bodies should carefully assess the degree to which the organization is supported by its own members, either through membership fees or voluntary effort. Service organizations wish to be consulted by government on programs and policies affecting the visual and applied arts, but, as we noted in Chapter 2, the strength of their influence should depend on how representative they are considered to be by the constituencies for which they speak.

Canada Council Grants

Since its founding, the Canada Council has conducted a full-scale program of aid to individual artists in all disciplines. These grants buy time to enable artists to carry out their work and provide financial assistance toward project costs. In 1980-81, the Council offered over 400 grants to individual visual artists (and in some instances to applied artists working in crafts) worth in total almost $2 million and accounting for over one-third of the total individual grants given to all artists. More generous allowances for the cost of artists' materials have recently been awarded by the Council. Arts grants are given on the recommendation of juries – generally composed of other artists and critics. In an attempt to ensure that artists from the various regions of the country are judged by jury members who are knowledgable about their work, visual arts juries include, as a matter of policy, members from different regions.

Most intervenors felt that the current system of Canada Council grants should be maintained and developed, since it represents an important means of support for the visual artist and the occasional craftsworker whose production is viewed by the Council as visual art. It is a fact, however, that grants and awards play only a secondary role in financing artistic creation and research in Canada. Most full-time professionals never receive a grant or award and of those who do, three-quarters receive no more than $1,000. Grants are a temporary and limited source of financing. They can, of course, be of great assistance at any given time in a career because they offer recognition and encouragement in addition to money.

The strongest and most frequent criticism we heard about the Canada Council's visual arts grants programs concerned its jury system. There were accusations of favouritism. Arguments were advanced intending to demonstrate an underrepresentation of women artists, Native artists, and artists from the various regions on juries, among grant recipients, and among artists whose works are purchased by the Art Bank. Such criticisms were stated more emphatically about the Art Bank and the visual arts juries than about any other facet of the Council's programs. We have considered these criticisms seriously. Nevertheless, despite its limitations, the jury system seems to be by far the most acceptable way of making difficult decisions among applicants competing for a limited number of arts grants or purchases.

As we stated in Chapter 2, in the section on the Canada Council, we urge the Council and other bodies using a jury system to ensure that jury membership reflects a balanced and representative cross-section of artistic and regional perspectives. *Critics, academics, other art professionals and collectors should be more involved in the adjudication process, and care must be taken to rotate jury membership frequently in order to counter criticisms of favouritism and underrepresentation. Excellence should be the only criterion for judging grant applications. But artistic excellence takes many forms, and these must all be given their due.*

The Contemporary Applied Arts

Innumerable works of art frequently escape our notice *as art* for one simple reason – they are also useful. These can be the utensils or pieces of furniture we use every day, the buildings in which we work or aspects of the streets in which we walk. Homes or post offices can be as important as art galleries or cinemas as places to see creativity on display.

We suggested at the beginning of this chapter that definitions distinguishing between the applied arts and the visual arts carry the danger of limiting our perceptions. Yet inevitably, we on this Committee found ourselves using the same, limiting terminology in order to make ourselves understood. Let us emphasize again that when we speak of the applied arts in this Report, we refer primarily to the creative disciplines of crafts, interior, industrial and graphic design, and the environmental arts of architecture, urban planning and design, and landscape architecture. In discussing these disciplines, we recognize that one common and distinguishing feature of their products is utility. Creators in the applied arts work not only with an awareness of the aesthetic criteria of the traditional fine arts, but with an added discipline imparted by the function that the work is intended to serve. For an applied artist, the utility of an object presents formal problems similar to ones facing sculptors and painters.

Although Canada has produced fine designers and Canadians have demonstrated an interest in good design, there is a clear necessity for more work to be done in stimulating public demand for good Canadian design in the applied arts. A strong federal policy of support for the applied arts can make good design an important aspect of commercial competition.

The federal government is a major client of Canadian architects and other environmental artists; the Department of Industry, Trade and Commerce funds Design Canada and the National Design Council; and recognition and financial support are provided to the Canadian Crafts Council and to other organizations of artisans, including Native craftsworkers. We have already recommended in this chapter that the collections and exhibitions of the proposed Contemporary Arts Centre include examples from the applied arts. On the same principle, examples of high quality applied artwork should be part of other federal collections, such as those of the National Gallery of Canada and the Canada Council Art Bank. Such examples could include one-of-a-kind craftswork, multiples, architects' and interior designers' drawings and maquettes, and industrial design prototypes. But in addition to these recommendations and suggestions, we urge that the applied arts should be given a new and important place in federal cultural policy.

A Canadian Council for Design and the Applied Arts
The Canada Council deals with the applied arts only peripherally. The utility that is an important discipline to creative designers usually places their work outside the Council's terms of reference. The Department of Communications provides operating funds for the Canadian Crafts Council, but does not extend financial support to individual artists. The federal government exerts its greatest influence on the applied arts through the National Design Council and its executive arm, Design Canada.

The history of the National Design Council is worth reviewing because in its history lie its problems. It began as the Industrial Design Committee in 1948, whose objective was to ensure the use of as much Canadian talent as possible in developing good design. In 1953, it became the National Industrial Design Council and acted as a committee of the National Gallery, sponsoring traveling exhibits and working with its Design Centres. Then, because of its intimate connection with industry, it was transferred in 1960 to the Department of Industry, Trade and Commerce where it was supported by the Office of Design Advisor. The Industry, Trade and Commerce Act of 1969 gave the department an improved industrial design mandate, and in 1970 the Office of Design Advisor became a departmental branch acting, in part, as secretariat to the Design Council. This branch became known as Design Canada in 1976.

Since the early 1960s the size and budget of Design Canada have dwindled, probably because of a lack of political priority given to a branch whose aims are relatively peripheral to department activities. On the one hand, Design Canada is responsible to the Design Council whose objective is promoting improved design; on the other hand, Design Canada is responsible to the department whose objective is to promote design in product, process and export market development. Although Design Canada has concentrated on industrial design, it has from time to time given support to other crafts professionals, graphic artists, interior designers and architects. However, its originally well-conceived programs have become ineffective. It does not control either its budget or its staff. We believe a better way for the government to provide necessary support to the applied arts in an effective, coordinated manner would be to support a strong and effective liaison and advocacy body. We therefore recommend that:

37.   The government should amend the National Design Council Act of 1960 to designate a Canadian Council for Design and the Applied Arts and fund the Council to a level that will enable it to fulfil its mandate. The Council should report to the Minister of Communications.

The Canadian Council for Design and the Applied Arts requires a mandate that includes: the creative development of the applied artist, fostering appreciation for applied artwork, establishing a productive relationship between applied artists and industry, and assisting with applied arts marketing. The proposed Council would absorb, build upon and expand all such programs currently conducted by the National Design Council and Design Canada. It would occupy a stronger position than have these two bodies vis-à-vis industry and at the same time find renewal through its status as a cultural organization for the applied arts. Representatives from both the arts and industrial communities would have a place on the Council's board of directors.

One of the important functions of the proposed Council would be to sponsor design competitions and offer support for developing product prototypes. We feel that government sponsorship of design competitions can do much to educate public taste and widen the domestic and foreign markets for Canadian applied arts. Another important function of the Council would be to establish open lists of professional artists and designers, available to both the private and public sectors and cross-indexed to meet the different purposes of industry and the arts communities. Establishing a registry of lists would also enable the Council to publish catalogues of artists working in various media and to collaborate in exhibitions with the proposed Contemporary Arts Centre and with other museums and service organizations. In time, these lists could serve as the foundation for an index of Canadian design and would be a valuable resource to university and college programs in design, art history and studio art.

In order to promote the relationship between applied artists and industry, the Council would support and coordinate workshops and seminars where crafts professionals and designers could work with manufacturers. It is important that applied artists be aware of industry experience in promoting fine design and improving the response of buyers to those designs. If these workshops and seminars were held at educational institutions across the country, the basis for schools of advanced design might eventually result.

In seeking to assist the individual applied artist, the Canadian Council for Design and the Applied Arts would support national professional associations and service organizations of applied artists which are demonstrably useful to their members. Such bodies would be assisted in carrying out research and action programs in the interests of professional development and in relationship with educational institutions, industry and government.

The Council would work through consultation and cooperation with the appropriate professional associations – for example, the Royal Architectural Institute of Canada, the National Indian Arts and Crafts Corporation, the Interior Designers of Canada, the Graphic Designers of Canada, the Canadian Crafts Council and with other federal departments and agencies. Expertise, enterprise and communication would be crucial for the development of effective Council programs for design and the applied arts.

The Federal Government as Client

Although, as we noted at the start of this chapter, government programs and policies have tended to separate the visual and the applied arts, we also noted that we wanted to lower barriers between visual and applied artists and between artists and the public. The Committee believes an extraordinary opportunity exists for the federal government to accomplish these objectives in a straightforward manner.

It is estimated that of the government's very large expenditures on new construction and renovation projects for federal buildings and leased spaces – for example, post offices, airports, offices, defence installations, prisons, utility plants, historic sites and embassies, among others – up to 25 per cent goes for building appointments, fixtures, furnishings and fine arts and craftswork, or somewhere between $100 million to $250 million a year. Federal government policy permits the use of foreign suppliers when there are no comparable Canadian sources for quality goods. Although the Committee recognizes that there are not always Canadian suppliers to meet all of the government's needs, we also believe there is no good reason why Canadian art and design should not, in time, become more competitive in both the world and domestic markets. We recognize, however, that there is need for a change of attitude concerning Canadian capability on the part of the public and the federal government, so that "buy Canadian" becomes not bureaucratic imposition but a perceived and desired standard of excellence.

The Committee believes strengthened federal support for Canadian art and design and the visible results of such support would do much to stimulate a more positive attitude toward Canadian art and design. Because federal buildings are an important presence in any community, large or small, the federal building program is capable of lowering barriers between artists and the public and, for that matter, lowering barriers between government and the public it serves. For example, we as consumers have come to regard chairs not only as seats to sit in, but also as art or craftswork of wood, fabric and metal, with qualities of line and design to be considered and valued. This is partly because Scandinavian design has been so effectively promoted by Scandinavian governments at home and abroad. Whether or not we like Scandinavian, Italian, or Bauhaus designs, our tastes have been influenced; some would say improved. If the federal government were to express a similar confidence in quality Canadian art and design by providing them with more exposure, more of us would begin to value them as something expressive of contemporary life and thinking.

The Canadian Council for Design and the Applied Arts will have as one of its important functions the promotion of quality Canadian art and design. Therefore, because we see the necessity of establishing, at the outset, a close and ongoing liaison between the Council's work and that of the government in planning expenditures for federal buildings, we recommend the following:

38.   The proposed Canadian Council for Design and the Applied Arts should ensure, to the greatest degree possible, that federal public buildings make extensive use of contemporary Canadian art and design. To that end, the Council would provide expert consultative services to all federal departments involved in building, leasing and renovation projects.

The intent of our recommendation is to enable the proposed Canadian Council for Design and the Applied Arts to act as an information coordinating body for all federal departments affected by the government's building program. The Committee believes that the present discussion within the visual arts and crafts communities favouring the reinstatement of the Department of Public Works' Fine Arts Program (1 % program) has drawn attention away from the many opportunities available to visual and applied artists within the full scope of the federal building program. The Department of Public Works, although an important builder of buildings, is not the only federal builder.

The mandate of the proposed Council will permit it to choose certain building projects, regularly identified from the official government *Estimates*, as candidates for design competition, prototype development and promotion. The Council's pivotal position within the federal building program will also enable it to identify and develop, in time, Canadian sources for art, design and supply for architects and directly involved federal departments. Further, because the Council will be able to assist federal departments in developing strong guidelines for the inclusion of contemporary Canadian art and design in their buildings, it will also be able to argue strongly that artists and architects alike should be involved at the start of all building design work. Public art programs for public buildings stand a better chance of obtaining public approval when artwork is installed as an integrated, necessary part of the building. The Committee believes that obtaining this recognition for fine arts and craftswork at the outset is extremely important. Clearly one of the difficulties with the former Department of Public Works program was that art sometimes appeared to be included as an afterthought to the building's design. The Council will also be able to make technical information and assistance available to artists undertaking federal commissions for visual art and craftswork.

We believe that an expanded "art in architecture" applied arts concept strongly advocated by the Canadian Council for Design and the Applied Arts will give us an effective government program for integrating visual and applied arts into our everyday lives. Such a program will ensure the presence of good Canadian art and design in all government buildings and make it accessible to a larger public.

By bringing together in one chapter both the visual and applied arts, we have sought to give prominence to the total aspect of our visual environment, be it architecture, city planning or our understanding of natural and technological surroundings. The visual and applied arts in Canada are steeped in popular tradition and open to innovative development. If our recommendations are put into practice, the next two or three decades should see important improvements obtained for the lot of artists, their public, and the intermediaries who present their work to us.

6

The Performing Arts

6

The Performing Arts

The performing arts are, in the first instance, a complex and (some would say) miraculous process by which composers, playwrights and choreographers make their vision known through actors, singers, instrumentalists and dancers, who may rely on yet another set of creative intermediaries, the conductors, directors and designers – all working together as a team to create a performance. Sometimes, indeed, two or even all three of these creative functions are combined in the person of a single artist.

A performance, almost by definition, is ephemeral. The moment when the actor speaks, the downbeat is given, the dance begins will never be repeated in just that way – ever again. Today through electronic technologies the moment may be caught and held forever. But the performance of it, still ephemeral, is unique.

For centuries, performances took place in the physical presence of audiences: in our time, film, sound recording, videotaping and broadcasting may bring them to thousands more spectators and listeners. Thus, the problems and prospects we discuss in our chapters on film, sound recording and broadcasting also touch closely on the performing arts. All these media have permitted the expansion of the audience to which performances can be distributed and have provided strikingly new ways to share and enjoy the performing arts.

Even so, the essence of the performing arts remains in the special relationship that develops between artists and their public in the theatre, concert or recital hall. In spite of the many advantages of electronic distribution, live public performances remain vital to a vibrant society, essential in their own right as well as for the continued development of vocal and instrumental music, drama and dance. Through them performers hone their skills and audiences refine their reactions; ideally, they share equally in the enjoyment of the performance. This field, furthermore, needs to proceed by trial and error, especially if inventiveness and creativity are to be favoured over repetition and habit. The reactions of audiences are therefore vital to the life of the performing arts. For these reasons, we emphasize in this chapter the task of strengthening bonds between artists and audiences.

Growth and Future of the Performing Arts

The growth and development of the performing arts in Canada over the last three decades has been impressive. At the beginning of the second half of this century, when the Massey-Lévesque Commission was concluding its review, professional theatres could be counted on the fingers of both hands. Only four cities had a symphony orchestra, and in the field of ballet there was not enough activity to justify a special study by the Commissioners. Moreover, concerts and performances took place more often than not in gymnasiums and poorly equipped school auditoriums. Though there was CBC radio, whose musical and theatrical programs provided work opportunities and whose influence on the performing arts was enormous, it was rare for artists to be able to earn their living solely through their craft. There were relatively few opportunities for a singer, an actor, a dancer or a musician to receive any structured professional training. So it was not unusual for talented artists to leave the country to study or make a career if they did not wish to give up their dream.

Since then, progress has been swift thanks to the dedication, self-lessness and enthusiasm of creative and interpretive artists, their teammates – including their unions – and their supporters. Around them have been built the service organizations, which have been promoters, information sources and catalysts.

Excellent training in the performing arts is now generally available in Canada, although the situation varies from discipline to discipline. Every province has at least one major performing arts centre, and many Canadian cities – and increasingly smaller communities as well – can boast acceptable facilities. Today thousands of professional performing artists work all or part of the year in hundreds of ventures: orchestras, theatre and dance and opera companies, nightclubs, radio and television. Aid for touring from many sources has enabled outstanding Canadian concert, theatre and dance productions to reach audiences across the country and abroad. Performing arts companies have grown not only in number but also in breadth of repertoire. It is true that the traditional forms are still often favoured by artistic directors and the public. Yet in each of the disciplines, in varying degrees, more progressive forms of expression are emerging, stimulated by the boldness of certain artists and groups and encouraged by the openmindedness of their public.

Paralleling the expansion in numbers of facilities and companies has been an undoubted growth in audiences attending live performances. According to statistics compiled jointly by the Canada Council and Statistics Canada, there were more than eight million paid admissions to the productions of the 184 largest professional performing arts companies in 1979. (This figure is derived from a survey of those companies receiving operating or project grants from the Canada Council and it does not include performances of amateur or semi-professional productions or popular music concerts. Were these to be included the figure would be many millions higher.) These figures are corroborated by other data. In a recent survey of audience attendance conducted by the Department of the Secretary of State, 21 per cent of adult Canadians claim to have attended at least one performance of classical music or dance during the course of a year, 27 per cent attended a live theatre performance and 31 per cent went to a popular or folk music concert. Even within this limited framework, it is clear that the performing arts in Canada, far from being an elite medium, enjoy a wide audience.

The recent history of the performing arts in Canada is therefore encouraging, but the current outlook has its sombre aspects. The flow of financial resources required to sustain the current momentum has slackened in recent years, often with dire results. In spite of the encouraging attendance figures we noted above, there is a need for further audience development. There are improvements still to be made in education and training and in physical facilities. And most of all there is an urgent need for a new emphasis on the presentation of the works of Canadian playwrights, composers and choreographers. Although some progress has been made, notably in theatre and modern dance, much more remains to be done.

The Creation and Production of Canadian Works
The structures we have put in place must now be properly maintained, developed and imaginatively used to foster the presentation of more works of an increasingly high quality by Canadian creative artists. To accomplish this we need not, and should not, close our borders or turn in on ourselves. The whole repertoire of foreign works from both the past and present belongs to us; to deprive ourselves of these would be to diminish our artistic and cultural life. But we must establish a healthier balance between works by foreign writers, composers and choreographers and those by Canadians. The balance may vary from discipline to discipline depending on its nature, and from company to company depending on its goals, but it is necessary to encourage the development and expression of our own artists' creativity.

Some advancement in the production and presentation of Canadian works has been achieved. In theatre, the change has been quite noticeable, to the point where some companies now offer exclusively Canadian repertoire. The situation is different and less encouraging in ballet, even though Canadian choreographers are more numerous than formerly. It is in music, particularly "serious" music, where things are least encouraging. Original works by Canadian composers are performed more often than before, but it is rare for them to make up a significant part of the programs of symphony orchestras. This situation is not peculiar to Canada, of course: it prevails throughout the Western industrialized world for all types of serious music. In all of these countries it is clear that it is not so much the nationality of composers which is the stumbling block as the newness of their works. Canadian composers find they have the most ready access to companies and groups which specialize in contemporary music; yet these groups tend to have very limited financial resources.

To encourage creation in all the performing arts, it will be necessary to win over the public to new works through regular performances under the best possible conditions. This may entail additional expense, since new works will often require more rehearsals, more artistic resources, and increased promotion when the work is ready for presentation. There is a need for more commissions, more opportunities to test ideas, more workshops and seminars. There is also a need for more artist-in-residence arrangements in performing arts companies, institutions and communities. These residencies provide income to artists and establish productive links with the public which are vital to the future of the arts and their enjoyment. The Canada Council has recognized these needs for many years, and has offered special grants for the commissioning of works by Canadian dramatists and composers and has given financial support to many choreographic workshops.

Such efforts in support of performing arts activity must be fostered if sufficient priority is to be given in federal cultural policies to the creation of works by Canadian creative artists.

In 1972, with a view to encouraging Canadian composers, the Canada Council required that 10 per cent of the programs of symphony orchestras subsidized by the Council should be devoted to Canadian works. Acknowledging that this requirement was imposed for good reasons and with the best of intentions, this Committee has nevertheless come to doubt the appropriateness of quotas in promoting the production of Canadian works in the performing arts. What is needed instead is a technique of funding support which permits a greater degree of decision-making freedom for companies than do quotas, yet achieves the objective of changing attitudes of both performers and audiences to new works. Hence we prefer a policy of financial incentives and recommend the following.

39.   The Canada Council should initiate a program of incentive grants related to the presentation of new Canadian works in the performing arts, the advertising and marketing of such works, and the increased cost of rehearsing and producing them.

As we have pointed out in Chapter 3, under the heading "The Government as Patron," a prime feature of incentive grants is that the terms of compliance are known in advance so that artistic directors can choose whether to accept them.

Establishing a Financial Base
The performing arts, taken as a whole, suffer from a perennial financial problem. As others have done, we might label this problem the "income gap," because it reflects the difference between income earned at the box office and the costs of mounting performances. We might also call it the "recovery ratio," because it measures the portion of production costs recovered at the box office in relation to what is obtained from other sources. According to

figures provided by the Canada Council and Statistics Canada, ticket sales and other earned income in 1979 accounted for roughly 50 per cent of the revenues of the 184 Canadian professional performing arts organizations included in the survey; 38 per cent was provided by governments and the remaining 12 per cent came from private donations and miscellaneous sources. These figures are consistent with data collected by other organizations.

This ratio of box office receipts to other sources of income has been stable for some years. It is, of course, an average and there are therefore many exceptions on either side of that average. In large cities, especially those with heavy tourist traffic, or in festival towns, some performing arts groups can amortize heavy costs over long runs. Individual companies sometimes even find themselves able to run profitable operations. The arrival of pay-television and the increasing popularity of other forms of on-demand home entertainment, through videodiscs and videocassettes, may boost the revenues of some performing arts companies just as recordings have helped musical organizations. But the impact of these developments, on average, is likely to be small, with the bulk of the new income generated going to only a few of the better-known organizations. For the performing arts as a whole, the recent average recovery ratio of about one-half is likely to prevail for the foreseeable future.

One way to deal with the income gap problem would be to reduce costs. But steps in that direction would almost certainly generate a downward spiral in which reductions in quality would lead to reduced attendance and, in turn, decreased box office revenues. In the performing arts, virtually the only way to reduce costs is to cut back on the number or size of the productions offered, because, as noted in Chapter 3, not very much can be done to increase productivity. As a result, audiences are deprived of the opportunity to see full-scale productions. Another consequence of such cost-saving measures is that fewer performers are employed, further reducing already low incomes.

To appreciate the impact of such cost saving on the incomes of artists, it is well to recall how low these incomes already are. For example, in 1980-81, the average annual income of a professional dancer employed on a full-time basis by one of our major ballet companies was $14,000. Professional dancers working with modern dance companies, though they must train every day, are often paid only for performance and rehearsal time. The average annual income of dancers in these companies in 1980-81 was $6,000. The situation is equally bleak for actors, singers and other interpretive artists, and for composers, playwrights and choreographers it is even worse. Few if any in the latter groups can reasonably expect to make a living from their creative activity alone, the chief exceptions being highly successful lyricists and composers of popular songs.

The task of introducing economies into the performing arts is complicated by the presence of unionized professions within production companies. At the beginning of this chapter we used the word "team" to describe the intimate relationship that exists among all performing arts participants, whether they be actors, directors, singers, pit musicians, backstage hands or house staff. While we recognize the importance of unions as advocates for their members, and understand the significance of the social gains represented by the union movement, we feel there is an ever-present and demonstrated need to keep in mind the ideal of teamwork. All members of the performing arts team count in the collective effort, and each draws strength from, and depends on, the others. If the approach to the work required for a performance is one of over-specialization or strict calculation of individual needs at the expense of the overall artistic effort, sooner or later the essential interdependence of team members is undermined. In the end all are losers: on stage, off stage and in the audience.

One often hears: if the performing arts cannot pay their way, why have them at all? We have suggested our answer in Chapter 3. Suffice it to add here that even by the simple measure of audience attendance, as we noted above, the performing arts are a source of entertainment, enjoyment and inspiration for large numbers of Canadians. Moreover, the unique nature of a live performance before an audience makes the performing arts, in a very real sense, irreplaceable. The social encounters they engender provide an effective antidote to the isolation increasingly felt by individuals in an electronic age. In addition, playwrights, actors, composers, instrumentalists, singers, choreographers and dancers who refine their skills through the presentation of live performances provide a necessary pool of talent for other vehicles of artistic endeavour – such as broadcasting and film. They are the wellspring of much other artistic and cultural activity. Providing a firm financial base for the performing arts in Canada can then be regarded as an important investment, in both human and material terms.

Multiple Funding Sources
In establishing a sound financial base, our preference is for a diversity of income sources: box office receipts, governments at all levels, and private donations from individuals, corporations and foundations. This preference, which reflects the way we already do things in Canada, represents a middle way between the tradition of nearly exclusive state support prevailing in most of Europe and the much more limited role of government in the United States. A multiplicity of funding sources guarantees a certain autonomy to the subsidized organizations by limiting the threat of control or interference by any one source. During our public hearings it was suggested to us that some of Canada's performing arts organizations are so prestigious and important to the cultural life of the country that they should be financed exclusively by the federal government which would, in effect, absorb the deficits of these companies. However, we have come to the conclusion that the principle of multiple funding sources should generally apply to minimize the threat of control. We make an exception in the case of the National Arts Centre, which has a specific mandate to serve the entire country and needs adequate and assured funds to do so, funds which appropriately come from the federal government. But for other organizations, we believe that the search

for support in their own communities and from various levels of government is an incentive to strive for artistic excellence and at the same time constitutes a powerful link to their audiences.

We have already recorded our views (Recommendation 9) on the need for augmenting the parliamentary appropriation of the Canada Council, the chief federal vehicle for assistance to the performing arts. Each province and territory, led by Saskatchewan and Alberta, has established a mechanism in the form of an arts council or a government department for providing support to cultural activities in general, and the performing arts in particular. Some municipalities were pioneers in assistance to culture and the arts. Montreal, for example, created its Arts Council even before the establishment of the Canada Council. More recently, other municipalities have shown concern about the health of the performing arts in their communities – a welcome and much needed source of revenue to arts ventures. This Committee hopes that municipalities, in spite of the limitations – and heavy demands – on their revenues will appreciate the essential contributions of the arts to the residents of their communities and, with the encouragement of local citizens, will find ways to increase their support substantially.

Although the private sector has become increasingly generous toward the arts, in the hierarchy of "charities" receiving business support the arts still rank very low. Moreover, assistance usually comes from large businesses more often than from medium and small ones, and tends to favour large arts organizations, where risk is low, over smaller groups where experimentation and innovative work are often more likely to be found. The Committee feels that business organizations could work to increase the extent of business support to the arts, particularly from small and medium-sized firms which are often reluctant to move into a domain in which they have little experience.

The Quest for Excellence and the Role of Boards
The search for additional sources of support is vitally important for the future of creative expression in the performing arts. To suppose that it is possible to maintain operations and facilities at their present level of activity and funding is to opt for the downward spiral we described earlier. Even performing arts organizations that are able to offer full seasons to practically sellout audiences, to employ artists full time for a full year and to play in fine halls are vulnerable to deficits. Virtually all of the most progressive and creative organizations are underfunded. All seek to improve, develop and achieve better results. The pursuit of artistic excellence is expensive, but the cost must be met.

The search for artistic excellence and its rewards doubtless motivates many citizens to serve on the boards of performing arts companies. Such boards are held accountable for the proper and responsible use of government funds provided through grants and must ensure that the arts organizations they serve maintain a healthy financial balance. However, their primary role is to give the necessary assistance and support to those who direct and manage such organizations so that the artistic and cultural goals the latter have set for themselves will be achieved. These goals undoubtedly attract board members to the organizations. Of great importance to any organization is the sensitive participation of board members in discussing and formulating such goals.

This Committee believes that members of boards of performing arts organizations, who volunteer their time, energy and expertise to the welfare of the organizations they serve, should be given all possible help in understanding their roles and responsibilities. We therefore urge the Canada Council and the Department of Communications to address the problems of boards of arts organizations and to evolve programs to help improve the operations of such boards and the selection of their membership.

Deficit Reduction and Capital Support

Some performing arts organizations have accumulated sufficiently large deficits that one can speak of a state of financial crisis in parts of the performing arts world. We need not be precise about the causes of specific deficits to recognize their severity and their potentially disastrous effects. Some argue that if grants had been indexed to the cost of living the deficits would not have arisen; others place the blame on the economic depression generally; a few others raise questions about the administrative competence of some of these organizations.

Statistics provided by the performing arts organizations and assembled by the Council for Business and the Arts in Canada show that for 110 organizations with revenues of over $100,000 a year, the total of the accumulated deficits at the end of the fiscal year 1980-81 was $7,630,467. This deficit position persists, it should be noted, in spite of special deficit-reduction grants from both provincial and federal governments, including some $3.8 million provided by the Cultural Initiatives Program of the Department of Communications. Any doubts about the seriousness of the situation have been dispelled by the announcement of several company closures. Without wishing to be too pessimistic, we are afraid that this is just the beginning of a list of closures which may contain the names of some of the most prestigious performing arts organizations in the country. The reduction or elimination of deficits is, of course, desirable, and we support measures which have that effect. But we note that the practice of simply erasing deficits could provide the wrong kind of incentives to companies: it may reward those who run deficits and penalize those who do not; it can therefore be an incentive to future deficits. Over the long run, a deficit-reduction policy linked to attendance figures or some other measure of accomplishment and effort would be much more healthy.

Looking for ways to enlarge audiences is, of course, a part of financial planning. If all theatre, ballet, opera and concert performances played to 100 per cent capacity, some of the financial problems of the performing arts would be alleviated, although not eliminated altogether. An empty seat for any performance is lost forever. But overriding these vital financial considerations, yet intimately connected with them, are artistic concerns. Full houses provide everyone in the performing arts team with the confidence needed to grow and improve artistically, while low attendance discourages artists and supporters alike. Moreover, high attendance proves to performing artists that their work is valued by society. For all these reasons, filling empty seats must be a high priority for all performing arts companies.

Although we feel that support policies for the performing arts should stress audience development in the largest sense and should encourage new Canadian creative work, we are also aware of the need to maintain and improve the existing physical facilities. Capital support programs should continue to be the responsibility of the Department of Communications. In federal capital programs, we are of the view that, in addition to the large population centres, consideration should be given to the smaller centres that do not yet have functional theatres or concert halls. In large centres, attention should be paid to the provision of medium-sized halls, a type of facility which is often lacking. There is also a need to upgrade existing facilities by replacing outdated or outworn equipment, a continuing problem even in long-established organizations with large budgets, which may be using what was regarded, not so long ago, as the latest in physical plant.

Building Audiences
Winning and holding audiences has always been a principal preoccupation of performing arts organizations. As we noted earlier, attendance figures for all performing arts disciplines are high, even though these statistics do not cover amateur productions or take into account the very large audiences that can be won through radio or television. A broadcast ballet, symphony concert, play or opera can reach an audience larger than the total attendance for an entire season in the organization's own hall, though, as we noted earlier, nothing yet can take the place of the unique, direct experience of a performance.

In Chapter 3 we call for a new nongovernment organization which, among other things, would assist in promoting Canadian cultural products. For performing arts companies, this assistance might take the form of providing expert advice on ticket pricing, helping with subscription and fund-raising campaigns, developing advertising and public relations approaches, or devising voucher schemes. All of these would help in building audiences.

Some organizations have sought to identify special target audiences. However, the special audience that deserves particular emphasis is children and youth. Performing arts companies should place a priority on attracting young audiences and should be ready to bring their productions, when appropriate, into the schools. We suggest this effort should be part of the regular outreach work of all performing arts organizations, not just those which specialize in works for young audiences. *We urge all performing arts companies and their supporters to pay special attention to the needs of young audiences, to devise special programming for those audiences where such does not exist in their own halls or in the schools, and to arrange for performances, open rehearsals and workshops for young people.*

Effective audience development activity of this kind will require the support of government. During the past 10 years, a great deal of interest in theatrical productions for young audiences has developed. The Canada Council responded to this interest by recognizing certain companies as "Theatre for Young Audiences" companies and increased grants to these companies, even during the recent years of financial restraint. These grants, however, remain relatively small. The Council should continue this support and seek other ways to encourage the access of Canadian youth to all the performing arts.

Education and Training

As indicated in Chapter 1 and discussed in our *Summary of Briefs and Hearings*, the question of education often arose during our hearings. Education is, in the first place, the essential cultural link between past, present and future. Both artists and audiences need a knowledge of what has gone before, to inspire the former to works of originality and to allow the latter to develop standards of aesthetic judgment.

The primary, secondary and post-secondary systems of education also have specific cultural functions – including the identification and encouragement of artistic talent, as well as the development of a sense of appreciation for our heritage and the arts. In the past this function was largely absent from programs of formal education. In spite of the fact that in recent years the arts have established themselves in educational institutions at all levels, the need to enlarge their role was a recurring theme in submissions to the Committee, from educators disturbed by the values being communicated through mass entertainment, from artists seeking a wider public, or from citizens wishing to see curricula changed to include more arts education. Through them, we found that there is a significant body of opinion in this country which holds that our school systems are doing an inadequate job of educating young people to appreciate the performing arts and of identifying and encouraging artistic talent.

On the whole we have to agree, and *we urge the relevant provincial authorities to make more prominent in school curricula the encouragement of an understanding of, and participation in, music, theatre and dance. As a long-term goal, the objective should be to see that every Canadian child has the opportunity to become literate in all the arts, to be able to appreciate music, painting and sculpture with understanding, view with a critical eye many different types of plays, films and television programs, and recognize the power and meaning of movement. Students should be able to feel there are positive values and social benefits to be derived from active participation in the arts as performers, creators, teachers or arts administrators.*

In recent decades Canada has taken immense strides toward providing advanced professional training in the performing arts. We now have a network of institutions for such training in theatre and dance, and a well-developed, if somewhat unorganized, structure of music education. Special mention must be made of Alberta's Banff Centre School of Fine Arts, now a full-scale year-round operation, which offers courses in the performing and visual arts, writing, and arts management. The Centre attracts teachers and students of international standing, and its enterprising and exploratory approach to training is to be applauded.

In dance, serious students need about 12 years of training. They begin when very young, usually under private teachers. Advanced professional training is provided by the schools created in association with the three major ballet companies – Les Grands Ballets Canadiens, the National Ballet of Canada and the Royal Winnipeg Ballet – and also by a few modern dance companies. These contribute a cadre of dancers to the profession. Many people associated with dance have reported to us that the level of private instruction offered to beginning dancers and the standards of private teachers must be raised. More and better training and retraining opportunities should be provided to independent dance instructors, and national standards and measurements need to be developed. *The major dance schools should be encouraged to assume a leadership role in devising goals for training and in developing suitable standards for dance instruction across the country.*

In music, too, instruction often begins at an early age. Studying with private teachers is the norm for beginners in most parts of Canada. In some of the larger communities, conservatories of music have sprung up, providing a central location for what is essentially one-to-one private instruction. Some of these, such as the Royal Conservatory of Music of Toronto, have developed full-scale music courses. Only Quebec among the provinces has established a provincially run conservatory system, offering free instruction to deserving students of music and theatre. The instructors in the six conservatories in the province are full-time teachers, linked with the public service. A substantial number of universities across Canada now have faculties and departments of music, offering degree courses with specialization in many fields of music, such as composition, voice and instruments, for students interested in performing or teaching careers.

Because early music training coincides with the official school years, much music instruction takes place outside regular school hours. In elementary and secondary schools in some communities, instrumental training has been established and school bands and orchestras add sparkle to school life. Some communities support youth orchestras, which have proliferated in recent years, and most participate in a biennial festival at Banff. The National Youth Orchestra and l'Orchestre des jeunes du Québec, the latter fully funded by the province of Quebec, provide excellent orchestral training, and their graduates regularly join the ranks of professional orchestras.

We heard from a number of people who advocated a National Music School, parallel in purpose and quality to the National Theatre School of Canada in Montreal, to serve the advanced music training needs of the country. A recent study commissioned by the Canada Council recommended that such an institution be established. We also heard from those who opposed the idea, arguing that it was necessary, first, to build up the potential in the many centres now providing music training. This Committee agrees with the latter group of intervenors. We feel that the situations in music and theatre arts training cannot be compared, and that the role played by the National Theatre School is unique.

Music training has a long history in most communities in the country. Yet within that tradition there is disorganization, mixing of standards and conflicting attitudes. Attempts have been made to set grading and examination standards. But there is still much more to be done to improve the quality of teaching at the earlier levels, clarify the relationship between universities and independently operated music schools, establish the financial responsibilities of communities and provinces to music training, and formulate acceptable standards and goals. The Committee therefore believes that, before the creation of a national music school can be considered, there must be a better understanding among the diverse elements that make up the existing music training milieu.

Training in theatre arts may begin in primary and secondary schools, as part of the school curriculum, and continue in the theatre departments of university fine arts faculties or conservatories. In addition, advanced professional training is given at the National Theatre School of Canada. This school was founded in 1960 to provide a full training program in acting, playwriting, stagecraft and set design for both English- and French-speaking students. The school has yet to develop a formal training program for directors, however – a serious gap, considering the prime importance of this profession in all the theatrical arts.

The National Theatre School was the subject of an intensive study conducted by A. Davidson Dunton for the Canada Council. The report, which was presented to the Council in January 1982, concluded that the school will have a "pertinent and important role in the theatrical life of Canada" to the end of this century, that it should remain a single co-lingual institution in Montreal and that grants to it "should be increased to meet present and projected costs as increased by inflation." The Dunton report also recommended that federal financing to the school should come from "a special fund for national artistic training institutions." This would be administered by the Department of Communications and would presumably not prejudice the continuation of provincial support to the school.

It is the Committee's view that advanced training in the performing arts is closely related to the development of high professional and artistic standards, and as such should be supported and evaluated by a staff of specialists able to judge the relationship between the training to be under-taken and the work produced by creative artists and professional companies. For this reason, the National Theatre School's federal funding should continue to come from the Canada Council.

Canada Council grants to the National Theatre School of Canada and the National Ballet School together exceed $2 million. The size of this amount leads us to single out these two institutions for particular comment. If it is true that quality education and training in the fields of dance and theatre are expensive, it is also true, in the case of both schools, that the results are grati-fying and worthwhile for the development of the performing arts in this coun-try. We therefore believe that it is necessary to provide the Canada Council with an appropriation large enough to deal properly with the needs of these schools, along with all the other demands on its resources.

40.   The Canada Council should continue to be the source of
       federal funding for the National Theatre School of Canada,
       the National Ballet School and such other professional train-
       ing programs as are appropriate to its mandate.

Training does not, of course, stop with graduation from a school. In one sense, performing artists are in training all their lives, with each new perfor-mance providing new lessons.

But there are two important stages in a creative or performing artist's career that are often neglected in discussions of training: first, the period of in-tense learning that goes on after the completion of formal schooling and the attainment of full professional status, and, second, the "sabbatical leave" that even seasoned professionals need during their careers for further training and refresher courses. *Accordingly, we urge that the creation of apprenticeship employment opportunities for young performing artists, as well as residen-cies for experienced artists who wish to hone their skills, receive more atten-tion from governments, professional organizations and training institutions.*

Some Problems and Successes in Dance, Music and Theatre

Dance: Rising Costs, Lack of Retraining Opportunities

Major ballet companies, each with a distinctive style and repertoire, have been established for some time in Montreal, Toronto and Winnipeg. Approx-imately 35 modern dance companies throughout Canada represent a broad spectrum of contemporary schools of dance. Other forms of dance – such as jazz, classical Spanish dancing, tap dancing and folk genres – have become popular and attract large audiences and participants alike.

Although the audience for dance is committed and growing, it is still comparatively small. For this reason dance companies, if they are to employ their dancers for a full season, cannot perform exclusively in one centre; they must tour. Each season the Montreal, Toronto and Winnipeg-based ballet companies try to arrange an extensive Canadian tour and an international tour, principally in the United States. Most dance companies now give many more performances while on tour than they do in their home community. With the costs of touring constantly on the rise, increasing the length of the season for home audiences becomes a crucial issue for dance companies. In that context, many of the briefs submitted to this Committee by the dance community stressed the role that the media, and particularly television and the new video technologies, could play in enlarging audiences for dance.

Working as a professional dancer is a full-time commitment; dancers must continue to train daily, whether or not they are performing. Incomes are low, and professional dancers can expect to remain at the peak of their careers for only about six years. On average, they retire from active performance in their 30s, at a time when many performers in music and theatre are beginning their productive careers. After that, teaching and coaching provide the only opportunities for continuing employment in dance.

This lack of job security, compounded by low earning capacity and the difficulty of resettlement into other employment after retirement from the stage, was identified by the Canada Council as a problem requiring prompt attention in an internal 1980 report, *The Art of Partnering the Dance – A Federal Pas de Deux*. We believe that the federal government, with leadership from the Department of Communications, should address this issue.

41.   The federal government should assist dancers and other
       artists who have short professional careers to resettle into
       allied professions where their artistic skills can best be put
       to use. All the relevant agencies and departments – such as
       the Department of Employment and Immigration – should
       be involved, and the Department of Communications should
       assume the leadership role.

The Canada Council, recognizing the importance of full-time employment for dancers and choreographers, and in the face of severe limitations on its funds, has in the last few years been compelled to consolidate its grants to dance companies. To meet the Council's requirements, companies must have demonstrated that they have administrative stability, audience support and professional resources, and must receive some provincial and municipal assistance.

Such a consolidation policy, although it may be necessary for a time, has inherent problems and dangers. Adequate sustaining support is provided to a few established companies only; funding for dance forms other than those of ballet and modern dance is not forthcoming; experimentation and the pursuit of new directions cannot be encouraged; growth and improvement for much of the dance community are therefore limited. Without the recognition attached to a grant from the Canada Council, companies have limited success in applying to other federal funding sources such as the Department of Communications and the Department of External Affairs. *This Committee therefore urges, in accordance with what we believe is also the view of the Canada Council, that the Council's consolidation policy for grants in dance be amended as soon as possible to extend the range of activity supported in this discipline.*

Music: Support for Canadian Composition

Canadian audiences today enjoy a lively and varied musical life. There are now well over 100 instrumental ensembles ranging in size from 95-piece symphony orchestras to classical quartets and early music groups. Opera has enjoyed a significant revival over the past decade and musical theatre has begun to flourish. In major centres there is a small but supportive audience for contemporary and experimental music which has been fostered by contemporary music societies. Many Canadian jazz musicians repeatedly win honours at the Montreux International Jazz Festival in Switzerland and as a result have often become known internationally before being known at home. Broadcasts and recordings produced by the CBC and Radio Canada International have helped to introduce Canadian performers and music to domestic and international audiences.

There has been a remarkable expansion of the popular music and entertainment industry in both the French- and English-speaking communities. Canadian entertainers and rock groups now enjoy national and international popularity, and Canadian groups appear regularly on the popular music charts both here and in the United States. Singers and rock groups from French Canada have been enthusiastically received in France. The annual presentations of the Juno and Félix Awards by organizations within the Canadian recording industry have become gala occasions which are shown on television. Folk music and country and western music are both extremely popular, and French- and English-language folk festivals attract large audiences in many parts of the country.

Choral music is performed widely. In addition to a few well-known professional choirs, there are literally hundreds of amateur choirs in communities all across the country, many benefiting from Canada Council support for the services of professional conductors, soloists, instrumentalists and workshop leaders. These choirs, like community orchestras, are an integral part of Canadian music life.

As we said earlier, perhaps the most critical problem in Canadian serious music today is the lack of exposure of the works of Canadian composers. The Canadian League of Composers has over 170 members who deposit a total of about 500 scores a year with the Canadian Music Centre. This Committee is deeply concerned that much of this music is seldom performed by Canadian orchestras, soloists and other ensembles and is therefore largely unknown to the Canadian public. CBC radio, alone among broadcasters, has consistently programmed and even commissioned Canadian compositions. We commend this effort and look forward to seeing even more effective methods of presentation. Sponsorship of concerts, commissions, competitions for new works and awards to composers to spend time in residence with orchestras and communities – measures that are currently supported by the Canada Council and provincial agencies – all help to increase the exposure of original Canadian composition. But persistence in such efforts over the long term is essential.

In this connection, the important role played by the Canadian Music Centre must be singled out. (A similar organization for theatre – the Canadian Theatre Centre – was in operation between 1960 and 1970 and then became inactive. It is now being reactivated by service organizations in both French and English Canada.) Founded in 1959, the Canadian Music Centre has become one of the best and most effective of such centres in the world. It currently has offices in Toronto, Montreal, Vancouver and Calgary. Its library, which it circulates freely to performers everywhere in order to stimulate performances, contains virtually all the music written by Canadian composers. It has recently launched a recording program to which we refer in Chapter 8 and has become involved in an imaginative project which will, among other things, convert its library of Canadian music into a form suitable for storage in a computer bank. The musical notations can then be summoned up on a monitor screen or printed out on paper, making the scores accessible wherever terminals are established – in schools, universities, libraries and other institutions. This will be a valuable addition to the other important services provided to Canadian music by the Centre. One further service we would urge the Centre to undertake – and governments to fund – would be the transformation into Braille of appropriate material from its library of Canadian compositions. Music is important to many blind people and they should have access to Canadian works in graphic as well as audio form.

42.   The Canadian Music Centre should be given adequate financial and other support to enable it to carry out its functions on behalf of Canadian music, including the promotion and dissemination of the works of Canadian composers and the employment of new technologies for the storage and use of musical compositions.

For centuries music publishing occupied a key position in the music world. Today, because of the high costs of printing, promotion and distribution of sheet music, and because active music-making in the home has given way to so much passive music-listening, the music publishing industry has declined. For composers of serious music, the availability to performers of their music in printed or other usable forms is still important, but for the publisher the investment in such ventures is extremely risky and the returns doubtful. We believe, however, that music publishers could play a more dynamic role. *Federal departments and agencies should reexamine their programs of support to music with a view to helping the music publishing industry achieve a more productive and effective role in the dissemination and promotion of Canadian music.*

Theatre: Development of Audiences and New Plays
The Canada Council now provides grants to over 150 professional theatre companies and organizations. In addition, there are a large number of non-professional companies which find their support locally or regionally. Many different types of theatre are being produced – for example, mime and puppetry, musicals, theatre for young audiences, experimental theatre – and independent commercial theatre production, including dinner theatre in some cities, is expanding.

Outside the "festival" towns, such as Niagara-on-the-Lake, Stratford and Charlottetown, theatre has flourished most in the larger centres because of the concentration of population, resources and opportunities. However, smaller cities have been able to establish their own independent companies to reflect the tastes and expectations of their communities, and in many instances they have succeeded in presenting theatre of superior quality, in spite of the limitations imposed by a small population base. To ensure that such growth will continue, *all levels of government should encourage and assist the operations of theatrical and other performing arts ventures in smaller cities in order to foster the development of local artists and stem the flow of talent and energy into a few metropolitan centres.*

One of the most exciting aspects of the theatrical boom in Canada has been the development of Canadian playwrights. In addition to the classical seasons offered by major festivals and the mixed repertoire presented by regional theatres, an impressive number of theatre companies now specialize in the production of contemporary, experimental productions and the work of regional playwrights. A few years ago, collective creations, in which actors develop plays from original sources, became an increasingly dynamic genre which has produced forceful social and political commentaries in dramatic form. In Quebec, a whole generation of artists in theatre cooperatives have chosen to devote themselves largely to collective work. Self-managed theatres have also mushroomed; here, as in collective theatre, priority is given to the creation of original work.

New and developing playwrights have been assisted in a number of ways. Support and encouragement is given by organizations such as the New Play Centre in Vancouver, Playwrights Canada in Toronto and the Centre d'essai des auteurs dramatiques in Montreal, which collect, print and distribute new plays and help in the development of new texts from rough drafts to final form through workshops and public readings.

Earlier we attributed this blossoming of playwriting to the interest shown by some theatre directors and companies in new Canadian plays. As an illustration of the talent that has been waiting for an opportunity to express itself, one has only to cite the results of the competition sponsored by the Floyd S. Chalmers Foundation for new Canadian plays performed professionally in the Toronto area. Within the first eight years of the competition, over 600 new Canadian plays were eligible for the award. Nevertheless, as the Guild of Canadian Playwrights pointed out to us, it is not possible for Canadian playwrights to live on royalty income alone, in spite of the increases in theatre audiences. In this field as in others, ways must be found to enable creative people to devote more time to their real work.

The Canada Council and the Performing Arts

In Chapter 2 we discuss the vital role played by the Canada Council in the cultural life of the country generally. The Council has assumed a special importance in the life of the performing arts.

Without the support and encouragement of the federal government through the Canada Council, many of the country's major performing arts organizations could not have survived the developmental period of the 1960s, let alone achieved the growth and artistic standards that have brought them national and often international acclaim. Although the provinces and municipalities have gradually assumed an increasingly important role, grants from the Canada Council have been the main source of public support for performing arts companies. Individual artists have continued to receive support through the Council's Arts Awards Service.

Changing Policy Priorities
Well over a decade ago the Canada Council recognized that performing arts organizations (like institutions in many other areas of our cultural life) would require continuing federal operating support to maintain their level and standard of activity. In accepting this responsibility, the Council committed a considerable portion of its annual budget to the continued support of established performing arts institutions.

Over the past few years, budgetary restrictions have created multiple problems for the Canada Council, with the result that it has been impossible to do much more than maintain the commitments already made. It has become increasingly difficult, for example, to assist younger companies or those working in newer art forms or in regions outside major urban centres. The Council has therefore found itself accused of being "establishment-oriented" and "insensitive" to newer companies just as they are beginning to find their audiences. At the same time, however, it has not been possible to increase grants significantly to established companies. Inevitably, serious deficits have begun to accumulate and, as we mentioned earlier, the very survival of some of the country's most prestigious performing arts companies is now being threatened. It would be regrettable indeed if the Canada Council, after playing such a vital role in supporting the performing arts, could provide no more than status quo funding. Such funding is not adequate to support the tried and true, nor dynamic and flexible enough to respond to the new. Council policies must evolve to reflect the changing situation in the arts.

For the performing arts, as for all other cultural disciplines, our Committee has recommended that increased stimulation of Canadian creative work and the development of resources and audiences in all regions must be the policy priorities over the next decade. In our opinion, the Canada Council must now reconcile these new priorities with the basic criteria long established for the operation of its performing arts programs and with its traditional commitment to provide "responsive" operating support. We recognize that it will require some adjustments on the part of both the Council and the subsidized organizations but the commitment must be made.

Touring Office Support for the Performing Arts
Although touring is extremely expensive in a country as vast as Canada, it remains an essential aspect of cultural exchange between the many communities and regions of the country. For many small communities, visits by touring artists and companies are often the only contact made with the professional performing arts.

When the Touring Office of the Canada Council was established in 1973, several functions were assigned to it. The agency was to serve the Canadian performing arts by providing information and consultation services, by acting as a booking agency and an impresario, and by offering subsidies for touring. The Touring Office has effectively fulfilled many of these functions.

The Touring Office has also encouraged its clients to learn how to arrange their own tours using, when possible, independent booking agents and local sponsors to whom the Touring Office has offered guidance. Tours subsidized by the Touring Office are now almost always initiated and managed by individual artists and companies. On a limited number of occasions, the Touring Office has initiated and financed, on a cost-sharing basis with provinces, special package tours for individual artists and companies.

The Committee agrees with the emphasis placed by the Touring Office on the creation of independent, self-reliant networks to promote and coordinate performing arts touring in Canada. Recognition of the role of the impresario and the artists' manager is relatively recent in Canada. Individuals working in this field still require support and efficient information services. A central computerized information system which provides cross-country access to current listings of artists and groups available for tours, potential sponsors and possible venues would greatly facilitate advance planning and national tour bookings.

In all of its activities, the Touring Office must continue to collaborate closely with provincial touring programs. Touring Office support is especially important for the French-language theatre companies whose touring possibilities are limited to Quebec (tours inside a single province are not at present subsidized by the Touring Office) and occasionally the other French-speaking regions of the country. In addition, the Touring Office should give consideration in its future planning to the needs of certain variety artists and jazz and folk musicians. It should also respond to requests for support for tours and festivals of performing arts productions for young people by developing a coherent youth access program. For international touring, the Canada Council would be deeply involved with the proposed international cultural agency recommended in Chapter 11.

Seed Funding, Parliamentary Funding
One initiative recently undertaken by the Canada Council is the Performing Arts Venture Capital Fund. This fund allows the Council to invest in productions in all performing arts disciplines, permitting the extension of runs and, it is hoped, engendering a measure of commercial success. Such a fund, we believe, is a logical extension of the deep involvement of the Council in the performing arts. By giving seed money support to commercial performing arts ventures, the Canada Council will reduce the pressure on the major subsidized companies to offer such programming to their audiences. This in turn will allow these companies to realize more fully their special responsibility to stimulate Canadian creative work. The establishment of the fund may have been ill-timed, given current economic conditions. In spite of some strong reservations voiced by segments of the performing arts community, we feel in general that the concept can have positive long-term effects.

As we state in Recommendation 9, the Canada Council is, and should continue to be, a primary vehicle through which the federal government provides assistance to the arts. And in view of the Council's importance to the performing arts, we would like to restate the essence of that recommendation here. *We believe that to fulfil its current responsibilities, and the additional ones we feel it must undertake, the Canada Council should receive a substantial increase in its parliamentary appropriation to permit new programs – as well as current ones – to be developed and sustained.*

The Council, in its presentation to us, has indicated that an appropriation about twice the present one is required. Although we would prefer not to be so specific, we would stress that the government's support should reflect the *real* as distinct from the *nominal* value of the Council's grants, with due regard for the consequences to the cultural life of Canada if this support is allowed to diminish.

The federal government showed initiative and awareness in establishing the Canada Council and its many other arts and heritage support programs. Because the government increased its support over the years, this
country was able to achieve a great many cultural gains in a markedly short
span of time. The government's continued understanding and relatively small
financial commitments can allow the momentum it has initiated to continue.

The National Arts Centre

In Chapter 3, "Marshalling Resources," we undertake a discussion of "government as proprietor." We make the point there and in other chapters that the
programs of state-owned enterprises such as the National Arts Centre
in Ottawa should complement those of nongovernment ventures in the
field. It is with that principle in mind that we have reviewed the role and programs of the Centre and make specific suggestions for its future.

The National Arts Centre was designed as the major centennial project
of the federal government "to develop the performing arts in the National
Capital region and to assist the Canada Council in the development of the performing arts elsewhere in Canada." It was completed in 1969 at a cost of
$46 million.

The Centre houses superb and versatile performing arts facilities. It has
highly skilled production and administrative personnel who have respect for
artists, their needs, and their aspirations for excellence. This combination of
technical and human resources makes the National Arts Centre one of the
finest performing arts institutions in North America. Its 1980-81 appropriation from Parliament totaled $10.9 million.

The Centre's three theatres have played to very good houses for nearly
all of their seasons. During its first 10 years the Centre staged more than
8,000 individual performances for which almost seven million tickets were
sold. More significant than these figures is the extent of the dramatic change
the Centre has made in the cultural life of the National Capital region.

Music at the Centre
From the beginning the Arts Centre planned to have its own orchestra – a
"concert-size" ensemble of 44 players that could tour easily, that would not
have to compete with the nearby Montreal and Toronto symphony orchestras, and that would be less expensive than a full orchestra. The
achievements of the National Arts Centre Orchestra under Mario Bernardi, its
first conductor, have been notable. It has been acclaimed not only in its own
home but also on tour in Canada, the United States and Europe. Its touring
began in 1970 and has been sustained annually ever since, with visits to
large centres in Canada and to small communities that cannot accommodate
big orchestras and therefore hear little live orchestral music. All of Canada

has benefited from the orchestra's performances, and it has earned a reputation as one of the best ensembles of its kind in the world. It has often commissioned composers to provide works for its repertoire and has made several recordings.

The creation of the orchestra has contributed significantly to the vitality of local musical life. Most members of the orchestra teach, either privately or in institutions in the area. Many play in chamber music ensembles outside the Arts Centre. The orchestra is also involved in the many state and diplomatic occasions which the National Arts Centre is called upon to organize.

In addition to its regular orchestral and chamber music concerts, the orchestra also plays for the annual summer opera season, "Festival Ottawa," which was begun in 1971. This Festival features presentations of three or four operas, a chamber music series and ancillary events of interest, attracting respectably large audiences. However, concerns have been expressed to us about this aspect of the Centre's activities. The 1982 opera season, for example, offered three operas and two additional works in concert version, for a total of 13 performances. Other Canadian opera companies feel deprived of a chance to participate in the Festival, and it is felt that too few Canadians benefit in view of the considerable costs involved in mounting such works. On the other hand, we can envisage a varied and exciting summer festival that can become an even greater attraction for both residents and tourists.

Theatre, Dance and Variety Programming

Resident theatre companies were formed at the National Arts Centre only in 1972, three years after the orchestra's debut. The first companies established were Hexagon and l'Hexagone, the English and French ensembles created (in the 1972-73 season) to produce theatre for young audiences. The English company was disbanded in 1976; as of the 1982-83 season, l'Hexagone will no longer maintain a resident company, but will, instead, become a co-producer of French-language theatre for young audiences, working closely with companies in regions where artistic and audience development are at an earlier stage. Through the l'Hexagone program, the NAC will offer these companies additional budgetary resources to engage outside professional and touring expertise. Co-productions will be featured as part of the Theatre for Young Audiences programming at the Centre.

It was not until 1977 that resident "mainstream" companies began producing plays for general audiences in both official languages. These companies toured the country in their first year to very mixed reactions and have not toured subsequently. The French company was disbanded at the end of the 1980-81 season, but the English company continues to contribute a reduced number of productions to the season.

Criticism of the National Arts Centre Theatre Company and of la Compagnie du Centre national des Arts has focused on the lack of a distinctive programming policy. NAC seasons have turned out to be no different from those offered by the major regional theatres, and they do not sufficiently reflect the diversity of theatre activity existing elsewhere in Canada. In addition, local professional theatre artists and groups have found it difficult to find a place in the activities of these two companies. Indeed, the almost overwhelming resources of the Centre have tended to impede the independent development of these artists.

The resident members of the NAC theatre companies have been less successful than the orchestra members in integrating their professional lives into the community life of the Ottawa-Hull region. This situation is undoubtedly due in part to the fact that few of the employment opportunities which usually supplement actors' incomes – such as television, film and advertising contracts – are available there.

Because the National Arts Centre has never had a resident dance company, dance is probably the performing art form most effectively showcased at the NAC. The "Dance Showcase Series" has succeeded in creating a sustaining and appreciative audience for dance. The major ballet companies in the country are virtually assured of an annual engagement in this series. Canadian contemporary dance companies, however, have not been well represented.

Variety programming fills about one-third of the NAC's schedule each year. Although the Centre sometimes invests and shares risks in that field, most of these shows are presented by impresarios who rent the facilities in order to present stars and groups, often from outside Canada. Revenues from such rentals account for a substantial part of the NAC's overall earnings.

In the future we would like to see many more Canadian companies and performers on NAC stages. An engagement there should be the cornerstone of all touring by these artists. Close collaboration between the National Arts Centre and performing arts organizations in other countries should be sought to assure a flow of worthwhile productions for touring throughout Canada. Quality international productions have always been of interest to Canadians and, as we noted at the beginning of this chapter, access to the international repertoire is an important part of our cultural lives.

Showcasing the Arts

Without a doubt the National Arts Centre has been successful in providing rich performing arts fare in the Ottawa-Hull region. It has been less successful, however, in fulfilling that part of its mandate which calls upon it to assist "in the development of the performing arts elsewhere in Canada."

We are pleased to note, therefore, that the NAC has announced its intention to adjust its programming policy to increase opportunities for the showcasing of theatre and dance companies from other parts of Canada. There are now many such organizations which meet high standards of excellence and which have the stature to display their work on a national stage. The National Arts Centre is a natural and obvious showcase for such work.

Co-productions can also produce beneficial results. An extensive program of co-production with established companies from other parts of the country could stimulate the creation of new works all over Canada, and would make available NAC production expertise and provide cost-sharing benefits. The results of such collaborations would provide interesting theatrical experiences for the patrons of the NAC and for those in the home theatre of the company involved, as well as for audiences elsewhere. What has already been accomplished along these lines is creditable, and we hope that the principle of co-production will become an established policy. A showcasing and co-production policy at the National Arts Centre would obviously require close collaboration with the Touring Office of the Canada Council.

An engagement at the National Arts Centre should become a confirmation, a high point, in the careers of individuals and companies. We agree with the view expressed in the National Arts Centre brief to this Committee that it has a "particular responsibility to arrange for the exhibition . . . of the most creative and technically accomplished work being carried out in the performing arts in Canada." We ask the Arts Centre to reexamine its policies and adjust its priorities toward that objective. For its theatre and opera activities, we ask it to substitute a showcasing mandate for its present one, which is built on the concept of resident companies and productions. We make an exception in the case of the resident National Arts Centre Orchestra, which is unique in the country. The orchestra provides a valuable service not only to its immediate community and to visiting companies, which may employ it as a pit ensemble, but also to Canada as a whole.

43.   The National Arts Centre should adopt a policy of show-
      casing the best available Canadian talent and productions in
      all the performing arts, in addition to outstanding artists
      and productions from other countries. It should forego in-house
      productions of theatrical and operatic works in favour of
      co-productions with other Canadian companies. The National
      Arts Centre Orchestra, however, should remain as a resident
      and touring organization.

We are ready to acknowledge that creative showcasing and useful co-production programming are not likely to be less costly than the current range of NAC activities. Nonetheless, *by assuming its role as the main national stage for all of the performing arts and by sharing its resources with companies and artists from other parts of the country, the NAC can greatly enrich cultural life in Canada.*

Radio and Television at the NAC

Over the years CBC radio has broadcast a substantial number of concerts by the National Arts Centre Orchestra. Television viewers have seen and heard the orchestra all too rarely, however, while the operas have been televised on only a few occasions and the theatre companies not at all. The CBC seems to be the only broadcaster interested in the offerings provided by the National Arts Centre, and mainly through its radio programming at that. The Centre's showcasing presentations, in particular, should be seen by all of Canada, and we hope that the CBC, pay-television programmers or other broadcasters will create television programs from that rich source.

In its brief to the Committee, the National Arts Centre stated that "as a national stage [it] must be brought to Canadians on a regular basis through the medium of television." We endorse this statement.

Policy Development in Concert

The performing arts are crucial to the cultural life of this country. It is also our opinion, confirmed by the results of our policy review, that all those involved in the performing arts in Canada – whether through professional, amateur, commercial or nonprofit operations – should be able to receive federal assistance whenever that assistance is necessary to ensure that the creative work of Canadian artists becomes more accessible to our own and to international audiences.

We believe, in addition, that all levels of government have a special responsibility to assist professional nonprofit performing arts organizations to achieve excellence in performance, and to attract larger, more varied and more critical audiences. All of these organizations provide opportunities for the production of works by creative artists – the composers, playwrights and choreographers whom we identified at the beginning of this chapter as essential members of the performing arts team.

To effect the quality and levels of federal government support we envisage, and to assist the federal cultural agencies to meet their own obligations on behalf of the performing arts, we stress the need for regular consultation by federal agencies with the arts community generally, and with provincial arts bodies, municipal officials and their arts councils, and the business community. Issues that should be addressed in such consultations include training, touring, matching funds, capital assistance, community arts activities and arts in education – to name only a few.

Developing a federal policy of comprehensive support to performing artists and performing arts organizations requires the nurturing of many complex and ongoing partnerships. We believe that this challenge must be met. Sustained support to the individuals and organizations working in the performing arts will provide more opportunities for Canadians to share in those special moments when the house lights are dimmed, the curtain rises, and the performance begins.

7
Writing, Publishing and Reading

_____
_____
_____
_____
_____
_____

7
Writing, Publishing and Reading

The title of this chapter reflects a fundamental thesis of our Report: that the creators and producers of cultural materials do not work in a vacuum, but are an integral part of a human community. In the context of literature, Margaret Atwood has stated our case for us most eloquently: "Writer and audience are Siamese twins. Kill one and you run the risk of killing the other. Try to separate them, and you may simply have two dead half-people."

We are speaking, then, about a symbiotic relationship among writers, publishers and readers. A writer may exist without readers, and a person without reading, but each lacks a major dimension of human contact. Publishers, for their part, make that contact possible.

Even this description does not do justice to a process that includes the roles played by editors, translators, designers, printers, booksellers, librarians and critics. All of these contribute in a unique and vital way, a fact that underlines the collective nature of the literary experience.

In Canada, governments have supported this collective enterprise to an increasing extent in recent years. They have done so without political interference in what is written, published or read – an approach that is just as essential to preserving freedom of thought and expression as it is native to Canadians' view of their governments' relationship to culture. The federal government in particular has provided that support directly to writers and publishers, leaving readers – the largest group – more or less alone.

There have been good reasons for this particular emphasis in cultural policy. Writers and publishers make up the first two links in the literary chain, setting the process into motion; without them, there would be little Canadian literature for readers to read, critics to analyze, booksellers to sell or printers to print. At the same time, writing and publishing are both extremely fragile activities economically in the relatively small English- and French-language markets in Canada. Those Canadians who choose to earn a living by writing or publishing books and magazines, particularly of an artistic or cultural nature, frequently work within economic constraints that necessitate a measure of financial support in addition to what the marketplace yields. But government cultural policies encourage and stimulate the suppliers of our literature essentially because the ultimate beneficiary is the Canadian reading public.

These policies have borne abundant fruit. As the Canadian Conference of the Arts reminded us, "Over the past 10 years there has been an extraordinary growth in Canadian writing and in the size and enthusiasm of Canadian audiences for new writing of all kinds by Canadians living in all parts of the country." By contrast, the authors of the Massey-Lévesque Report concluded 30 years earlier that "among the various means of artistic expression in Canada, literature has taken a second place, and indeed has fallen far behind painting." They went on to ask, almost plaintively: "Is it true, then, that we are a people without a literature?"

Such a question need scarcely be asked today. In quantity, quality and public interest, both at home and abroad, Canadian literature has attained a state of development unimagined in 1951. The same may be said of the publishing, bookselling, library and critical professions which sustain our literature. These are manifestations of a maturing society for which the credit does not belong to governments or their policies; but it is certainly true that government actions have played a significant supporting role. Far from being the country portrayed in the Massey-Lévesque Report as "hostile or at least indifferent to the writer," Canada now provides numerous forms of support at the federal and provincial levels for authors and their publishers. In return, the country is more than amply rewarded with a substantial variety of books and periodicals in both official languages which reflect the Canadian people to themselves and to the rest of the world.

The members of the Massey-Lévesque Commission would have been happily astonished had they been able to foretell the national and international recognition that would be won by Canadian authors in the 1970s and early 1980s: Margaret Laurence, Anne Hébert, Robertson Davies, Yves Thériault, Irving Layton, Antonine Maillet, Margaret Atwood, Marie-Claire Blais, Farley Mowat, André Langevin, W.O. Mitchell, Gaston Miron, Mordecai Richler, Jacques Godbout, Mavis Gallant, Réjean Ducharme and Leonard Cohen are only a few who come to mind, in addition to those singled out for earlier recognition by that Commission: Gabrielle Roy, Morley Callaghan, Roger Lemelin, Hugh MacLennan, Gratien Gélinas and Earle Birney. Clearly, the written and published word is flourishing in Canada, signifying that the spirit of artistic and intellectual freedom is alive here as never before.

In our travels across the country and in our own deliberations, however, we have become convinced that there is no room for complacency about these matters, and have detected a number of serious gaps and omissions in existing federal policy which urgently need to be remedied. In the case of writers, we believe that their financial reward has been woefully inadequate considering the public benefits received. As for readers, we are persuaded that their interests as consumers of Canadian literature have been neglected (perhaps inadvertently) by federal government policy, a concern that will lead us to suggest ways of improving both public awareness of and public access to Canadian publications. We will also suggest ways in which publishers can be assisted to perform their cultural role.

The Literatures of Canada

Productivity and artistic maturity in Canadian writing might reasonably be said to have proceeded hand in hand since the days of the Massey-Lévesque Commission, and indeed to have followed a certain progression through the various literary forms during the past three decades. In the earlier years of that period, the most substantial and most interesting body of work probably belonged to our poets. By the mid-1960s, however, fiction had established itself as an equally fertile and variegated form in both our official languages. And during the past decade – say, since the arrival of Michel Tremblay's plays on the Montreal stage and the original performances of George Ryga's *The Ecstasy of Rita Joe* or James Reaney's Donnelly trilogy – Canadian drama has begun to display strengths similar to those found in our poetry, novels and short stories.

Other equally important branches of literature are also thriving: history, biography, social and political criticism, artistic criticism and children's literature. Popular authors as well as scholars have all made their distinctive contributions. Strengths in these fields once seemed more potential than actual, but are now being realized in a steady flow of publications emanating from virtually all parts of the country.

Such a varied and steady flow would not be possible without a diverse network of professional book and periodical publishers. From the small and somewhat unhopeful contingent that visited the Massey-Lévesque Commission public hearings, the Canadian publishing community has grown in several significant ways. Today there are book publishers in every province, some specializing in works by the writers of their particular region. Among the new regional houses are several French-language publishers located in New Brunswick, Nova Scotia, Ontario and Manitoba. And among the English-language houses, several have built on a regional base to develop an enthusiastic national market for their works.

Another aspect of the evolution in Canadian book publishing has been a degree of editorial specialization unknown in the 1940s or 1950s. In addition to the regional presses, we now have both English- and French-language publishers specializing in history, politics, women's issues, children's literature, art books and how-to books. We have publishers serving the popular tastes of the mass market, but we also have literary presses in many parts of the country producing small printings of exciting and often sophisticated new work by poets, playwrights and fiction writers. All these types of publishers – some of them large, but many of them relatively small in scale – add a vital creative dimension to the scholarly lists of the university presses, the textbooks of educational publishers and the output of more general "trade" houses.

Although some of the largest book publishing companies are foreign-owned, chiefly in English-speaking Canada, today's industry contains a substantial majority of firms owned in this country. Indeed, Canada possesses a remarkably well rounded domestic publishing industry. That fact is all the more striking considering the relatively modest size of our two markets, the enormous amount of competition within those markets from books imported from the United States, France and the United Kingdom, and the extremely difficult economic times. Canadian book publishing, then, is a success story – at least in cultural terms, if not often in financial ones.

A similar story may be told about magazines and periodicals. Canadians now have access to an impressive cross-section of periodicals of their own. These range from newsmagazines through broadly based consumer magazines to publications appealing to all manner of specialized interests, whether artistic, scientific or recreational. Some of these are scholarly journals, while others are "little magazines" whose openness to experimental work in art and literature is so essential to a living culture. The emergence of regional voices has also been a recent factor in magazine publishing, and several magazines aimed at the narrower market of a city, a province or a region have experienced success.

The periodical industry as a whole, however, resembles the book publishing industry in demonstrating more frequent cultural successes than financial ones. Again, a small population spread across a vast geographical area in two linguistic markets, sometimes overwhelming foreign competition, rising costs and a depressed economy combine to make life precarious financially for magazine ventures, particularly new ones.

In the end, Canadian publishing ventures of all types have been sustained by the creativity of writers and the interest of readers. These forces have converged just at a time when electronic imagery might seem to be diminishing public concern with the written word. Yet there has been renewed interest in exploring and expressing the Canadian reality precisely through books and magazines. Far more Canadians than ever before are becoming writers and publishers, and in the process providing alternative voices to the products of a mass electronic and print culture emanating chiefly from the United States. And Canadians have proved ready for a richer diet of books and magazines of their own in the post-television age, while still keeping their minds and borders open to publications from other lands.

Government Support of Literature

In recognition of these trends, the federal government increasingly placed financial resources at the disposal of Canada's writers and publishers from the late 1950s onwards.

The first federal organization to provide this type of support was the Canada Council, which immediately after its establishment in 1957 began making individual grants to creative writers, scholars and a few publishers of books, literary and artistic magazines, and scholarly journals. In the years that followed, the Council's support to writers and scholars expanded, until in 1972 it undertook the major programs of assistance to publishing which continue to this day, administered in part by the Council and in part under the aegis of the Social Sciences and Humanities Research Council. Since then, the Canada Council has received the means to assist the promotion as well as the publication of Canadian books and periodicals; measures to assist the foreign marketing of Canadian books have been taken; a co-publication program has been instituted at the Department of Supply and Services to cooperate with the private sector in publishing books, in both official languages, originating from federal departments; and the Foreign Investment Review Agency has become concerned with limiting any further expansion of foreign ownership in the Canadian book publishing industry. An attempt to strengthen the periodical press was undertaken in 1976 with the passage of Bill C-58, an amendment to the Income Tax Act to enhance the attractiveness of advertising in Canadian periodicals and broadcasting outlets. Finally, in 1979, a major new development program for Canadian book publishing was launched within the Arts and Culture Branch of the Department of the Secretary of State. Transferred to the Department of Communications in July 1980, with that department's assumption of responsibility for arts and culture, the program includes substantial support for sales and marketing of Canadian books, as well as for structural and professional improvements within the industry.

Provincial governments, too, provided new forms of direct assistance to literature during the 1970s and early 1980s. Particularly large commitments were made by the governments of Ontario and Quebec, where the greatest concentrations of professional writers and publishers are located, but governments of other provinces also became involved as the literary professions expanded within their jurisdictions.

It is impossible, of course, to quantify the precise relationship between the advent of these forms of government support and the expansion of writing and publishing during the past 25 years. Nevertheless, it is significant that government assistance has remained an encouraging and enabling factor, rather than a directing or controlling one. The degree of government involvement in supporting writing and publishing is considerably greater in Canada than in other nations that share our cultural heritages; citizens of those countries might conceivably ask if the various governments in Canada do not exercise too much influence on what is written and published here. They could be told unequivocally, however, that Canadian governments have not sought to use their programs of support as levers of censorship or propaganda, and that such a policy is consistent with the wishes of the Canadian people.

Writing

Writers are an individualistic breed, and it is difficult to generalize about them with accuracy. It is even more difficult in a society like Canada's where there are two official language groups with their own distinctive literatures. Canadian authors writing in French and in English work within different, if intersecting, literary traditions; perhaps even more fundamentally, they write by and large for different audiences with different sets of experience and expectations. Market conditions facing Canadian writers and their publishers also differ according to language. The French-language market is considerably smaller than the English-language one, but more concentrated geographically and therefore less costly to service. When Canadian writers or publishers look to the international market, those writing in English find their largest foreign audience just over the border, while those working in French must reach across the Atlantic.

Regardless of language, the briefs we received from writers and their professional associations contained strikingly similar themes and concerns, tending to concentrate on incomes and economic justice. There was little doubt in the writers' minds that the federal government should be concerned with these matters. The basic issue as they saw it might be summed up in the question: "Are Canadian writers receiving a fair return for the benefits that the public derives from their labours?" Their answer was a categorical no, and they placed the onus squarely on the federal government to do something about the problem.

Critical attention and media recognition have been coming to Canadian writers as never before, but they are not enough to live on. We have been enriched immeasurably by our storytellers, poets, playwrights, historians and social and political writers, and have gained in self-knowledge from their work. But do we give enough back? Do we reward our authors adequately, not only in return for past accomplishments but so that they will be encouraged and enabled to continue producing in the future? The submissions we received argued that authors continue to be under-remunerated for the physical and spiritual energies they invest in their work, and this Committee agrees with that view.

Although the problem is partly a result of market conditions and the narrow financial margins in publishing, it is apparent that authors are unfairly treated in certain respects that are the domain of public policy. Consequently, writers are less adequately rewarded, on average, than the various other professionals whose livelihood they make possible. In spite of the enlarged audiences for their work and the undeniable usefulness of grants to buy time from other duties, authors are scarcely more able now to function as full-time professionals than they were in the time of the Massey-Lévesque Commission. To illustrate this fact, a study prepared by the federal Department of Communications and based on Statistics Canada data for 1978 (the most recent available) shows that the median income from all writing sources of full-time writers (defined as devoting more than 30 hours a week to their writing) was $7,000: a figure that was less than half the median income for all Canadian wage-earners in that year. In the case of those writers earning the majority of their writing income from book royalties, the median income from all writing sources was a mere $3,000. This situation is not only unfair, but a waste of creative resources. When writers are hindered from realizing their creative potential, Canadians are deprived of the full benefits that their authors can provide.

Not all the problems facing writers are amenable to solution by government. Whether an author or book or periodical is critically successful, or widely read, or receives a grant, is not a matter for legislation. But this Committee advocates that insofar as government is able to remedy existing abuses or enhance financial recognition on the basis of equity, it should do so. We endorse the position of the Writers' Union of Canada, stated at one of our hearings, that since writers do not have a fixed income, they need as many sources of income as possible. Financial reinforcement, however, is not the only issue at stake: we would also like to see increased exchange between our two literatures and expanded professional development opportunities for writers.

Increasing the Flow of Income
There are at least two main ways in which the federal government could increase financial rewards for writers: through grants and through payment for public uses of writers' work.

Writers' Grants
In writing, as in other fields of artistic creativity during the past 25 years, individual grants have been particularly effective in producing completed works that have attracted significant public attention. A Canada Council or provincial government grant has often provided the free time needed by a professional author to finish a work in progress (although it is also true that most published manuscripts are written without the benefit of grants).

The Canada Council provides grant support in two broad categories of literature. "Creative" writers in the fields of poetry, fiction and drama can apply for the Council's Arts Awards, while writers with nonfiction projects may seek assistance from the Council's Explorations program. Our Committee has received no persuasive arguments that substantive changes are needed in the Arts Awards program for creative writers. In the case of assistance for nonfiction writers, however, there is a genuine case for change. The Explorations program has funded hundreds of valuable projects over the years in many disciplines and in all parts of Canada. The problem is that the average level of financial assistance it provides is considerably below the amounts set for awards for "creative" writers; hence professional writers of nonfiction are effectively discriminated against in obtaining assistance for their work, which may be every bit as "creative" as the work of novelists or playwrights.

Professional nonfiction authors, however, often with many years of experience and even many books to their credit, have increasingly turned to Explorations for help. Probable sales in the Canadian market do not permit a publisher's advance to be large enough to defray the author's true expenses in the course of a long-term writing project, and a grant is often necessary to permit a book to be written. Unless such authors are scholars, in which case they can approach the Social Sciences and Humanities Research Council, Explorations is usually the only federal program available.

The various branches of serious nonfiction (including such categories as history, biography, children's literature and social, political and artistic criticism) have major significance within a mature literature. Canadians have shown outstanding ability in all of these areas, but these authors are not assisted as adequately as are "creative" writers.

44.   **The Canada Council should put assistance to professional nonfiction writers on the same footing as assistance to fiction writers, without diminishing support to the latter.**

Payment for Public Use
The other principal way the government could increase financial rewards for writers is through payment for public use. At present, authors are not adequately or fairly compensated for such uses of their work, particularly in two cases: library borrowing and photocopying.

Ten countries in the Western industrialized world – the United Kingdom, Australia, New Zealand, the Federal Republic of Germany, the Netherlands, Sweden, Norway, Denmark, Finland and Iceland – already operate systems to compensate authors for library use of their books. These countries consider that authors are deprived of normal payment for services rendered if, after a one-time royalty payment on the sale of their book to a library, they receive no further remuneration, no matter how many times the book is borrowed.

There is considerable variation in the systems in place in the various countries, particularly in the nature of the payments to authors and the methods of calculating these payments – that is, whether on the basis of library holdings or actual borrowings. Generally speaking, funds are provided for these programs directly by the national governments as a lump sum, rather than being collected in the form of dues from individual borrowers. But the intent is the same in each country: to provide financial reward to authors for the benefits accruing to the public from library borrowing of their works.

In Canada we have no such system, but since 1976 the Canada Council has been studying the idea of a Canadian adaptation, and in 1981 presented a proposal to the government for a payment for public use scheme based on library holdings. The proposal was drawn up with the assistance of an advisory committee of writers, librarians and publishers, and involved the cooperation of both French- and English-language library communities and associations. The latter fact is especially significant since the Canadian library communities, like their counterparts in other countries, initially opposed the idea on two grounds: that it would drain library resources if librarians had to administer a complex, circulation-based system; and that the notion of a lending right or a compensation payment implied that libraries had been abusing authors and their rights, which librarians insisted was not a true reflection of the facts. In the end, Canada's librarians felt that their reservations had been accommodated and endorsed a scheme of increased financial rewards to writers based on library holdings data.

This Committee commends the Canada Council for the extensive and conscientious labours on behalf of Canadian authors represented by its payment for public use proposal. In particular, we feel that the Council was correct in removing the question from the context of Copyright Act revision: inclusion of payment for public use within the ambit of Canada's international copyright obligations would mean a heavy flow of payments to foreign writers, which would substantially dilute payments to Canadian authors and add enormously to the workload and expense of administering the system. The type of scheme proposed by the Council represents an important contribution to fairer dealing between the Canadian public and our authors.

We wish to take the payment for public use concept further, however, and extend it to another major use for which authors are now denied fair compensation: the widespread practice of photocopying.

What could be called "the reprography revolution" has come about not only as a result of the almost universal use of the photocopy machine in offices, schools, universities, libraries and other places, but also because of new technologies of information storage and retrieval including word-processing and videotex. This revolution is of undeniable value to society and its members (including writers), but the losers are the very people who created the information and ideas in the first place – the authors themselves, who receive no financial reward for often quite extensive uses of their work over which they have no control. Legally, such uses are prohibited by the existing Copyright Act; but in practice, the provisions regarding illegal reproduction are quite unenforceable against the unthinking habits of hundreds of thousands of otherwise law-abiding citizens. The problem, then, is how to find a practicable and mutually satisfactory way for the public to compensate creators for reprographic as well as library uses.

45. The federal government should establish immediately, outside the copyright regime, a program to provide payment for both library and reprographic uses of the books of living Canadian authors. The basis for calculation of such payment should be the annual royalty payments to living Canadian authors.

While we respect the work done by the Canada Council, we are concern-ed that the benefits to authors of its proposal, including a maximum contribu-tion of $300 per title, are little better than token. The Council's own sampling of Canadian libraries indicates that only 12 per cent of English-language titles and 18 per cent of French-language titles would qualify their authors for this maximum contribution. Furthermore, through its provision for benefits in every year in which a title remains on deposit in libraries regardless of how often (if ever) it is borrowed, or how little the author may have produced in the meantime, the scheme would tend to reward past efforts over current cre-ativity – a tendency which, we submit, would misdirect the emphasis of public policy.

Like the Canada Council scheme, the approach recommended by this Committee provides benefits to Canadian authors in a neutral way, involving no value judgments of literary or other merit by the government. Unlike the Council's scheme, however, our proposal contains a measure of relationship between creation and use. Because it keys payments to authors' royalty statements from their publishers, our proposal offers four advantages:

- It is more likely to stimulate further creativity, since royalties are a more accurate indicator than library holdings of whether an author is currently productive.
- No book in print and actively selling would be excluded, whereas a scheme based on library holdings will exclude many such titles.
- It can embrace the idea of compensation for reprographic uses, since royalty payments provide some indication of how much in demand a book is and therefore constitute a valid basis for compen-sating authors for both library borrowing and reprographic uses by the public.
- The scheme can be adapted to other categories of creators who suf-fer a similar lack of compensation for public uses of their works, such as composers.

We acknowledge that one group of authors would benefit more from the Canada Council's proposal than from our own, namely, those whose books have gone out of print. Authors will receive nothing from our scheme for an out-of-print title, since such titles no longer earn royalties. Nevertheless, we do not believe that annual public payments can be justified simply because titles continue to occupy space on library shelves, from which they may or may not be borrowed. If there is a significant level of continuing public use, titles will tend to be kept in print by their publishers and will therefore be eligible for inclusion in our scheme. We can only repeat that we feel the public interest lies in rewarding and encouraging the maximum relationship between cre-ativity and public use. The federal government's priority should be to compen-sate authors who are currently productive, rather than to rectify the errors of the past.

A second objection that we anticipate to our proposal is that by implicating reprography within it, we are condoning unrestricted photocopying and other means of reproduction without regard for copyright law. To that criticism we would reply that, for the foreseeable future, there is no way of compensating creators *directly* for actual instances of reproduction of their work; yet authors are being victimized daily by this shortcoming in society's laws and practices, and are the group most vulnerable to it financially. Therefore we believe that the federal government should adopt some measure of redress, even if it is only an interim measure until a more adequate and direct form of compensation can be devised, and it is in that spirit that we put forward our recommendation.

Because the scope of our proposal is broader than that of the Canada Council's payment for public use scheme, a considerably larger budget would be required than the amount envisaged by the Council for the first year of its scheme ($1.3 million). We hesitate to mention an exact amount, but a reasonable target might be between 50 and 100 per cent of Canadian authors' royalties, depending on the category of publication. Such a budget would be in the range of several million dollars – not an unreasonable amount, we submit, for the Canadian public to spend in recognition of intellectual and spiritual benefits received from its authors, and as an investment in their future productivity.

Although we do not intend to describe a detailed administrative structure, we do believe these seven points of principle should be respected:

- Our recommendation for a basis of compensation different from that proposed by the Canada Council should not be used by the federal government to delay introduction of a compensation program, which is urgently needed and merited by Canada's writers.
- Authors who are already amply rewarded by the marketplace in a given year should have their benefits from the program limited, either by imposition of a ceiling or by graduated participation rates that decline as their royalties rise.
- Because of the existence of high peak years in authors' royalty earning patterns, recipients of the program should be permitted to have their payment for a given year averaged over a period of three to five years.
- Categories of publication that are important from a literary point of view but poorly remunerated, such as poetry and drama, should be given a greater weight within a graduated scale of benefits.
- The categories of publication eligible for such a program require definition. Considerations that should be uppermost include Canadian authorship and, broadly speaking, the cultural or creative nature of the types of publication eligible. As is the case with the Canada Council's program of publishing assistance, these criteria would exclude how-to guides, manuals, cookbooks, dictionaries and materials intended primarily for classroom use.

- Consideration should be given to assigning the administrative responsibility for such a program to the federal government's primary agency for dealing with writers, the Canada Council.
- Although this scheme provides direct assistance to writers only, it is not intended to imply exclusion of publishers from any future copyright regime that may be devised to establish collectives of professionals for the purpose of compensating copyright holders for reprographic uses.

Literature and Language

The past 15 years have seen a gradual but steady increase in the number of Canadian titles published in English or French translation. Canada now has a community of highly skilled professional translators, including some specializing in the difficult and creative work of translating literary works in poetry, drama and fiction. The availability of these translations has been an important element in enriching the literary and cultural experience of many Canadians. Most of these titles have been translated with the assistance of the Canada Council's translation grants program.

Undoubtedly, more could be done to build on these accomplishments and to expand Canadians' interest in and knowledge of the literature and society of the other official language group. We must stress that any such efforts by the federal government should be undertaken not to further national unity or any other political purpose, but as a non-political form of cultural exchange. We have two specific recommendations in this area, as follows:

46. The Canada Council should raise the per-word rate paid to literary translators, which is the basis for its translation grants, to a level commensurate with rates paid to professional translators of industrial and government documents.

Such an increase is essential as a matter of justice and also as a practical matter so that capable translators will continue to be attracted to this type of work. If they are not, fewer works will be published in translation and Canadian readers will be the poorer.

47. Federal agencies involved in assisting publication should provide additional financial incentive to book and periodical publishers for issuing work translated into English or French from the other official language.

Such publications tend to suffer larger deficits than similar works published in the original language, and financial recognition of this fact should be built into funding allocations.

Professional Development of Writers

Writing is often described as a lonely profession. Indeed, it may be that the relative isolation of writers and the absence, until recent years, of a strong writers' lobby have been factors leading to the neglect of their interests addressed earlier in this chapter.

In Canada, the writer's isolation takes several forms. There is the usual condition of the profession in which writers, like painters but unlike performing artists, work apart from their audience. Writers are often equally cut off from other writers with whom they could share the agonies and ecstasies of the craft. And overlying both these conditions is the geographical isolation from each other experienced by Canadians in all walks of life.

In recent years, steps have been taken to offset the Canadian writer's isolation and to bring authors closer both to their readers and to each other. For their part, writers have established new professional associations (and maintained older ones) from which they derive considerable benefits: personal contact with colleagues, pooling of professional resources and information, and stronger positions for negotiating and lobbying with publishers and governments. For its part, the Canada Council has funded various promotional projects of these writers' organizations and has administered a program of public readings, which has brought Canadian authors face to face with their readers on many hundreds of occasions each year. The Council also operates a writer-in-residence program on a cost-sharing basis with post-secondary educational institutions. This program, complemented by various provincial government programs for artists-in-schools at the elementary and secondary levels, provides students with the opportunity to learn from professional writers at first hand, and gives the writers the rejuvenating experience of working with young people.

These are highly beneficial activities for all concerned. We urge government arts funding bodies to continue them and, where deemed justifiable, expand them with additional funding. There is, however, one area related to all of these but distinct from them where we believe a fresh approach would be fruitful: the professional development of writers.

Our aim here is to make it possible for writers, even well established ones, to expand their professional horizons if they see fit, and to learn something new about the various branches of their craft. Our last wish would be to produce sameness, predictability or orthodoxy in Canadian writing, or to propose a centralized and centralizing institution such as a National Writers' School. Instead,

48.   Federal assistance for workshops and seminars that bring writers together to learn from one another should be expanded and increased. Special emphasis should be placed on meetings between writers from different literary genres.

We have in mind occasions varying in duration from a few days to a few weeks, held in various settings in a variety of locations throughout the country and attended by writers who may be at different stages of their careers, but who are interested in imparting what they know to others and in learning new skills themselves. A novelist interested in writing for the stage, for example, or a playwright wanting to develop screenplays for film or television might attend these sessions, drawing on the experience and expertise of invited visiting writers.

These professional development occasions, then, would be of short duration and relatively inexpensive; they could make use of existing facilities and would be designed to answer the needs of specific groups of writers, as perceived by the writers themselves. Opportunities should also be created for writers from the two official language groups to bridge their isolation from each other for mutual artistic benefit.

If writers prove receptive to this idea, guidelines for such a program could be developed cooperatively by writers' groups and the Canada Council, and program funding could be provided by the Council. It seems to our Committee that such a program would have a beneficial long-term impact on the quality and quantity of writing being done in all forms, by giving writers the opportunity to challenge themselves and to grow.

Publishing

Authors need publishers almost as much as they need readers. Even before the invention of movable type, authors depended on intermediaries – clerics and scribes – to copy their works and put them into circulation. Now a book or magazine publisher can deliver an author's words to a potential audience of a thousand or a million, and new forms of electronic publishing via videotex systems and computer printout are becoming more of a reality every day. But publishers can be far more than intermediaries or mere delivery systems: they may have a fundamental and profound influence on what writers write and what readers read. They can be creative partners with authors in developing story and book ideas and shaping manuscripts; frequently publishers and their editors approach writers with concepts for books or articles that they want written. Consequently, publishers and publishing have been the focus of a good deal of cultural analysis, policy-making and public funding in this country in recent years.

Naturally this observation applies to the daily press as well as the book and periodical publishing industries. The newspaper industry, however, does not come under our Committee's mandate; the daily press has recently been the subject in its own right of a federally commissioned study, the Royal Commission on Newspapers, which reported in August 1981. For the purposes of this document, then, our concerns with publishing extend only to the book and periodical fields, especially those elements within them of a creative or intellectual nature, which are the most sensitive culturally and, at the same time, the most vulnerable economically. There are other areas of print culture such as the business press and educational publishing which, while extremely important in themselves, must be beyond our purview.

Both book and magazine publishing in Canada have achieved the editorial and regional specialization necessary to express the many aspects of our diverse society. Integral to this diversification has been an increase in the number of Canadian-owned publishing enterprises. Multinational publishing companies, by and large, have remained on the margins of this particular cultural evolution, since their presence in Canada is motivated more by business goals than cultural ones, and since they are excluded from the benefits of most federal and provincial assistance programs.

Such diversification in publishing has been facilitated by the ease of entry into the profession and the existence of government support. However, a price has been paid in national and regional markets that are relatively small and inundated with both imported and domestic products: low or nonexistent profits on the part of many Canadian-owned publishers (although by no means all). It *is* possible for publishers to make profits in Canada – for example, by concentrating on how-to books, specialized magazines catering to affluent consumers, romance fiction and certain kinds of textbooks, as well as importing the books of foreign publishers. But it requires a peculiar combination of editorial acumen, professional skills, and personal ingenuity and sacrifice, as well as government support, to make any money or even to survive financially by publishing original Canadian books or periodicals of cultural significance. Such publishing is not inherently profitable: on that point a divided and sometimes fractious publishing community has been able to agree. The Association des éditeurs canadiens pointed out that in spite of current forms of government assistance, "the situation of a number of publishing houses remains extremely precarious. This is particularly true of those houses that publish only works of literature." (Our translation.) The implication for government policy is clear. As the Canadian Book Publishers' Council stated during our public hearings, "In the area of literature . . . for at least the foreseeable future, there will be many culturally important books whose publication requires direct subsidy."

Publishers themselves are the first source of subsidy for this type of publishing in both the book and magazine fields. In an impressive number of cases, they have mortgaged personal assets to publish Canadian writers and have subsidized their publications from their own pockets. It is after a concrete commitment of this sort has been demonstrated that government steps in to support Canadian publishers. All publisher support programs require a track record of some nature, either titles or issues published or sales achieved, as a criterion of eligibility. Federal support comes from several sources: chiefly the Department of Communications, the Canada Council and the Social Sciences and Humanities Research Council. In 1981-82, federal programs disbursed a total of some $16 million in grants and direct financial contributions for book and magazine publishing, of which approximately $13 million went in support of book publishing.

Although publishing in Canada, particularly book publishing, has a reputation of being heavily subsidized, this amount of direct federal support is quite modest when placed in context. It represents, for example, only about 1.3 per cent of estimated net federal expenditures on culture for 1981-82 of $1.2 billion. Or it can be compared to the $931.7 million estimated by Statistics Canada to have been the wholesale value of the book market in Canada for the year 1980 (the most recent estimate available), of which $256.7 million is estimated to have been in sales of Canadian publishers' own books.

Government financial support does not appear to make publishers either wealthy or particularly profitable. A recent study of its membership by the Association of Canadian Publishers confirms this view. One reason for this may be that public subsidy constantly draws new and relatively untried players into the game, reducing the aggregate level of profitability as well as the average subsidy to any individual firm. In any event, it is true that most types of public subsidy in Canadian publishing represent an incentive to undertake kinds of publication which are not inherently profitable.

In the absence of government support, Canadian publishers who are now financially sound or making significant profits would probably survive, but the same cannot be said of their current publishing programs. There would no doubt be sufficient publishing skills and sufficiently developed markets to ensure the publication of certain kinds of Canadian books for which there is high popular demand. But if government support to publishing were eliminated, the saving would scarcely be noticed, while much that is culturally valuable, although not profitable, in Canadian life and literature would be placed in severe jeopardy. Much of the richness and variety that Canadian readers now enjoy in their literary experience would disappear. The result would be a truncated publishing industry whose survivors would be forced to publish only the safer commercial properties and to rely more heavily (in the case of book publishing) on sales of imported titles. Many of these survivors would be the larger and more diversified firms for whom publishing Canadian authors might have to become, relatively speaking, a sideline. Thus authors would lose too. Many smaller publishing houses and periodicals whose primary or sole activity is publishing Canadian authors would be pushed to the crisis point; they would have to change their publishing goals, their very raison d'être, or face extinction.

Our conclusion is that this would be a highly undesirable outcome. If there is a public cost in supporting the publishing infrastructure we now have in order to ensure the availability of a wide range of works by Canadian authors, then there is an even greater cost if we eliminate that support. *Our Committee wishes to affirm, therefore, the fundamental social and cultural value of continuing direct federal assistance to Canadian publishers of both Canadian books and periodicals.*

Book Publishing

Although the level of activity in Canadian book publishing has risen during the past decade with the support of government, certain problems of the profession remain and will not easily disappear. Some can be alleviated through further initiatives by government and by the profession itself, while others will in all probability continue, complicating the business of being a Canadian book publisher whether in the English- or the French-language market.

Book publishing is, in the first instance, an easy business to enter. Remaining in the business for a significant length of time, however, is a much more difficult matter. Early success and growth in book publishing (as in other industries) can often usher in a whole new set of problems, as the entrepreneur seeks working capital to finance expansion. Enlarged premises, overheads and inventories can seldom be financed out of profits alone.

Even if a publisher's list has been profitable, with sales figures on most titles passing the break-even mark, two very troublesome practices of the book retailing system hamper the realization of those profits: relatively slow payment of accounts (commonly up to 120 days or more) and the policy of returning unlimited quantities of unsold books for credit. Both these practices not only complicate a book publisher's financial planning and sometimes very survival, but discourage two potential sources of working capital: individual investors and Canadian banks.

Bankers are disinclined to accept publishers' inventories of books as collateral. Moreover, publishers usually lack those other assets that investors or bankers would find acceptable – buildings, land or machinery. These factors, combined with the uncertainty of a book publisher's accounts receivable, lead the financial community to see the publishing community as a doubtful risk.

This has been a traditional obstacle for the industry, and for many publishers it continues to be one. But it is a problem especially for publishing companies owned in Canada and operating mainly or exclusively in the Canadian market. These firms have consistently found that they have far less access to investment capital or bank credit in their own country than have multinational publishers backed by parent companies' assets. As a result, Canadian-owned publishers have experienced a serious competitive disadvantage. This is far more than a business dilemma: it has grave cultural consequences, because it is precisely the Canadian-owned sector of the industry that undertakes the lion's share of publishing of Canadian authors. For example, Statistics Canada has released figures from its survey of the book market to show that out of 5,668 titles published in Canada in 1980, 4,731 or 83.5 per cent came from Canadian-controlled firms.

Government Support to Book Publishing
A decade ago, roughly speaking, governments in Canada began intervening to ensure the survival of a Canadian presence in book publishing. Among

the major initiatives taken were granting programs by the Canada Council, the Quebec Ministère des Affaires culturelles and the Ontario Arts Council; the bookstore accreditation system in Quebec; and the Ontario government's loan guarantee and interest subsidy programs for Canadian-owned, Ontario-based book publishers. Today, every provincial government has programs to fund book publishing in one way or another, and a major program has been launched by the federal Department of Communications which applies an industrial development approach to book publishing. Most of these programs feature eligibility requirements concerning Canadian ownership and authorship. The reason for these requirements is that the ultimate purpose of the programs is not economic, but cultural; the aim has been not to create more jobs or contribute to the Gross National Product (although both have happened as an indirect result), but to ensure that Canadian authors in all fields of literature have access to professional publication and to their primary or nearest market, the Canadian public. In essence, the Canadian-owned publishing sector has been governments' chosen vehicle for delivering Canadian books to Canadian readers.

Because of the simultaneous presence of these various forms of government support for book publishing, it can be difficult to trace specific effects on the industry back to particular programs. One way of measuring the net effect of these programs, however, is to examine the share of the Canadian market held by Canadian books. The Statistics Canada market surveys have shown that in the latter half of the 1970s, Canadian publishers' own books maintained one quarter to slightly more than one quarter of the total domestic market for books: in the most recent year for which figures are available, 1980, as we have mentioned, that share was $256.7 million out of $931.7 million, or 27.5 per cent. Most encouragingly, sales of Canadian publishers' own books increased by 23 per cent over the previous year, compared to an increase of only 11 per cent for imported books. The ability of Canadian books to perform in this fashion must undoubtedly be traced to the creative abilities of their authors, but also in large measure to the continued existence, productivity and marketing efforts of Canadian-owned publishers assisted by government programs.

Some would disagree with the policy of directing most government assistance to Canadian-owned firms, and argue that the best way to support Canadian authorship would be to assist any publisher able to get those authors to market, regardless of the firm's ownership. Such an approach ignores several basic facts about the book industry in Canada, the performance of firms within it, and the nature of the author-publisher connection.

There is the fact, just mentioned, that multinational firms already enjoy a substantial advantage over Canadian-owned publishers in their access to working capital; in many instances their parent companies are wealthy corporate giants operating on a global scale. Similarly, the Canadian branches of multinational firms begin life here with the enormous advantage of sales revenues from the parent company's product lines – the Canadian market for which in many cases was originally developed by a Canadian agent or distributor before the multinational elected to assume greater control by establishing its own branch in this country. With assets like these, such companies scarcely need subsidizing by Canadian government cultural programs.

Equally important is the matter of motivation. Most Canadian branches of multinational publishers do not have as their raison d'être the publishing of Canadian authors. They are here first and foremost to achieve the greatest possible market penetration for the parent company's products and to return satisfactory profit levels to their head offices in the United States, France or Britain. Although honourable exceptions exist, very few foreign-owned companies publish Canadian novelists, poets or playwrights; and in two fields of publishing that have recently flowered in Canada, regional writing and children's literature, the contribution of multinational publishers has been extremely limited, where it has existed at all.

All of this is not to denigrate the accomplishments of foreign-controlled publishers in this country, but to explain some of the reasons why most federal government assistance to book publishing has been weighted towards firms owned in Canada which demonstrate a primary commitment to Canadian authors. Implicit in this commitment is the acceptance of high editorial costs, which are not borne by book importers and which cut into profit margins. By supporting Canadian-controlled publishing houses, governments support the continuation and development of Canadian writing in many forms, as well as the reading public for Canadian works.

At the same time, foreign-controlled publishers are in no way hindered from publishing such Canadian works as they see fit, while Canadian writers may receive government grants or awards regardless of whether they publish with a Canadian-owned or foreign-owned house. This seems to our Committee to be an appropriate as well as an eminently practical policy for a federal government to pursue in this field, so long as it is applied in a manner consistent with principles of freedom of expression. It is also a policy which in the past decade has produced demonstrable cultural gains. By ensuring the spread and survival of our publishing communities, federal and provincial governments have fostered the existence of Canadian and regional literatures of considerable scope and increasing maturity. But there is, as always, room for improvement.

The federal government, unlike certain provincial governments, has been reluctant to use fiscal measures such as loans, loan guarantees or investment incentives as strategies for supporting book publishing. Instead, its chosen instrument has been subsidies. This is true of not only the relatively older granting programs of the Social Sciences and Humanities Research Council and the Canada Council, but also the Canadian Book Publishing Development Program established in 1979 and now administered by the Department of Communications. It would seem that the federal government has shared the banks' view of book publishing as a bad business risk and rejected long-term financial commitments in favour of the year-to-year cycle of awarding subsidies. Even the Federal Business Development Bank, with its mandate to assist growing small businesses, has steered clear of involvement with publishing.

Of the $13 million in federal direct subsidy to book publishing mentioned earlier, over 90 per cent comes from two sources: the Department of Communications and the Canada Council. The approaches taken by these two organizations are markedly different in their methods and impacts. Their ultimate intent and stated purpose in policy terms – to support Canadian book publishing and, by extension, Canadian writing – is the same, but their strategies in pursuit of that objective are quite divergent. There is nothing wrong with that, of course, provided cultural goals are being met. But it is our view that these programs can be better designed and coordinated in order to pursue cultural goals more effectively.

Broadly stated, the Department of Communications' Canadian Book Publishing Development Program attempts to build companies, while the various Canada Council programs for publishing attempt to build books and authors. The Council bases its major support program, the annual block grants for book publishers, on the specific quantity and general quality of titles considered to be of cultural significance, receiving an assessment of these matters by a jury of leading professionals. The department, on the other hand, avoids cultural value judgments and keys the major part of its assistance to the sales figures of eligible companies. The Council provides reward and incentive for achievement in literary, regional and children's publishing; the department offers reward and incentive for success in sales and marketing of books, with little regard for their content. The Council excludes certain types of books from its considerations, such as how-to guides, cookbooks and educational materials designed for the classroom; the department embraces all of these categories, and also titles by foreign authors if they have been published and printed in Canada by an eligible publisher.

Both these programs have a great deal of validity in their different ways. Both programs have been extremely important to Canadian book publishers, ensuring the survival of some and the steady growth of others. It is highly unlikely, for example, that we would have seen the regional and thematic diversification of book publishing without the Council's programs. And without the departmental program, more than one productive and culturally important Canadian publishing house might not have lived to fight another day.

There are also serious limitations to both programs. By concentrating on title content and output to the exclusion of a publisher's overall financial situation and business needs, and stressing ease of entry into its programs, the Canada Council, after 11 years of block grant funding, has ended up spreading its resources more and more thinly across an ever widening spectrum of publishers. For some years now, the block grants have fallen drastically short of even the specifically cultural needs they were meant to serve. The program administered by the Department of Communications was intended partly to counterbalance this deficiency, but has in fact benefited mainly the larger and more profitable publishers, those with sales volumes of from $1 million to $20 million a year. Because of its emphasis on company size, this program provides little or no assistance to a part of the publishing spectrum which may show only modest sales but is vitally important culturally. Included in this last group are many regional, literary and other specialized presses.

This analysis shows the effects of basing support for book publishing too narrowly on either title output or sales figures – that is, on either content or demand. Neither preoccupation constitutes a sufficient approach. If we adapt to publishing policy the central message of this Report about creators and audiences, it becomes clear that cultural policy-makers should be concerned with both content (what writers write) and demand (what readers read). Within government support programs, then, publishers merit assistance not as final beneficiaries, but as the essential link without which writers and readers would not connect.

A Cultural Policy for Book Publishing
The approaches to book publishing taken by the Canada Council and the Department of Communications have not been articulated and presented by the federal government as being complementary to each other in any but the most perfunctory manner. Instead, there has been an unfortunate tendency within government cultural circles and the publishing industry itself to see the two approaches as incompatible and even antithetic. We feel that this type of thinking about federal cultural policy is likely to be counter-productive. It seems to us well within the realm of possibility to devise a subsidy program that embraces both content and demand simultaneously in a coherent attempt to serve cultural objectives. Such a program need not ignore the real financial needs and scale of operations of publishers, as the Canada Council tends to do, or the cultural and artistic context of publishing, as the Department of Communications tends to do. Nor would such a program, *if adequately funded*, be forced to make false dichotomies between large and small publishers, or "commercial" and "cultural" ones. The program would represent a clear statement about writing, publishing and reading as a complex cultural experience requiring a policy sensitive to the many variables within it.

49.   For the long-term future, the federal government should adopt a cultural policy for support to book publishing which would contain two major components: a comprehensive subsidy program geared to the twin elements of content and demand; and, in a supporting role, an economic development program as underpinning to the industrial structure of book publishing.

We envisage the subsidy program adopting the Canada Council's criteria for eligibility of titles, in order to direct the funds clearly towards the culturally significant portion of a publisher's activities. It would thus exclude guidebooks, how-to books, cookbooks and the like; it would give emphasis to works of Canadian literature for both adults and children, as well as belles-lettres in the domains of history, society, criticism and so on, by Canadian authors only. Grant allocations should reflect the numbers and cultural contribution of such titles as in present Canada Council practice; but in equal measure they should reflect the sales *of those same cultural titles*. In this way, the best of both the current approaches would be combined, but targeted clearly to the cultural element of a publisher's list. This would eliminate the present misdirection of support by the Department of Communications' Canadian Book Publishing Development Program to publishing activity that does not require or justify subsidy from federal cultural funds, such as publication of works by foreign authors. As for the location of this cultural subsidy program, it would be consistent with the views we expressed in Chapter 2 on the arm's-length principle if it were administered by the Canada Council.

The second component of the policy, an economic development program, should complement the subsidy program rather than compete with it for funds or influence. The economic development program would perform specific industrial support functions not served by the subsidy program and would be administered by the Department of Communications. The program's objective would be to strengthen the industrial structure of Canadian book publishing in order to assure the industry's ability to fulfil its cultural role. Included would be a continuation or expansion of the following four functions of the existing departmental program:

- Assistance for both collective industry and individual company projects for domestic book distribution, with continued high priority for the introduction of a Canadian adaptation of the computerized book ordering and stock information system known as teleordering, in order to improve the service provided in both official languages by Canadian publishers to booksellers, libraries and their customers;
- Foreign rights marketing and export assistance, to further the presence of Canadian writing and publishing abroad for the attendant cultural and economic benefits;
- Professional development of book publishing personnel;
- Research and documentation for the book industry.

The economic development program would also assume two major new functions to be discussed in a moment:

- Funding research into adaptations of new technology to book publishing, whether in the areas of ordering and distribution or electronic publishing itself;
- Administering a limited and highly selective loan or loan guarantee program for qualified publishers.

A future federal policy for book publishing such as we have outlined would strike an equilibrium between cultural and industrial needs, strengthening our publishers in their cultural role to meet the challenges to survival and growth in the 1980s and 1990s. For the short term, however, we must acknowledge that, as we write, federal programs for book publishing are in place and functioning; in particular, the program administered by the Department of Communications appears likely to extend its activities at least until 1985. As we have suggested, the subsidies provided by that program to book publishers do not in some respects address cultural needs or objectives with sufficient directness. Specifically, the program's financial contributions related to sales volumes of highly commercial titles, textbooks and books by foreign authors manufactured and published in Canada do not constitute reward or incentive for undertaking Canadian publishing of appropriate cultural significance, and may merely be adding to the recipients' profits without ensuring cultural benefits. In order to remedy this problem we recommend that:

50.   In the short term, the Canadian Book Publishing Development Program of the Department of Communications should adjust its criteria for eligible titles to reflect the same categories of culturally significant books assisted by the Canada Council.

A Loan Program for Book Publishers
A few words of explanation about our proposals for a loan or loan guarantee program and a new technology program are called for here; the former idea is particularly heretical in the context of federal support to publishing. As noted earlier, even though book publishing is an industry, the federal government has preferred to support it with subsidies rather than the type of fiscal measures applied to other industries. This is understandable to the extent that book publishing attracts many practitioners whose motive is not profit but cultural expression; it is not a particularly profitable field at the best of times, and indeed has had its share of business failures. On the other hand, some Canadian firms earn respectable profits in the book business, while others that run closer to the break-even level are soundly managed. Canadian book publishing could be said to have suffered from a bad press on the score of its financial management.

It is noteworthy that the governments of both Ontario and Quebec have not shied away from extending loans or loan guarantees to qualifying Canadian book publishers. Indeed, for publishers in Ontario, the loan guarantee program is widely considered to be (in the words of the trade paper *Quill & Quire*) "the most useful government support strategy in operation." This is because it provides not a quick once-a-year injection of cash from a program that may or may not continue in the years to come, but sustained access to the working capital which banks so often deny Canadian publishers. In addition, the Ontario loan program provides a subsidy of half the prime rate of interest.

Although federal government policy-makers have rejected such an idea for book publishing in the past (as they have turned down tax incentives for investment in publishing), we feel that it now deserves to be reconsidered. One of the premises behind the Department of Communications program was that a cash-poor industry required injections of working capital to put it on its feet. If the premise proves correct, then by 1985, as a result of six years of such injections, at least some Canadian publishing companies will be in a position to be treated like responsible businesses. In that event there should be no reason, given full and accurate information and informed judgment about a Canadian publisher's financial soundness, and a good understanding of the nature of the book business, why the federal government should not feel able to become involved, in a gradual and selective manner, with guaranteeing or extending bank loans to qualifying publishers. The Department of Communications is developing extensive documentation on the financial histories of the publishing companies it supports. This information, combined with a financial assessment of a company's future plans, would enable the program's administrators to assess applications knowledgably and to limit the risk to the public treasury. Banks could be provided with a government guarantee for a specific portion of a publisher's line of credit. Consideration should be given to providing an interest subsidy as the Ontario program does, to ease the burden of debt in these times of high interest rates. In some cases, coordination with provincial governments providing a similar type of assistance would be an absolute necessity. But in the case of publishers deemed risk-worthy, the provincial and federal governments would be strengthening each other's judgment in the matter and sharing whatever risk might be involved. For publishers located in provinces that do not provide such guarantees, the federal program would be providing a measure of equalization of opportunity. We refer the reader to Recommendation 10 for a discussion of how the Federal Business Development Bank might be involved in the planning and operation of such a loan program.

It must be acknowledged that it will be of doubtful utility to many Canadian publishers to assist them to go further into debt. But there are three highly desirable advantages to a federal loan scheme for some Canadian publishers at least – those with a track record of sound financial management and profitability. In the first place, a loan program would assist them to move toward a greater degree of self-sufficiency, reducing their requirement for subsidy as a source of working capital (although, as noted earlier, it would not eliminate that need for certain types of publication of a culturally significant nature).

A second advantage of the scheme is that it would provide the federal government with a tool for assisting educational publishing, without encroaching on provincial jurisdiction over school curricula. At present, the Canadian Book Publishing Development Program of the Department of Communications includes a component for supporting textbooks and related learning materials. Because the program disburses these funds as a percentage of eligible sales but does not require the funds to be applied to any specific educational publishing activities, it is impossible to determine how, or indeed whether, this support actually benefits educational publishing. Federal subsidies to specific textbooks, on the other hand, would almost certainly be opposed by provincial governments as an incursion into their jurisdiction. But loans related to educational publishing programs would enable the federal government to provide support to the development, production and marketing of Canadian learning materials for Canadian schools without actually becoming involved in the content of those materials.

A third advantage of a loan scheme relates directly to our other proposal for a program component concerned with new technology. As publishers adapt to technological change in various aspects of their operations – order processing, word processing, typesetting and electronic forms of publishing itself, especially in the realm of educational materials for both home and classroom – new types of capital investment will be required. Since such investments will be critical if Canadian publishers are to remain competitive in products and service within a changing industry, they should be prime targets for assistance through loans.

New Publishing and Distribution Technologies
As to the new technology program itself, it should focus on two broad areas, at least initially: book ordering and distribution, and electronic publishing. Teleordering systems in the United States and Britain have demonstrated how the computer can streamline the cumbersome, slow and inefficient process whereby bookstores and libraries obtain books (and information about inventory and in-print status) from publishers and wholesalers. U.S. wholesalers are already providing such services directly to some of their Canadian customers, a situation that threatens not only Canadian publishers and agents, who are bypassed and thus lose import business, but also Canadian books themselves, which are seldom included in the databases. Perceiving the urgent necessity for a Canadian version of these systems, the English-language book industry has secured assistance from the Canadian Book Publishing Development Program for feasibility studies and start-up funding. A new program component dealing specifically with technological adaptations for book publishing would carry on from these promising beginnings, ensuring that adequate funding is provided to continue the structural development and technological updating of such a national system in both languages.

The other area for action includes the whole spectrum of computer adaptations of the publishing process – computer-assisted learning and on-demand publishing being two of the most promising growth areas. We received a most original and stimulating brief on the latter subject from the Coach House Press and the literary periodical *Open Letter* in Toronto. That brief prompted us to think of the computer as a tool for revolutionizing not only manuscript preparation, typesetting and the servicing of customer accounts, but also the very process whereby readers obtain their literature. A future was described to us in which bookstore or library patrons could receive on-the-spot printouts of the desired publications from vast computer databases. Such a future is entirely conceivable given the rapid pace of technological development and would be especially useful in providing rapid and inexpensive access to reference materials, technical information and out-of-print literary works. At the moment it seems unlikely that such developments could render obsolete the physical book or the bookstore as we know it, since the book format – particularly in paperback – is portable, inexpensive and therefore the most practical means of packaging literature for which there is some popular demand. But precisely because the pace of technological change is so rapid, we hesitate to predict the shape of things to come. We must content ourselves with urging government policy-makers to ensure that all writing and publishing support programs remain flexible enough to accommodate, wherever possible within their criteria and methodology, changes in publication formats and processes that occur in the years ahead.

The Government's Co-publishing Program
Finally under the heading of book publishing, we wish to draw the federal government's attention to a most valuable program which appears in some danger of falling into regrettable neglect: the program of the Publishing Centre, Department of Supply and Services, for co-publishing government-originated books with private publishers. This program gives Canadians access at a competitive price to much useful and interesting research developed by departments of their federal government. Canadian publishers are invited to submit tenders for the right to publish such manuscripts, which then receive professional design, production and marketing through the bookstore and library systems instead of languishing outside public view.

It has come to our attention that the Department of Supply and Services has pursued this program with something less than vigour; the full capacity of private publishers to participate in the program has not been exploited, especially in the French language. This seems to us an unfortunate and wasteful under-utilization of both public and private resources which might be more imaginatively combined for the benefit of Canadians.

51.   The Department of Supply and Services should operate its co-publishing program more energetically, seeking the participation of federal departments and Canadian publishers to the limit of their interest and capability.

Magazine Publishing
The distinctive role that magazines play in our culture was identified with precision by the Special Senate Committee on Mass Media (the Davey Committee) in 1970: "Magazines are special," the Committee's report stated. "Magazines, in a different way from any other medium, can help foster in Canadians a sense of themselves."

Magazines serve specialized audiences that other media – newspapers and television, for example – cannot reach. Magazines speak to and for new constituencies, creating a sense of community among readers who share common interests. The cultural benefits to a society as dispersed and diverse as Canada's are obvious.

Much that we have said about the creative successes and business difficulties of book publishing applies with equal force to magazine publishing. Nevertheless, there are important differences between the two. Unlike book publishers, magazine publishers have a product that is highly defined, specialized and immediately recognizable, and they issue it on a regular, repetitive cycle. Unlike books, magazines must build and maintain a following over the long term. Most magazines must also win over a second group essential to their survival: advertisers.

Problems of Capital, Distribution and Competition
Ideally, success with readers should lead to success with advertisers and thus to business success. But magazine publishing is not that simple. There is ample evidence in the form of good Canadian magazines and periodicals that have faltered or disappeared over the years to suggest that a magazine does not survive just because its readers like it. It must also face and overcome at least three orders of problems: capital shortages, distribution difficulties and foreign competition.

Because a magazine must build up circulation and advertising over the long term while appearing promptly and regularly, a large proportion of its capital is required up front. During the time it takes to become established, relatively little cash is flowing in from copy sales, subscription sales or advertising. Thus initial capitalization is crucial if the publication is going to have a fighting chance. At the same time, magazine publishers are carrying on a parallel struggle against inflationary price increases. In briefs to us, they reported recent annual increases in paper costs at well over 20 per cent (a problem shared, of course, by book publishers), while postal rate increases have added greatly to the mailing and promotional costs of magazines distributed mainly by subscription. Magazine publishers have not felt able to pass on these increases in their entirety to their readers and advertisers. It is no wonder that magazine publishers, in the words of the Canadian Periodical Publishers' Association, "live at the ends of their nerves and their bank lines."

Physical distribution is another difficult problem for magazine publishers. Even if the preferred method of sales and distribution is subscriptions, which can be serviced through the mails, many magazines need to establish their presence on newsstands in order to gain enough visibility to attract readers and advertisers in the first place. Newsstand distribution is, however, monopolized by wholesale firms that control access to the retail accounts; if a magazine is not considered salable enough by such distributors to be worth handling, it will not penetrate the newsstand market to any significant extent. This problem is multiplied for periodicals that depend on reaching a broader audience, since they must arrange separate distribution deals in each major urban or regional market. It is not surprising, then, that some of the Canadian magazines that have been most successful financially in recent years have been those based on a local market – a single city, province or region. Nor is it surprising that the other eminently successful phenomenon in periodical publishing recently has been the controlled-circulation magazine, which is delivered free to homes in selected neighbourhoods and thereby avoids the problems of newsstand distribution and display.

To some extent these latter two types of magazines also avoid the third major problem facing Canadian magazines: foreign competition. A foreign magazine cannot replace a Canadian one based on the life of a particular city or region. Nor are foreign magazines likely to challenge Canadian controlled-circulation magazines in their own markets. On practically every newsstand in Canada, however, foreign magazines of many kinds outnumber their Canadian counterparts by 10 to one or more. And whether the magazine is American, French or British, it is assuredly enjoying the economic advantage of having its editorial, design and administrative overheads paid for by sales in its home market. Thus the publishers are simply shipping low-cost additional copies into Canada, which they regard as merely a profitable extension of the home market. The Canadian magazine, on the other hand, usually attempts to recover all its costs from sales in the Canadian market alone.

Not all these problems can be solved by government, or even addressed by a single level of government; regulation of wholesale distributors of magazines, for example, is a matter for provincial jurisdiction. Nevertheless, the problems are inextricably linked. Government action to remedy even one of them would undoubtedly have a beneficial influence on all the others. However, federal government assistance has not been extended to magazine publishing as generously or in as many forms as it has been to book publishing. This situation therefore represents a fourth order of difficulty for Canadian periodicals: the relative lack of government measures of support.

As we examine government measures of support for periodicals, it is useful to categorize magazines into three broad types: the large-circulation consumer magazines with copious advertising and proven financial viability; special-interest magazines with a narrower market but genuine commercial possibilities; and literary, artistic, scholarly and scientific periodicals, usually with small circulations, minimal advertising and little hope of becoming self-sustaining, much less profitable.

The last group is clearly the main beneficiary of existing programs, whether federal or provincial. Federal grants are accorded to periodicals in that group by the Canada Council for literary and artistic periodicals; the Social Sciences and Humanities Research Council for scholarly journals in the humanities and social sciences; and the National Research Council and the Natural Sciences and Engineering Research Council for scientific journals. Grants from those sources are seldom, if ever, large enough to launch their recipients on the road to self-reliance; they are seldom even sufficient to allow them to pay their contributors and editors more than token fees (although admittedly contributors to scholarly and scientific journals usually do not require payment). As we have been told by publishers more than once, the real beneficiaries of such grants are often printing companies, since without subsidy the publications might not appear at all. The other beneficiaries, of course, are writers and readers, for whom these magazines are an irreplaceable forum for artistic and intellectual exchange and discovery.

For the other two broad groupings, no programs of direct assistance are available. There are the reduced second-class postal rates for magazines, but these we view first and foremost as a form of support to readers, as we will explain in the final section of this chapter. The major federal initiative to assist these two groups of magazines in recent years has been an indirect measure, an amendment to the Income Tax Act passed in 1976.

The effect of this amendment was to disallow tax deductions for advertising placed in foreign media but directed primarily at Canadian audiences – including advertising purchased in any Canadian edition of a foreign magazine. Among other things, the legislation resulted in the closing of the Canadian branch of *Time*, and in increased Canadian ownership and content in *Reader's Digest/Séléction du Reader's Digest*, which publishes in this country in both English and French.

This change to the Income Tax Act had the general intent of redirecting to Canadian magazines some of the considerable advertising revenues that had been flowing into multinational coffers. Although it is impossible to quantify the precise amount of advertising so redirected, the magazine community told us that this step by the federal government had a favourable impact on the climate for Canadian periodical publishing; *Maclean's* has acknowledged that otherwise it would not have felt able to undertake its transformation from a monthly consumer magazine to a weekly newsmagazine, while the Canadian Periodical Publishers' Association said in its brief that the legislation "had a psychological effect of great value in our industry." Meanwhile, Canadians can still freely obtain the regular U.S. edition of *Time*, albeit without the four or five pages of Canadian news formerly carried by the Canadian edition.

But such a legislative step – although an important one to have taken – hardly constitutes a federal cultural policy for periodicals. The grant programs of the funding bodies mentioned above certainly do not extend to all types of periodicals that can be considered culturally significant or that have difficulty sustaining themselves in the free market. For example, by restricting its eligibility criteria to literary, artistic and children's magazines, the Canada Council's periodicals program excludes many magazines publishing on subjects – history, politics and society, for example – that are considered perfectly eligible under its book publishing programs. Does the Council, and through it the federal government, believe that these subjects are valid concerns of cultural policy in book form but not in periodical form? It hardly seems possible. Rather, the explanation would appear to lie in the fact that the Council has not been given the necessary funds by the government to undertake a more ambitious or comprehensive approach to assisting periodical publishing. Book publishing was chosen for such treatment beginning with a federal cabinet policy decision in 1972; periodical publishing has not received the same priority.

We feel that this situation constitutes a serious inadequacy in federal policy for Canadian writing, publishing and reading. Periodicals, like books, are an integral element of that continuum. Periodicals provide a training ground for new writers, often giving them their first opportunities to make contact with readers. Periodicals also serve as a forum for new expression and exploration of ideas by more mature authors, and are frequently the seedbed for books, television programs and films. As well, they create a sense of cultural community among readers with common interests.

We believe therefore that periodicals must be accorded a new and higher priority within federal publishing policy. It is not sufficient for that policy to help Canadian book publishers survive so they can perform their cultural functions, while leaving Canadian magazine publishers to fend for themselves. It seems to us eminently logical that federal policy and strategy for magazines should follow the same lines that we have proposed for book publishing.

52.   The federal government should enlarge its commitment of support for Canadian magazines through both the Canada Council and the Department of Communications. The Council should establish a two-pronged system of grants based on the twin elements of content and demand, similar to the re-designed subsidy program already outlined for book publishing. The department should initiate an economic development program for the magazine industry similar to the one recommended by this Committee for book publishing.

For the Canada Council, the budget for the new funding program should be adequate to permit the following three steps. First, eligibility criteria should be widened so that grants can be awarded to periodicals dealing not only with literature, the arts and children's interests, but also with the other subjects of cultural significance deemed eligible for book publishing assistance. Second, grant allocations should be determined using twin budgetary elements based on 1) quality of content and 2) evidence of demand, as we recommended earlier for book publishing. And third, amounts of individual periodicals' grants should be sufficient to ensure that henceforth writers and editors can be paid on a more adequate professional scale and the magazines themselves can be more adequately promoted to readers.

The economic development program for Canadian magazines, like its counterpart recommended for book publishers, would contain components for funding distribution projects, professional development, and industry-wide research and documentation. The research component would permit the establishment of an annual statistical survey of the magazine industry –

something we regard as particularly important, since at present there is a dearth of reliable and comprehensive information on the industry available to policy-makers. While the foreign rights marketing and export assistance components of the book program might not be as appropriate or necessary for the Canadian magazine industry, the new technology and loan program components assuredly would be. Loans or loan guarantees should be considered only for magazines with a sound business record and would, we trust, reduce their need for subsidy.

The Department of Communications has now embarked on a major study of the Canadian periodical industry. We urge the government to take the results of that study into account in designing, in consultation with the industry itself, a support policy along the lines we have suggested in order that Canada's magazines may play their role in our life and literature to the fullest.

Reading

All our recommendations about writers and publishers will, if implemented, also benefit readers. Nevertheless, we feel that readers themselves deserve a greater place in federal cultural strategy. A public policy of support for writing and publishing makes little sense unless the members of the public are able to benefit from the consequences of that policy. If it is government policy to encourage a diversity of literary and cultural expression through publication, the products of that diversity must be made accessible to Canadians.

Public Awareness and Access
Two cardinal issues, then, in writing and publishing as in every other field of cultural policy are public awareness and public access. As we have indicated earlier in this document, we have been much concerned with both these matters throughout our deliberations. We believe that in a country such as Canada, whose population is so extended geographically and at the same time so inundated by publications from other countries, governments have a responsibility to facilitate public awareness of and access to indigenous works.

That responsibility is not only federal. At the earliest stage of public awareness, provincial governments bear the responsibility for ensuring that the education system encourages a familiarity with our writers among young people. And in a very direct sense, provincial authority embraces the public's access to Canadian books and periodicals through jurisdiction over libraries and retail outlets, including bookstores and newsstands. In Quebec, for example, the provincial government has had an impact on the availability of Quebec books by requiring that book purchases by public institutions (chiefly schools and libraries) be made from accredited bookstores, which in turn must be Quebec-owned and carry a certain level of Quebec publications. This requirement, instituted in 1971 (and recently broadened to include accredited publishers and distributors as well as booksellers), may have something to do with the estimate by Statistics Canada that Canadian books (including textbooks) held 40 per cent of the French-language market in Canada in 1979, but only 24 per cent of the English-language market. In Ontario, to cite another example, the provincial government has encouraged public awareness and access with its Halfback discount scheme as an incentive to purchase several kinds of Canadian cultural products.

At the federal level, the measure of longest standing to improve public access to the written word has been the low (second- and third-class) postal rates for newspapers, periodicals, books and other mail of a cultural nature. The substantial subsidy from the Department of Communications to the Canada Post Corporation which makes these reduced rates possible has the effect of reducing and equalizing the postage costs of printed matter received by all Canadians, no matter how far they may live from the point of publication or mailing. It should be noted also that these rates apply to any printed materials mailed in Canada to Canadian readers, regardless of the publication's nationality or content. Therefore the postal subsidy is applied to a vastly greater range of publications than are eligible under the government's programs of direct assistance to publishing described earlier in this chapter.

It has been tempting, in these economically troubled times, to consider recommending the outright elimination of the postal subsidy to non-Canadian publications, to redress partially the economic disadvantages that Canadian periodicals face in competing for Canadian readers; indeed, such a course was urged on us several times during our hearings as a valid tool of cultural policy. We have decided against such a wholesale recommendation because we believe that ease of access to reading materials of all kinds is an important principle of our society. However, *we note that the degree of the postal subsidy was reduced for non-Canadian magazines early in 1982, and we support this policy direction, provided it is accompanied by a continuation of substantially lower postal rates for Canadian publications.*

We have also been drawn to consider whether the postal subsidy (the exact calculation of which has been a matter of some dispute within the government, but which was reckoned to amount to some $189 million in the 1981-82 fiscal year) should be removed from the Canada Post Corporation and used by the Department of Communications for other cultural purposes. We have decided against recommending this course of action also. It would remove a cultural benefit that the Canadian taxpayer has enjoyed virtually since Confederation. Moreover, the burden of paying the additional postal charges resulting from the subsidy's removal would fall directly on readers (particularly for newspapers and periodicals) and on bookstores and libraries (particularly in the case of books, on which the retailer or library must pay shipping costs). Indirectly the burden would fall on already troubled publishers, because their products would become more expensive to consumers.

Other federal measures for books and periodicals already contain an emphasis on public awareness and access, an emphasis that we trust will be maintained. These include the Canada Council's promotion and distribution program, its book purchase and donation program, and National Book

Festival, as well as the marketing components, already discussed, of the Department of Communications program for book publishing. Beyond these existing activities, we would like to see the federal government's cultural agencies and programs making more thorough and concerted efforts to stimulate readers to read – and, in particular, to read the work of Canadian writers in magazine and book form. This aim can be accomplished in two ways: by disseminating more and better information about Canadian writers and their works, and by making those works more readily available.

In reality, we fully realize that reading is a learned pleasure and habit; reading as a preferred activity must precede a taste for reading specifically Canadian materials. Moreover, the reading habit is most easily acquired in a reading environment, and in the creation of such an environment educators and librarians play leading roles. We have chosen, because of the particular mandate of this Committee, not to issue recommendations regarding either the education systems of Canada, which are under a combination of provincial and municipal jurisdictions, or the conduct of public library systems, which are in a similar position (although we comment on the National Library in Chapter 4, "Heritage"). We cannot avoid, however, the necessity of noting how crucial it is that both educators and library professionals realize the high social responsibility they hold in this regard, and that they do their utmost not only to create a reading environment for Canada's young people, but one in which Canadian materials are prominent. This responsibility implies, as an essential first step, the presence of Canadian books and magazines in significant quantities in our schools and public libraries.

Stimulating Demand for Canadian Literature

Federal jurisdiction can, however, touch other prime influences that shape a positive attitude toward reading Canadian authors: the home, the media and the marketplace. Such federal measures would be predicated on an observable but anomalous fact: although Canada has a wealth of good writers, their works are often not widely known or easily obtainable, even in our major cities. We on this Committee have been much concerned by this fact. We have considered to what extent it represents a failing on the part of book and periodical wholesalers and retailers, given that quality Canadian works exist in ample quantity; and we have seriously considered whether the federal government ought to step in to provide some sort of alternative retail or direct-mail merchandising operation, in order to give Canadians more adequate access to their own publications than is currently provided by the marketplace. We have discarded this option, however; we believe that the federal government should support and reinforce Canada's cultural distribution structures, rather than compete with and thereby undermine them. If, for example, the wholesaling or retailing sector came forward with a promising proposal of its own for a Canadian book club – a distribution mechanism that is badly needed in Canada – then the federal government should not hesitate to support it through existing assistance programs. At the same time, the federal government is in no position jurisdictionally to regulate these distribution structures; it must restrict itself to providing positive encouragement to the marketplace on behalf of Canadian authorship.

53.   **The federal government should pursue a broad policy of stimulating public demand for Canadian publications through awareness and incentive measures, with the objective of increasing that demand so that book and periodical wholesalers, retailers and librarians are encouraged to make Canadian products more widely available.**

An essential first step in achieving this wider availability is adoption by the book industry of electronic ordering systems, already partially under way, as mentioned earlier in the chapter, since such systems can make Canadian publications easier for booksellers and librarians to obtain. But increased efficiencies in distribution are only half the battle; by themselves they will not necessarily widen the choice of Canadian titles available to readers outside the categories of new releases and bestsellers. The chances of retailers' stocking a greater variety of Canadian books and magazines will be improved only if the consumer is knowledgable and motivated enough to demand them. In building this awareness and motivation, we foresee a key role for the non-government organization for marketing Canadian cultural products which we have advocated in Chapter 3, "Marshalling Resources."

The advertising and promotion role that we have described for that organization would reinforce and extend publishers' own marketing activities on behalf of particular titles. But it would also generate public interest in reading Canadian writers in general, including areas where exciting new growth is occurring, such as children's literature. In addition, we have envisaged an activity for the marketing and promotion body which would be especially useful in stimulating public demand for Canadian writing: a national voucher scheme providing customer discounts on Canadian cultural products, similar to the Ontario Halfback program which has proved effective in attracting readers into the marketplace to buy Canadian books and magazines. Another valuable function of this organization would be in conducting ongoing assessments of readers' needs and interests, and feeding back the knowledge gained to the professional associations of writers, publishers, booksellers and librarians, for dissemination to their membership. These associations are particularly well organized in the Canadian literary world and should be fully consulted about the planning of the marketing and promotion organization, as well as other aspects of federal policy development.

The other potent force within federal jurisdiction for reaching readers and potential readers is the Canadian Broadcasting Corporation. We would like to see the Corporation make available to Canadians more regular programming that deals specifically with their authors, books and magazines.

We believe that such programming would not only make Canadians more in-terested in Canadian authors and more likely to seek out their works, but would also make good television. As an example of such programming of high quality and interest, we can cite the program "Apostrophes" from France, which receives an enthusiastic reception on TVFQ in Quebec. In addi-tion to providing a regular program of this kind on both its English and French networks, the CBC should make a sincere and concerted effort to become more knowledgable about and sensitive to developments in Cana-dian writing and publishing, so that these can find their way whenever ap-propriate into program content throughout the system.

A Balance of Voices

Sharing in two of the world's great literary languages, Canadians are extraor-dinarily fortunate in having access to a wide range of books and periodicals from other parts of the world. Few countries have borders as open as ours to international publishing. The only danger implicit in this situation is that the very economic and marketing strength of those nations that freely export their publications into Canada can overpower the indigenous book and periodical. That is why the federal government must act to support the posi-tion within the Canadian market of our own writing and publishing resources – for without them, we are like a people without a voice.

We have recommended a number of ways in which that voice can be strengthened, not in order to silence other voices, but in order that our own can be clearly heard. We believe that if our Committee's recommendations are followed, they will assure Canadian readers of access to a balance of Canadian and international writing appropriate to a free society, and will assure the continuation of a vibrant and growing literature.

8
Sound Recording

8

Sound Recording

Sound recording, like broadcasting, with which it is closely involved, has become a pervasive feature of the social and cultural landscape. Recordings – whether on discs or tapes – are with us at many times and in many settings, both private and public. Sometimes we play them on sound equipment in our own homes, but just as often we hear them broadcast over the radio or publicly aired in restaurants, department stores, elevators or airplanes. If we wish, we can even listen to recorded sound while jogging, bicycling or walking down the street.

What we hear on record can depend on personal taste or merely on circumstance. The content may consist of any number of types and styles of music; it may also consist of the spoken word. Sound recordings can appeal to mass audiences, young or old, or be interesting to only small segments of the population. But whatever their content, they share the convenience of being relatively inexpensive and highly portable, and therefore accessible to many: a sound recording is a movable concert hall, stage or classroom, available for enjoying in the place and at the time of the listener's choosing, able to leap time and space to bring the individual into intimate touch with the artist.

Because of these properties, sound recording is a profound force for expanding and democratizing the enjoyment of art, especially music. Young people in particular are touched by this phenomenon. It has often been observed that listening to records or tapes, either directly or on the radio, is the normal way for contemporary youth to encounter music. We have been told that Canada has one of the highest per capita rates of record consumption in the world. Canadians in 1980 spent an estimated $580 million on records.

Clearly sound recording is one of the seminal cultural influences of our times, making music happen "on demand". Yet, paradoxically, the sound recording industry has not usually been included among other cultural industries when major support policies were being considered by the federal government. As described elsewhere in this document, the government has devised policy tools to assist the other cultural industries – book publishing, magazine publishing and film – which have produced demonstrable cultural gains. But in the case of sound recording, such measures have been few. The Canadian Broadcasting Corporation operates a valuable program in which it records some types of Canadian music; the Canada Council provides a small amount of production assistance for "serious" music recordings; the Department of Communications, through a grant to the Canadian Independent Record Production Association, has made possible the introduction of a computer catalogue service (now available through Telidon) for record stores; and in the past the Department of Industry, Trade and Commerce occasionally helped record companies to participate in international record marts. As helpful as these measures are, they constitute only the bare beginnings of a federal policy for Canadian sound recording.

Records and Radio Broadcasting

The one exception to the general rule of federal inaction in this field – and it is a highly significant exception – was the introduction in 1970 of the Canadian content regulations for AM radio. Devised by the federal agency responsible for regulating the broadcast media, the Canadian Radio-television and Telecommunications Commission (CRTC), this measure had the purpose of increasing the exposure to audiences of Canadian performing artists, composers, lyricists and their recordings. In the process, a powerful stimulus was provided to Canadian production of the types of records played by AM stations. The CRTC required that 30 per cent of all music played on those stations be Canadian. For the purposes of the regulations, a "Canadian" recording had to satisfy two of the following four conditions: "the instrumentation or lyrics were principally performed by a Canadian; the music was composed by a Canadian; the lyrics were written by a Canadian; and the live performance was wholly recorded in Canada, or was wholly performed in Canada and broadcast live in Canada."

This single step by the federal government released an immense volume of creativity in the Canadian music world – especially in the popular music field. Many new performing groups were created, recording studios emerged, record producers proliferated and many small companies were formed, leading eventually to the development of a substantial Canadian record production industry. Above all, much new music was created. A new crop of Canadian singers and musical groups arose in response to the content regulations, reaching large audiences at home and around the world, with the result that some of our "pop" artists and groups are stars not only in the eyes of Canadians, but to fans in other countries as well.

Among the most conspicuously successful are Anne Murray, Diane Dufresne, Gordon Lightfoot, Robert Charlebois, Bruce Cockburn, Diane Tell, and Kate and Anna McGarrigle. Years of solid effort by Canadian rock bands have also produced spectacular success recently for groups like Rush, April Wine, Triumph and Loverboy. Their popularity can be measured in gold and platinum records (sales of 50,000 and 100,000, respectively), launched through extensive radio airplay – striking examples of the essential interdependence of radio and record sales, and evidence that if Canadian musical talent is sufficiently exposed on radio, it receives an enthusiastic audience response. The Committee believes that content regulations for television could have similar effects.

Radio as a means of promoting Canadian recording artists has had a somewhat different history in the English- and French-language markets. By the late 1960s Quebec's chansonniers, playing in cafés and boîtes à chansons, had established a strong rapport with a growing audience. Their songs reflected a new-found sense of pride and self-confidence among Québécois, and the chansonniers became local heroes and stars, moving out of the clubs into the Place des Arts for sellout concerts. Some record companies – notably Columbia (now CBS) Records, and the Canadian company Select Records – recognized the market potential in this phenomenon and began to build up what eventually became substantial catalogues of recordings by chansonniers. Soon radio stations responded to the new movement. While some stations continued to program American songs, some with French lyrics, or played recordings from France, others began to play the chansonniers regularly and helped develop audiences and a record-buying public for Quebec songwriters. This important cultural development was by no means due to the efforts of all of Quebec's French-language radio stations. A good portion of the French-language market before 1970 was as ripe to benefit from Canadian content regulations for AM radio as was the English-language market. Today, in Quebec, as well as in English-speaking Canada, record producers need to seek large international markets in order to be profitable. And the problems of the Quebec record industry with respect to market size and costs of production and promotion make the content regulations a necessary stimulus to the French-language market also.

In English-speaking Canada the regulations played a major role from the start. They stimulated not only audience demand for Canadian recordings, but creative effort as well, and made it possible for Canadian musicians to become successful recording artists at home. Today, the AM regulations are regarded by virtually everyone in the Canadian music world in both language groups as a federal government measure that should be maintained, in order to assist Canadian pop artists to continue to flourish and to achieve a better equilibrium between Canadian and international recordings in radio and, thus, in the marketplace.

The CRTC's Canadian content measures cannot by themselves, however, be construed as a sufficient policy for Canadian sound recording. That fact becomes clearer from consideration of the structure and problems of the record market in Canada.

The Canadian market can be characterized as having a mass-market sector and a specialized-market sector. The former consumes nearly 90 per cent of the amount spent annually by Canadians on recordings; it embraces the various categories of pop music, from rock to country to "middle-of-the-road" pop standards and light classics. Such recordings can have worldwide appeal, capturing audiences in the hundreds of thousands and generating substantial profits. But the mass-market sector is also characterized by high financial risk and fierce competition, with the result that a few large multinational corporations tend to dominate both production and distribution, in Canada and around the world. The mass-market sector of the recording industry has been the beneficiary of most of the market growth in recorded music generated by the Canadian content requirements for AM radio.

The remaining 10 per cent constituted by the specialized market is shared by all forms of "serious" or "classical" music, as well as jazz, traditional folk music, most children's records, the spoken word (including poetry and drama), and electronic and experimental music. Records in this market – although occasionally enjoying success on a mass scale – generally appeal to a restricted audience. In the classical music category, nearly all records feature the relatively familiar concert repertoire of the past. Even on the rare occasions when Canadian artists, ensembles and orchestras are featured on these recordings, the music they play is hardly ever written by Canadian composers.

Record companies have taken various approaches to solving the problem of the small market for specialized recordings. One is to select artists and music from the specialized field with the potential to cross over into the mass market. The Canadian independent producer, Boot Records, for example, successfully launched both the Canadian Brass and the guitarist Liona Boyd into the Canadian mass market with extensive promotion. However, as often happens when such a strategy succeeds and the performer's appeal is established, multinational companies absorbed these artists into their own catalogues.

In the case of recordings of symphonic music, substantial subsidies are needed in order to make the investment attractive even to the largest record companies. Until now, subsidies have been provided through special fundraising efforts, and sometimes through grants from the Canada Council. Even so, a contract with a multinational company does not guarantee large sales, financial success or international distribution. It is true that there are benefits in the form of enhanced reputations for the Toronto Symphony, which records for CBS Records, and the Montreal Symphony, which records with Polygram – a company specializing in classical music recordings through its worldwide operating unit, Deutsche Grammophon. (The latter company accounts for 50 per cent of all classical record sales in Canada.) But given the small market for such recordings and high production expenses, it is easy to understand why, even with modest subsidies, recording contracts for symphony orchestras are relatively rare. This is unfortunate, given the fact that recordings function virtually as calling cards, or symbols of recognition, for performing artists and composers today.

If the audience for specialized Canadian recordings is to grow, as we believe it should, new initiatives will be required involving incentives and encouragement from the federal government. We have described the role of radio in increasing the opportunities for the Canadian public to hear and respond to Canadian recording artists in the popular music field. We are convinced that similar measures for specialized recordings, once instituted, will reveal a much larger demand for those recordings than had previously been assumed to exist.

In addition, while the Committee supports the existing content regulations for AM radio programming, we believe that they place too little emphasis on the creative act of composition. When a Canadian artist performs music written by non-Canadians, not only do the royalties go abroad, but musical composition in Canada is not stimulated. More weight should be given to Canadian creative components in music recordings for both the mass and the specialized markets. Recordings have an importance to a composer today not unlike that of the published manuscript of the past.

54.   The CRTC should continue to apply Canadian content regulations to AM radio programming, but the stipulations dealing with the Canadian creative components of broadcast recordings should be strengthened. In addition, the CRTC should reexamine the present regulations for FM radio and devise ways to increase the performance of Canadian specialized recordings on both AM and FM radio.

Production, Distribution and Marketing

If quality Canadian recordings are to be available in sufficient quantity and variety for AM and FM stations to play, and Canadians to enjoy, federal policy must also concern itself with production, distribution and marketing issues.

In the specialized market a recording of symphonic music, which necessarily involves musicians' fees to many players, carries initial production costs of $50,000 or more. In addition, the record producer must cover promotion expenses and provide adequate warehousing, shipping and billing, all without sufficient scale to reap significant economies. And even though a sale in Canada of 5,000 classical music albums represents a "hit," such a sale returns to the producer and his backers only about half their expenses. Facing a loss of $25,000 or more with each "successful" recording, the venture makes no business sense, unless international sales can make up the difference. As a result, very few, if any, Canadian recordings of symphonic music can be made without subsidy. Chamber music and recital recordings cost less, at least in artists' fees, and stand a better chance of being produced, but high marketing expenses make these equally unattractive as investments. In the absence of government support or private subsidy, virtually the only way such specialized records reach the market is either through internal cross-subsidization, whereby companies produce the records by subsidizing the losses with profits from other areas of the business, or through intensive international marketing. Even then, only large integrated companies – those that have diversified into several or all aspects of the recording business, such as manufacturing, distribution, music publishing, record clubs and even retailing to stabilize sales and profits – can afford these measures.

In Canada, the largest record companies are subsidiaries of foreign-owned multinationals, which first established themselves in this country to sell the products of their parent corporations. Besides being large, well-financed and highly integrated, these companies face few barriers to the pursuit of their business goals. They manufacture records and tapes in Canada from imported master tapes, the import duty on which is assessed at the value of the raw tape, although the contents may have cost tens of thousands of dollars to produce. The four largest of these companies dominate the Canadian market, accounting for almost 80 per cent of all record sales in Canada. On the other hand, the 100 or so small Canadian-owned record companies are responsible for producing over half the records with Canadian content. These firms must bear not only artists' fees and studio, promotion and other overhead costs in their entirety, but must also contend with the sheer physical and financial limitations imposed by the geographically dispersed yet relatively small Canadian market.

In other words, Canadian-owned record companies face problems similar to those confronting the Canadian-owned sector of the book publishing industry. In the case of sound recording, the marketplace is controlled by fewer but larger foreign conglomerates, while the Canadian sector is even weaker and more fragmented than in the case of book publishing. Distribution problems are also greater. Since Canadian-owned distribution operations have generally been unable to compete effectively, Canadian record producers find it expedient to turn to the multinationals for distribution and related marketing services which independent producers are unable to afford on their own.

Some Canadian recordings distributed in this fashion move into the international marketplace, conferring upon Canadians artists and groups the status of international stars. However, the ambitions of Canadian composers, songwriters and performers generally are more likely to be realized through the sustained efforts of the Canadian independent producers. While it is true that the multinationals produce recordings of Canadian artists for both the French- and English-language markets in addition to distributing Canadian records, the primary policy of their head offices remains the sale in Canada of recordings that they have produced elsewhere. In view of this situation, the Canadian independent record producer and distributor should be supported and strengthened as the best means of delivering Canadian recording artists to Canadian audiences.

Ninety per cent of all recordings are bought through retail stores. "Full-line" record stores devoted entirely to the sale of recordings tend to acquire their stock directly from record distributors. Department stores and other retail chains selling a variety of products are supplied by a "rack-jobber," a sub-distributor who selects and services their stock and takes back all unsold records for credit. Rack-jobbers now account for over two-thirds of all records bought in Canada. Since their interest lies in the most rapid possible turnover of stock, they tend to limit their choice of records to the widely promoted products. Rarely does one find lesser-known Canadian pop or classical artists – and, even more rarely, Canadian compositions – on their racks.

55. The federal government should assist Canadian-owned companies to distribute and market recordings of "pop" music and of specialized materials recorded by Canadian artists through a loan program or other appropriate forms of subsidy.

56. The federal government should ensure that, for specialized recordings only, subsidy programs are established to assist Canadian-owned companies to produce recordings by Canadian performers, with special consideration given to recordings of which the material is written by Canadians.

For many years the CBC has been active in the recording field. As early as 1946, Radio Canada International began to produce records of Canadian music and artists for distribution abroad through arrangements with broadcasters in foreign countries and through Canadian embassies. RCI's series of boxed sets, each devoted to the works of a single Canadian composer under the title of *Anthology of Canadian Music,* is a notable example. The CBC became active in the domestic record market in 1967, when it began to make recordings for broadcast in order to provide its radio producers with Canadian artists and works as an alternative to imported recordings. As a prime employer of Canada's musical talent and the owner of a powerful promotion vehicle, the CBC eventually offered these recordings to the general public through what is now called CBC Enterprises for the English radio and television networks, and the Ancillary Rights Service for the French network.

The CBC is most active in the field of recorded classical music, although some lighter popular music can be found in its catalogues; CBC Enterprises now offers a selection of close to 400 classical albums and 70 to 80 pop albums. We perceive no serious conflict with private-sector interests if the CBC were to continue to market such records more aggressively. Any concerns about unfair competition from the public sector should be offset by the CBC's practice of leasing its products for distribution by commercial companies. In fact, when it comes to recordings for specialized markets, the CBC should consider offering its own distribution services to independent producers of suitable Canadian materials.

57. The CBC should increase its production of quality recordings by Canadian artists and improve its promotion and distribution of such recordings, extending these services to suitable recordings made by independent Canadian producers.

The CBC is not the only organization active in promoting Canadian recordings. Since 1963, Standard Broadcasting, as a service to other broadcasters, has produced what it calls the Canadian Talent Library, consisting mainly of middle-of-the-road music; it also offers to commercial record companies distribution rights to its catalogue. The Canadian Music Centre, a non-profit national service organization devoted to promoting the works of serious Canadian composers, has recently inaugurated a record production program. This endeavour requires effective distribution and government funding. The Canadian performing rights societies – Composers, Authors and Publishers Association of Canada (CAPAC) and Performing Rights Organization of Canada (PROCanada) – have sponsored valuable record promotion activities. The Juno, Félix and Moffat Awards have been important. And the promotion efforts of the Association du disque et de l'industrie du spectacle québécois (ADISQ), the Canadian Academy of Recording Arts and Sciences (CARAS), the Canadian Independent Record Production Association (CIRPA), the Academy of Country Music Entertainment (ACME) and others must also be mentioned.

Some Canadian radio broadcasters, in honouring their commitments to the CRTC to promote Canadian talent, have organized concerts by rock and pop groups. Recently a few of the larger broadcasting organizations established a fund, to be administered by CIRPA, which will provide forgivable non-interest loans, to be repaid out of income, to Canadian-controlled record companies for up to 50 per cent of the cost of producing master tapes. It is expected that many other broadcasters, as well as other parties interested in the same objective, will also contribute. The fund will focus on pop recordings that can be broadcast widely on radio, probably providing only limited assistance to specialized recordings. The Committee encourages this kind of nongovernment support and hopes that other plans can be devised that blend with equal effectiveness business self-interest and the general public good.

Recording artists in the pop music field – without government support – promote and maintain a close relationship with audiences through live performances and touring, which in turn promote record sales. This interaction between concertizing and recordings is not nearly as pronounced in the specialized music field. A closer working relationship should be established between entrepreneurs, record producers or distributors and such federal bodies as the Canada Council Touring Office, the National Arts Centre and the Department of External Affairs, which arrange and promote concerts.

On the international front, annual trade fairs such as MIDEM (Marché international du disque et de l'édition musicale) at Cannes and others in the

United States offer excellent opportunities to develop sales in foreign countries and to make co-production, exchange and distribution arrangements. It is important for Canada's status in the international community and for the careers of Canadian artists – to say nothing of the economic benefits – that foreign sales of Canadian sound recordings should flourish.

58.   The federal government should assist Canadian record producers to improve the international marketing of their recordings through various means including attendance at marketing fairs.

One crucial aspect of record marketing is the record jacket; attractive jacket design often helps to sell a recording. Such design work also offers creative opportunities to visual and graphic artists, and the Committee suggests that the Contemporary Arts Centre, proposed in Chapter 5, which is to be dedicated to the development and promotion of contemporary visual art in Canada, should provide opportunities for the exhibition of work especially created for this genre.

Technology and Recording

Since sound recording is a technologically based phenomenon, new developments in electronic technology have an obvious relevance to its future. This is true of both the recording process itself and the distribution of records.

The quality of Canadian record production is enhanced by the existence of recording studio facilities meeting international standards of excellence. Studios have opened in many parts of the country, and some meet those standards. As new technologies and equipment are introduced, most recently involving digital recording and manufacturing techniques, these studios need to equip themselves to remain competitive in quality with those in other countries. However, each new development imposes considerable financial burdens on the studios, making it especially difficult for the Canadian operations to adapt. The federal government, through the Department of Communications, must keep abreast of problems in this area; in particular it must assess the impact of customs duties on Canadian-owned studios' ability to acquire new sound recording equipment and decide whether removal of the duty could help those studios without adversely affecting Canadian manufacturers. In addition, with this same goal in mind we believe that

59.   Canadian-owned sound recording studios should be assisted to acquire and upgrade recording equipment through an expansion of existing loan programs, possibly established in association with the Federal Business Development Bank.

New technology also has a great influence on the distribution and retailing of recordings. The rental business in sound recordings is growing alongside the rental of videocassettes. Cable operators are beginning to offer access over their wires to specific recordings selected by users, who are then billed for the service. In the near future, whole libraries of recordings and video images implanted on micro chips could be selected by buyers via satellite or other communications devices. "Home record stores" in the United States are already offering consumers the opportunity to tape, in their homes, musical works provided by the store. As we noted earlier, the Canadian Independent Record Production Association, through a grant from the Department of Communications, offers a catalogue service via Telidon computer terminals to assist record stores to order Canadian recordings. Indeed, most aspects of the industry – from production and distribution to marketing and retailing – will likely be transformed by such technological advances.

The growth in the use of audiocassettes has already raised serious legal and copyright problems. As audiocassette recorders have come increasingly into use, the purchase of blank tapes has grown. Cassette users are making their own copies of recorded music either from borrowed records or radio broadcasts. This widespread practice not only seriously affects record production and sales, but also deprives copyright owners of their rightful royalties. It is difficult to establish a fair and practical mechanism to compensate record companies and recording artists for the significant loss of income caused by this practice. Some countries have levied special taxes on the sale of either recording equipment or blank tapes, assigning the funds thus collected to professional collectives for distribution to copyright holders.

We can envisage one effective way in which a levy on blank audiotapes could serve the goal of stimulating increased sales, and thus increased production, of Canadian recordings. A fixed levy – to be assigned to a fund, administered preferably by a nongovernment body – would be paid by every purchaser of a blank tape. In return, the buyer would receive a voucher, redeemable at the value of the levy (or a multiple thereof) towards the purchase price of a "Canadian recording," with that category of products being fully defined and identified. Retailers would then be reimbursed for the value of the voucher by the record company, and the record company would be reimbursed by the fund. A similar plan could associate a levy on videocassettes with a fund to assist Canadian film and video production.

60.   The federal government should empower a nongovernment, Canadian cultural products marketing organization to administer a discount voucher scheme, based on a levy on sales of blank audiotapes and videocassettes, to stimulate the sale and production of Canadian sound recordings and film and video productions.

The ease with which recordings can be copied has led to the associated problems of piracy and counterfeiting. An enormous business has been built in some countries, including Canada, on the unauthorized duplication in large volume of commercial record albums, tapes and cassettes. Labels, jackets, design and record notes exactly resembling the original product are offered for sale as the genuine article. Even when the vendors of these stolen properties are caught, Canada's out-of-date copyright laws carry such small penalties that the offenders are not deterred. Canada, like other countries, must impose legal penalties harsh enough to make such activities really impractical. Our recommendations on revision of the Copyright Act are to be found in Appendix 2 of Chapter 3.

The Copyright Act also contains provisions for the compulsory licensing of sound recordings. It removes control over their musical content from creators and copyright holders and gives any record company the right to record any music once an initial recording has been authorized, as long as the copyright holders, in the wording of the Act, are paid a royalty of "two cents for each playing surface on each record and two cents for each perforated roll or other contrivance." Since long-playing records, unforeseen when the Act was passed in 1924, contain 15 to 20 minutes of music per side, it has long been evident that the Act needs extensive revision – a process that is finally under way. If compulsory licences are to be retained, the rates of royalty payment obviously need to be substantially raised and brought into line at least with rates in other countries. Alternatively, such compulsory conditions could be removed and rates left to be set through negotiations between copyright owners and record companies.

The Federal Government and Recording

The foregoing analysis calls for federal government recognition of the cultural importance of the Canadian sound recording industry and a stronger commitment to assist the industry in bringing Canadian artists before the public. We believe that our recommendations to that end represent important objectives for the government to pursue in the years ahead, so that this particular cultural industry can be assisted to perform the service of which it is capable.

Although we have not attempted to assign every recommendation to a particular government body, it is appropriate that the Department of Communications, which has established a place for sound recording in its cultural industries directorate, should continue to be deeply involved in monitoring developments in sound recording and consulting widely with participants in the industry in order to shape adequate responses to valid cultural needs. Particular roles in policy development and the delivery of programs must be played by the various bodies that are or should be engaged with the industry: the Canada Council, the Federal Business Development Bank and the

Departments of Industry, Trade and Commerce, Finance, External Affairs, and Consumer and Corporate Affairs. But the Department of Communications should be the catalyst in activating the participation of these departments and agencies within a broad federal policy for sound recording. No matter what the future may bring in the form of new technologies and market pressures, Canada's artists will continue to need this medium to create for and to reach their public.

9
Film

9
Film

Film is a preferred form of art and entertainment for millions of people around the world. From the early days of silent film, through the advent of the "talkies" in the late 1920s and into our own times, the prolific output of Hollywood has continued to dominate the lucrative international movie market. This may affect Canada more than than any other country because it shares with the United States a common border and, for a majority of the population, a common language, and because it has been unwilling to control the access of any foreign film producers, distributors or exhibitors to the Canadian market. Although it now has a film production industry of its own, Canada remains an integral component of the United States market. Neither the production of the National Film Board (NFB) nor of the Canadian Broadcasting Corporation (CBC) has attempted to challenge the domination of our television and movie screens by U.S. feature films.

The Canadian government's first important venture into film production occurred with the founding of the National Film Board in 1939. Not until then were films *about* Canada *by* Canadians made in any quantity. For the most part, these first Canadian films were short documentaries and animated films which have won for the NFB an enviable international reputation over the years. The government's second important venture occurred with the move of the CBC in 1952 into television programming. However, Canadian television programs, whether made by the CBC or by private Canadian networks, are typified by public affairs, sports, light entertainment and news production. They are not often, or often enough, film or video drama.

When the Massey-Lévesque Commission surveyed the Canadian cultural scene in 1951, it noted, "for general film entertainment, Canadians want commercial features; and in this field there is practically nothing produced in Canada." The Commission found cause for concern in that situation. It termed film "not only the most potent but also the most alien of the influences shaping our Canadian life," and it distinguished between more and less benign U.S. influences on our culture when it stated: "The urbane influences of Carnegie and Rockefeller have helped us to be ourselves; [but] Hollywood refashions us in its own image." The Commission's comments were written before the widespread advent of television into Canadian homes. Television has expanded further the influence of U.S. mass entertainment. The substantial part of English-language Canadian television programming filled by movies is almost entirely American in content; French-language television displays only a somewhat better but parallel situation with foreign films.

The reason is simple. Until the 1970s, a feature film industry did not exist in this country to any degree. We lacked the financial resources, the essential underpinning for such an industry, because the Canadian audience is limited in size. The lack of adequate access to distribution and exhibition facilities in Canada has made the audience for Canadians films even smaller. All of these factors tend to make Canadian feature film production unprofitable. It took two major steps by the federal government to begin to change this situation for feature films.

In 1968 the Canadian Film Development Corporation (CFDC) began to provide public financing for Canadian films. Between 1968 and 1974 the CFDC's financing helped stimulate the feature film production effort in Canada. In 1974 and again in 1976, the federal income tax regulations were amended to grant a 100 per cent Capital Cost Allowance (CCA) for "certified feature films" and to allow investors to shelter part of their incomes by deferring taxes in proportion to the CCA. Between 1978 and 1980 feature film production boomed. By taking these two steps, the federal government demonstrated the value of public participation in the Canadian film industry. However, in spite of the increase in the number of films produced in the late 1970s, the industry has not yet established a solid economic foundation – one based on a dependable relationship between film production and film distribution.

There is no doubt that the critical problem for Canada's filmmakers is breaking into their own domestic market. We were told at our hearings that the Canadian market for film is a rich one, that Canada is Hollywood's largest foreign customer. But in the words of one film producer: "We don't have the same access to our own marketplace that others do." A healthier situation for Canadian film, both culturally and financially, would be one permitting Canadian and international audiences the regular opportunity to see and support the works of Canadian filmmakers. This will not happen in the foreseeable future without concerted support from the federal government.

Structure of the Film Industry

As a creative endeavour, film is collaborative; many kinds of artistic and technical skills are required to produce a finished product. As an industry, too, film is collaborative. There must be a working relationship among the three major elements of production, distribution and exhibition. Without such a relationship, a film may be made but not seen. In Canada the tripartite industrial relationship all too often does not work well.

Filmmakers – the directors and producers, screenwriters, actors, cinematographers, composers, designers, film editors – all share the needs of artists in other media. Like other artists, they may lack regular work and income, critical understanding and audience acceptance. They also have particular problems of their own. The tools and services of the filmmaker's trade engender very high costs, when one considers the expense of cameras, film, videotape, editing machines, lighting and sound equipment, animation stands, supporting casts, technical crews, and the use of film and recording laboratories. All of these production elements combine to make film a costly form of cultural expression.

In Canada, both private and public funds are invested in film production. Government participation is channeled through the production budgets of the NFB and the CBC or Canada Council grants. Most independent producers and their backers seek and receive the benefit of public assistance from the CFDC or the Capital Cost Allowance tax incentives or both, although a few independent producers choose to go it alone.

Shooting and editing a film, adding music and sound effects and making copies for distribution are only the beginning. The film must be promoted and marketed, first to the exhibitors – chiefly theatre chains and television networks – and then to the public. This is the role of the distributor, who may therefore play a key role in determining a film's success, even to the point of influencing content and production. Because the distributor plays such an important role and because there are such high financial stakes involved in producing films, it is advantageous if film producers can control their own distribution. For this reason the major production studios in the United States operate their own national and international distributing arms. Until United States antitrust legislation forced a change in 1949, the studios also owned the means of exhibition, the cinema houses. A strong corporate integration structure continues to guarantee that Hollywood studios have marketplace access and increases the attractiveness of investing in Hollywood films. On the other hand, the very integration which attracts money to Hollywood films also makes it difficult for any independent producer (which by definition includes Canadians) to compete in the North American market. Few Canadian producers own their own feature film distribution arms, and such companies handle only a small percentage of the distribution in Canada. If a Canadian film producer is unable to secure a commitment from a distribution company, often Hollywood-based, access to many exhibition markets will not be available. Moreover, the risks entailed in investing in that film will increase.

A Canadian film producer's chances of convincing a United States distributor to promote and market a film are enhanced if the distributor believes the film has a large potential market. In the last year or so a number of Canadian films did find their way into world distribution through major U.S. distribution houses (*Porky's, Quest for Fire, Paradise, Ticket to Heaven*).

The distributor looks for films which can achieve the largest net revenues. The exhibitor has the same concerns in that the selection of films to be shown is made on the basis of attracting the largest audience. For these reasons Canadian film producers may make what many Canadian critics call "American" films but which are, in fact, no more nor less than mass-market films. Decisions about the future of a Canadian producer's films are thus often made by powerful distributors concerned with marketing films throughout the world, not just in Canada. Canadian films which are judged to be of limited marketability are simply not considered.

We acknowledge this dilemma. However, the mass-market dilemma is one of the major barriers to the growth of a genuine Canadian feature film industry. Canadian-produced films will be distributed and exhibited in Canada if ways can be found to compensate for a small market size, a situation no different from that facing the Canadian recording industry.

The problem we are describing cannot be resolved by a policy requiring Canadian ownership of theatres. Indeed, the case of Odeon Theatres – the chain of cinema houses acquired by Canadian interests from the Rank Organization of London, England – gives us ample evidence of a more likely situation if there were such a policy. Shortly before Odeon was acquired by Canadian interests in January 1978, the company stopped honouring a voluntary agreement with the federal government to program a certain quota of Canadian films, an agreement the federal government had negotiated in 1975 with both Odeon and Famous Players Theatres. Although American-owned Famous Players has failed to honour the agreement in full, Odeon has dissociated itself from it entirely, perhaps because it is Canadian-owned and feels protected as such from the need to be more responsive to Canadian films.

The nature of the exhibition market itself is also changing. Today, the major market is often television, unlike a few years ago when the predominant film market was the movie theatre. The television market will become even more significant in 1983 when pay-television is introduced in Canada. Another factor changing the film market is the freedom of choice and privacy of home viewing afforded by films in videocassette and videodisc format.

Canadian Film Production

When most Canadians think of film, it is the dramatic feature film shown in theatres or on television that comes to mind. Yet production of films in Canada has centred in great measure on other types of film. Documentaries of all kinds, including those made for educational purposes, for training, industrial public relations and tourism have been important outlets for film-makers, as have television commercials. All of these have been termed by some who wrote to us the "backbone of the film industry in Canada," providing the basis for the operations of most, by far, of the film companies and a steady source of their revenues. Some, especially those producing educational films, have found a market for their product in the United States and other countries.

Another noteworthy type of film is the "personal" film, made by artists seeking to use and develop the film/video medium as a means for personal, individualized expression. Such film artists have found support from granting agencies such as the Canada Council and those in provincial governments. In all, Canada has had a sustained record of quality non-theatrical film production, especially since the Canadian government formed the National Film Board as its own production agency.

Some of the NFB's production found its way into cinemas as "short subjects" to accompany feature films, but this field has never been adequately developed as a market for Canadian film producers, although there is a move today in that direction. When it comes to feature films themselves, Canada began very slowly. Between 1943 and 1959 only 37 feature films were attempted here, about two films a year. In the next decade the average rose to four or five a year. Because Canadian governments were unwilling or unable to intervene to alter the situation, the level of production remained unusually low for a country so enamoured of film. Other countries have provided remedies for similar situations by directly funding production and distribution services. In many instances they have imposed an exhibition quota for films produced within the country, or levied a box office tax on all films shown in order to provide revenue for redistribution to national film production. In Canada, however, the federal government has been unable to adopt similar strategies because the theatrical exhibition of film falls under provincial jurisdiction. No general federal-provincial agreement on the subject has been reached to date.

Canadian Film Development Corporation

During the 1960s pressure to nourish a feature film industry in Canada began to build. In response, the federal government decided to supply financing for independent production. The instrument chosen to implement this strategy was the Canadian Film Development Corporation. The CFDC was established in April 1968 with a revolving $10 million fund earmarked for equity investment, loans, awards and grants related to Canadian feature film production. The result was a leap in production from the four or five feature films a year of the early 1960s to an average of over 20 a year between 1968 and 1974. In its first year of existence, the Corporation helped launch only three films; but by the 1972-73 fiscal year, it was assisting in the financing of 33 features, of which 20 were made in English and 13 in French. Canadian films, especially those in the French language, were beginning to achieve national and international critical acclaim.

During its first five years, the CFDC's main emphasis was on equity investment in Canadian film, usually limited to half the budget of any film; in addition, in placing its investment, it gave prime consideration to the yield on

the investment, as any banker would. In 1972 the CFDC added a special program to assist, by deferring its cost recovery, the production of low-budget
films. By 1973, however, many investors had become disillusioned with the
Canadian film production industry. The return on investment in Canadian
film was low, and old complaints about the lack of an assured market for
feature films were heard again. The number of films in production declined.
But there was a new complaint as well: the federal tax incentives offered to
Canadian investors did not differentiate between investment made in foreign
films and investment made in Canadian films.

Capital Cost Allowance for Feature Film Investment

The stage was set for the next major federal initiative. In November 1974,
amendments were announced to the Income Tax Regulations which extended the 100 per cent Capital Cost Allowance to investments in feature films
that the government certified as "Canadian." To be certified Canadian, a film
project had to satisfy the Department of the Secretary of State, which first administered the scheme (it is now handled by the Department of Communications), that it employed Canadians in key creative and technical positions. A
point system was used to determine eligibility. In addition, it was required
that a certain percentage of production funds be spent in Canada by Canadian firms. Private capital was attracted into Canadian films because it
created a tax shelter for investors, enabling them to deduct 100 per cent of
their investments in certified features from their taxable income and, thereby,
defer taxes until profits were earned. As a result, another leap in production
occurred. In 1979 there were 67 certified feature films in production. Then
production dropped. By 1980 there were only 59 certified films in production
and in 1981, just 37. The decline has continued into 1982. Having been party
to the production of over 460 feature films since 1968, neither the CFDC nor
the private investors have been able to escape or avoid the boom or bust
climate for Canadian film production. They may even have exacerbated it.

Investors attracted to Canadian films by the Capital Cost Allowance
provisions found, as did the CFDC, that most Canadian films lose money. Of
the $26 million in financing provided by the CFDC during its first decade, only
$5 million was earned back by the CFDC. In the case of the CCA-assisted films,
private investment capital was organized by banks and investment houses
with little experience in the film business. Many producers tried to establish
themselves quickly as a match for well-established U.S. operations. They frequently channeled money into high-budget productions with expensive international stars. Although a few were successful, many of these films were box
office flops; others did not receive the opportunity to be even that, because
their theatre or television distribution could not be arranged.

One could assess these problems as nothing more than the economic
growing pains of an infant industry. But, from a cultural point of view, there
are other problems, too. The mandate of the CFDC is not only "to foster and

promote the development of a feature film industry in Canada," but also to promote the making of films with "a significant Canadian creative, artistic and technical content." Many critics believe tax-shelter movies serve the former objective far better than the latter. Although the tax shelter attracted investors to Canadian film, it also attracted promoters interested in earning high fees for their contributions. Investor resistance to Canadian film promoters grew in 1980 because the large fees paid to investment brokers, lawyers and accountants, over and above those paid to stars and directors, were leading to greatly increased film production budgets. Costs in many instances were so high they could be recovered only with a highly successful worldwide distribution program. As a result, far fewer films have been produced since 1980. The Canadian films that do manage to go into production today are likely to be produced by those with experience and a reassuring track record.

Although the films in production in the late 1970s were financed by Canadian investors and subsidized by the Canadian public through tax shelters, they were films intended for a mass-market, North American audience, not a Canadian one, with the added presumption that Canadians preferred such films. Leading roles were played by U.S. stars. Toronto masqueraded as Washington; Montreal became Chicago. Such films did employ large numbers of Canadian actors and creative and technical personnel. Nonetheless, industry critics charged that Canadian talent was used chiefly in subordinate positions. The Committee is convinced that the federal government's film policy should do more than fight unemployment. If two of the objectives of that policy are – as we believe they are and should continue to be – to enable Canadians to create fresh and distinctive Canadian films, and to enable audiences in Canada and abroad to see those films, then experience to date has proved that the film tax incentive cannot by itself achieve either of those objectives.

A second consequence of the tax incentive demonstrates the same point. French-language feature films, as we have noted earlier, enjoyed a vigorous period artistically during the early 1970s. At that time, the CFDC helped finance approximately two French-language films for every three English-language films produced. This situation changed with the introduction of the 100 per cent Capital Cost Allowance tax incentive. Few French-language films benefited from the tax incentive because, as was noted in the 1976-77 CFDC annual report, "there was a continued reluctance on the part of investors to finance French-language films since their international market potential is more limited than for the English-language films." The average French-language film budget was substantially lower (often below $500,000, with some of the earlier films budgeted below $200,000) than the English-language films (which often cost over $3 million). Yet in 1978 and 1979 almost two-thirds of the French-language films made were produced without benefit of the tax incentive.

A third consequence of the film tax incentive was its impact on the role of the CFDC. As the Capital Cost Allowance incentives stimulated the flow of large amounts of private capital into English-language Canadian features, the role of the CFDC as an investor became considerably less significant. The CFDC changed its emphasis from providing equity financing for lower-budget Canadian features to one of providing interim or bridge financing for films to be financed eventually by private investors using the tax shelter. This change affected the way the CFDC attempted to achieve its objectives when making decisions to invest. The CFDC became a banker looking to investment brokers for recoupment. In 1981, the CFDC broadened the scope of its programs to in- clude not only support for commercial feature films but also for short films and video productions, something it had not done before, and for documen- taries and television dramas. If these changes mean that cultural values begin to play a greater part in the CFDC's financing decisions, then federal film policy may be moving in a desirable direction.

The National Film Board as Pioneer

Canada's strong record in non-theatrical film production has already been mentioned. For many years the National Film Board was the primary source of Canadian film production. In its initial phase, the NFB's activities were geared to the war effort. Following that period, it redirected its production ac- tivities to include short films of high artistic and technical quality while still continuing to fill the film needs of government departments, at their expense and according to their needs.

The NFB has been a world pioneer in developing such film and video techniques as three-dimensional film, the use of hand-held cameras, synthetic and stereophonic sound, sound synchronization techniques, and a variety of animation techniques. The NFB has served as a training ground and ex- perimental laboratory for many of Canada's filmmakers who have achieved international reputations: Norman McLaren, Claude Jutra, Gilles Carle, Michel Brault, Tom Daly, Sidney Newman, Anne-Claire Poirier, Colin Low, Kathleen Shannon. The NFB has helped train much of the broad base of technical and creative talent active throughout Canadian film production. It has helped other countries in similar ways. Important, too, has been the NFB's engage- ment with Canadian social issues through, for example, its "Challenge for Change" series and the work of Studio D, its women's unit. A high point in the NFB's history of imaginative ability and achievement was reached with its Labyrinth pavilion at Expo 67 in Montreal. A large collection of international awards attests to the NFB's prestige.

It is impossible to imagine the history of filmmaking in Canada without the initial, nurturing presence of the NFB. However, today the NFB no longer occupies a central position in Canadian film. It continues to issue film and video productions from its facilities in Montreal, to distribute its products through a network of 27 offices across Canada and abroad, and to procure films for government departments. But it is independent production which now attracts many of the skilled filmmakers who once were drawn to the NFB. This is true not only of television commercials and feature film production, neither of which the NFB was ever expected to produce, but true also of the documentary film, in which the NFB was once preeminent. Even within the public sector, the NFB's mandate "to interpret Canada to Canadians and to other nations" has been increasingly assumed by the CBC's news and public affairs programming.

The Canadian Film Market

The best available data from Statistics Canada tell an instructive story about filmmaking and film distribution in this country. According to 1980 figures, the most recent ones available, the largest revenue source by far for Canadian film and video production companies in the private sector was the television market. There were 292 production companies in the private sector, and 27 had annual revenues of over $1 million. These companies reported that more than 30 per cent of their revenues came from selling and renting television programs and almost 41 per cent were derived from television commercials, for a total of 71 per cent. Less than 24 per cent of their revenues were derived from non-theatrical sources – such as schools, libraries, government, industry and private individuals – and the smallest revenue source of all was the theatrical market, the movie theatre chains and independent cinemas. Only 3 per cent of the production companies' revenues came from feature films and a bit more than 2 per cent from shorts.

The private sector film and video distribution companies reported a very different picture. In 1980, the distributors received 47 per cent of their revenues from the theatrical market. But of that 47 per cent, less than 3 per cent was generated by Canadian film and video productions and, in the television market, which represented 42 per cent of the distributors' revenues, Canadian production occupied less than 8 per cent of the 42 per cent. Although the non-theatrical market was also the smallest revenue source for distributors, at 11 per cent, Canadian production generated over 41 per cent of that 11 per cent.

From these figures it is clear a very serious distribution bottleneck faces our film and video productions. The problem is greatest in the largest segment, the theatrical market. The theatrical market is highly integrated with the United States market; both Canadian and U.S. theatres are supplied chiefly by distribution companies which are integrated with the major Hollywood studios – Columbia Pictures, MGM-United Artists, Paramount Pictures, Twentieth Century-Fox Films, Universal Films, Warner Communications. These studios have the greatest control over what theatres exhibit because they control the "blockbuster" Hollywood releases, which are what the theatres want.

Statistics Canada also reports that in 1980 foreign-controlled distribution generated 72 per cent of the theatrical revenues in Canada and 65 per cent of the total distribution revenues. In that same year, the six largest United States production-distribution companies distributed only a few Canadian feature films. The organization representing these companies in Canada, the Canadian Motion Picture Distributors Association, told us at our public hearings in Toronto in July 1981 that the distribution of Canadian features by major U.S. companies had improved. However, it is still evident that the distributors' greatest self-interest lies in promoting a Hollywood-type product in the Canadian marketplace. They have little commercial interest at present in distributing Canadian films if the primary market is Canada because, as we pointed out earlier, the distributors believe more money will be made by distributing films to a mass North American market than by developing a uniquely Canadian market for Canadian films. To change this situation would require the participation of several federal agencies.

A New Film Policy for Canada

We hope to see distinctively Canadian films made with high artistic and professional standards. We also hope that Canadian and international audiences have an adequate opportunity to view these films. The twin issues of production and marketing, content and demand, are equally important to us. Nowhere are these two issues more intertwined than in the area of film and video. Both film and video production and the government's film policy itself have survived their birth trauma and troubled childhood. Both are now ready to embark on a new maturity.

No single federal policy instrument is enough by itself to encourage a healthy Canadian film industry, from either the cultural or commercial point of view. A Canadian feature film, produced for even a reasonably low budget, will, it is assumed, earn some of its revenues from distribution in theatres and through pay-television sales, but it will probably also need help from the CFDC, the CBC and other federal agency programs. *We urge the government to evaluate its film policy instruments, each one in relation to the others, in order to see them all as a package able to channel public and private funds into the making of distinctively Canadian films for Canadian and world audiences. Public and private resources must complement each other.*

Financing Film Production

In spite of its shortcomings in serving Canadian cultural values in film, the Capital Cost Allowance tax incentive has proven capable of attracting the large amounts of capital required for making feature films. And in spite of its financial limitations, a federal organization such as the CFDC is in place and ready to serve the objectives of a renewed Canadian film policy. What is now required is a pragmatic partnership between these two resources to finance the production and distribution of good and attractive Canadian films for audiences everywhere.

Some genuine emphasis in government policy must be restored to the words "good" and "Canadian." Only Canadians will make Canadian films. Therefore, the criteria by which films are judged eligible for Canadian government assistance, whether by the CFDC or by the administrators of the certification system, must ensure not only substantial majority participation by Canadian creative personnel but also Canadian control of production. As for "good" films, a new way of dealing with questions of quality must be introduced into government film financing decisions. This goal can be accomplished by providing the CFDC with a mandate and resources to play a more aggressive role in government film policy. Close working relationships and consultations with filmmakers are essential. Finally, there must be decisive government action to ensure effective public distribution of the films whose creation is being financed with the public's money.

A Canadian film policy structured along these lines would recognize in fact what has long been acknowledged in theory – namely, that such a policy is motivated by cultural goals and only secondarily by industrial or commercial ones. This approach would counter a widespread tendency to assume that the United States audience and the mass-market values of the distributors serving that audience are the only arbiters for Canadian commercial audiences. Two salient facts have been missing from the debate on Canadian film policy. First, some Canadian films would be able to support themselves in the Canadian market alone *if* they were made with moderate budgets, had adequate access to distribution and exhibition throughout that market, and were assured government financial assistance in the early stages of production. Second, it should be remembered that internationally celebrated directors such as Kurosawa, Bergman, Truffaut or Fellini have made an impact on the world in part *because* their films are so quintessentially Japanese, Swedish, French or Italian.

We believe that additional federal funding will be needed by the CFDC if we are to produce quality Canadian productions for television and cinema screens. We also believe a substantial demand for assistance is justified until profitable markets are established. With these considerations uppermost in our minds, we recommend the following.

61.   The Canadian Film Development Corporation should have its role and budget substantially enlarged so that it may take bolder initiatives in financing Canadian film and video productions on the basis of their cultural value and professional quality.

In assessing these latter two considerations, the CFDC must not itself become an arbiter of Canadian content or taste; we anticipate the CFDC drawing consistently on the advice of a broad and varied range of film professionals to guide its financing decisions. The CFDC should also resort to the full range of financing options provided for in its Act – the subsidies and loans as well as the equity investments – to fulfil its cultural mandate. The CFDC would not be expected to recoup its funds quickly or even at all in some instances, although there is no reason why films selected by the Corporation for encouragement because of their cultural values should not also be chosen by private investors who seek profits. Good films can also be profitable ones.

Filmmaking, as we have already noted, requires large quantities of capital. Films cannot be produced without a large infrastructure. For that reason, some government fiscal instruments should be designed to encourage the investment of private funds in the development of independent Canadian production companies. Fiscal instruments that foster one-shot film projects should be avoided in favour of those which can promote a sustained film production industry over the long term. Now that some experience has been acquired with the Capital Cost Allowance, this objective should be more readily attainable.

62.   The Capital Cost Allowance tax incentive for investment in Canadian film production, or at the very least some equivalent incentive, should continue to be used in order to channel private capital into Canadian filmmaking.

Fiscal instruments which seek to channel large sums of money to a particular project are more efficient if very few restrictions are placed on their use. The larger the number of restrictions, the smaller the volume of funds attracted by the fiscal instrument. There is, in other words, a trade-off between the cultural objectives sought by the certification requirements and the industrial or commercial objectives of attracting funds to the industry. The greater the certification requirements, the less efficient the instrument. Striking the right balance is important. It is because we believe fiscal inducements are not very efficient cultural instruments – although they are efficient industrial tools – that we believe the CFDC should play a larger role in filmmaking activity, over and above any current fiscal inducements.

In areas of production outside the feature film field, we would expect the CFDC to exercise rigorously the part of its mandate which empowers it to finance short films and video productions. We anticipate then that documentary and other "small" filmmakers would turn to the Corporation as their principal federal source of production assistance.

We also think it is reasonable to propose that the operations and project funding of film organizations and film cooperatives should be provided by the CFDC, a responsibility currently exercised mostly by the Canada Council. We believe there is much to be gained from bringing the many aspects of the film and video world into close contact with each other because of the interdependence that characterizes that world. The efficacy of service and umbrella organizations could best be measured by a CFDC which would be functioning within the heart of the industry; even film cooperatives could benefit in the long run from such a relationship. On the other hand, the activities of what we had earlier called "film artists," whose concerns may fall within either the film or video medium, should continue to seek funds from the Canada Council. We assume that the CFDC would seek advice on its funding decisions from the filmmakers and from all agencies involved in film activity, including the Canada Council and the National Film Board.

Finally, the certification and other aspects of the operation of the Capital Cost Allowance tax scheme for film should continue to be administered by a small, efficient staff within the Department of Communications. That department should be able to monitor these functions closely.

Financing Film Distribution

Such measures as we have recommended for strengthening the cultural content of Canadian film production must be complemented by similarly strong action to ensure Canadian films access to Canadian screens. Because the major foreign-controlled distributors in this country have not shown sufficient interest in Canadian films to assure a promising future for a truly indigenous production industry, we believe that Canadian filmmakers' best hope lies in allying themselves with a Canadian-controlled, strong distribution industry. The capital necessary to build up participation by Canadians in this aspect of the industry – namely, marketing Canadian films successfully to Canadian theatre and television audiences – could be provided directly or indirectly by some or all of the following methods:

- Subsidies could be provided by the Canadian Film Development Corporation or the Department of Communications on the basis of a percentage of a qualifying company's revenues from distributing Canadian films. This method could be designed using as a model the sales and marketing incentive for Canadian book publishers which has been established by the Department of Communications.
- Loans could be extended to Canadian-owned distributors, either from the Canadian Film Development Corporation or through the Federal Business Development Bank. These loans could be guaranteed by the CFDC, scaled to the company's distribution of Canadian films.
- An incentive equivalent to the Capital Cost Allowance for production could be extended to investment in Canadian-controlled film distribution companies, scaled to their distribution of Canadian films.

63. The federal government should provide the Canadian-controlled film distribution industry with the economic strength to market Canadian films successfully to Canadian and foreign audiences through all channels of exhibition and sales.

In addition, we propose that the National Film Board's foreign distribution and sales function be integrated into a new "Film Canada" operation with the Canadian Film Development Corporation as the responsible operating agent working closely with other departments and agencies. The present NFB offices outside Canada, at least the appropriate and effective ones, would form the basis for this operation. The new organization would assume most, if not all, of the functions now performed by the NFB, the Department of External Affairs, the Department of Communications and the CFDC itself for promotion, sales assistance and exhibition of Canadian films outside Canada. As we note in Chapter 11, "International Cultural Relations," under the section on promoting and marketing abroad, a start has been made on presenting a unified approach in international markets by three of these bodies: the Department of Communications, the CFDC and the NFB. An extension and consolidation of this initiative into the operation we are proposing seems appropriate.

Film Canada would concern itself with the international prospects for all Canadian films from all sources because we have no wish to limit the viewing of Canadian films solely to Canadian audiences. Filmmakers as individuals, not just federal or provincial government offices, would be able to take advantage of the services offered by Film Canada. Any increased international exposure of Canadian productions from whatever source will be in Canada's best interests, to say nothing of the benefits to be earned from sales outside the country. In some instances such sales are absolutely essential to the ability of some film projects to recover their costs. For such ventures it can be a matter of "export or die." In any case, the possibilities for wide sales, stimulated by a greatly increased worldwide demand for film and video software, could make a significant difference to Canada in economic terms if our potential in film production, promotion and distribution can be realized. Film Canada should aim to make that possible.

The Film Festivals Bureau now operating within the Department of Communications should be part of this new operation. This would enable support for domestic film festivals as well as participation in international events to be better coordinated with all other film activities and interests.

If the film industry is strengthened economically, it will have a chance to become profitable, to attract private investment and, at the same time, to serve an important Canadian cultural objective.

Exhibition of Canadian Films

The area of theatrical exhibition is under provincial government jurisdiction; nevertheless, we cannot omit some comment addressed to the provinces on this central point. We believe provincial governments have a responsibility to their own citizens to make a home for Canadian films in Canada, whether by exhibition quota, levy or any other means they consider appropriate. If the federal government continues to play its part in fostering the development of indigenous Canadian film, the provincial governments may see their own roles more clearly.

A New Role for the National Film Board

The course of recent events has altered the historic place and role of the National Film Board. The Board's output of new work no longer represents a significant film experience for the Canadian public. Its short films are seldom shown in Canadian theatres because theatre owners do not believe these films have audience appeal. Nor are current NFB productions a staple of either television programming or even the curricula of educational institutions in Canada. The NFB's displacement from centre stage has occurred for a number of reasons, of which institutional inertia is not the least important.

Three decades ago, the Massey-Lévesque Commission recommended that the NFB "develop its research and experimental work in documentary films and especially in films designed for information and instruction." In 1951 the NFB's legislation was redefined and its resources and facilities expanded. At that time the NFB had strong support from the individuals and public bodies presenting briefs to the Massey-Lévesque Commission. At our own public hearings in 1981 we did not find that same level of support. Much has changed in the world of film and video since 1951. Television news and public affairs programming and private sector film and video production have all assumed much of the NFB's function in providing "information and instruction," as well as in "interpreting Canada to Canadians."

The National Film Board's situation becomes particularly questionable when we consider its high level of funding. In 1981-82, it spent about $66 million, $48 million of which was provided by a parliamentary appropriation. Some $28 million of its budget went into the production of 57 original films and 45 other audio-visual items; another $16 million was spent on its distribution operations and facilities. As a point of comparison, in the 10 years between 1968 and 1978, the Canadian Film Development Corporation invested a total of only $26 million in Canadian films; in 1979, according to a study on the film industry prepared for this Committee, the actual cost to the federal treasury of the 100 per cent Capital Cost Allowance tax incentive for film investment was probably not more than $14.5 million; and in 1980-81, the Canada Council's entire budget for individual artists and organizations in film and video was less than $2 million.

We suggest the time has come for the government to reappraise and redefine the mandate of the National Film Board in a manner consistent with its historic role as pioneer and leader in the film industry. The NFB's share of the federal government's resources for film cannot be justified if judged by the cultural benefits Canadians now receive from the NFB. We recommend a new direction for the NFB because we are convinced it is possible to build on the Board's current strengths in order to allow it to contribute significantly to Canada's film needs in the 1980s and beyond.

64.   The National Film Board should be transformed into a centre for advanced research and training in the art and science of film and video production.

There is a need for research in the field of the moving image, and the National Film Board should be in the vanguard of that research. The Board's original mandate required it "to engage in research in film activity and to make available the results thereof to persons engaged in the production of films." In carrying out its responsibility, the NFB earned a position as a leader in the evolution of cinema. We would like to see the NFB emerge in the future as the unquestioned leader in this field, a role it is well equipped to fill, provided it is allowed to concentrate on that goal and equipped with sufficient resources for the purpose.

Filmmakers who have shown an interest in new communications technology and techniques have all too often worked in a vacuum. The proposed new NFB would reach out to users and other research centres, collecting and disseminating useful information. Workshops and seminars would help to spread information about the Board's activities, and to relate its work to all aspects of film and the film industry. Because its research would be planned and implemented with the participation of related federal agencies, provincial film and broadcasting bodies and the private sector, the NFB would contribute to a wider pooling of knowledge and the effective exploitation of the resulting benefits. In our view, such a centre would enable Canada to play an innovative role in the film and video technologies that are so critical to the cultural life of this country.

Centres for advanced research inevitably become centres for advanced training. We would like to see the NFB develop as a centre with training activities that extend and complement those of Canada's educational institutions. If successful, the new NFB would attract aspiring young filmmakers of unusual talent and ambition, as well as experienced film artists seeking artistic renewal. We believe filmmakers from other countries would also be attracted to such a centre. It is in line with Canada's, and the NFB's, traditional generosity that the Board would lend its expertise to filmmakers in Third World and other countries, and would invite them to hone their skills here.

The new NFB would continue to be engaged in film and video production as part of its training and research. But it is our conviction that its production should be limited to what would be required by these activities. The experimentation with new techniques, the innovative work in new areas, the training of filmmakers – all would determine the level of production to which the NFB becomes committed. The role we envisage for the NFB will enable it to achieve a new prominence in the world of film and video arts.

As a new mandate for the NFB is realized, a number of the Board's current operations can be assumed by other federal agencies.

- All film and video needs of federal government departments, now handled by the National Film Board on their behalf, should be filled by independent producers.
- The Department of Supply and Services should set up a coordinating and advisory service to handle tenders and supervise contracts to independent producers under Treasury Board scrutiny. Close working relations between independent film producers and departmental employers should be encouraged.
- As described earlier, the NFB's foreign distribution and sales functions should become part of the Film Canada operation under the auspices of the CFDC. The NFB's present offices would become centres for the sales, promotion and viewing of Canadian film and video production, both public and independent.
- Over the past 40 years, the NFB has accumulated a valuable film library which should be available to be seen by Canadians. We believe the realization of the distribution potential of these films falls well within the operating mandate we are proposing for the CBC in Chapter 10. Given control over the NFB film library, its maintenance, packaging and repackaging, the CBC could widen the distribution of NFB films to Canadian audiences. We anticipate that before long the cumbersome and costly method of showing visual materials on film stock will be replaced by the use of videodiscs or videocassettes, a more easily managed format for inexperienced users. We would like to see our hundreds of public and school libraries become more effective distributors of audio and video productions than the 27 NFB offices have been in recent times. We propose that the CBC become responsible for that development, melding its own library with that of the NFB. The actual maintenance of the film vaults and the safe preservation of the NFB film library should be assumed by the Public Archives of Canada, which has already accessed hundreds of hours of CBC radio and television programs.
- In the field of still photography, the NFB's technical, processing and commercial activities should be taken over by the Department of Supply and Services, including the functions of the Canadian Government Photo Centre and the NFB Photothèque. The valuable collection of stills which is available for a fee to government departments and commercial users alike should be maintained and developed as a useful service.

- The pioneering and much-praised achievements of the NFB Photo Gallery should be built upon. The Contemporary Arts Centre, which we have proposed in Chapter 5, would become a suitable venue for that collection, providing an exhibition space that links still photography with other contemporary art forms, and developing publications, catalogues and other promotion devices to encourage a better understanding and acceptance of the art. This Centre would, in effect, take over the principal activities of the NFB Still Photo Division.
- The government would be advised on film activities and policies not exclusively by the National Film Board under its new mandate, but also by the Canadian Film Development Corporation, the Canadian Broadcasting Corporation, the Canadian Radio-television and Telecommunications Commission and the Canada Council.

Creative Leadership

We are confident that the measures we have proposed here and in Chapter 10 will result in more films and video materials being made on behalf of enlarged and receptive audiences inside Canada and elsewhere. We have sought to clarify the roles to be played by government participants in the film industry which will provide a more fertile environment for Canadian producers and distributors to make and promote films that reflect Canadian sensibilities. This in turn will mean that Canadian writers, directors, designers, editors, composers, performers and technicians are more likely to have a medium within which they can work and thrive.

As in most other areas of the arts, Canada has proved that it can generate film artists and technicians of the highest calibre. Until now the best of them have had to seek their livelihood elsewhere, depriving Canada of their talents. Hollywood's studios and boardrooms are well populated with Canadian performers and directors; the film and television screens in the United States, France and Britain attest to that. It is time to lure these artists back. We must ensure in future that talented Canadians remain in Canada, so that Canadian audiences and the domestic industry can benefit directly from their efforts, and so that the rest of the world can enjoy what these artists produce from the vantage point of their own land.

10
Broadcasting

10
Broadcasting

Television and radio broadcasting have preoccupied us a great deal throughout our deliberations. The fact that we, and those who submitted briefs to us, expended much time and thought on this complex and challenging subject is a reflection of its importance in contemporary life. Canadians actually see more films and dramatic productions on television than in cinemas or theatres, and for most people, radio is a major source of music. Through the broadcast media we also obtain news, information and commentary that influence our attitudes to many issues of the day – social, political, scientific and cultural. It is no exaggeration to say that broadcasting continually colours and even shapes the way we see the world around us.

Our broadcasting system itself has been a central issue of public debate for several decades now. Canadians care deeply about broadcasting because they expect so much from it. Yet at the same time, there has been a struggle to maintain a vigorous Canadian presence within a broadcasting system that is so plentifully supplied with popular foreign programming.

That particularly Canadian struggle received its greatest challenge from the introduction of network television in the 1950s and from the later spread of cable services. Today the Canadian broadcasting system faces challenges of perhaps equal magnitude resulting from continuing and rapid technological changes. As always, such changes bring with them opportunities and dangers; the emerging broadcasting environment will change the ways in which television and radio programs are delivered and received, but it will also challenge our creative talents and our collective resolve. If we respond imaginatively, this Committee believes that the prospects for a genuine improvement in quality Canadian cultural expression will be greatly enhanced. If we respond too timidly, it is difficult to assess how great the damage will be, but we are convinced that it will be significant.

We shall examine the nature of some of these technological changes, describe the problems now facing the Canadian broadcasting system and recommend ways of achieving the goals that we believe the system should have. Because television is where most of the changes are taking place, we shall concentrate on it particularly, though not exclusively.

The Emerging Broadcasting Environment

In the best of circumstances, forecasting the future is a risky business; when everything seems to be changing at once, it is even riskier. But the following list of the changes that the broadcasting environment is likely to undergo in the next decade or so includes several developments that are already under way. The formulation of rational and effective cultural policies for broadcasting requires an understanding of these changes and their consequences. The intelligent public discussion of broadcasting issues makes such an understanding imperative.

Here are some likely features of the emerging broadcasting environment in the very near future:

- The number of Canadian households served by cable television will probably increase by the year 2000 to nearly 85 per cent of all households. The percentage of cable subscribers able to receive more than the 12 basic channels, through the use of converters or cable-compatible television receivers, is likely to grow from 30 per cent in 1980 to close to 100 per cent in 1990.

- A variety of new cable-delivered home services – such as emergency medical alert, burglar and fire alarm, banking, catalogue shopping, information and distance-learning programs – will soon be provided.

- At least one out of four Canadian households, it is expected, will own either a videocassette or videodisc unit capable of recording and playing television programs and films.

- Telidon-type videotex terminals will be more widely used, accelerating the use of interactive services involving two-way communication. Such services will be distributed by cable, fibre optics, telephone, terrestrial transmitters and Direct Broadcast Satellites (DBS).

- Satellites will transmit more powerful signals than at present, enabling them to be received by small, low-cost earth stations or "dishes." By 1986, several satellites originating from the United States will probably be in operation, sending messages directly into homes through dishes whose cost will be no more than that of a colour television set. The signals from such Direct Broadcast Satellites will spill over into Canada, becoming available to most of our population, although some of these signals will require a decoding unit to "unscramble" them.

- A dramatic increase in user-pay services – both of the pay-per-channel and pay-per-program variety – will occur. Service will be provided through several cable "tiers," each offering a distinct package of services.

- Audio and video retrieval systems permitting the user to call up specific programs will become common. Electronic video games and music are already being sent to some cable subscribers from a centralized computer.

These changes will have important consequences for broadcasting in general and for Canadian broadcasting in particular. If these consequences are disregarded by policy-makers they can cause serious damage to Canadian creative expression and culture. But if they are properly taken into account, they can usher in a new era of development for Canadian creative talent and for the participation and enjoyment of Canadian audiences. We focus on two of these consequences in the next few pages, because they appear to us to be the most important for a critical evaluation of current Canadian broadcasting policies and for the formulation of strong workable alternatives. Other effects, important in different contexts, are mentioned only briefly.

Increased Program Choice
The first and possibly the most important effect of the emerging broadcasting environment is that viewers will have a greatly increased choice of programs. To an extent, the control over programming is passing from the hands of broadcasters to viewers and listeners. This phenomenon, which has been taking place increasingly for many years, results in a fragmentation of audiences which is often observed with a jaundiced eye by broadcasters.

This fragmentation of audiences – or, to put it more positively, the increased capacity of viewers to watch programs of their own choosing – is not solely a technological phenomenon. It is true that the technology will enable viewers to choose among a hundred channels (some provided as a basic service, some for a price), to rent or buy a large variety of videocassettes, to call up programs, games and other services from centralized computer memories. But that freedom of choice will also be derived from the fact that viewers will pay for what they watch, whereas under the prevailing arrangements, programs are paid for by public funds and by advertisers, so that viewers have to take what is given them.

When broadcasting is partially or wholly paid for by advertising, broadcasters search for the largest possible audiences. Large audiences mean high ratings and therefore large advertising revenues. Since there is a limited number of channel or station outlets, many potentially good programs are not produced. Even though there might be an audience large enough to allow them to be produced profitably, there are other programs with even larger audiences that are still more lucrative and these win out. If television programs were sold to audiences, as in the case of pay-television, broadcasters would, in many instances, search for and find profits with relatively small audiences.

As we shall see in more detail later, the search for the largest possible audiences has shaped many of the features of broadcasting as we know it today: large networks, syndication of programs, broad similarity of content at any time period, and a lack of specialization in types of programs.

With audience fragmentation – or freedom of choice for viewers – the nature of networks will change. Already new types of networks are appearing, such as those being established to provide pay-television services, as well as new cable networks such as the ATV-2 service in the Atlantic region. Television broadcasters will probably become more specialized in the production of programs, provided they have a market large enough to yield a profit. Thus there will be much more variety in the television programming fare available, satisfying many more minority tastes. The key task for Canadians will be to exploit the new possibilities in an enlightened way, and this Committee welcomes the opportunities that the emerging environment offers for Canadian creative talent, present and future.

Broadcast Regulations and Balanced Programming

A second consequence of the emerging environment will be its effect on Canada's broadcasting regulations, from policies for the licensing of stations to Canadian content requirements. As the new environment takes shape, it is inevitable that the role of the regulator will change. In the past it has been possible to use regulation to exert a major influence on the broadcasting system; but with so many new programming sources available to the consumer, regulation of broadcasting as an instrument of policy will be transformed.

Canadian network television began 30 years ago. But for some time before that, many Canadians living near the United States border had been buying television sets and antennae to pick up American shows. In 1952, at the inauguration of Canadian Broadcasting Corporation television services in Montreal and Toronto, there were already some 146,000 television sets in Canadian homes. The motive for launching television in Canada was to provide a Canadian alternative to U.S. programs. The CBC proceeded to establish a microwave delivery system that eventually carried its programs over a 4,000-mile communication network into more and more Canadian homes. Because it was the only service in many regions, because of the great interest of Canadians in American television programs, and because of the desire to compete for the station loyalty of border residents, the English network of the CBC filled about 40 per cent of its schedule with foreign – mostly American – programs. The proportion for the French network was about 25 per cent. Practices to regulate the use of the limited frequencies for television were adapted directly from radio, where they had been introduced very early to control use of the airwaves.

Partly to demonstrate the government's desire to remain at arm's length from CBC programming decisions, and partly to reduce the cost of CBC television to the public purse, revenues were to be sought from two sources: advertising and licence fees paid by television viewers. This strategy had the effect of forcing the CBC to compete for audiences at a time when it was also being influenced by United States broadcasting styles. The CBC's first competition came from U.S. border stations and soon extended to private broadcasters in Canada. As early as 1953 a private English-language station opened in Sudbury, followed a year later by a private French-language station in Quebec City. By 1958 there were 36 private stations operating in this country.

Although the viewer licence fees were abolished in 1953, to be replaced by an excise tax of 15 per cent on television receivers and parts earmarked for the CBC, the advertising component of the financial strategy remained. Advertising has been kept as a source of revenue for CBC television to this day. Yet its presence can no longer be justified on the grounds that it keeps government at a distance, because gross advertising revenue represents only about 16 per cent of the Corporation's income. We shall examine the effects of that mode of financing later in the chapter.

One of the elements of the philosophy of Canadian broadcasting regulation that is still with us today is the view that there is a "single national system" in which privately owned broadcasting is supposed to cooperate or at least coexist with the state-owned network. (Until the creation of the Board of Broadcast Governors in 1958, the private broadcasters were actually regulated by the public network.) Associated with the notion of a "single national system" is another principle which still plays a central role in regulation, that of "balanced programming." Balanced programming was intended to produce a mixture of programs with something for everyone in the course of a week.

A new Broadcasting Act in 1968 made it clear that the broadcasting system as a whole, including both elements – the publicly owned and the privately owned – had to provide balanced programming. The rationale for this prescription was that many Canadians had access to only one service, usually the CBC, and were entitled to the mixture of programs that other Canadians enjoyed, including news, public affairs, sports, variety entertainment, American comedy and drama, and so on.

In the future broadcasting environment described earlier, all Canadians will have access to a multiplicity of television channels. A continuation of the Broadcasting Act's principle of balanced programming by the CBC will lead only to a duplication of programs, a phenomenon that is already too much with us. As we emphasize later on, what Canadians need from the CBC is an alternative to private broadcasting. That is the only way to have true balance in the broadcasting system as a whole, in the spirit of the 1968 Act.

One ingredient in the "balance" which has always created a special problem and which flows from one of the objectives of the Broadcasting Act is Canadian content. The problem of Canadian content stems from two facts: first, it is much cheaper to acquire a foreign program than to produce a domestic one of equivalent quality; and second, foreign, especially U.S., comedy and drama tend to attract larger audiences than Canadian equivalents because they can be more heavily promoted and because the larger market to which they are sold makes it possible to invest larger sums in their production, thus often enhancing their appeal.

We leave for later discussion the analysis of regulatory practice for Canadian content. We simply note here that the introduction of cable television in the late 1950s massively aggravated the problems of regulation with respect to Canadian content. Cable has advantages over conventional off-air reception. It can provide clearer pictures because it overcomes the difficulties created by obstacles, such as mountains and high buildings, that interfere with signal diffusion, and it also makes possible the reception of programs that are out of reach of the typical home antenna. Canadians subscribed to cable for these reasons. But another motivation, which soon dominated all the others, was the opportunity to receive U.S. stations showing programs from the three big networks – the Columbia Broadcasting System (CBS), National Broadcasting Corporation (NBC) and American Broadcasting Company (ABC) – and documentaries, music and drama from the Public Broadcasting System (PBS) network. Once Canadian cable services were authorized, a flood of American programs poured onto Canadian television screens.

In the new broadcasting environment, these problems of Canadian content will be multiplied. Large numbers of Canadians everywhere will be able to rent or buy videocassettes and videodiscs from stores as close as their newspaper and magazine stands, making the world's movies and television programs instantly available. With the use of small satellite dishes able to receive U.S. signals, we will have access to shows and games distributed all over North America. It will then become much more difficult to regulate Canadian content effectively. Under such circumstances, the only alternative would seem to be a completely different approach to the Canadian content question.

Problems of the Present Broadcasting System

Section 3 of the Broadcasting Act of 1968, which is still in force, describes the government's objectives in broadcasting. These can be summarized as follows: the broadcasting system is to be a "single system," to be "effectively owned and controlled by Canadians" so as to "safeguard, enrich and strengthen the cultural, political, social and economic fabric of Canada." It should offer a varied, comprehensive choice of programs, permitting a "balanced opportunity for the expression of different views on matters of public concern." The programming of each broadcaster is to be of "high standard," "using predominantly Canadian creative and other resources." The system must provide educational services.

The Canadian Broadcasting Corporation is required to offer services in English and French, which should be extended to, and serve the needs of, all parts of Canada. It must also balance "information, enlightenment and entertainment for people of different ages, interests and tastes." It must promote the "exchange of cultural and regional information and entertainment." Finally, the CBC must "contribute to the development of national unity and provide for a continuing expression of Canadian identity."

To achieve these objectives, the federal government has two instruments: the Canadian Broadcasting Corporation, of course, and the Canadian Radio-television and Telecommunications Commission (CRTC), which is the body that regulates the CBC, the private broadcasters, cable television and telecommunications.

It is not easy to determine the extent to which the objectives listed above have been achieved. The task is difficult partly because the objectives are vague and largely unmeasurable, and partly because they are inconsistent. For example, the broadcasting system is "effectively owned and controlled by Canadians," but has that safeguarded, enriched and strengthened the cultural fabric of Canada? Does each broadcaster use "predominantly Canadian creative and other resources"? Are the needs of regions adequately served by the CBC? The answers to all such questions depend on how the terms are defined.

This Committee, however, believes that those objectives which are properly cultural have not, on the whole, been attained as fully as they could have been. The Canadian broadcasting system probably serves industrial and economic objectives fairly well. But as a dynamic promoter of Canadian creativity, as an intermediary between creative expression and Canadian audiences, it has not done as well as it should have. The reasons for this shortcoming are not to be sought in the motivations or competence of individuals. Nor is it the search for profits or the desire for individual job security which is at fault, but rather the operation of economic forces, human mechanisms and counterproductive public policies – all of which can be altered.

In the pages that follow we shall consider each of the major components of the Canadian broadcasting system individually. We begin with the CBC and the private broadcasters, after which we examine cable and satellites and conclude with a discussion of the CRTC.

The Canadian Broadcasting Corporation
The CBC is a large organization broadcasting in both French and English. It owns and operates 31 originating television stations and 62 originating radio stations. The CBC also has arrangements with 31 television affiliates and 81 private radio affiliates to deliver a portion of CBC programming to areas where it does not own a station. With 304 television and 666 radio rebroadcast transmitters the CBC spreads its signals into smaller communities. It operates a shortwave international service – Radio Canada International – which is described in Chapter 11, "International Cultural Relations," and a Northern Service for radio and television which broadcasts to the Yukon and the Northwest Territories and to the most northerly regions of the provinces. Finally the CBC delivers, via satellite to cable television systems, the House of Commons debates in both official languages.

According to its annual report for 1981-82, the CBC's current expenditures totaled $792.6 million for that fiscal year. Parliament provided $598.5 million of that sum; $131.5 million was earned from advertising sales; $12.2 million came from other sources including interest, the sale of international rights and other marketed products; $45.9 million was accounted for by expenditures that did not require cash outlays, such as capital depreciation and amortization, provision for vacation pay, etc.; and a deficit of $4.5 million was registered. In addition, Parliament appropriated $66 million which was used to finance depreciation and other of the above items. The CBC employs about 12,250 people in television and radio.

The foregoing facts provide some indication of the Corporation's size and the amount of the federal government's expenditures on culture it absorbs. They also suggest its potential importance for cultural policy. Given these facts and the responsibilities they imply, it is not surprising that the CBC has been the largest single employer of Canadian performing and writing talent for many years. The development of that talent can be credited especially to both the French and English services of CBC's AM and FM radio networks. These have long been providing music, drama and literature to Canadian audiences; commissioning new works from writers and composers; sponsoring competitions, public concerts and music festivals; presenting live concerts played by Canadian orchestras; and producing broadcast recordings featuring Canadian musicians and some Canadian music.

The Use of In-house Talent
Unfortunately we cannot credit CBC television with the same creative initiative and intellectual leadership as we do CBC radio. It is true that Canadian television production teams have been able to develop within the Corporation, and that occasionally Canadian orchestras, opera or dance productions and theatre companies are featured on CBC television. It is also true that a number of drama series produced by the CBC have provided outlets for talent, and that efforts have been made to provide a training environment for new talent of all sorts. But on the whole, relative to the total sums expended, the contribution of CBC television to Canadian cultural expression has been meager. Of course comparisons with the private networks in these matters are flattering to the CBC, since private broadcasters do too little to promote cultural activity. But we do not think it appropriate to evaluate the CBC's performance in this way. We should rather like to draw attention to the CBC's modest use of the large pool of Canadian talent that we know is available and waiting to be drawn upon.

To obtain some quantitative appreciation of the use made by the CBC of outside talent, we note that in 1981-82, CBC radio and television networks combined, in all their services, paid out less than 9 per cent of their total expenditures in fees to musicians, writers, actors and performers, a percentage that falls to 6 per cent when non-unionized freelancers are excluded. Less than 2 per cent of total expenditures were made outside Ontario and Quebec. These are small numbers, which we suspect would be even smaller in terms that are truly meaningful if the CBC's accounting practices provided definitions for the terms used in reporting how its money is spent.

This Committee fully endorses the criticism heard during our public hearings that CBC television is not sufficiently open to Canadian creative talent and, more importantly, that it does not foster the growth of that talent sufficiently. We believe that the CBC should, in fact, act as a magnet attracting creative talent from all over this country, and should provide opportunities for critical, dissident, daring and original voices that otherwise have no means to be heard.

Clearly the CBC relies too much on in-house talent. We do not believe it does this because it is badly intentioned or because it wants to deny access to "outsiders." It is not motives that are at fault but institutional dynamics. Good intentions, in whatever amount, would do nothing to resolve the serious problems the CBC now faces. The reason why institutions like the CBC tend to rely to such a great extent on in-house services relates to the privileged position of one sort or another which those organizations occupy in society. Because some are able to operate as monopolists (sole suppliers) or quasi-monopolists, they eliminate virtually all the pressures of competition to operate more efficiently – such as eliminating wasteful practices, cutting back on redundant and unproductive personnel and, in general, searching for more effective ways of doing things. The result is a hardening of creative arteries and protection of the institutional status quo. The CBC is that type of over-protected operation. It is not a monopolist, but the fact that it receives so much of its gross income from Parliament effectively shields it and its employees from having to respond to changing circumstances.

There is another element which is important to consider in explaining the particular position of the CBC. In seeking, quite rightly, to defend its arm's-length status and also, but with much less justification, in fighting to retain a position of power within the Canadian broadcasting system, the CBC has developed a tradition of secretiveness which extends to virtually every arm of its activities. This secretiveness has shielded it from criticisms which could have helped it to deal more effectively with its problems of bureaucratic inertia and its sorry labour relations, and could have assisted it toward a sounder relationship with the arts and culture of Canada at whatever stages of development they may be. This is not a new phenomenon. The reports and decisions of the CRTC are witness to this fact, as are the reactions of the CBC to the recommendations these contain. The Corporation's attitude was decried by the Committee on Broadcasting, chaired by Robert Fowler in 1965, a Committee that seems to have had access to more information and to more analysis and documentation from the CBC than was revealed to this Committee during our 11 encounters with officials of the Corporation during our public hearings.

We are aware that CBC management is deeply concerned about its inability to make more effective use of the cultural and artistic talent of the country, and about its apparent helplessness to serve as a force in developing strong new talent through television. The protracted strikes of the National Association of Broadcast Employees and Technicians (English services) and the Syndicat des techniciens du réseau français (French services) in 1980 and 1981 over the capacity of the CBC to use "outside" talent testifies to that fact. The settlement, which essentially guaranteed that there would be no reduction in "in-house" production, was not very helpful in resolving the problem, since only a fraction of new money can be allocated to "outside" production.

Effects of Advertising on Programming
A second serious problem of CBC television – one that we heard about throughout the entire country during our public hearings – is how little it differs from other broadcasters. To put the issue in exaggerated form, CBC programming has become almost indistinguishable from the fare offered by other television networks. The statement is exaggerated because, as we have noted earlier, the CBC does present a variety of programs which private broadcasters do not, but the proposition contains more truth than fiction. Section 3 of the Broadcasting Act, it will be recalled, requires "balanced" programming on the part of the CBC – an objective that necessarily tends to lessen its ability to provide a distinct programming alternative.

However, the main force that robs the CBC of a more distinctive character is not the Broadcasting Act but the search for larger audiences, which it must undertake in the competition for advertising revenues. When the new "broadcasting environment" we described at the beginning of this chapter has moderated the influence of the advertising market on programming, it will be much easier to appreciate fully the multiple effects of that mode of financing on programs. Nevertheless, there is enough evidence to allow us to form a judgment now.

It is important to stress that the effects of advertising on programming are not closely related to the volume of advertising: the effects are much the same whether these revenues account for a small or a large fraction of a broadcaster's gross income. These effects go beyond the fact that commercial messages occupy so many minutes per hour of screen time. More importantly, the resort to commercial revenues has a profound influence on the kinds of programs that reach the screen in the first place, especially in prime time. Without any direct intervention by sponsors in production or programming decisions, producers make programs and broadcasters schedule them with a view to achieving the real purpose of commercial broadcasting – namely, the delivery of large audiences to paying advertisers.

This process has two consequences: first, it induces producers to make programs that have great similarity to each other, and second, it leads all Canadian broadcasters – including the CBC – to compete with each other for the acquisition of those foreign, mostly American, programs that are expected to draw large audiences. This, incidentally, drives up the price of those programs. Competition between the CBC, CTV and Global networks and some independent broadcasters for American programs means that Canada pays considerably more for those American shows than does the United Kingdom, for example, with a market nearly three times the size of Canada's.

It is possible to appreciate further the effects of advertising by examining what has happened to CBC radio since it dropped advertising in 1974-75. One result is that CBC's radio programming on both its AM and FM networks has become distinctive rather than imitative. It addresses many kinds of minority interests and has carved out a special programming role of its own, becoming the main source of radio drama, serious music, children's shows, public affairs, and science, literary and arts coverage, in addition to its first-rate news coverage. Whether by coincidence or not, these changes have been accompanied by increases in the size of audiences. Nationally, the CBC's English AM network share of audiences rose by 50 per cent between 1973 and 1980. In the Toronto and Vancouver metropolitan areas, the increases were 100 and 133 per cent, respectively; in the Montreal area, the increase was 20 per cent.

An additional and striking measure of the effects of advertising on programming can be obtained by observing the difference between the programming of commercial television stations, to which we must add the CBC, and the provincial educational stations of Radio-Québec, TVOntario and Access Alberta.

As long ago as 1974, the CRTC argued that "commercial activity deflects the CBC from its purpose and influences its philosophy of programming and scheduling. It must, in the Commission's considered opinion, be reduced or even eliminated entirely." We concur with this view, and would emphasize that a reduced reliance on advertising is not sufficient: it must be eliminated.

We are aware that the search for programs that attract large audiences has been exacerbated by the CBC's agreements with its 31 affiliated television stations, which extend its coverage to about 20 per cent of the general population, and deliver approximately one-third of the CBC's total French-and English-language television audience. Although the affiliate agreements confer the benefit of low-cost coverage, they present two serious disadvantages. They do not provide for transmission of the entire network schedule, or even all of the culturally significant CBC-produced programs. In addition, the agreements are a continuing source of frustration for both parties. "From the Corporation's point of view," the CRTC wrote in its 1974 renewal decision, "the use of private affiliates restricts the network's flexibility and results in limited or constrained distribution of some CBC-produced Canadian programming. The affiliates, on the other hand, complain that the CBC reserves the largest amount of peak viewing hours for its network programs without distributing to the affiliates a sufficient proportion of the revenue from sales within these programs." Five years later, the Commission's 1979 decision noted an irony in the fact that "public financial support is provided to some affiliates to assist in a partial distribution of CBC Canadian network programming, while at the same time the CBC schedules U.S. mass entertainment programming, especially in peak viewing hours, to ensure such partial distribution."

One of the important effects of the combined reliance on "in-house" production and advertising revenue has been a reduction in the CBC's ability to devise programming that truly fulfils its role and objectives as a public broadcaster. It has been argued that the heart of broadcasting is programming and that other questions, such as the locus of production and whether advertising is used or not, are peripheral. We believe the issues that may appear peripheral from a given angle are really central, since they determine how the heart beats, how programming is done.

Loss of Audience Support
A third problem faced by CBC television, especially its English service, is that it is losing audience support. Between 1968 and 1980, according to CRTC and CBC figures, the share of the audience watching CBC English-language television fell from 35 to 18 per cent, while that of its affiliated stations fell from 12 to 5 per cent. In the same period, CTV audience share rose from 25 to 30 per cent, and that of the US channels from 24 to 32 per cent. (These percentages do not total 100 because independent and other stations are not included.) The picture is a bit brighter for French-language television: from 1968 to 1979 the audience share for CBC French-language television rose from 40 to 42 per cent while that of its affiliated stations declined from 12 to 3 per cent, and that of TVA (Télédiffuseurs associés) rose from 48 to 53 per cent. (These percentages do not total 100 because independent and other stations are not included.) The picture is a bit brighter for French-language television: from 1968 to 1979, the audiences watching CBC-owned stations rose from 40 to 42 per cent while those watching its affiliated stations declined from 12 to 3 per cent, and the audiences for TVA (Télédiffuseurs associés) rose from 48 to 53 per cent. These figures take into account programs such as hockey and football games, "specials," and variety shows, as well as American programs, all of which attract a large number of viewers.

To deal with some of these problems, the CBC has proposed adding a new half-hour per week of Canadian drama to its television schedule and to offer on cable, through a second service labeled CBC-2/Télé-2, a repackaging or rebroadcasting of certain of its Canadian programs, supplemented with some new productions. The philosophy underlying such a proposal is that more exposure of Canadian programs would increase audience size and foster a greater interest in these programs.

We certainly concur with the intent of this projected move. All the recommendations of this Report are predicated on the belief that if Canadian creative work is encouraged and made available to Canadians it will be appreciated. We believe, however, that the idea underlying the proposed second CBC network is too timid, because it does not really address the needs of the emerging broadcasting environment as sketched out earlier in this chapter. That new environment will require more specialization, more repackaging and rebroadcasting and, in particular, much more original production than envisaged by the second network proposal.

The Private Broadcasters
The private television broadcasting system is made up of 26 English stations affiliated with the CTV network, 6 French stations forming the TVA network, 31 CBC affiliates and 23 independents. The private radio system consists of 349 AM and 144 FM stations, for a total of 493. There are 101 French stations, 392 English stations and several networks. (If we add the 41 AM and 24 FM CBC-owned stations, we obtain a grand total of 558 radio stations in Canada.)

Virtually all the revenues of private broadcasting come from advertising. In 1980, according to Statistics Canada, these totaled $610 million for television and $392 million for radio – over $1 billion altogether. Television accounted for some 23 per cent of the total amount expended on advertising in

Canada, and radio 15 per cent. Together these media absorbed over 38 per cent of advertising expenditures in Canada for that year.

In radio many of the stations are group-owned, with the largest groups reaping almost half of total revenues. According to Statistics Canada, total employment in 1981 in private radio broadcasting stood at 9,693, reflecting its size and importance in the system.

As television wooed audiences away from it, radio adjusted quickly. It became almost exclusively a local service, airing local news and information, disc jockey programs, and some talk shows. Today the system is in virtual equilibrium, with growth occurring only in the number of FM stations to accommodate the steady increase in the acquisition of FM receivers. The concentration on "pop" music, which makes up so much of private radio's programming, is offset by the CBC, which no longer competes for the pop audience and has been able to establish a separate programming niche for itself. There is general satisfaction with the nature and quality of the Canadian radio service, which is perhaps best illustrated by the fact that only about 1 per cent of Canadian audiences listen to non-Canadian radio stations.

Private radio is regulated by the CRTC, which requires that AM stations program Canadian music in 30 per cent of their air time devoted to music (see Chapter 8, "Sound Recording"). Regulations governing FM radio are motivated by a desire to avoid duplication of programming and to encourage alternative approaches. Regulations therefore prohibit simultaneous broadcasting of AM programs on FM and require a certain amount of "foreground format," so that "the intrinsic intellectual content of the matter being broadcast is entirely related to a particular theme or subject" in blocks of at least 15 minutes. The regulations also call for the CBC and private FM stations linked with an AM station to allocate 20 per cent of their broadcast time to such programming between the hours of 6:00 a.m. and midnight; the proportion for the private independent stations is 12 per cent.

Like private radio, private television is supported almost entirely by advertising revenues. In 1981 private television employed 6,841 people in programming, production, sales, promotion and administration. Although not quite as large as the CBC, the private system is nonetheless a large and significant element in broadcasting, as indeed it should be in promotion and expression of culture in Canada generally.

A Responsibility for Cultural Programming
Private television is regulated by the CRTC, and from the point of view of cultural policy the most significant regulatory requirement is Canadian content. The main characteristics of Canadian content quotas are examined below (under the heading of the CRTC). Suffice it to note here that, although these quotas were resented initially by private broadcasters, they have not been particularly constraining.

One's expectations of the cultural program content of private television are not very high, and these are usually borne out. Private television uses little Canadian talent and expends few resources to develop new talent. The airwaves and cable are regarded as carriers to be exploited for profit. Few private broadcasters seem to display a sense of responsibility for the development of the arts and other aspects of cultural life in Canada, notwithstanding the content regulations.

The CRTC has persisted, nonetheless, and has even attached specific conditions to the granting or renewal of private television licences. For example, in a recent decision regarding the CTV network, the CRTC stated that: "It is a condition of this licence that 26 hours of original new Canadian drama be presented during the 1980-81 broadcasting year, and 39 hours of original new Canadian drama be presented during the 1981-82 season." The CTV network appealed this decision, which was upheld by the Federal Court of Appeal; the Supreme Court has recently upheld the original CRTC decision.

The question was, and remains, how best can the private television system fulfil its cultural responsibility? We acknowledge that the Canadian content rules and conditions of licence are costly to the private broadcasters because implementing them may cut into profits. But no one – still less the public authorities – should confine an analysis of program performance to the costs imposed on broadcasters by these rules and conditions. There are at least three other measures of public policy which are designed to maintain or improve the profitability of private television broadcasters, and these have to be considered together with costs.

The first is Section 19.1 of the Income Tax Act, which disallows as a business expense advertising by Canadian companies on U.S. stations that send signals into Canada. Second, there is the CRTC's ruling which permits a Canadian station to substitute its own advertising for that of a U.S. station whenever the two stations are broadcasting the same show at the same time. Since this means that American advertising messages are deleted under the circumstances, the ruling simply maintains or even increases the Canadian broadcaster's audience. Third, there is the tax shelter asssociated with the 100 per cent Capital Cost Allowance on investments in Canadian film and video productions, including those for television. (We discuss the Capital Cost Allowance and its effect on the film industry in Chapter 9.)

Consider first Section 19.1 of the Income Tax Act. As noted, the provisions of the Act disallow the claiming of advertising expenditures on foreign stations as a business expense for taxation purposes, but by the same token, they allow deduction of these expenditures when programs originate on a Canadian station irrespective of the fact that the advertising is placed on U.S.-produced shows. Consider next the CRTC's substitution ruling. This regulation probably militates against the interests of Canadian producers, since it encourages the purchase of American shows that will appear in prime time, at the same time that those shows are programmed by the originating U.S. networks. Since these shows elicit premium rates, the prospects for Canadian-produced shows in those same time periods are seriously reduced. Finally, there is the tax shelter. Whatever the value of this measure from a cultural point of view, relatively little use of it is made by producers of television programs because of the limited demand for Canadian shows.

There can be no doubt about the value of these three measures to private broadcasters. From the point of view of this Committee, which sees cultural policy as the promotion of creative and artistic expression as well as the access of audiences to that expression, these measures have to be viewed as elements of an industrial policy, not a cultural policy. It is imperative that in setting content requirements and in granting licences, the CRTC consider the costs and benefits of *all* measures affecting private broadcasters. Private television broadcasting, in our view, does have a cultural responsibility – to provide information and quality entertainment.

Cable and Satellite Systems
There are 505 cable systems licensed by the CRTC throughout Canada, each one a monopoly in the area it serves. These systems reach about 4.5 million homes and in 1980 generated revenues of $352 million. The industry is highly capital-intensive, with fixed assets in 1980 valued at nearly $390 million. Although Canadians are already large purchasers of cable services, the pattern of growth continues – from 46 per cent of homes in 1977 to 50 per cent, 52 per cent and 55 per cent in the following years. Canada is now one of the most "cabled" country in the world; 59 per cent of all Canadian households were subscribers to cable television at the time of writing.

Cable operators currently offer their subscribers a number of channels; only about 130 of the 505 Canadian systems offer the full 12 channels on the "basic" service. The CRTC requires that priority space on these channels be allocated to Canadian stations, and the clearest spots are assigned to the CBC. In most locales the cable operators offer U.S. network programming through American stations, and it is to receive this service that most householders subscribe to cable in the first instance.

Many subscribers also rent or buy converters, which open up a selection of many more channels. Some 83 cable systems offer supplementary channels for converters, providing up to 30 channels and a variety of services. Not all the stations carried by cable operators to fill these channels offer different programs; there might be CBC or CTV programs on two or more stations, as well as duplication resulting from the simultaneous broadcast of U.S. programs by Canadian stations. But for those who use converters in the major centres, there has been a shift from channel scarcity to channel abundance. As time goes on, the variety of entertainment and information provided on cable channels will increase sharply. Some new television sets have built-in converters with a capacity of 122 channels. When programming becomes available on these channels, the effect on viewing habits and therefore on programming and advertising will be dramatic.

In March 1982, the CRTC inaugurated a new type of cable service when it issued licences to six pay-television programmers to sell their fare to homes ready to pay the price. Two companies were licensed to provide a national service, the remaining four to operate within specified regions. Pay-television is expected to begin operations in Canada in early 1983, with subscribers paying a monthly fee that will be split between the programmer and the cable operator or other exhibitors. It is expected that this service will stimulate further cable subscriptions. The CRTC has required Canadian program production from pay-television licensees according to individually applied formulae, and a special requirement has been worked out for the multilingual licensee in British Columbia.

As early as 1971 the CRTC asked cable operators to allocate a portion of their revenues to Canadian program production, encouraging them to establish community channels in order to satisfy certain local needs. Later attempts by the CRTC to get 10 per cent of cable revenues committed to community programming were not generally accepted. Independently, the CRTC's attempts to get broad cable industry commitments to establish channels for repeating Canadian programs were not acceptable to broadcasters.

At present, virtually the only major contribution made by cable television to Canadian programming is through activities on community channels and through some limited, but notable, special cable channels and programs. Examples are: children's and multilingual channels; programs teaching the French language; coverage of selected community and political events; carriage of the parliamentary proceedings produced in both official languages and distributed via two satellite-to-cable networks by the CBC. In the Montreal area, Télécable Vidéotron has been allowed to experiment with a variety of new services which are provided on separate channels – such as arts and entertainment, science, education, sports, and children's and recreation programming.

The cable industry should be able to contribute more to Canadian creative video production. It is true that the CRTC has consistently refused to allow the cable industry uninhibited entry into program production except for community operations. Beyond the protection it gives to the profits of broadcasters, this policy is a guaranteed buffer against the inherent conflict of interest facing a cable carrier that has to choose between its own production and that of a competitor. If the CRTC and the Bureau of Competition Policy of the Department of Consumer and Corporate Affairs had the mandate and the will to enforce conflict-of-interest guidelines, it might be possible to contemplate with some equanimity the idea of carriers becoming producers and broadcasters.

But because both bodies have so far not been rigorous enforcers, either because of a failure of will or lack of coercive authority, one must assume that if carriers become producers there will be little to prevent them from giving priority to their own programs when conflicts of interest arise, as they are bound to do. In this regard, it is important to point out that "experiments" such as the one connected with Télécable Vidéotron, mentioned above, do not and cannot test anything, nor prove anything relevant to the question because they are being conducted outside a competitive context. Hence one cannot evaluate what would happen under actual conditions of competition.

Nevertheless, means should be sought to put some of the revenues from cable television at the service of Canada's program creators, on whose output Canada's cultural activity in this medium depends. The business of delivering video and audio signals must be not an end in itself but a means of achieving cultural goals. The ease with which imported messages can be acquired makes cable carriers critical players who must fulfil their proper role.

In addition to Canada's leadership in cable, the Canadian government and its agencies have been and continue to be pioneers in the development of satellite services. Telesat Canada was the Western world's first operator of domestic satellites, and the CBC was the first public broadcasting agency to provide satellite-delivered programming. The first operational Anik satellite was used by the CBC to provide services to northern communities.

Unfortunately, as has been the case with other technical pioneering efforts, Canada seems to be losing its preeminence in satellite use to other countries, notably the United States. This is occurring in spite of the fact that CANCOM (Canadian Satellite Communications Inc.) is now licensed to carry multichannel radio and television programs via the Anik A-3 satellite to remote areas. In addition, Canada's Anik C is the first satellite system with sufficient power to make practical a Direct Broadcast Satellite (DBS) mode – that is, one that will enable services sent directly from the satellite to be received by individual homes through a small and inexpensive dish.

If cable television posed a threat to Canadian broadcasting because of its importation of U.S. television stations, it is sobering to contemplate what the impact will be when a host of U.S. services can be received via satellite anywhere in Canada – not just in locations near the border or where cable systems exist. Restrictions are not the solution. In the long term no government or regulatory agency can, or should, prevent the public from obtaining access to the foreign programs and services it wants. *But if Canada is to retain a programming presence in its own broadcasting and telecommunications system, it must use all its technological and creative resources to provide Canadian programs and services that Canadians want to see and hear, programs that are competitive in quality with those from other countries.*

Canadian Radio-television and Telecommunications Commission

The Canadian Radio-television and Telecommunications Commission (CRTC), the successor to the Board of Broadcast Governors (BBG), is the regulating agency of the federal government for broadcasting and telecommunications. Two of the many activities that the CRTC regulates are particularly important from the point of view of cultural policy – namely, licensing and Canadian content (although some licensing rulings are subject to cabinet appeal).

CRTC decisions on the number of broadcasting licences and, most importantly, on the method of allocation of these licences to applicants, are among the determinants of the profitability of broadcasting operations in Canada. More specifically, by restricting the number of licences, by attaching weaker conditions to a licence, or by deciding not to auction licences to the highest bidders, the CRTC can raise the value of a licence. Its decisions can also have the opposite effect.

Historically the CRTC has paid considerable attention to the economic viability of outstanding licences in deciding whether or not new ones should be issued and in this way has made itself a party to the profitability of Canadian broadcasters. It has also attached performance requirements to licences, perhaps as a quid pro quo for the high profits. But in general these requirements for better performance have not been rigorously enforced.

The inherent conflict here, as in many other areas of cultural policy, is between an industrial and a cultural strategy. If the airwaves, cable systems and other common carriers are to be exploited to achieve the largest possible addition to Gross National Product (GNP), then cultural and artistic objectives are impediments to those who benefit from a larger GNP and who will then seek to have the impediments reduced. It is important that this conflict between industrial and cultural goals be acknowledged. The tendency of federal cultural policies, so apparent in the licensing practices of the CRTC, to stress the complementary nature of these goals instead of their competitiveness is generally counterproductive from the point of view of culture.

Canadian Content Requirements
As an instrument used by the CRTC to implement cultural objectives, Canadian content requirements deserve special attention. The first Canadian content requirements for television were implemented by the Board of Broadcast Governors (BBG) in 1960. After public hearings, the Board announced that 55 per cent of all broadcast time must be Canadian in content and character. Protests by private broadcasters were immediate. In response to those protests, the averaging period was altered from one week to four weeks and no special quota was imposed for prime time. The transition period was extended, with no quota the first year and only 45 per cent in the second. The full requirement of 55 per cent was to be effective in 1962.

To appreciate both the strength of the protest and the weakness of the BBG, it is useful to consider how broadly Canadian content was defined. This history is significant, because it summarizes the attitude of private broadcasters toward cultural objectives and the position of the regulatory body.

"Canadian" production was defined (in 1960), rather generously, as follows:

- any program produced by a licensee and to be broadcast by the licensee;
- news and news commentaries;
- broadcasts of events taking place outside Canada in which Canadians were participating;
- broadcasts of programs featuring "special" events outside Canada and of general interest to Canadians (the funerals of Sir Winston Churchill and of President John F. Kennedy, the World Series, etc.);

- one-half of programs produced in Commonwealth countries or in the French language;
- programs, films or other productions made in Canada.

In March 1962, the BBG wanted to return to its 55 per cent rule, not only overall, but also during prime time (6:00 p.m. to midnight). Protests flared anew. In May, the prime-time quota was reduced to 40 per cent and then waived altogether for the summer months (as was done again in 1963). Commonwealth and French-language productions were given full credits and programs from Commonwealth and French-speaking countries dubbed in the other official language were given one-quarter credit.

In 1965, the situation had reached a point which led the Fowler Committee on Broadcasting to charge that even though private broadcasters earned very high rates of return, they were not providing the services contemplated in the Broadcasting Act. That Committee charged also that the BBG had come to represent only the interests of broadcasters.

The next step in developing Canadian content requirements was taken in 1968 with the creation of the CRTC (at that time, the Canadian Radio Television Commission; the change in name, although not in acronym, took place in 1976). New regulations, which were aimed more at controlling foreign content than Canadian content, were announced in 1970. They required a 60 per cent quota of Canadian programs both for the whole day and for the period between 6:30 p.m. and 11:30 p.m., averaged on a calendar quarter. They also proposed restricting the maximum amount of programming from any one foreign country to 30 per cent and eliminated the special treatment of French-language, Commonwealth countries and "special" feature programs.

If there had been protest in earlier years, the reaction this time resembled a bitter attack; the powers of the CRTC were questioned and the possibility of court action mentioned. Private broadcasters put pressure on the Commission through the press and through the parliamentary caucuses. In 1971, the CRTC caved in. Prime time was redefined as 6:00 p.m. to midnight, the limit on programming from a single foreign country was raised to 40 per cent, and the averaging period was changed from calendar quarters to a full year.

Private broadcasters maintained the pressure. In 1972, the CRTC announced further relaxations. Private broadcasting now had to achieve only 50 per cent Canadian content in prime time (while the CBC continued at 60 per cent), and all restrictions against program importations from any one country were completely abolished. Preferred treatment was accorded to productions of Commonwealth and French-language countries.

This gloomy account clearly indicates that the method of regulating content which has been used for the last 20 years does not work. Some other solution must be found to ensure that cultural values and goals are not completely expunged from private broadcasting.

Content regulations were disliked by broadcasters because they reduced profits, and liked by others (such as actors and musicians) because they raised their earnings. These are legitimate concerns, although not necessarily the most helpful in ensuring quality of cultural expression. Content regulations have been attacked on the grounds that they are a manifestation of economic nationalism – like the National Energy Program or the Foreign Investment Review Agency. Arguments based on that kind of reasoning have sometimes been put forward as a way of disguising self-interest, but they have also been advanced as bona fide intellectual arguments.

Whether they are a manifestation of nationalism or not, content regulations cannot be identified with other nationalistic policies. Let us consider two "goods": oil and television programs. The first is a homogeneous product, in that users of oil in any of its forms will not know whether it comes from Saudi Arabia, Venezuela, Nigeria or Alberta. From the point of view of satisfying needs and requirements, there is no such thing as national oil. If one country or region stops producing oil, supplies from any other will satisfy consumers equally well. Cars do not run better, homes are not warmer and fertilizer is not more efficient if the oil used is Canadian or Mexican.

Television programs are a completely different type of product. No two programs are alike. If they are good, they reflect something vital, insightful and dramatic about their subject. As a result, Italian television programs are different from German, British and French ones. Co-productions are possible, but Italians do not make Japanese programs, nor Japanese Canadian ones. In the realm of culture, Canada cannot import Canadian products.

The above is not a defence of existing Canadian content rules, which clearly do not work. It is, however, an argument for forcing some of the very large profits that accrue to private broadcasters into the production of Canadian cultural and artistic products. If Canadians do not produce their own writing, music, theatre, films and television programs, no one else will.

Setting Cultural Goals for Broadcasting

All the components of Canada's broadcasting system – the public and private broadcasters, the cable and satellite delivery systems – must be made to work together to reach important cultural objectives. The government's regulator, the CRTC, must see to it that such cultural goals are in fact pursued and, as much as possible, fulfilled. How, then, can the broadcasting system as a whole achieve these goals coherently?

The key element in the system, fundamental to its operation, is the publicly owned broadcaster – the voice of the public's interests, the expression of Canada's multifaceted reality. We must have a public broadcaster to provide original and stimulating programs that private broadcasters will not provide because they may not be profitable; to ensure that Canada's artists and producers are encouraged to develop new ideas, new forms of entertainment, new program concepts; to be involved with developing technologies and engaged in video and audio experimentation. We need a public broadcaster free to reach audiences, in Canada and elsewhere, through all possible means. *In short, we need a better, more vital, more courageous CBC.*

The CBC as Public Broadcaster
This Committee regards the CBC as the heart of broadcasting in Canada. As Canadians we have built up many expectations about the CBC as a medium through which we learn about ourselves and the world. We have asked it to weave together the many and diverse strands of our society's finest accomplishments. We have used it as the instrument on which our creative artists could learn to play. We have asked it to provide an outlet for the intellectual and creative energies that have burst forth in all regions of the country. The CBC has been able to succeed remarkably well in some of these assignments; in others it has failed.

As we have indicated in the preceding pages, we face a critical moment in our broadcasting history. This moment demands that we release our programming potential to express itself in Canadian programs of quality and character – programs that Canadians will want to watch and will relate to because they reflect parts of themselves. If we do not do this consistently and in large measure, we are in danger of losing for all time the 50-year fight to establish and retain a broadcasting voice that is our own.

In order to tackle the job, we need a CBC that is strong yet flexible, able to concentrate its energies on essentials, open and responsive to opportunities, ready to draw on the store of existing talent in Canada and the exciting array of new talent which will inevitably come to the fore when the chance to create and perform presents itself.

All through our history Canadians have been ready and able to respond in an extraordinary way to new challenges. Talent blossoms when the opportunity to express it arises. The CBC can provide that opportunity if it becomes, once again, Canada's leading broadcaster, a prime force in furthering the evolution of Canadian self-expression. To achieve this end, we propose a series of changes in the CBC which arise from the analysis we have set out in the preceding pages.

Advertising and Affiliation Agreements
In the light of our previous discussion, the Committee recommends the following:

65.   CBC television should discontinue selling air time for commercial advertising.

66.   CBC television should discontinue its affiliation agreements with private television stations.

We argued earlier that the need for advertising revenue exerts a profound pressure on CBC programming decisions to fill prime time with U.S. programs. It is fundamentally important that CBC television be released from that constraint, so that its programming options can be considered only in terms of the best interest of Canadians.

The expedient of broadcasting CBC television programs to all communities through affiliated private stations has resulted in agreements that have also affected CBC programming adversely. It has been cheaper to arrange for affiliates to carry portions of the CBC schedule to some parts of the country than to build and operate stations in those places. Because private broadcasters depend on advertising revenue, the affiliates resist carrying programs with a limited audience and especially programming that does not carry advertising, such as a number of CBC public affairs shows. The initial resistance to carrying the English-language public affairs program "The Journal" during prime time is a case in point. Because affiliates do not earn enough money from carrying CBC programs, the CBC pays those stations compensation on a negotiated basis. In 1981-82 these payments totaled $11.6 million.

In addition, because of pressure from affiliates and advertisers, the CBC carries U.S. shows in prime time not only to earn revenue for itself but also to provide the opportunity for revenues for its affiliates. As a result, we have the ironic situation in which the CBC not only gives financial assistance (much of it being taxpayers' money) to private affiliates to carry a portion of its programs, but also itself carries shows imported from the United States to ensure this limited distribution of its own programming.

In some cases, the CBC could discontinue its affiliation agreements without undue hardship or disruption for the private stations. The latter can fill their schedules from other sources and perhaps develop new relationships with other private stations or networks. In other localities, special arrangements would have to be made, involving buying out the affiliate if necessary.

In those instances in which disaffiliation would be appropriate, CBC television programs would reach areas now served by the affiliated stations in several ways. In some localities, low-power rebroadcast transmitters could be used; in others, linking satellite to cable or to low-power transmitters might be effective. Eventually, Direct Broadcast Satellites will offer yet another delivery alternative. Care should be taken to avoid the loss of local service, and existing arrangements should therefore be maintained until alternative modes of delivering them can be put into effect.

CBC Television Programming
This Committee wants the CBC to provide a genuine alternative to the programming policies of private broadcasters and we believe that many Canadians want the same thing.

Over the past 25 years, observers of the Canadian broadcasting system have been consistent on this one point: the need for the CBC to provide a distinctive Canadian service and to provide encouragement and outlets for Canadian creative talent. The CBC, in its proposal for CBC-2/Télé-2, noted that the Corporation itself has repeatedly called for television programs that "spring from our cultural roots, that... reflect life as it is lived and experienced in our many cultural and regional communities. It means a full spectrum of programming... more and better serious and popular dramas, an emphasis on the development of variety stars, many more and better children's programs and the full range of programming for diverse minority interests." Alphonse Ouimet, a former president of the CBC, called for "complementary" programming, "to serve at the same time all tastes and needs and not just those of some artificial mass." What Mr Ouimet meant was that the CBC should not strive to provide homogenized mass entertainment, like that produced by the U.S. networks and Canadian private networks, but a diversity of specialized and distinctive programming attuned to different segments of the population with specialized and distinctive interests.

For a long time the CBC has not been the only player in Canadian broadcasting. Even the imperative under the Broadcasting Act to provide "balanced" programming can be criticized, as we have criticized it, since very soon television programmers will be offering specialized services: "vertical" channels programming only sports, religious broadcasts, feature films, children's shows, multilingual services, arts coverage, and so on. Some of this is already happening and more will be forthcoming with pay-television programming in 1983. The fate of television networks themselves is in question, at least in their present form and character.

Under such conditions, we think the time has come for the CBC to act decisively, to concentrate all its energies on building programs in response to public needs. Programming concepts and ideas should flow from diverse sources, tapping Canada's creative resources. The objective should be to stimulate the production of attractive, entertaining and informative Canadian shows that will win viewers.

The number of channels to which the CBC has access should therefore respond to programming needs. As the CBC itself notes, "although many Canadians have a wide choice of television stations, we really don't have much choice in television programming." In the Corporation's proposal for CBC-2/Télé-2, it outlined types of programming that it considered to be missing from the Canadian television system, and listed suggestions it had received from the public. Following is a summary of these.

The CBC might be expected to provide:

- a truly Canadian alternative to American programming;
- an end to the excess of sports coverage on television;
- programming in specialized areas such as business, the arts, international affairs and politics;
- more cultural programming, including more dramas from Canadian theatres;
- more regional programming and expression of regional points of view;
- programs explaining our cultural diversity and shared experiences;

- more Canadian films and high-quality documentaries;
- more criticism, news and analysis of theatre, music, dance, books, films;
- more opportunities for performing arts companies to gain television experience;
- more exchange between English and French programming;
- national viewing of materials produced by provincial television agencies;
- experimental programming and new ways of dealing with the visual arts;
- classical foreign series;
- repeats of outstanding programs.

It is a fine catalogue and is in line with comments that we heard about the CBC during our own public hearings. However, we must stress that, in the view of this Committee, the programming policies of the CBC must encompass not only the arts and specialized programs but also popular and mass entertainment: comedies, soap operas, light dramatic series, variety shows and children's programs. As a programmer, the Corporation should be able to call on all of Canada's creative production and performing talent.

In the past, the CBC has been burdened with far too many responsibilities: building the hardware necessary to reach audiences, constructing program schedules, producing the programs described in those schedules, and delivering them to audiences through its network of owned and affiliated stations. We indicated in the previous section, "Problems of the Present Broadcasting System," some of the difficulties which such structural integration has created. To achieve substantial improvements in programming, and to ensure that such programming sufficiently utilizes the cultural potential of Canada, this Committee is convinced that a much larger proportion of the CBC's television budget must be allocated to using outside production talent. We have sought to find a way of determining what would be the appropriate share of the CBC schedule to be given over to outside programming and also who would see that such a share was respected in practice.

We have come to the conclusion that an ideal proportion of outside programming is not, in principle, definable. But, more importantly, we have concluded that even if such a formula were to exist, its implementation on a day-to-day basis would be an unnecessary intrusion into program decision-making.

67.   With the exception of its news operations, the CBC should relinquish all television production activities and facilities in favour of acquiring its television program materials from independent producers.

It is essential to be clear about what this recommendation does *not* say. First, it does not transfer the CBC to the private sector, nor does it place the public corporation in the hands of independent producers. As the 1965 Fowler Committee stressed, "The only thing that realty matters in broadcasting is program content; all the rest is housekeeping." In our recommendation, programming decisions remain firmly in the hands of the CBC. Second, our proposal does not mean that the CBC, as programmer, is a passive recipient of what the independents will decide to produce. We trust that the public programmer will be attentive and responsive to ideas that originate with the independents, but we emphasize that programming should be controlled by the CBC and that many ideas for commissioning new programs will originate in the public corporation.

By becoming solely a programmer, the CBC would clarify its purpose and direction. Many of the talented people it has developed would move into private operations of their own, producing programs for the CBC. It is impossible to guarantee that the transition process would be a smooth one, since it would inevitably entail a certain amount of disruption and realignment of human resources. But if the changeover were carefully planned, new production companies, new facilities, studios and services (many presumably to be created, owned and run by ex-CBC staff) would quickly respond to the opportunity to produce programs for the Corporation and for other exhibitors and users. As a result, we see emerging in time a much larger production universe than now exists.

Most of the television studios in the country are owned by broadcasters, public and private. We would like to see more of these facilities acquired by non-broadcasting interests, by producer and producer-oriented service companies, thus reducing the danger of self-serving decisions being made by broadcasters. The studio and other technical facilities released by the CBC could gradually be acquired by such interests.

Transmission facilities could be owned and operated by a subsidiary operation within the CBC or, better still, assigned to an independent agency, with the CBC having such access as it needs for its operations. In the hands of such an agency the facilities could be shared – rented to public, private and community programming operations as they become available. This might be especially helpful in building up the prospects for increased local programming, a subject we discuss below.

We recognize that if the CBC relinquishes all television production (except for news) and relies on contracts and arrangements with independent producers to obtain its programs, the operation of "natural" economic forces will lead to a concentration of production in Montreal and Toronto and possibly one or two other centres. If this were allowed to happen, our main goal would not be achieved, since the vast reservoir of actual and potential talent outside these centres would not be tapped in ways most beneficial to the rest of Canada. To obviate this tendency,

68.   A proportion of the CBC's programming budget should be allocated specifically to the commissioning of programs produced in the various regions of the country.

Although the objective of our recommendations is a public television corporation that is an alternative to private broadcasting and one that will genuinely reflect Canada's character, we do not wish the CBC to be closed to programs and materials from other countries. Nor would we want the CBC to be precluded from undertaking, through independent producers, certain coproductions with other countries. Much television production outside of Canada is of high quality but never reaches Canadian screens. The CBC's programming should rectify that situation and bring the best in television programming, from whatever country, into Canadian homes.

69.   CBC programming, though developed primarily from Canadian sources, should nevertheless include imported programs or co-productions of some programs of interest and excellence which would not otherwise be available to Canadians.

CBC Television News
Television news should continue to be produced within the CBC. Additional resources should be invested in the news service, not only to extend coverage and technical quality but also to raise the level of journalistic skill so that greater objectivity and depth of treatment can be achieved. The use of more CBC foreign correspondents, for example, would improve the confidence that Canadians have in the Corporation's news service. Raising the standards of news coverage would in turn contribute to the growth of a better informed and more aware public.

CBC Radio
During our public hearings we heard many favourable comments about CBC radio service in both languages. We do not propose changes in the CBC's handling of the radio aspect of its mandate. The Corporation should, however, remain sensitive to new developments in the delivery of radio programming – such as the use of cable and satellite systems – and adapt to new modes of delivery as they become practical.

Although we are not recommending that the CBC discontinue its own radio program production, we believe that it is in the public interest to encourage the development of an independent radio production potential in Canada. This view is consistent with our desire that the greatest variety of programming ideas find their way into the system.

Northern Service
Like CBC radio, the Northern Service for radio and television broadcasting should be retained as a production operation within the CBC. A special type of expertise and sensitivity to cultural, linguistic and social issues are essential in

providing this service. Native people should have a strong voice in shaping the policies and operations of a service which so directly affects their lives and communities. *Additional resources seem to be justified, and we would urge the CBC Board to give the future development of the Northern Service careful and concerned attention.*

Radio Canada International
The CBC should retain its international service, which we discuss in Chapter 11, "International Cultural Relations." Radio Canada International, which already reaches countries in Europe, Africa and Latin America, should be provided with the means to enlarge its service to countries on the Pacific rim which are not now being served.

Regional and Local Programming
The mandate of the CBC requires it to provide programming that reflects each region of Canada to itself and to the rest of the country. In addition, although it is not a requirement of the Broadcasting Act, the CBC provides local programming to communities in which it operates stations. There is some confusion, even within the CBC, about how local and regional programming should be clearly defined and differentiated.

In earlier days, the CBC provided the only production capability worthy of mention in many of the regions it served. Out of its own budgetary resources, the CBC developed production facilities in St. John's, Halifax, Moncton, Montreal, Toronto, Winnipeg, Edmonton and Vancouver. (Although at present the Prairie Provinces are served from Winnipeg, a new production centre is projected to open in Regina in the Fall of 1983 to serve Saskatchewan.) These regional facilities are backed up by sub-regional centres and local stations in Corner Brook, Goose Bay, Labrador City, Sydney, Charlottetown, Moncton, Quebec City, Ottawa, Windsor, Saskatoon and Calgary (Fredericton has only production facilities). These in turn are supported by an extensive network of television rebroadcast transmitters strategically located to extend service to virtually the entire population of Canada.

But today the CBC is no longer alone in providing regional programming. Private broadcasters have been extending their reach into many communities, cable systems are bringing more channels into more homes, and soon satellites will allow television signals to be received even in remote and isolated areas. At the same time, production facilities have grown and cable operators have studio facilities in many parts of the country designed to provide opportunities for community-based programming. Further, the talent and capability to produce and exploit the medium have proliferated through the growing number of film and television training centres and cable community channels, and through experience acquired in the production of commercials, documentaries and industrial films.

The needs of local television programming can now be filled in a variety of ways, some of which will be examined below in the section on private broadcasters. If local programming is given a fairly precise definition, the CBC provides very little in the way of local programming, except for local news. For example, in the Atlantic provinces, the schedule normally offers 81 hours per week of national programs (which include 8 hours of regional contributions), 31 hours of regional programs, but only one to three hours of local productions.

Recommendation 68 on CBC television programming aims to stimulate production from regional sources and to provide an outlet for underused creative production talent. There would thus be a better opportunity to integrate regional program materials into the national distribution network, since the search for program ideas and materials would be the core of the CBC's operations.

Local television programming, as we indicate below, could be provided more effectively through a combination of sources not including the CBC. The Corporation would therefore be able to give more time and attention to national and regional programming. Local radio programming should be sustained and continued by the CBC.

70.   In its television services the CBC should rededicate itself to providing regional programming, but should phase out local programming as soon as alternative local broadcasting facilities are in place.

English and French Services
From the beginning, the CBC has maintained services in Canada's two official languages. But the two services are quite separate and parallel to each other, even if their central administration in Ottawa is common to both. That parallelism has been accentuated by the extensive production activities of the Corporation in English and French. We do not believe that our recommendations will automatically bring the two services closer, nor do we suggest that the two be fused into one. Such a step would not be feasible, nor culturally productive if it were.

But once the CBC concentrates all its activities on programming, we would expect a substantially increased level of exchange and collaboration between its two language services. Beyond that, many programs could be dubbed for distribution by both services. It should be possible in many instances to avoid having to build different operations solely on the basis of language.

71.   As a matter of policy the CBC should encourage the greatest possible collaboration, cooperation and exchange between programmers in the French and English services in order to make the best use of human resources and to permit a truly significant exposure of programs produced in both languages to all Canadians.

Marketing Operations
For some time the CBC has marketed its products through what is now called CBC Enterprises for the English radio and television networks and, only recently, through the Ancillary Rights Service for the French networks. These marketing arms promote and sell materials produced by the CBC – including television programs and, mostly through mail order, records, books and similar products. We would like to see these activities pursued with more vigour. CBC programs, records, films, books, information materials and entertainment items of various kinds should be sold, or rented as appropriate, in all formats through retail and other outlets. Under expert management, the marketing operations should earn revenues for the CBC. In Chapter 8, "Sound Recording," we note the importance of these marketing units for the distribution of specialized recordings.

The CBC is also the principal outlet for the presentation of National Film Board films. In Chapter 9, "Film," we propose that the CBC should assume responsibility for the distribution of the NFB's library of films. Such distribution would fit appropriately into both the proposed programming and marketing functions of the CBC. In this connection, the CBC should undertake to repackage the appropriate NFB films, seek out markets all over the world, and make available this valuable library of films to Canadians.

72.   The CBC should enhance its marketing operations in order to exploit the maximum domestic and international marketing potential of its materials and those of other producers.

Audio and Video Archives
Audio and video materials form a vital part of Canada's heritage. In spite of the concern and effort of a few dedicated collectors, however, much of that valuable material has been or is being lost. The accent on the immediacy of much of radio and television production tends to produce indifference to its preservation, even among those who are in the broadcast media. The problems related to the preservation of these materials are great, as we were reminded during our hearings, but they demand a solution.

Fortunately, some first steps have been taken. In 1959, the CBC began to preserve its sound recordings in Toronto and Montreal. In 1975, it made an arrangement with the Public Archives of Canada for the collection and preservation of its broadcast materials, to which other documentation was added in 1981. Thanks to this agreement and with funding for the purpose, the vast repository of CBC materials began to be processed. Unfortunately, the operation was curtailed when funds ran out. Nevertheless, a system for handling such materials has been established, providing a basis for future archival development.

According to the Association for the Study of Canadian Radio and Television, an organization which has concerned itself with better sound and video archives, the CTV television network has assembled an estimated 18,000 hours of videotapes awaiting cataloguing. The Canadian Association of Broad casters has made its members aware of their responsibilities in this area, though a comprehensive program still remains to be developed.

Time is an important factor: backlogs must be dealt with before these materials disappear forever, and preservation of future collections and the pro vision of public access to them must be undertaken. The job is massive and re quires assistance from many sources. Given the widely scattered origins of the materials, even within the CBC, not only must the Public Archives become more deeply involved, but agreements should also be made and projects undertaken with provincial and other archival services. It is estimated that about $10 million would be needed to deal with the backlogs alone within the CBC and CTV collections, but since this process would take several years, the annual financial burden would not be heavy.

To deal with this serious problem, and in view of the time constraints involved,

73.   The federal government should immediately provide funds to the Public Archives of Canada to enable it to deal with the serious problem of the collection and preservation of audio and visual archives and to operate a soundly based, ongoing archival program in this area.

The Public Archives of Canada should work closely with all those who have audio and visual archival materials, especially broadcasters and film pro ducers, as well as with provincial and other repositories, to coordinate and facilitate the efforts in this field. The Public Archives should continue to serve the archival needs of the CBC and should, as we have suggested in Chapter 9, undertake the management of the National Film Board vaults and archival materials.

A New Broadcasting Act

Our recommendations for the CBC call for a reconsideration of its mandate. But the restructuring that we propose should not be construed as diminishing the autonomy that the CBC enjoys. We have argued in Chapter 2, "Government and Culture," that it is vital for the CBC to be free of political influence in its pro gramming decisions. At the same time we are conscious of the fact that some of the changes we recommend have been proposed in the past by others, in cluding the CRTC, to little effect.

Frankly, we worry that a continued effort to maintain the status quo may lead the Corporation to react negatively to our suggestions. Too many Canadians are beginning to question the very need for a public broadcaster such as the CBC. Our recommendations are intended to preserve the valuable experiences gained throughout the long and productive history of the CBC, so that these can be strengthened and built upon in a new and vibrant operation that is able to face the future and to contend effectively with its demands.

Many of our recommendations could be implemented within the present legal framework provided for the Corporation and for the other elements that make up our broadcasting system. However, taken together, our proposals represent a significant departure in direction sufficient to warrant new legislation.

74.   A new Broadcasting Act should be presented to Parliament.

Private Broadcasters and Increased Canadian Programming

Private broadcasters in Canada have been well served by the protection offered them by public regulations. Even within the current economic climate, and although individual operators may be suffering downturns in profit, advertising sales are high and profitability over the whole industry is healthy. However, there is little to indicate a relationship between industry health and improved Canadian programming in either television or radio.

Competition from new delivery systems will affect private broadcasting, but an inherent flexibility should enable the system to adapt to new conditions, as it did when cable television emerged. Our concern is not with the ability of private broadcasters to adjust to the new environment but with the contribution that they can and should make to the cultural life of Canada.

The withdrawal of the CBC from the advertising market and from the competition for U.S. programs, both of which we have recommended, would provide several advantages to the private broadcaster. For one, the departure of the CBC from the market for foreign programs would most likely make it possible for Canadian private broadcasters to buy such programs at a lower price. More significantly, well over $100 million in advertising revenues would become available. It is probable that a large part of those funds would be absorbed by television operators within the CTV, TVA and Global networks and by other independent stations. Some way must be found to convert some or all of these additional funds, and a significant portion of private station profits, into better Canadian program production.

In the recent CRTC ruling on pay-television licensing, the conditions imposed on the licensees called for a commitment to Canadian programming which differed from standard Canadian content regulations, although they resemble prior efforts by the CRTC. Currently, Canadian content is measured only in terms of time allocated within the schedule. The new approach adds a requirement to spend a percentage of gross revenues and a percentage of programming budgets on Canadian shows. We believe that this approach makes good sense and will make a definite impact on the quantity and nature of the programming produced by the private sector.

We have noted several times that, in general, programs emerging from private broadcasters do far too little to enhance our sense of ourselves and our culture. Their coverage of news and sports is good, but little else of cultural value is produced with any consistency. We believe that much more is possible and should be required of the private broadcasting community.

75. The CRTC should require private broadcasters to allocate substantial percentages of their programming time, programming budgets and gross revenues to new Canadian program production.

In the pursuit of this objective, the CRTC might find it necessary to make its requirements for the scheduling of Canadian programs more precise and rigorous. At the same time, if the fraction of gross revenues and programming budgets which the private broadcasters are required to devote to Canadian programs is sufficiently large, these broadcasters may be induced to produce attractive Canadian shows, which they would then find in their own interest to display in prime time. The test of any regulation in this area will be a decision by private broadcasters to air their own programs in prime time.

We also believe that the additional revenues that would accrue to the private system, once the CBC ceased to carry advertising on its television programs, should be used for increased production at the local and regional levels. The annual CANPRO awards, which highlight productions emanating from private broadcasting stations, indicate a high level of production talent whose efforts often deserve wide exposure.

This move toward increased Canadian programming could be accomplished in several ways. One possibility is that, in markets where it is feasible, private station owners could be required to program, as a condition of their licence, a second channel whose content would be all, or nearly all, Canadian and on which they could sell advertising.

A variation of this concept would open up a second channel to entrepreneurs willing to provide a new, predominantly Canadian service. There would be open competition to provide this service. The bidders might be the local private station, affiliates of other networks, and others desiring entry into this field. Approval would be granted only if plans for Canadian production and programming were satisfactory. To be effective, performances would need to be strictly policed and the approval of licences withdrawn and opened to new bidders if programming promises were not fulfilled.

76. The CRTC should permit the establishment of new, private local television services in those communities able to absorb them, and use its licensing powers to ensure that these new services contain almost exclusively Canadian programs.

A third possibility is the introduction of a tax on profits which would be earmarked for upgrading the quantity and quality of Canadian programming. Beyond the problems of devising such a tax, however, there are the problems related to earmarking, which we have analyzed in Chapter 3, "Marshalling Resources."

The largest single television advertiser is the Canadian government. At present, federal advertising expenditures are associated with U.S. programs on Canadian television stations on the basis that these programs attract the largest audiences. Such are the dictates of efficiency, at least as long as only one objective is being considered. Should the government choose to allocate a reasonable part of its advertising budget to Canadian programs that are attracting large Canadian audiences, even if these audiences are not as large as those viewing American shows, the government would not only provide a further incentive to private broadcasters to invest in Canadian program production but could also set an example to other advertisers.

The Challenge of a Multi-level Cable System

Approximately 80 per cent of all households in Canada have easy access to a cable television connection in the sense that the cable "passes" near their homes; and, as we have already noted, 59 per cent actually subscribe to a cable service. The cable system is therefore a prime delivery mechanism. Off-air transmission – the traditional way to receive television signals – no longer governs the way we look at broadcasting.

The CRTC has not allowed the cable television industry to engage directly in program production, beyond the provision of community channels and services. When cable first arrived on the scene it was considered a threat to the off-air broadcaster. Recent history, however, has shown that the two delivery systems can work together to their mutual advantage. Now satellites are seen by some as dangerous intruders into the system. But already there are signs that a combination of cable and satellite systems could provide equal or greater coverage than is being provided currently, thus putting even isolated and remote parts of the country within reach of broadcasters. Various kinds of data, security and other services could be offered, in addition to entertainment and consumer information. As ever, the questions are not merely technological but cultural: which programs will be offered to and seen by Canadians?

Proliferation of cable systems has increased Canadians' access to U.S. television programs, and the use of cable converters increases this access still further. Without cable, viewers can receive off-air signals from Canadian network broadcasters like the CBC, CTV, TVA or others, depending on the province of residence. Since the production and transmission of these signals are financed either by public appropriation or by advertising, viewers are provided with a practically free service. Looking at one more program does not cost them anything more, beyond a few cents of electricity and wear and tear on the television set. By purchasing cable service, at an average cost of about $7 a month, viewers can increase the number of channel choices to eight or twelve (the "basic" service) and improve the quality of the picture on their sets. For an additional $5 or so a month (or an outright purchase price of around $100), a converter increases the number of choices still further.

Early in 1983, viewers will have the option to purchase yet another level of service from cable companies, when pay-television is offered for a probable price of around $15 a month for the first pay channel, with discounts applying to additional channels. To receive pay-television programs, which will be delivered to cable companies by satellite in a scrambled form, a decoder will have to be bought or rented. Soon, for an additional sum, non-broadcast services such as banking, house protection, shopping, etc., will add another level to what is available. Before long, viewers will probably also be able to buy individual programs instead of whole channels of service.

Thus we are already entering a multi-level, or tiered, system in which viewers have freedom of choice in paying for what they use. As the number and types of these new cable services increase, their pricing and marketing will become more complex, and the tendency of cable companies to use popular foreign programming to attract subscribers will increase as well. For this reason it will be necessary to ensure two things: that Canadian programs are scheduled in adequate quantities and at appropriate times, and that Canadian program production is increased as a result of the introduction of the new services.

In effect, then, it will be necessary to regard the entire programming offered by any cable system in the same light as we now regard a broadcaster's service. Of particular concern to this Committee is the need to maintain all Canadian non-discretionary services – national, regional and provincial networks, independent stations, community channels, educational services, House of Commons coverage – as part of the basic service of all cable companies.

77.   Any CRTC policies on multi-level, or tiered, cable service must continue to ensure that the first priority on the basic cable service is given to designated Canadian services. In addition, a substantial portion of all other tiers of service offered to cable subscribers must be Canadian.

We believe that every effort should be made to reduce the fee charged for the basic cable service to the lowest possible level. Furthermore, the federal government and the cable industry should consider a policy of hooking up to cable systems all households that are now "passed" by cable and offering them this basic, low-cost service. Our purpose here, as elsewhere in this Report, is to give encouragement to Canadian creativity by providing our creators with enlarged audiences. Recommending a favoured position for Canadian-based channels within the cable television system is a major step in this direction.

Our position on increased Canadian programming suggests that we should advocate an open and unlimited policy for Canadian television producers and that, in particular, we should recommend that cable companies produce and distribute their own programs. But the inherent conflict of interest placed on carriers who are also producers forces us away from making that recommendation. We are ready to acknowledge that, in the short run, production of Canadian programs could increase, but only at the cost of very probable long-term reductions of such production. Nor do we believe that the problem posed by conflict-of-interest situations can be resolved by such legal devices as arm's-length companies, because the degree of autonomy must be monitored and enforced, and we have serious doubts, for reasons given earlier, about the resolve to do this. Prudence and the logic of this position therefore dictate the following:

78.   The CRTC should encourage cable companies to improve their community channel operations, but cable production must remain limited to such programming.

Local Television Programming
References have been made throughout the earlier parts of this chapter to local programming. We have indicated that private broadcasters should substantially increase their production activities, providing much more access to independent production talent in their communities. This Committee wishes to underline its particular concern for this aspect of broadcasting in Canada. At the local level, the provision of opportunities to develop and produce programs is fundamental to the thrust we advocate so strongly, namely, that the future of broadcasting in Canada depends on our ability to generate productions that reflect and concern us. Nowhere is this more vital than in the area of what is termed local broadcasting.

This Committee fully shares the concern so often expressed to us during our public hearings about the improvement of local service and the development of local talent. When we propose, in Recommendation 70, that the CBC discontinue the small amount of local programming it currently undertakes, it is in order that the CBC might then be able to provide producers with increased access to its system, through the additional time and funds it will have available for the stimulation of new production.

Our proposals on additional cable-delivered stations to be made available to private broadcasters should provide further opportunities for production talent. The additional revenues – $100 million or so – to be earned by private broadcasters when the CBC ceases to sell air time for commercial advertising should be directed in large part to new productions. Whether this is achieved by regulation or otherwise, the goal in all these developments has to be found in the fundamental needs we have described.

The cable system offers further possibilities. In 1979, 467 cable companies provided community channels and 276 operated studios (156 with colour facilities). On average, about four hours of programming a day are produced by these community channels. Local groups are also given access to cable facilities for television programming. However, much more can be done; the CRTC already requires that cable facilities, equipment and expertise be made available to communities as a condition of cable licences, but the Commission has not been firm in administering these conditions. It had been hoped that cable operators would allocate 10 per cent of their revenues towards the operation of community channels; generally this has remained an unrealized hope.

Nevertheless, a great variety of opportunities have been opened up in the brief history of cable community programming. Many individuals and groups have become involved, technical training and outlets for local talent have been provided and encouragement given to local entrepreneurship. In communities where colleges and schools offer some television training, students have become not only operators but have also helped train citizens in the use of cable television cameras and equipment. Community groups in some areas virtually control the entire community channel activities, while in others the cable companies do most of the production emanating from community sources. In many places the community channel provides the only local television service. The diversity of approaches and ways of dealing with local conditions is one of the strengths of community channel operations.

Of special interest to this Committee is the fact that, through the cable system's community channels which can create new relationships between the public and television, the Canadian broadcasting system has one of its few alternatives to mass entertainment and information in which the viewer is merely passive. In the community channel operations, direct participation by members of the community in all aspects of programming is not only possible, but the norm. As a result, programming policies are attuned to a remarkable degree to specific local needs and aspirations. Even in their present underdeveloped stage, community channels have sometimes been able to develop program ideas that have been picked up by off-air commercial broadcasters.

The Committee has concluded that cable community channels must continue to be developed and strengthened, and suggests three areas in which improvements should be sought: there should be a greater contribution and commitment by cable companies, a search for additional and diversified sources of funding, and increased efforts to establish closer relationships between communities and operators of community channels. To that end we recommend the following:

79.   Cable television operators, as a condition of licence, should be required by the CRTC to allocate a significant percentage of gross revenues toward the facilities and programming of community channels.

80.   The CRTC should encourage the establishment of Local Programming Leagues wherever community channels are available to the local community.

The Local Programming Leagues would be nonprofit organizations composed of representative groups and citizens within each community. If incorporated as charitable organizations, they could appeal to a variety of sources for financial support. The allocations by cable companies which we propose in Recommendation 79 would provide basic operating funds. Increased funding could be sought from provincial and municipal governments, the Canadian Film Development Corporation (see Chapter 9 "Film"), other federal agencies and local private and business sources.

The Leagues should be deeply involved in local programming. They would seek to improve its quality and its sensitivity to local needs and to provide encouragement and opportunities to local talent. The licence would continue to be assigned to the cable operator, who would be accountable for fulfilling its conditions. The League could, in some circumstances, seek other distribution outlets for its programming needs.

Cable companies providing important local services in communities that have no other local broadcasting service should be able to use off-air facilities in the form of supplementary transmitters for the purpose of improving their coverage.

In making these proposals we seek to achieve three principal objectives: a better broadcasting service in line with the interests of local residents, more opportunities for performers and producers to test themselves and to grow, and more involvement by citizens in ensuring television's usefulness in their lives.

Developing a Policy for Satellites and New Production

There are some strange ironies to be observed in Canada's approach to the satellite question. Canada has been a pioneer in the use of satellites for broadcasting purposes. Long before the United States and other countries began to look seriously at the potential of satellites, the CBC was using Canada's Anik series of satellites to serve the North. Yet Canada now seems to be almost reluctant to build upon and exploit this early lead. We are now preoccupied with controlling the entry of foreign satellite signals and programs into Canada, instead of recognizing that this new technology provides unprecedented opportunities for us to increase the distribution of new Canadian programs and services, not only domestically but internationally.

The United States has dramatically shown how satellites used in conjunction with cable systems can bring audiences the kind of program diversity which our own Broadcasting Act expects from the Canadian system and which thus far has eluded us. Furthermore, when Canada launches Anik C in late 1982, this country will move to the forefront of new satellite technology, making it possible to offer, among other new services, the economical transmission of broadcasts directly to individual homes. Ironically, the first users of this type of service (Direct Broadcast Satellite Service) could be U.S. entrepreneurs. It is one thing to be concerned about the high cost of technological development and the inordinate emphasis it has received in relation to our underfunded program production activities. But it is vital to recognize that the wise use of technology extends the opportunity for creative communication and expression and is an essential component of Canada's present and future cultural endeavours.

Canada must be able to look to its public and private institutions to respond to these challenges, and government policies must be flexible enough to allow for considerable individual initiative. To the program producer and distributor, these technological systems represent new program dissemination possibilities to be considered along with all the other systems – such as cable and videodiscs – now becoming available. Consequently it is important not to retard such new developments as satellite systems, nor single out any one system as being the "preferred" system of program and service delivery.

There are some very specific actions which must be taken now. The Committee has already referred to the vital need to undertake more research in programming and has suggested in Chapter 9 how the National Film Board may be reconstituted to serve this need. In addition, we have proposed for the CBC a primary role in programming within the expanding broadcasting and communications system. These two public institutions should be fully alert to the potential of new satellite systems, taking that potential into account in their long-range planning. For example, a much closer ongoing coordination with the telecommunications satellite corporation, Telesat, is highly desirable, to encourage the evolution of new technological systems that can serve programming objectives.

The federal government and the CRTC must see their roles as custodians of a multifaceted program distribution system in which extended range and diversity is sought. It is essential to be open to all ideas, to encourage new systems development, and to see every new advance not as a cause for concern but rather as an opportunity for creative enterprise.

81.   The Canadian government must develop a clear and coherent policy for the orderly development of satellite capabilities and put such technologies and the funds they can generate to the service of new Canadian production.

A Strengthened CRTC
The licensing and regulatory powers of the CRTC exert a powerful effect on broadcasting in Canada. These powers should be used with firmness and determination in enforcing the delivery of promised performance by licensees in respect of Canadian programming.

Licensing and Cultural Objectives
The CRTC has generally shied away from applying the ultimate penalty for non-performance in cultural matters – the revocation of, or refusal to renew, a broadcaster's licence – for fear of depriving a community of services. With new broadcast ventures continuing to proliferate, that fear need no longer be a factor in many of the CRTC's licensing decisions. The need to protect the business concerns of private broadcasters is not as important as the need for new Canadian program production. Non-enforcement of any promise, pledge or assurance is an incentive to further non-performance. Conversely, the only way the CRTC can show that it places cultural objectives on a par with, or

higher than, industrial or commercial objectives is through strict enforcement of promises with respect to cultural matters. It must remind broadcasters that they are licensees, not owners, of the airwaves.

82.   The CRTC must strictly enforce conformity to all conditions of licence.

The Broadcasting Act, in its present form, has been a source of friction between the CBC and the CRTC. The Act gives the CBC a specific mandate and the authority to carry it out. The CBC is also licensed by the CRTC, but that licence cannot be suspended or revoked. When the two agencies find themselves in adversary positions on some subject, the CBC has managed to get its own way.

83.   The proposed new Broadcasting Act should give clear authority to the CRTC in matters related to the CBC.

In Chapter 2, "Government and Culture," we discuss the power of cabinet ministers to provide policy direction to agencies. Although we are firm in our conviction that agencies need to be strongly shielded from political direction, we note that the conditions surrounding the CRTC as a regulatory body put it in a different position. We disagree with that aspect of the present Broadcasting Act which disallows policy direction while enabling the government to challenge individual CRTC decisions on granting or renewing of licences. We repeat our position here.

- The cabinet's right to challenge licensing decisions should be removed.
- The minister should have the right to offer general policy directions under certain conditions: prior consultation with the CRTC and the tabling of the policy view in the House of Commons. The CRTC should, however, be able to hold public hearings on the issue in question prior to the policy direction being formally given.

84.   The proposed new Broadcasting Act should confirm the total independence of the CRTC from political intrusion in matters relating to licensing, but permit direction by the minister on matters of general policy, under certain specified conditions.

*The federal government does not play any direct role in educational broadcasting, except that through the CRTC it licenses educational services. In order to reduce the danger of political control or undue political interference in educational broadcasting, these licences are given to independent bodies

---

*The Committee records an abstention on this matter (up to and including Recommendation 85) by one of its members, Joy Cohnstaedt, Deputy Minister, Cultural Affairs and Historical Resources, Province of Manitoba. That department is responsible for provincial telecommunications policy.

operating at arm's length from provincial or municipal governments, although they may be funded entirely by such governments. Thus educational operations such as TVOntario, Radio-Québec, Access Alberta and others are licensed by the CRTC. Cable systems also provide channels to educational broadcasters, including those based at universities.

The ownership of broadcasting operations by political bodies presents certain dangers. Political influence on programming decisions must be minimized, in order to protect the integrity of the broadcasting system against accusations of being used for political ends or presenting views biased towards one political or social cause. Although provincial educational broadcasting undertakings have shown genuine interest in the promotion of Canadian programs, provincially administered cable activities have shown the opposite tendency, apparently wishing only to provide access to American programs. It is in the Canadian interest that cultural goals in broadcasting be pursued by these enterprises. For these reasons,

85.   The CRTC should continue to license provincially and municipally based broadcasting undertakings.

Encouraging Alternative Radio
In the course of our public hearings, radio was criticized for shortcomings in its programming much less than was television. CBC radio in particular was widely lauded. In Chapter 8, "Sound Recording," we have already noted the dependence of radio on recorded music and vice versa; we have also noted how little attention is paid by radio programmers to serious music. Our recommendation to the CRTC in that chapter is aimed at increasing the performance on both AM and FM radio of Canadian specialized recordings.

When FM radio emerged as an alternative to AM broadcasting, the CRTC sought to make FM programming "different," a way of providing an alternative for listeners who complained about the nature of the AM service. Their criticisms had noted AM radio's repetitiveness, stridency, triviality, undue commercialization and imitativeness. To avoid these tendencies, FM licensees were required to provide a certain amount of "foreground" programming, were forbidden to simulcast in cases where the licensees operated both FM and AM stations, and were generally encouraged to provide greater diversity, substance and quality in their programming and to limit the amount of commercial advertising. It was hoped that in response to such pressures, broadcasters would create new ways of dealing with subjects that private radio had ignored. There were other hopes. It was expected that independent radio production would develop, that exchanges, syndication operations and even networking would result. Little of this has happened. The program exchange service of the Canadian Association of Broadcasters is as limited in its scope as it has always been.

The CRTC should persist in its efforts to make private radio programming more diverse and imaginative. Given the fact that most Canadians now

*own FM receivers, the CRTC should reconsider its FM licensing procedures,
making it easier for small entrepreneurs with different ideas to enter the field.*
The costs of preparing an application and of submitting it are sometimes so
high that such entrepreneurs are almost barred from entering the market. This
situation, while protecting profits of existing operators, also impoverishes the
whole sector by limiting its openness to new ideas.

One group, the community and campus-run stations, already provides
valuable alternatives to the fare provided by private commercial stations.
Community and campus-run stations are also usually very different from each
other, and that diversity should be encouraged. Such radio stations not only
provide an important local service through their information programs, but
also encourage experimentation and offer opportunities for new talent to
develop. Many of these stations operate in small communities and in the
North; as a result they often provide vital exchanges between small, isolated
groups. Others are located in urban centres serving special groups. Still other
stations function in universities, often operated by students. All share the problem of being seriously underfinanced.

Some departments or agencies of the federal government have at times
provided assistance to these stations, usually for special projects. The Quebec
government, the only provincial government to do so, has provided funds
toward the basic operation of many stations within the province; but even in
those cases, the financing has proved to be both insufficient and lacking in
continuity. Private fund-raising is difficult for such ventures, and the sale of
advertising would often be antithetical to their interests even if it were
permitted.

86. Federal and provincial governments should seek ways to
     assist community and campus-run radio stations to alleviate
     their financial difficulties and to stabilize their operations.

Advisory Committees for Performance Assessment
Dialogue between a regulatory agency such as the CRTC and the public is very
important. The constituency that watches and listens to programs should be
heard clearly alongside the professionals and businessmen of the media. The
public can provide a useful evaluation of broadcast or cable services that are
presumably designed for their benefit, and some mechanism for the regular
sharing of views with the public would be an asset to the supervisory and
regulatory roles played by the CRTC.

We would like to see advisory committees formed by the CRTC to which
the agency would have regular and consistent access. These committees
should be representative and wide-ranging enough in their activities so that a
thorough feedback system would be in effect, providing an efficient and accurate public assessment of broadcasters' performance. The ancillary impact
of such an operation on individual broadcasters and the networks could be
considerable. Just knowing that their work is seriously and continuously being

assessed would affect broadcasters' daily decision-making. Since much volunteer effort would be involved, the operation of such a network of advisers should not be costly. The process would not downgrade public hearings, which should remain the core of the CRTC evaluative process. In fact, participation by such advisory groups in the CRTC's public hearings would be both appropriate and valuable.

87.   The CRTC should set up Advisory Committees in each province to assist in performance evaluation of licensees and to provide advice and reaction from a local perspective on all broadcast activities.

Funding Public Broadcasting

Concern was often expressed to us at our public hearings about the portion of the federal government's cultural expenditures consumed by the CBC. In the eyes of many, this amount is inordinately large. Hopes were often voiced that even a small part of the CBC's budget could provide major benefits if it were reassigned to other federal cultural agencies, all of which operate on a small fraction of the funds available to the CBC.

There are no simple ways of establishing whether net savings to the government would result from the recommendations we have put forward on broadcasting in general and the CBC in particular. Very substantial savings are indicated by some of the measures we advocate; these derive from staffing adjustments, disposition of physical plant, realignment of services, shifts in priorities and tightening of operations.

On the other side of the equation, there is the proposed loss of CBC advertising revenue, the cost of breaking with the affiliated stations and, most of all, the cost of commissioning more high-quality programs. It is extremely difficult to add up benefits or losses on either side and arrive at a useful answer. Time considerations add to the dilemma. When will certain actions begin? How long will they take to complete? What will be the condition of our economy at the time?

The problem of acquiring the necessary funds raises other issues. In Chapter 3, "Marshalling Resources," we have set out our views on such questions as special taxes, levies and other means of acquiring funds for particular cultural purposes. This Committee wants the government to act responsibly to achieve a stable ongoing financial commitment to the cultural activities that are essential to the well-being of Canadians. A strong Canadian programming presence is undoubtedly one such activity. In the briefs presented to us, we heard ideas on the accumulation of special funds through taxes earmarked to provide financial support for Canadian television and film productions. One of these ideas took the form of a tax on cable billings; another a tax on blank audio and video tapes; yet another a levy on television set sales. The most frequently heard suggestion was a levy on cable subscriptions, with the income going to the CBC or to a production fund in the hands of the Canadian Film Development Corporation or some other agency. This has been called, perhaps inaccurately, a "universal pay" television system and was advocated by several intervenors at our hearings.

The government may, indeed, choose to use any or all of these funding devices. We would prefer, however, to have the necessary funds for cultural purposes come out of general tax revenues, thus avoiding the pitfalls that we have described in Chapter 3.

The CBC has often voiced a plea for assured funding from the government over a period of years. At one time the government promised five-year appropriations, but that promise has never been fulfilled. Other agencies, such as the Canada Council, have also asked for multi-year funding in order to serve the needs of their clientele better. In recent years, the Federal Policy and Expenditure Management System has required all agencies to provide a three-year projection of their financial needs. We hope that this process can eventually lead to an arrangement enabling the government to provide appropriations for the CBC and other cultural agencies for periods longer than the one-year cycle on which they now must function.

Whatever the pattern and whatever the source of funds, we urge that enough financial support be provided to enable the activation of the creative potential of Canadians. In that context, the CBC is vital, and Canadians should be vigilant that they do not cheat themselves of the great benefits to be derived from a properly motivated and well-operated public broadcasting system.

11
International Cultural Relations

_____
_____
_____
_____
_____
_____

11

International Cultural Relations

The importance of international cultural relations was set out most persuasive-
ly by the Social Sciences and Humanities Research Council of Canada in these
words:

> "It would be folly to try to build our culture in isolation: we would
> be denying a trait common to all active cultures – universality. We
> must all therefore participate on the international scene – artists,
> humanists, social scientists – to augment the sum of knowledge
> and the works of art which constitute the worldwide cultural assets
> of humankind."

As part of its assessment of the direction Canadian cultural policy should
take in the decades ahead, the Committee sought comments and information
about Canada's cultural relations with other countries. We asked intervenors
what cultural image of Canada they thought should be projected abroad. In
more than 150 briefs, they answered this question and many also told us of
their aspirations to test their talents before new and challenging audiences
abroad and of their dissatisfaction with present arrangements for assisting
them to do this.

Earlier sections of this Report have shown the diverse and energetic
character of all aspects of Canadian cultural activity. The pool of talent in every
field is large enough, as it has been for many years, that Canadian artists can
reach out to foreign audiences without depriving those at home. Indeed, the
ambitions of Canadian artists of all kinds to measure themselves and to
mature in their chosen discipline can only be met by performing or exhibiting
abroad for larger audiences that are both informed and critical. In the Committee's view, future federal cultural policy must include extended and innovative
programs to support Canadian artists who, with their distinctive voices, want
to speak not just to Canadian audiences but to international audiences as well.

This desire of Canadians for wider exposure of their talents is not a recent phenomenon. The Massey-Lévesque Commission received much the same message 30 years ago.

Since then, informal cultural exchanges between Canada and the world outside have increased greatly. Canadians now make innumerable personal contacts throughout the world through tourism, work and study abroad, and through the international affiliations of their professional and fraternal associations. Through all of these contacts, Canada becomes a little better known overseas. The formal promotion of knowledge of Canada abroad, however, is a government responsibility assumed primarily by the federal government but to some extent also by some of the provinces. Both levels of government have designated agencies and undertaken activities to advance their particular and sometimes incompatible interests.

The past 30 years have seen a rapid increase in the number of federal agencies with statutory authority to participate in international aspects of cultural policy. While not necessarily complete, the list of agencies active in this area today includes the following: Department of External Affairs (incorporating components of the Department of Industry, Trade and Commerce), Canada Council, Department of Communications, National Museums of Canada, National Arts Centre, Radio Canada International, National Film Board, Canadian Film Development Corporation, Canadian International Development Agency, Ministry of State for Social Development, Canadian Commission for Unesco, Social Sciences and Humanities Research Council, National Research Council, Medical Research Council, National Library, and Public Archives of Canada.

Despite all this activity by other agencies, the cultural community in Canada identifies international cultural activities as a responsibility primarily of the Department of External Affairs. It is true that External Affairs has the most visible program and administrative arrangements to project the Canadian image abroad, but its involvement in international cultural relations, although long-standing, came about by default. As the Massey-Lévesque Commissioners observed, much of the department's work in this area was assumed

"because of pressure both from within and without the country and for want of any other available agency. Neither the officials concerned nor the public are entirely satisfied with the resulting improvisation."

Submissions made to this Committee clearly demonstrated that this dissatisfaction has not diminished. We have come to the conclusion that the legitimate aspirations of the Canadian cultural community to be exposed to international audiences have not been satisfactorily combined with the diplomatic objectives of the Department of External Affairs. We are convinced that there must be an increased commitment by the federal government to developing the informed, positive interest of other countries in Canada and in the work of its artists and scholars.

In our opinion, the Department of External Affairs has made no more than a good start towards this goal. Its progress has been hampered by the limited recognition given to the value of cultural activities within the present departmental structure. Inevitably, the political concerns of foreign policy predominate to the detriment of Canada's international cultural relations when budgetary and administrative decisions are made. The Committee is convinced that only an agency outside the existing departmental organization can make the substantially increased and more broadly based effort required to achieve important but diverse objectives in the field of international cultural relations. We shall have a good deal more to say about this later in the chapter.

The Development of International Cultural Relations

Canada's Commitment to Cultural Cooperation

Cultural cooperation or cultural diplomacy is a concept that has been fostered by the United Nations Educational, Scientific and Cultural Organization (Unesco) and adopted by a large number of countries with whom Canada has friendly relations, providing a rationale for the development and exchange of cultural contacts among countries. The articles of the Declaration of the Principles of International Cultural Cooperation formulated at the Unesco conference in 1966 state that international cultural cooperation covers "all aspects of intellectual and creative activities relating to education, science and culture." Such cooperation may assume various forms: bilateral, multilateral, regional or universal. Regardless of the form, the aims of these activities, according to the Declaration, should be "to spread knowledge, to stimulate talent, and to enrich culture."

Cultural cooperation has not always been one of the objectives of Canadian foreign policy, which has traditionally been rooted in economic, commercial and political considerations. Over the last 20 years, however, the objectives have been broadened until, in the words of the Department of External Affairs, "Today the development of international cultural relations is an essential dimension of our diplomacy."

Under the administration of the Department of External Affairs, Canada maintains diplomatic relations with 162 countries through a network of 117 posts located in 79 countries, at the latest count. The continuing, identifiable Canadian presence in these foreign countries is to be found in the embassy buildings and the official residences of Canadian representatives, many of them now designed by Canadian architects. At each post, works from the department's extensive collection of Canadian art are on display and a selection of Canadian books, periodicals, newspapers and reference materials is available to the public.

All of these things are an accepted part of representing Canada abroad but, in themselves, are insufficient to project a well-defined image of Canada, or to extend knowledge and understanding of Canadian life and attitudes. These are functions of specific programs within the Department of External Affairs.

Recognition of the substantial commitment many countries were making to the development of cultural relations led the department to establish a Cultural Affairs division in 1965 as part of the Public Affairs Bureau. This bureau was dismantled in 1979 and two separate bureaus were set up to take responsibility for information and cultural relations. The Information Bureau now handles public relations and general information activities, while Canada's contributions to cultural cooperation are looked after by the Bureau of International Cultural Relations.

The structure and activities of the latter bureau are of particular interest to the Committee. The bureau has four divisions, two of which (Academic Relations, and Cultural Affairs – Arts Promotion) carry out programs inspired by specific aims of cultural cooperation. The Cultural Affairs – Arts Promotion division continues the long tradition of External Affairs of sending representative work of Canadian creative artists and performers on tour abroad. The Academic Relations division, set up in 1975, provides support for intellectual activities directed toward achieving increased understanding of Canada abroad.

In the artistic field, the department's activities include assistance to professional arts organizations in negotiating engagements and making tours abroad, exhibitions of Canadian art, lecture tours by writers and other artists, film screenings, book donations, assistance in market development and visits to Canada by foreign artists, critics and impresarios. On the academic side, the Canadian Studies program encourages and supports interest in teaching about Canada in "selected universities" as well as providing money for scholarships, fellowships and scholarly exchanges.

The Committee looked at the staff and work of this bureau in Ottawa and abroad, including the cultural centres in Paris, Brussels and London, a specialized art gallery in New York and display centres in several large capital cities where Canada maintains diplomatic missions. While our recommendations are directed chiefly to the Department of External Affairs, we also have comments to make about the international activities of some other federal agencies with an interest in cultural affairs. Nor can the increasing provincial activity in international cultural relations be ignored.

Federal-Provincial Cooperation

While the Committee believes that there should be strong federal leadership in international cultural activities by Canadians, we recognize that there are provincial interests to be considered as well. Through established arts councils or departments responsible for arts and culture, the provincial governments have in recent years increasingly sponsored local groups wishing to perform abroad, in many cases to strengthen a distinctive provincial cultural image. Provincial interests are also frequently reflected in Canadian delegations to Unesco meetings and international conferences relating to education and cultural matters, and provincial cabinet ministers are sometimes designated leaders of delegations.

This increased provincial participation in international cultural conferences has not been without problems. If delegations are to be well prepared, the selection of delegates must be agreed upon long enough in advance for briefings to take place, and for a team approach to develop. Invitations to form delegations for international meetings involving the provinces must be given and responded to promptly to allow time for proper briefings to be arranged and for differences of opinion on conference issues to be reconciled. The provincial point of view to be represented at international meetings arising from Canada's cultural agreements with other countries should form part of the overall Canadian position being presented.

There has been an improvement in the exchange of information between federal and provincial governments on their interests in international cultural relations in recent years. The Committee considers highly desirable the formal and informal consultative meetings that now take place between federal and provincial officials concerned with international cultural affairs. In our view, such consultation would be even more effective if artists or their representatives were included in these discussions whenever appropriate. The choice could be made on the recommendation of artists' organizations or provincial arts councils.

Although these consultative meetings are helpful for cultural affairs, they do nothing to solve problems arising when educational affairs must be taken up. Federal officials from departments and agencies concerned with scholarly activities could usefully be invited to participate. Provincial representation might also be invited from the ministries of education and the Council of Ministers of Education – Canada, and its staff. This serious omission in communications with the provinces should be corrected promptly.

88. The Department of External Affairs should extend federal-provincial consultation on international cultural affairs to include officials of other federal departments and agencies concerned with education, provincial departments of education, representatives of the Council of Ministers of Education – Canada, and the academic community.

Selecting Canadian Talent for Presentation Abroad

A variety of methods is used in the selection of Canadian art for international exposure. In the visual arts, guest curators and gallery owners from individual Canadian galleries are often associated with specific exhibitions and invited to make selections. Curators from abroad sometimes make selections when an exhibition is co-sponsored by a foreign exhibition centre. The Canada Council

Art Bank has occasionally assisted in the organization of a touring exhibition, and the Department of External Affairs has a number of small permanent collections of its own continuously on tour.

Authors and performing artists seeking assistance to present their work also make formal applications to External Affairs which are referred to an Advisory Committee on Foreign Cultural Relations. This committee, entirely made up of public servants representing the federal cultural agencies, gives advice about the artistic quality of the company, group or artist and about the appropriateness of the tour for the applicants and the countries to be visited. The International Cultural Relations Bureau organizes and participates in the committee's meetings, assisted by representatives of the National Museums of Canada, representatives from the International Relations section of the CBC and the Arts and Culture Branch of the Department of Communications, and the heads of sections of the Canada Council and the National Arts Centre as appropriate.

Effective and equitable decisions about which artists to assist are admittedly difficult to make. The Committee accepts the argument that if too many consultations are entertained, the selection process will be unworkable. At the same time, those involved in it should be seen to be free from bias and to be well-informed about the quality of performance to be expected from the applicants.

The Committee considers it desirable to open up the selection process a little. While informal consultations certainly take place already, there will surely be occasions when outside expertise from the professional arts community should be called upon formally to assist the Advisory Committee on Foreign Cultural Relations.

89. The composition of the advisory committee designated to review applications from Canadian artists, performers and craftspeople seeking financial and administrative assistance to present their talent outside Canada should be expanded to include, when appropriate, knowledgable individuals from the professional creative arts community.

There is also the question of what criteria are to be used in the selection process. In our Discussion Guide *Speaking of Our Culture,* we asked, "What cultural image of Canada should be projected abroad?" We received many suggestions in response to this question which helped focus our thoughts in preparing the following observations. They may also be of interest to provincial or private sponsors of Canadian touring artists.

To begin with, selections should be tested against two basic questions. What will the chosen form of presentation tell people abroad about Canadian culture? And to what degree will the foreign experience enrich the artistic careers of the Canadian performers who travel abroad?

Ballet companies and other performing artists told us that touring out-side Canada is essential if they are to acquire and retain an international reputation. The Montreal Symphony Orchestra drew our attention to the fact that an international reputation serves to instil pride throughout the country and to develop support in the home community. Selection criteria should be designed to ensure that Canadians can be proud of those who receive federal assistance to perform or display their work before international audiences.

Many intervenors advanced the view that groups which present material reflecting the ethnic and multicultural character of Canada should be assisted. Nor should it be forgotten that there is great interest abroad in the traditions and artistic activities of Canada's indigenous peoples. Exhibitions of Inuit sculpture and prints have been successfully toured abroad for many years by the Department of External Affairs. More opportunities could now be given to Indian artists and performers as well. And as the Commissioner of Official Languages reminded us, having two official languages is a great asset – one that is perhaps undervalued in Canada. Selecting talent to tour abroad is made much easier expressly because we have artists who perform in English and in French. Our official languages offer exceptional access to the international community.

The question of support for amateur groups traveling abroad was frequently mentioned by intervenors and requires some comment. Amateur groups usually find their own funding and make their own arrangements for tours abroad. In any event, they are not eligible for financial assistance from the Department of External Affairs, which accepts applications only from "professional artists who are Canadian citizens" or from "professional ensembles or companies who have achieved recognition and are based in Canada."

A case can be made for federal sponsorship of tours abroad by amateurs who have achieved a high standard of performance. "Full-time professionalism is not an inevitable touchstone of art," as one intervenor wrote, and amateur groups often make a people-to-people impact that professionals do not. The Committee considers that the overriding criterion in such instances must be the degree of excellence attained in the chosen field of performance. External Affairs should help groups that meet this criterion. Even if the financial help that can be given to such groups is modest and only occasional, they should be encouraged to make their touring plans known to the International Cultural Relations Bureau, so that Canadian diplomatic posts abroad can be told they are coming. Canadian amateur groups might then sometimes be invited to perform at Canadian cultural centres abroad, thereby contributing to the variety of programs presented.

Canadian content also figures among the criteria used by External Affairs in awarding grants. Canadian writers and visual artists meeting foreign audiences obviously have no problems with this criterion, but performing artists do. It would be unrealistic to insist that groups performing abroad under federal government sponsorship be required to present programs entirely made up of original Canadian material (music, choreography, and so on). However, External Affairs does give priority to applicants who propose to present "high quality Canadian works or productions which reflect Canada's current arts scene." It must be acknowledged that it is sometimes a gamble to take material to foreign audiences which have no frame of reference for such material. Sadly, some productions which have been successful in Canada have failed before foreign audiences for this very reason.

90.   Among the Canadian companies, groups or artists eligible to receive federal support for international tours and projects, the following should be given priority:
Canadians who have received recognition in Canada and who will benefit materially and professionally by foreign experience;
Professionals, in the broadest sense, meaning not only those whose principal employment is the pursuit of their art but also those who have demonstrated excellence in performance;
Canadian artists and performers representing the cultural traditions of Canada's Native peoples and ethnic communities who can introduce foreign audiences to their specialized art forms.

Recruitment and Training of Personnel

If Canada is committed to the concept of cultural cooperation and intends to give cultural relations equal status with economic, commercial and political policies, this should be reflected in the personnel practices of the Department of External Affairs. Positions in cultural affairs must be staffed with strongly motivated, highly qualified and well-trained people. Yet it was abundantly clear from the comments of intervenors that inadequacies in the numbers and training of staff assigned to this activity, particularly in posts abroad, were often the cause of their dissatisfaction. Given the limited budget and the minimum priority assigned to international cultural relations within External Affairs, it is remarkable that any specialization in this field has developed at all. No formal career stream for cultural affairs officers has existed, although there have always been foreign service officers who found this work to their liking when assigned to it. Some have consistently sought these assignments.

Specialized cultural affairs jobs are mostly found at headquarters. The assignment of staff in missions abroad to carry out cultural affairs responsibilities is very haphazard. Full-time cultural affairs officers are attached to only a few missions in major centres. The common practice is to assign a junior Canadian officer to supervise a locally engaged employee. Canada has been well served by its locally engaged employees abroad who in many cases have devoted their entire working lives to furthering Canadian interests. It cannot be denied, however, that such personnel start with a disadvantage which particularly affects cultural promotion.

Canadian-based political affairs officers assigned to cultural affairs may devote a good portion of their time to this work if they are personally interested, but other duties will always compete for their attention. Often the officers do not stay in the post long enough to develop or exploit effective collaboration with the resident cultural community, the professional promoters or impresarios, or the scholarly community. As one intervenor told us, foreign service officers engaged in cultural activities have energy and enthusiasm. They may evidence goodwill but, because they lack expertise, they fail to understand the needs of Canadian performers and artists going abroad and are of little help in cultural marketing.

The amount of attention paid to cultural affairs in missions abroad is ultimately a reflection of the degree to which the head of post believes this activity can support and extend the other Canadian interests promoted by the mission. If the head of post recognizes that cultural and academic affairs merit support, much can be accomplished. Even with limited resources, information can be collected and contacts made to help Canadian performers.

The Committee is convinced that there must be a fundamental change in the approach to the recruitment and training of officers for the cultural affairs activities of External Affairs. The department has shown no reluctance to allow the development of specialization in economic and legal career streams within its organization. Since the recent amalgamation of international departmental services, specialized trade and immigration career officers have also been brought into External Affairs. It is now time that a cultural affairs career stream should be fully recognized and fostered.

Competitions for positions in international cultural relations should obviously emphasize appropriate scholastic background and experience. It was suggested to the Committee that additional training might include an assignment, for a full posting period of one to two years, to either another federal cultural agency like the Canada Council or the National Arts Centre, or to the management side of one of the major artistic companies or even to the office of a Canadian artistic management organization. Officers coming back to Canada from a posting in cultural centres abroad would also benefit from such a home assignment. No academic background can provide the same degree of sensitization to the needs of the artistic community as a shared experience in cultural production management of this type.

91.   The Department of External Affairs should formally designate cultural affairs as a distinctive career stream within the foreign service and provide appropriate recruiting standards and training facilities to ensure its development and continuation.

Cultural Centres and the 20-Year Plan

While facilities required to implement cultural policies abroad are not as important as the people who run them, they must be available. From the Department of External Affairs brief and subsequent discussions, the Committee learned that cultural activities will be extended according to a detailed 20-year plan.

The cultural centres already established or designated for several cities abroad are of key importance to this plan. Such centres are associated with Canadian diplomatic missions but are not necessarily located within actual chancery or consulate premises. The centre in Paris established the prototype and has been in operation since 1969. Similar centres are now open in London and Brussels. In New York, the cultural affairs section of the Canadian Consulate-General opened a centre for contemporary Canadian art, the 49th Parallel Gallery, in 1981. Preparations to open a centre in Bonn and later in Mexico City are well advanced. When capital costs can be met, others will be set up in Los Angeles, Tokyo and Sydney and also in a South American capital.

Each cultural centre will also be a training and resource centre to which officials assigned to cultural affairs duties in a geographically related group of Canadian missions can apply for assistance. Each centre is considered an "operational base" competent to serve Canadian interests in arts, letters, academic and cultural promotion. Ideally, each centre should also have the capacity to carry out an appropriate academic role in support of Canada's international educational responsibilities. This capacity has been provided in London but some other centres have yet to undertake these duties.

The current director of the cultural centre in London has described the essential purpose of the cultural centre as it is conceived at present: "We aim to maximize the cultural presence of Canadians in this country. We serve as facilitators and resource people. We provide information on all aspects of the arts in Canada. We seek to generate an atmosphere in which cultural exchanges between Canada and Britain become increasingly possible."

Cultural centres abroad are guided by the objectives of headquarters, but local directors are given great freedom to select and arrange the annual calendar of events in their centre. However, they do not have very much to spend. The budget for all cultural activity in New York in 1982-83 is $120,000, while operating costs of the three European centres will total $560,000: $60,000 for Brussels, $200,000 for London and $300,000 for Paris. Each centre has a small staff of one or two Canadian officials assisted by locally engaged employees.

The International Cultural Relations Bureau considers that these centres can substantially improve the presentation of Canadian cultural programs. It is anticipated that a stable audience will be built up over time at each location. Opportunities to perform or exhibit at these centres will be available to developing artists. The centres can also use some of their own financial resources to help Canadian touring companies put on additional performances while in the area. Programs organized by Canadian cultural centres can be linked to other Canadian promotions in trade, tourism and sports to generate a much greater total impact. How well cultural centres succeed in improving both the content and style of their cultural programs will depend, of course, to a large extent on the sensitivity of their staff to the needs of Canadian creative artists. *The Department of External Affairs should be commended for its long-range plan to open and operate Canadian cultural centres abroad as operational bases from which to extend and improve the presentation of Canadian cultural activities in foreign countries.*

International Cultural Exchanges

Canada needs exchanges with other countries to widen its choices and stimulate its creativity, as the Canadian Commission for Unesco emphasized in its brief. In fact, Canada participates in many overlapping but complementary cultural exchanges, both formal and informal. Formal bilateral cultural agreements have been negotiated between Canada and a number of countries including Brazil, Italy, Belgium, France, Japan, Mexico and the Federal Republic of Germany. The themes covered are cooperation, friendly relations and development of understanding through cultural connections on a broad scale. Specific areas of activity are usually designated; these may include education, social affairs, youth, sport, film and artistic exchanges. In the case of the Soviet Union, cultural affairs are covered within a General Exchanges Agreement. Continuing but less formal consultation on cultural matters takes place at annual meetings with the United Kingdom, the Netherlands and China. In addition, Canada exchanges scholarships in specialized studies with several other countries.

Bilateral exchanges open up opportunities for foreign experience and assure a measure of patronage by the host country. The Department of External Affairs provides the financial support to carry out the bilateral cultural agreements it negotiates and organizes provincial participation in any joint consultations arising from them. The various sections of the Canada Council arrange support for tours and exhibitions of foreign artists in Canada resulting from the agreements on behalf of External Affairs. The costs are met by that department.

The External Affairs brief reminded us that at present "many other countries are investing State-to-State relations with increasing importance." The Committee has some reservations, however, about formal cultural agreements. These agreements should be recognized for what they are – essentially political documents. Precisely because they are structured, the cultural component is vulnerable to manipulation for political reasons. The Canadian artist wishing to perform or exhibit abroad should be assisted, not thwarted, by any cultural agreement negotiated by the Department of External Affairs.

The Committee supports one special case which would require some bilateral negotiation. The Inuit Tapirisat of Canada put before us their view that "federal policy should contribute to easier access by Canadian Inuit to the culture of their fellow Inuit in the circumpolar world and among one another within Canada." There are approximately 100,000 Inuit in all, living in Canada, Alaska, Greenland and Siberia. The Inuit Tapirisat brief argued that:

"art, artifacts, handicrafts, broadcasts, films, foodstuffs, books, records, performances, videos and tapes from other Inuit, should, for the purposes of the Canadian north... not be treated as 'foreign'... Without the free exchange of cultural materials between *all* Inuit, the market will be so small that cultural development will be extremely difficult."

We believe that this is a reasonable request which merits further consideration.

92. The Department of External Affairs and the Department of Indian and Northern Affairs should explore methods by which barriers preventing the free exchange of cultural materials between Canadian Inuit and their fellow Inuit in the circumpolar world may be removed.

At both federal and provincial levels, there is much interest in pursuing the possibility for cultural and scholarly exchanges resulting from the fraternal connections Canada has with members of the Commonwealth and La Francophonie. Various institutions organize official opportunities for multilateral cooperation in educational and cultural affairs (in addition to science, technology and sport). In addition, in both international associations, numerous nongovernment organizations have been formed to foster mutual interests and cooperation in specialized fields. Cultural and academic exchanges within La Francophonie and the Commonwealth are particularly valuable to both Canada and the other member states, many of which are Third World countries. Exchanges arising from these close ties of friendship and common language should be sought out and supported by the Department of External Affairs and other relevant federal agencies.

Another important multilateral forum through which Canadian cultural concerns can be expressed is Unesco, of which Canada is a founding member. The Department of External Affairs is responsible for official representation of Canada at the Paris headquarters of Unesco. The Canadian position on subjects debated there is coordinated within the International Cultural Relations Bureau, while Canadian support for Unesco's development aid projects in Third World countries is channeled through the Canadian International Development Agency (CIDA).

There is, however, another dimension to Unesco's activities. The Massey-Lévesque Commission was asked to advise the government how Canada could contribute fully to that organization and receive full benefit from the association. As a result of the recommendations in the Massey-Lévesque Report the Canadian Commission for Unesco was established as a separate agency associated with the Canada Council, which provides secretariat and budget. The Commission is therefore another arm's-length body, but beyond its internal organization, it has a membership of more than 100 nongovernment organizations and individuals who share its varied concerns. Government departments have consultant status. The Commission describes itself in its brief as "an interdisciplinary liaison and advisory body capable of drawing in Canada on a vast network of expertise and human resources from public and private sectors." The Commission can also draw on links with other national commissions of the member states of Unesco.

It seems to the Committee that the potential usefulness of the Canadian Commission for Unesco has not been fully exploited by either the Commission itself or the government agencies it has the capacity to assist. This is in part a result of the separation of the Social Sciences and Humanities Research Council from the Canada Council in 1978. The Commission remained an autonomous division of the Canada Council and liaison with the SSHRC has, as a consequence, diminished. This is regrettable. The Commission should seek to strengthen its direct contacts with all federal and provincial agencies interested in cultural policy. The Commission has the capacity to contribute to government programs in education, culture and research. It offers a forum where the interests of nongovernment organizations on these subjects and others can be explored. The Commission should be more persistent in making government agencies aware of its potential usefulness. We endorse the work of the Canadian Commission for Unesco and urge both federal and provincial governments to call upon it more often.

The Commission's brief supported the evidence put forward by many other intervenors that customs regulations, border regulations and tax liabilities enforced by many countries constitute a barrier to the unrestricted interchange of cultural products. We encourage the Canadian Commission for Unesco to continue to press, through its international contacts, for changes in regulations which impede international cultural activities.

We learned from the Commission brief that Unesco has actively sponsored "the compilation and coordination of research in cultural statistics and the development of cultural data banks." The need for more and better research and data in the field of the arts was forcibly brought home to this Committee in its own work, and we therefore welcome this Unesco initiative.

The Committee believes that Canada should foster exchanges particularly with countries of the Third World as part of our cultural policy. Cultural exchanges are an essential dimension of the assistance channeled through the Canadian International Development Agency (CIDA) and the international aid organizations which Canada supports. We were reminded by the Unesco Commission that, unlike most of the countries of the industrially developed world, Canada has experienced many of the problems which Third World countries now face, such as

"the problems of dealing with a pervasive and overwhelming foreign culture, of trying to develop a strong metropolitan culture without sacrificing the hinterland, of guaranteeing the cultural integrity of Native peoples and other minority cultural groups."

Third World countries know that Canada has dealt with many of these problems and has achieved high international standards in the arts and in mass communications within a very short time. The Commission's brief argued that Canadian experience should be shared and suggested that a multilateral agency such as Unesco is a good instrument for this, both because of its international links and because of its links with the Canada Council. While the Committee agrees that cultural exchanges with Third World countries could well be arranged through the Unesco Commission, direct bilateral arrangements should also continue and expand.

Some federal cultural agencies have for many years shown an interest in Third World countries. Radio Canada International broadcasts to Africa, Latin America and the Caribbean. The National Film Board has frequently cooperated with the Canadian International Development Agency on projects. As we said in Chapter 9, we see an expanded role for the NFB as a training and research institution for film production in which students from the Third World could participate. There is a long tradition of Canadian assistance in education carried out by CIDA, the Canadian University Service Overseas (CUSO) and its French-language counterpart (SUCO). We were told by the Canadian Crafts Council that "there is a demand for short-term technical assistance to the Third World in crafts and appropriate technology." The Crafts Council is pursuing this with CIDA and other nongovernment organizations. Undoubtedly other examples of fields for fruitful bilateral cultural aid could be cited.

We have a strong conviction that cultural exchanges with Third World countries should be expanded. We entirely agree with the eloquent argument in the brief from the Université de Moncton which stressed the need to improve communications between Canada and the countries of the Third World in the interests of world peace and international justice.

The Committee agrees that international cultural exchanges on both the bilateral and multilateral level are essential for the full development of Canadian cultural life. The Committee therefore encourages the initiatives of the Department of External Affairs in the negotiation of cultural agreements.

93.   Multilateral and bilateral cultural exchanges with countries of the Third World should be actively sought by all federal cultural agencies in cooperation with the Canadian International Development Agency, the Department of External Affairs and the Canadian Commission for Unesco.

94.   The Canadian Commission for Unesco should strengthen its direct contacts with government agencies concerned with cultural policy. Additional resources should be allocated to permit this expansion of its activities.

Making Canada Known Abroad

"Ignorance of Canada in other countries is very widespread," wrote the Massey-Lévesque Commissioners. This condition has changed little in the ensuing 30 years. However, the National Film Board, Radio Canada International and the Department of External Affairs' Bureau of Information and Academic Relations division are working to correct this situation. In addition, the programs of the Canadian Commission for Unesco and academic and professional exchanges arranged by federal departments and agencies help to make Canada better understood abroad.

From the time it was set up in 1939, a primary purpose of the National Film Board has been to illustrate Canadian life for foreign audiences and to increase international understanding through specialized subject coverage. National Film Board productions are distributed internationally through offices in London, Paris, Sydney, New York and Chicago. Copies of NFB and other Canadian films have been deposited in every Canadian diplomatic mission for local distribution.

Radio Canada International is an organization that is little known within Canada. Of the federal agencies attempting to increase knowledge of Canadian life abroad, it undoubtedly has had great impact on foreign audiences. Although it is difficult to estimate the size of the audience reached by its signal, the service transmits daily shortwave broadcasts in 11 languages to audiences on four continents, and reaches still wider audiences through recorded programs on tape and disc, distributed to foreign radio stations.

Radio Canada International is unusual among national shortwave broadcasting organizations in that it is not directly controlled by government. The Department of External Affairs proposes target areas and languages, while RCI is entirely responsible for the editorial content and programming of the 175 hours it broadcasts every week. It receives its funds from Canadian Broadcasting Corporation appropriations, justifying its budget requirements in broadcasting terms.

95. It is imperative that the editorial independence of Radio Canada International be maintained in any new financial arrangements that may arise from changes in the operation of the Canadian Broadcasting Corporation.

For 40 years, Radio Canada International has proven itself to be an effective instrument for increasing understanding and knowledge of Canada in many parts of the world. The range of its broadcasts is, however, limited by the capacity of its transmitter at Sackville, New Brunswick. It can direct broadcasts only to those countries within reach of that signal – that is, mainly in Europe, Africa and Latin America. At present, RCI is giving no serious consideration to extending its coverage by installing additional facilities for shortwave transmission to Asia and the Pacific. It is surely time for the organization to expand its activities in this direction, using existing commercial facilities in Western Canada to start with and taking advantage of advances in communications technology for new permanent installations when practical.

96. Radio Canada International should extend shortwave broadcasts as soon as possible to countries in the Pacific and Asia through transmission facilities in Western Canada.

The Bureau of Information of the Department of External Affairs is engaged in communication activities to elucidate Canadian foreign policy objectives. To counteract the misconceptions about Canada conveyed by the popular press, television and radio in other countries, the External Information division of this bureau uses films, exhibits, speeches, seminars and publications, and sponsors tours of Canada by foreign journalists. A modest cultural program which allows missions abroad to make book presentations and, on occasion, to invite Canadian performers to contribute to the celebration or promotion of a special event, is also part of this essentially political public affairs activity.

The Academic Relations division of External Affairs also promotes knowledge of Canada. The department was very slow to recognize that information and public affairs activities should be supplemented by programs emphasizing Canadian scholarship. As recently as 1969, the *Times Literary Supplement* could truthfully declare, "Canada has done little, especially externally, to eradicate its traditional reputation for philistinism." The public relations orientation of the department's external information activities was documented in a report released in March 1976 *(To Know Ourselves, Report of the Commission on Canadian Studies*, prepared for the Association of Universities and Colleges of Canada). This report recommended increased encouragement and support for a Canadian Studies program abroad as a crucial new element in future activities.

In 1975, following consultation with the Commission on Canadian Studies, but before its report appeared, the Department of External Affairs established a formal Academic Relations division with responsibility for the development of Canadian Studies programs in selected foreign countries. This division is now a part of the Bureau of International Cultural Relations.

The division's Canadian Studies program aims to inject some Canadian content into the education systems of selected countries. Research and publications are commissioned and financial encouragement is given for teaching, faculty enrichment and curriculum development. Some printed materials about Canada are made available for distribution and some scholarships are awarded. In addition, Canadian Studies Associations on the academic level in several countries have been encouraged and given a limited degree of financial support, and a program for visiting foreign professors brings scholars from abroad for short-term teaching assignments in Canada.

While funds allocated for this purpose have not been generous, money from the Canadian government has led to the introduction of Canadian Studies programs in the United Kingdom, the United States, France, the Federal Republic of Germany, Japan, Italy, Belgium, Australia and Ireland. Approximately 400 universities in these countries now offer courses on Canada to an estimated enrolment of 20,000 students. Cultural agreements with a number of other countries provide for academic and scholarship exchanges. Acting on one of the recommendations of the report *To Know Ourselves*, the department in 1978 formed an advisory committee for Academic Relations composed of Canadian university faculty members to give the division guidance on academic but not administrative matters.

At present over 50 per cent of the Academic Relations division budget is spent in Europe, including Britain, while about 11 per cent is spent in the United States. *The overwhelming importance of our relations with the United States strongly suggests to us that a program which aims at increasing knowledge of Canada among future American decision-makers merits extraordinary effort and should be supported accordingly.*

Although the programs are new and assessment is therefore difficult, the Committee has concluded that the programs of the Academic Relations division are not only undervalued but also inadequately funded. Working through schools and universities to extend understanding of Canada in other countries is admittedly a long-term proposition, but it is an important and worthwhile endeavour. Canadians traveling abroad for artistic, academic and business reasons are likely to be more successful in foreign countries if Canada is known to be a country rich in human as well as material resources.

This has not yet been adequately recognized in the Department of External Affairs, even though over the relatively brief life of this program a good beginning has been made with limited resources by a few dedicated officials. Cooperation with nongovernment organizations such as the Canadian Mediterranean Institute and the Shastri Indo-Canadian Institute in the field of Canadian scholarship has already been fruitful. Contacts of this kind should be sought out and supported. The potential reward in terms of increasing awareness of Canada abroad is enormous.

97. The extension of knowledge of Canada in other countries is a fundamental element in federal cultural policy. The Department of External Affairs should therefore assign additional specialized staff and increased financial resources to the Academic Relations division to permit the development of innovative Canadian Studies programs in new geographic areas as well as to strengthen Canadian Studies programs now in place.

Promoting and Marketing Abroad
It was primarily with an eye to the marketplace that visual artists broached the matter of international relations with us during our hearings. The Canadian Book Publishers' Council told us, "There should be no adversary position between culture and commerce. Our culture is a salable commodity." We received a similar message from record companies, filmmakers, craftsworkers and the whole range of performing artists.

In fact, federal agencies now have a wide range of programs to promote Canadian talent abroad. Two departments of the federal government assist Canadian publishers to market books by subsidizing attendance at international book fairs. Popular recording artists are assisted by Radio Canada International, which distributes the winning records from the Juno and Félix competitions held by the English- and French-language associations within the Canadian recording industry to 2,000 radio stations abroad. As a result of collaboration between Radio Canada International and Canadian consulates in the United States, several educational and public radio stations have carried recorded programs by Canadian popular artists. Canadian Broadcasting Corporation representatives promote sales of CBC television productions to other countries. Canadian films are promoted by two federal agencies, the National Film Board and the Film Festivals Bureau of the Department of Communications. The Film Festivals Bureau not only gives grants to assist Canadian films to compete but also organizes press and marketing offices at film festivals to promote them. A joint information and public relations operation has been undertaken, involving the National Film Board, the Canadian Film Development Corporation and the Department of Communications. Under the name "Film Canada" it presents a unified promotion and information approach at international film markets. In the United States, a successful start was made in Los Angeles in March 1982.

Canadian performing and visual artists who receive assistance from the Canada Council tour or exhibit extensively in the United States – a market that both the Council and Canadian artists consider to be a natural and vital extension of the Canadian market. The Canada Council also contributes both money and expertise for infrequent extraordinary exhibitions of Canadian art abroad, such as the one mounted jointly by Canada and West Germany at the Akademie der Künste in Berlin in 1982-83.

The work of the Cultural Affairs – Arts Promotion division of the International Cultural Relations Bureau is entirely directed toward promotion of Canadian talent abroad. It is guided by objectives approved by cabinet in 1974 which state that its activities should "reflect internationally the growing creativity and scope of Canadian culture and... promote as an extension of domestic cultural policy, the export of Canadian cultural manifestations abroad." The objectives further state that the division should, in association with the Academic Relations division, "improve professional opportunities abroad for Canadian artists and scholars."

The grants which External Affairs awards to Canadian performing and visual artists and to Canadian writers to tour abroad reflect these promotion objectives. In the assessment of applications for assistance, External Affairs gives priority to proposed tours which are of "at least two weeks' duration and part of a sustained effort to create permanent circuits for Canadian artists in specific areas; which have commitments from recognized and reliable sponsors who will guarantee reasonable revenue in relationship to the local market"; and which are "organized by professional Canadian agents or tour coordinators."

Other promotion grants have brought European impresarios to Canada to see Canadian productions and sent Canadian impresarios to professional conferences where they could negotiate contracts for their clients, or enabled them to travel abroad to evaluate possibilities for future tours.

Radio Canada International is doing its part to promote Canadian performers. Working with both the Department of External Affairs and, more recently, directly with Canadian artists' representatives, RCI will announce tours by Canadians in its regular shortwave broadcasts to the countries where they are to perform. Audiences in these countries will also be reached through the distribution of recordings made by the artists, and through broadcast interviews recorded by the artists for RCI before they leave Canada on tour.

The potential of this program in terms of promotion and publicity is substantial. It depends for its realization, however, on timely, accurate information. This free service to Canadian artists opens up opportunities for audience development considerably. The Committee commends this initiative and joins Radio Canada International in its hope that good use will be made of it by artists and their managers.

While this is not an inclusive list of federal activities directed toward the promotion and marketing of Canadian talent and Canadian cultural products, it does demonstrate that there are programs in place to do this job. However, the Committee was repeatedly told that much more is required.

Much of the unhappiness felt by Canadian artists with the efforts made on their behalf abroad can, it seems to us, be traced to misunderstandings about what can reasonably be expected from External Affairs posts abroad. Canadian officials can make appointments and introductions, but further arrangements must be made by professional managers whose business it is to understand the product and gauge the capacity of the local market to accept it. This is true both for promotion of performing artists and for marketing of the work of visual artists and craftspeople.

The role External Affairs assumes is that of facilitator, an appropriate role in our view and one that the department could more often assume. In foreign capitals, for example, External Affairs could extend contracts to local impresarios to work with the management of Canadian companies throughout their tours, or could enter into contracts for services from local art market specialists to organize Canadian exhibitions.

The department should also encourage officials responsible for trade promotion in posts abroad to direct their considerable expertise toward the marketing of cultural products. Operating in 91 different foreign posts, trade commissioners are trained to identify opportunities and to assist Canadian businessmen to take advantage of them. There is no reason why they should not assist in the marketing of Canadian cultural products. The possibilities for collaboration between cultural affairs and trade promotion should be improved by the fact that trade development has been housed directly within the administration of the Department of External Affairs since January 1982. Canadian private sector business interests and Canadian performing artists could collaborate much more often than they do. This is not an untried idea by any means. Some major trade promotions have included a cultural component, and for years some Canadian companies have generously assisted Canadian performers to tour abroad.

Cultural promotion abroad requires not only specialized knowledge of Canadian artistic accomplishments but also sensitivity to foreign political and cultural environments, as the Department of External Affairs reminded us. The successful promotion of Canadian cultural activities in foreign markets demands the support and active involvement of experienced officers of that department at home and abroad and also the combined energies and perspectives of specialists, drawn from Canada's top creative, administrative and entrepreneurial talent. Recognition of the requirements is only part of the solution. In the interests of the Canadian artists seeking international sales and recognition, we urge the Department of External Affairs to follow its own good advice with all possible speed.

98.   The Bureau of International Cultural Relations of the Department of External Affairs should involve itself more actively in the promotion of Canadian artists in other countries. In doing so, it should take full advantage of the expertise that exists in the International Trade divisions of the department and that is available on contract from professional arts managers in Canada and abroad. It should seek the active cooperation of interested private sector corporations in the promotion of cultural activities in those countries where such collaboration is likely to advance both trade and cultural objectives.

A New Direction for International Cultural Relations

The Canadian cultural community judges the motives of the Department of External Affairs correctly when it asserts that cultural cooperation with other countries helps to create favourable conditions for the achievement of Canada's foreign policy objectives. Funding from the External Affairs "envelope" to support the work of the Bureau of International Cultural Relations is currently justified on these terms.

Certain conditions must be met by those who apply for assistance from External Affairs to tour internationally. Proposals will be considered from professional companies, groups and artists based in Canada who are Canadian citizens and "have achieved recognition." Priority will be given to tours which will "professionally enrich the individual or company and bring it greater international recognition." This implies a commitment by External Affairs to the advancement of Canadian creative artists which the cultural community apparently finds inadequate.

The Department of External Affairs was the focus of a good deal of adverse comment in briefs sent to us. Some of this comment is attributable to current restraints on federal spending. While the department's financial commitment to international cultural relations has been firmly maintained, the costs of international touring have soared. The National Ballet of Canada, for instance, told us that they could not tour outside North America "without the continuing support of the federal government through the Department of External Affairs. Unfortunately, the amount of financial support given us, however generous it may appear in absolute terms, has not increased in the last nine years. Costs of such international tours have tripled in that same period." If fixed administrative and personnel costs are excluded, funds available to the International Cultural Relations Bureau for programs and grants have been held to just over $7 million since the mid-1970s. This has meant that many legitimate requests for assistance have not been met, that extended tours by major companies have been reduced and that younger artists and companies must wait their turn to tour.

Another point of criticism was that the artistic community is not represented on the advisory committee which reviews applications for assistance in touring and other international cultural activities. Without such representation, it is perhaps inevitable that many of the selections made by External Affairs on the advice of the advisory committee should be considered ill-advised by those outside the selection process.

There are strong and legitimate aspirations within the Canadian cultural community which are not being adequately assisted by the present External Affairs grants system. Canadian writers, artists, craftsworkers and scholars need to test themselves and their creations before international audiences in order to develop and to widen the demand for their work. They need international experience to advance their careers artistically and financially. The work of making Canada better known abroad in order to further cultural objectives is not easy. International audiences, for the most part, have a plethora of cultural diversions and interests from which to choose. They give their support and thereby accord stardom to only a few outstanding artists in any field. When international approval is given to a Canadian artist it is a source of gratification not only to the artist but to audiences at home as well. The Department of External Affairs has not convinced either the Canadian cultural community or the Committee that it fully recognizes these national implications of its essential role as the federal agency responsible for the introduction of Canadian creative artists to international audiences.

99. Although federal funding for the presentation of Canadian cultural activities in other countries has some relevance for the achievement of diplomatic and trade objectives, substantially increased expenditures would be justified for reasons relating to the professional development of artists, to the opportunity to increase their financial rewards and to the pride of all Canadians in their achievements.

Proposal for an International Cultural Relations Agency

At present, no organization other than the Department of External Affairs has appropriate funding to channel support to Canadians wishing to develop an international audience for their work. Yet the Canadian cultural community is evidently of the opinion that its interests are not being met by a department whose primary responsibilities are diplomatic and political, and not cultural. A number of intervenors proposed that an entirely new agency should be set up to promote Canadian talent abroad. The British Council, the Goethe Institute and the Alliance française were all held up as models for a federal international cultural affairs agency independent of the Department of External Affairs. Speaking from their own arm's-length positions, both the Canada Council and the National Arts Centre proposed such an agency in their briefs. The NAC went so far as to suggest an organizational structure, a name (the Canadian Arts Promotion Organization) and even an acronym (CAPO). This proposal envisaged CAPO as "a government organization staffed with experienced members of the arts community and interrelating with the Department of External Affairs." Some form of shared responsibility was also favoured by other intervenors with extensive experience of provincial and federal assistance to the arts.

In considering how an accommodation between the desires of the cultural community for more international exposure and the political responsibilities of the Department of External Affairs could be made, the Committee was conscious of the fact that other federal agencies already have the statutory authority to take on an expanded role in the promotion of Canadian talent and scholarship in other countries if they choose to do so. This is true particularly of the Canada Council, the National Arts Centre and the Social Sciences and Humanities Research Council. We were urged by several intervenors to consider expanding the activities of the Canada Council Touring Office into the international field. Indeed, the Chairman of the Canada Council stated in his 24th Annual Report, 1980-81, that the Council hopes to provide grants for international touring as soon as funds permit.

The brief from the Department of External Affairs forecast that arguments in favour of an alternative agency for international cultural relations would be made by other intervenors and discounted them. However, if the following paragraph is a true reflection of departmental views, External Affairs apparently sensed that the legitimate aspirations of the Canadian cultural community might be more satisfactorily combined with the foreign policy priorities of the department.

"Canada's cultural relations with other countries have assumed increasing importance for its citizens. The need for a global external
cultural policy – one that establishes principles, identifies priorities
and integrates plans of action – is more and more apparent. So
also is the need for a much more dynamic approach to cultural
diplomacy in an increasingly competitive international environment."

The Committee has, however, come to the conclusion that the Bureau of
International Cultural Relations is too restricted by the fact that it is part of the
Department of External Affairs to be able to execute the "global external
cultural policy" described as ideal in the quotation above. Both cultural affairs
and academic relations programs were for a long time overshadowed by the
larger, more directly foreign-policy-oriented, Information programs. Since these
activities were removed from an overriding Public Affairs Bureau and placed
within a Bureau of International Cultural Relations, they have had status in
name but have not been given a significant increase in appropriations or been
assigned additional trained cultural affairs officers. Nor are academic relations
accorded the same prestige as cultural affairs within the bureau.

Cultural cooperation has been accepted world wide as an element in
diplomatic relations. Many countries will discuss arrangements for cultural
presentations or scholarly exchanges only on a state-to-state basis, because all
their cultural activities are controlled by the state. On the operational level, certain aspects of presentation of Canadian talent abroad and the extension of
Canadian Studies will always require the cooperation and assistance of officials in Canadian missions abroad. It was consequently apparent to us that
for any agency responsible for Canada's international cultural relations an
association with the Department of External Affairs is not only unavoidable
but genuinely desirable.

We therefore agree that international cultural relations activity should
be administered outside the Department of External Affairs but should remain
under the ministerial direction of the Secretary of State for External Affairs. It
should be strengthened and given an identity of its own, able to respond to
the calls made upon it by its minister to act as the Canadian coordinator for
cultural cooperation with other countries. It must also be able to respond to
the needs of Canadian artists and scholars to present their work before international audiences. We suggest that this agency might be called the Canadian
International Cultural Relations Agency. We consider it important that the chief
executive officer of this agency have a rank equal to that of a deputy minister.
In making appointments to this prestigious position it should be remembered
that the incumbent will represent Canadian cultural and academic interests internationally. This new agency should have a clearly defined mandate, but a
mandate alone is not enough. We consider it essential to retain the confidence
of the cultural community in Canada. We therefore propose that an advisory
board, representative of those cultural and academic interests to be served by
this agency, be appointed to guide it. At the same time, the two existing advisory committees should be retained and strengthened, as we have already

suggested above. These two committees provide specialized advice on applications and suggested extensions of academic relations programs. Direct and useful liaison with other federal cultural agencies and with the academic community is thereby maintained.

Not all the components of the present Bureau of International Cultural Relations would necessarily move to the new agency. To pursue the objectives we see as its responsibility, the Cultural Affairs – Arts Promotion division, the Academic Relations division and the Programmes and Cultural Agreements section should become the core functions. It would seem appropriate, however, for the Historical division and the Multilateral Relations and Sports division, which have a stronger attachment to foreign policy objectives, to remain within the formal departmental organization.

In April 1982, a task force under a former Public Service Commissioner was created to survey the international activities of all government departments and agencies, as part of the implementation of the reorganization and integration of the foreign policy and the international trade sectors announced in January 1982. This task force will, we assume, identify units within other departments and agencies directly concerned with international cultural affairs which might possibly be added to the proposed Canadian International Cultural Relations Agency. The Committee has already recommended that the distribution offices of the National Film Board be more closely associated with the cultural centres abroad, that the new marketing organization recommended in Chapter 3 assist in the promotion of Canadian cultural products internationally, and that the function of the National Museums of Canada international office be included as one of the activities of the Canadian International Cultural Relations Agency.

The authority which the Canada Council has to sponsor international tours is *not*, in our opinion, incompatible with the mandate we propose for the new Canadian International Cultural Relations Agency. Arrangements for cooperation with the Canada Council would continue and indeed should be strengthened by the new agency. Both agencies should be able to assist Canadian creative artists to take advantage, in particular, of the immense U.S. audience so easily reached from Canada.

The Committee has considered the relationship of the Canadian Commission for Unesco to the new agency. In our view the Commission should for the time being retain its independent status within the arm's-length administration of the Canada Council. It was established to act as a national commission of a United Nations body working entirely with governments at both levels as well as with nongovernment organizations in Canada. We suggest, however, that the Canadian Commission for Unesco might be more appropriately associated with the Canadian International Cultural Relations Agency once it is established and has demonstrated that it too is an arm's-length agency.

In recommending an independent agency, the Committee wishes to stress that the new body should maintain close and harmonious relations with the Department of External Affairs, in particular with the Information Bureau and with divisions in the International Trade area. Those cultural centres already planned or in existence would naturally fall under the supervision of the new associate agency. However, it is reasonable to expect that in smaller missions abroad, foreign service officers would represent the interests of the Canadian International Cultural Relations Agency in the same way they now represent the Canadian International Development Agency in posts where no CIDA officer is attached. The head of post should consider international cultural relations as much a part of the job as aid, trade and immigration, each of which have program and reporting responsibilities to specialized divisions at headquarters, both inside and outside the actual departmental structure. This should be reflected in the annual appraisals of performance of both the head of post and any officer on the staff responsible for cultural affairs. The Canadian International Cultural Relations Agency would benefit from participation in the department's annual assessment of accomplishment and future objectives for each country where Canada has representation (called the "country program" review) and should be invited to so participate.

The advantages of giving international cultural relations this new but associated status would, we believe, be substantial. The new arrangement would afford officers greater freedom to develop a distinctive career path in international cultural affairs. It would also extend consultation and coordination among provincial governments and the Canadian cultural community involved in supporting cultural activities overseas. Close liaison with the other federal cultural organizations would continue.

100. The Cultural Affairs – Arts Promotion division and the Academic Relations division of the Bureau of International Cultural Affairs should be separated from the Department of External Affairs and given independent status as the Canadian International Cultural Relations Agency, reporting directly to the Secretary of State for External Affairs.

101. The proposed independent but associated agency of the Department of External Affairs, the Canadian International Cultural Relations Agency, should be directed by a chief executive officer with the rank of deputy minister, guided by an advisory board drawn from the Canadian cultural and academic community. It should be given adequate resources in dollars and person years to permit it to represent effectively not only the diplomatic interests of the Secretary of State for External Affairs but also the interests of Canadian artists and scholars seeking to present their work in other countries.

The Committee makes these recommendations in the conviction that the interests of both the federal government and the Canadian cultural and academic community will be better served by a new approach to international cultural relations. Cultural relations with other countries must do more than merely support Canada's foreign policy objectives. Our cultural attainments as well as our trade and economic capacity should be recognized by as much of the world as possible. To achieve this, Canadian creative artists must be given the opportunity to demonstrate that they can attract and sustain the approval of audiences anywhere.

12
Recommendations

_____
_____
_____
_____
_____
_____

12

Recommendations

The page number on the right refers to the location of the recommendation in the text.

Chapter 2 – Government and Culture

1. The status of federal cultural agencies should be defined in a   34
   new Cultural Agencies Act, in recognition of the fact that government activity in culture and the arts is subject to special
   considerations requiring a distinctive measure of autonomy. The provisions of this statute should prevail wherever
   they may conflict with those of the Financial Administration
   Act or the proposed Government Organization Act.

2. To the extent that the functions of cultural agencies and   38
   offices require the exercise of impartial, critical judgment in
   the support of cultural activity, they should be exempt from
   political direction in the form of ministerial directives of either
   a general or specific nature.

3. Freedom from ministerial and central government agency   38
   direction in financial and personnel administration should be
   granted to all cultural agencies which, under their mandates,
   exercise a high degree of responsibility for the economy, efficiency and effectiveness of the operations they direct –
   namely, the National Film Board, Canadian Film Development
   Corporation, Social Sciences and Humanities Research Council
   and the proposed Canadian Heritage Council – in the same
   manner as is now granted to the Canada Council, the National
   Arts Centre and the Canadian Broadcasting Corporation.

4.   In recognition of the accountability of cultural agencies to   41
      Parliament and the Canadian public for the interpretation
      and execution of their respective mandates, each agency must
      develop appropriate measures for the disclosure of its plans
      and performance, including the preparation and publication
      each year of a corporate plan and an annual report which,
      in their form and content, will stimulate public interest and
      permit informed judgments.

5.   Appointments to the boards of directors of cultural agencies   44
      should be made with an overriding concern for the appoin-
      tees' experience in the fields of concern of the agency and
      their demonstrated broad-ranging interest in cultural matters.
      Attention should also be paid to ensuring that the boards as
      a whole are generally representative of Canadian society.

6.   Chairmen of boards of cultural agencies should be appointed   45
      be the Governor in Council, after consultation with the board,
      to ensure an effective working link with the government and
      Parliament. Chief executive officers should be appointed by
      agency boards, or at the very least appointed on their recom-
      mendation, as witness to the responsibility of the boards for
      agency care and management.

7.   The Government of Canada should include in the portfolio of   48
      the minister responsible for the cultural agencies a mandate to
      act as a central reference point in cabinet for cultural matters –
      in effect, an advocate before government on behalf of the arts
      and culture community. This mandate would leave with
      cultural agencies and other departments – particularly the
      Department of the Secretary of State – the responsibility for
      developing cultural policies and programs within their res-
      pective areas of concern.

8.   A primary function of the federal department housing the Arts   52
      and Culture Branch is to assist in providing the environment
      in which cultural life may flourish and the cultural agencies
      may best achieve their purposes. In the course of advising
      the minister on broad cultural policy directions, departmental
      officials should pursue this primary function by fostering com-
      munication and consultation, providing an accurate knowledge
      base for cultural activities, and assisting artists and cultural
      groups to make the fullest use of appropriate technologies.

9.   The federal government should regard the Canada Council as   56
      a primary instrument of support to the arts. Accordingly, it
      should augment the Council's annual parliamentary appropria-
      tion, having regard for the real, as distinct from the nominal,
      value of the Council's grants and sustaining support and for
      the consequences that will follow if the real value of that sup-
      port is allowed to diminish. Parliamentary appropriations must
      be of a magnitude that will permit new initiatives, both inside
      and outside the Council's current areas of support, to be
      developed and sustained.

Chapter 3 – Marshalling Resources

10.   The Department of Communications, in consultation with the   80
      Federal Business Development Bank, should promote the use
      by cultural enterprises of the financial and managerial services
      of the Bank and consider, jointly with such cultural agencies
      as the Canada Council and the Canadian Film Development
      Corporation, how the needs of the Bank for expertise and risk-
      sharing in respect of cultural activities might be met.

11.   In view of the distinctive merits of voucher schemes for sub-   81
      sidizing public attendance at cultural events and purchase of
      cultural products, the federal government and its agencies
      should include such measures in their programs of cultural
      support.

12.   Tax provisions respecting the employment status of artists   84
      and such matters as the calculation of their costs against in-
      come, the valuation of works given for public use and enjoy-
      ment, and their entitlement to income averaging must afford
      equitable treatment in comparison with those applicable to
      other classes of taxpayers.

13.   Public funds for the support of cultural activity should as a   94
      general rule be financed from general revenues. The earmark-
      ing of revenues from a specified source for a specified use
      should be employed only when there is a close correlation
      between the incidence of the financial burdens imposed and
      the distribution of benefits, and its adoption as a means of
      cross-subsidization should be avoided.

14.   The federal government should assume a leading role in   95
      fostering the creation of a nongovernment organization
      designed primarily to devise initiatives and provide impetus
      in the marketing and promotion of Canadian arts.

Chapter 4 – Heritage

15.   The Government of Canada should establish an arm's-length   107
       agency to be known as the Canadian Heritage Council, to be
       a visible champion of heritage interests in Canada, recognizing
       the importance and particular characteristics of those inter-
       ests, to promote heritage arts and sciences and to support
       heritage institutions.

16.   The National Museums of Canada, guided by its Board of   108
       Trustees, should retain supervisory responsibility for the four
       existing and any proposed federal heritage custodial institu-
       tions in the National Capital Region or elsewhere. It should,
       however, relinquish to the proposed Canadian Heritage Council
       responsibility for the various categories of grants and assis-
       tance now given to nonprofit museums throughout Canada
       under the Museum Assistance Programmes, for the continu-
       ation of the National Inventory of the cultural heritage, and for
       the Canadian Conservation Institute – all of which are at present
       administered and funded by the National Museums of Canada
       as part of the National Programmes.

17.   Existing federal legislation relating to the designation of his-   109
       toric sites should be strengthened to compel heritage impact
       studies to be carried out and reviewed before any such site
       is sold, developed or in any way altered from its present use.

18.   The Department of Indian and Northern Affairs, as the federal   109
       department which administers the Northwest Territories,
       should review the existing Northwest Territories Archaeological
       Sites Regulations with the Archaeological Survey of Canada
       and the National Historic Parks and Sites Branch. It should
       proceed at once to develop a comprehensive heritage preser-
       vation act which clearly states the responsibilities and obliga-
       tions of government, industry, special interest groups and in-
       dividuals for the prehistoric and historic archaeological
       resources of the Northwest Territories, and gives recognition to
       the interests of Canadians in the Northwest Territories to re-
       tain such materials in the context in which they were found
       whenever possible.

19. The annual sum appropriated for grants made by the Cana-   112
    dian Cultural Property Export Review Board should properly
    reflect the unpredictable and high prices of the international
    art market. Unspent balances from this appropriation should
    be carried forward to succeeding fiscal years and the Cultural
    Property Export and Import Act should be amended to pro-
    vide authority to do this.

20. The Canadian Cultural Property Export Review Board should,   113
    while retaining its independent status, be associated for ad-
    ministrative purposes with the proposed Canadian Heritage
    Council.

21. In recognition of the fact that conservation is a vital national   114
    aspect of heritage, the proposed Canadian Heritage Council
    should give special consideration to requests for grants which
    will ensure that every region of Canada has access to regional
    conservation facilities. The Canadian Conservation Institute
    should report directly to the Canadian Heritage Council and
    receive its funding from appropriations made to the Canadian
    Heritage Council. The Canadian Conservation Institute should
    give priority to research into new conservation techniques, the
    results of which it should share with all Canadian heritage
    institutions.

22. The National Inventory program and the Canadian Inventory   116
    of Historic Buildings should be completed as soon as possible
    to facilitate collections management, exhibition planning,
    research and education activities based on heritage collections
    throughout Canada. The proposed Canadian Heritage Council
    should assume continuing responsibility for the National Inven-
    tory program and the Canadian Inventory of Historic Buildings.

23. The proposed Canadian Heritage Council should encourage   119
    and support the dissemination of heritage materials
    throughout Canada, and in order to do so should assume
    from the National Museums of Canada direct responsibility for
    grants now given under the Museum Assistance Programmes.
    To facilitate access to nonmovable heritage, the proposed
    Canadian Heritage Council should cooperate with the National
    Historic Parks and Sites Branch of Parks Canada, and with the
    Heritage Canada Foundation, and should assist activities of the
    Heritage Canada Foundation financially if requested.

24. The proposed Canadian Heritage Council should support in-   120
    itiatives to develop training programs in professional heritage
    management.

25. Encouraging volunteers in heritage organizations by offering   121
    them special training is money well spent, and grants for the
    purpose of training volunteers should now be made through
    the Museum Assistance Programmes of the National Museums
    of Canada and, ultimately, by the proposed Canadian Heritage
    Council. In addition, recognized national heritage service
    associations should be eligible for financial assistance toward
    the cost of annual meetings and publications.

26. Suitable buildings should be provided for the National   122
    Museum of Science and Technology, the National Museum of
    Natural Sciences, the Public Archives of Canada and the Na-
    tional Library of Canada as soon as possible, in line with the
    accommodation priorities established by these institutions for
    the heritage collections for which they are responsible.

27. There should be increased federal assistance to smaller   123
    heritage institutions, including the National Exhibition Centres.
    Other levels of government, interested individuals and cor-
    porate sponsors should consider commensurate increases in
    support.

28. The Board of Trustees of the National Museums of Canada   128
    should be given full responsibility for the operation of existing
    and future national heritage institutions in the National Capital
    Region or elsewhere, for staffing those institutions and for
    negotiating acquisitions for its various collections from a non-
    lapsing account to which annual appropriations for this pur-
    pose are made.

29. The Public Archives Act should be revised, following consulta-   132
    tions with provincial and private sector archivists, to reflect
    national needs of archival institutions throughout Canada.

30. A National Archival Records Commission, to be responsible for   132
the coordination and encouragement of programs devoted to
the preservation and use of historical records in the care of
archives throughout Canada, should be established as an independent body associated with the Canadian Heritage Council for administrative purposes. The cost of carrying out the
national objectives of the National Archival Records Commission should be included in parliamentary appropriations provided for the Canadian Heritage Council.

31. In addition to establishing a Canadian Heritage Council   136
(Recommendation 15) the federal government should give consideration to setting up other federal heritage institutions such
as maritime museums, a national aquarium, arboretum, zoological garden and botanical garden. The proposed Canadian
Heritage Council should be called upon to give advice about the
establishment of these long-awaited heritage institutions.

32. The proposed Canadian Heritage Council should be given in-   138
dependent authority for staffing and be otherwise constituted
to be able to operate with the maximum autonomy feasible
for an arm's-length agency.

33. The proposed Canadian Heritage Council should promote   138
liaison among various federal departments and agencies
involved in heritage, among all levels of government and
between government and the private sector.

Chapter 5 – Contemporary Visual and Applied Arts

34. The federal government, through its cultural agencies, should   146
increase the funds available to public art galleries for the purpose of exhibiting contemporary Canadian art.

35. The Government of Canada should establish a Contemporary   148
Arts Centre, with the same status as its four national
museums, dedicated exclusively to the collection, exhibition,
touring, promotion and development of contemporary visual
art in Canada.

36. The federal government should stimulate private demand for   151
contemporary Canadian visual art through incentives to purchase and should apply special depreciation allowances to
purchases of works of art by any Canadian artist, not just living Canadian artists, and to all transactions involving these
works, not just initial purchases.

37. The government should amend the National Design Council   163
    Act of 1960 to designate a Canadian Council for Design and
    the Applied Arts and fund the Council to a level that will
    enable it to fulfil its mandate. The Council should report to the
    Minister of Communications.

38. The proposed Canadian Council for Design and the Applied   165
    Arts should ensure, to the greatest degree possible, that
    federal public buildings make extensive use of contemporary
    Canadian art and design. To that end, the Council would pro-
    vide expert consultative services to all federal departments in-
    volved in building, leasing and renovation projects.

Chapter 6 – The Performing Arts

39. The Canada Council should initiate a program of incentive   172
    grants related to the presentation of new Canadian works in
    the performing arts, the advertising and marketing of such
    works, and the increased cost of rehearsing and producing
    them.

40. The Canada Council should continue to be the source of   181
    federal funding for the National Theatre School of Canada, the
    National Ballet School and such other professional training
    programs as are appropriate to its mandate.

41. The federal government should assist dancers and other   182
    artists who have short professional careers to resettle into
    allied professions where their artistic skills can best be put to
    use. All the relevant agencies and departments – such as the
    Department of Employment and Immigration – should be in-
    volved, and the Department of Communications should
    assume the leadership role.

42. The Canadian Music Centre should be given adequate financial   184
    and other support to enable it to continue to carry out its
    functions on behalf of Canadian music, including the promo-
    tion and dissemination of the works of Canadian composers
    and the employment of new technologies for the storage and
    use of musical compositions.

43. The National Arts Centre should adopt a policy of showcasing   192
the best available Canadian talent and productions in all the
performing arts, in addition to outstanding artists and productions from other countries. It should forego in-house productions of theatrical and operatic works in favour of co-productions with other Canadian companies. The National Arts Centre
Orchestra, however, should remain as a resident and touring
organization.

Chapter 7 – Writing, Publishing and Reading

44. The Canada Council should put assistance to professional   204
nonfiction writers on the same footing as assistance to fiction
writers, without diminishing support to the latter.

45. The federal government should establish immediately, outside   205
the copyright regime, a program to provide payment for both
library and reprographic uses of the books of living Canadian
authors. The basis for calculation of such payment should be
the annual royalty payments to living Canadian authors.

46. The Canada Council should raise the per-word rate paid to   208
literary translators, which is the basis for its translation grants,
to a level commensurate with rates paid to professional
translators of industrial and government documents.

47. Federal agencies involved in assisting publication should   208
provide additional financial incentive to book and periodical
publishers for issuing work translated into English or French
from the other official language.

48. Federal assistance for workshops and seminars that bring   209
writers together to learn from one another should be expanded and increased. Special emphasis should be placed on
meetings between writers from different literary genres.

49. For the long-term future, the federal government should adopt   217
a cultural policy for support to book publishing which would
contain two major components: a comprehensive subsidy program geared to the twin elements of content and demand;
and, in a supporting role, an economic development program
as underpinning to the industrial structure of book publishing.

50. In the short term, the Canadian Book Publishing Development   219
Program of the Department of Communications should adjust
its criteria for eligible titles to reflect the same categories of
culturally significant books assisted by the Canada Council.

51. The Department of Supply and Services should operate its co-   222
publishing program more energetically, seeking the participation of federal departments and Canadian publishers to the
limit of their interest and capability.

52. The federal government should enlarge its commitment of sup-   226
port for Canadian magazines through both the Canada Council
and the Department of Communications. The Council should
establish a two-pronged system of grants based on the twin
elements of content and demand, similar to the redesigned
subsidy program already outlined for book publishing. The
department should initiate an economic development program
for the magazine industry similar to the one recommended by
this Committee for book publishing.

53. The federal government should pursue a broad policy of   230
stimulating public demand for Canadian publications through
awareness and incentive measures, with the objective of increasing that demand so that book and periodical wholesalers,
retailers and librarians are encouraged to make Canadian products more widely available.

Chapter 8 – Sound Recording

54. The CRTC should continue to apply Canadian content regula-   239
tions to AM radio programming, but the stipulations dealing
with the Canadian creative components of broadcast recordings should be strengthened. In addition, the CRTC should
reexamine the present regulations for FM radio and devise
ways to increase the performance of Canadian specialized
recordings on both AM and FM radio.

55. The federal government should assist Canadian-owned   241
companies to distribute and market recordings of "pop"
music and of specialized materials recorded by Canadian
artists through a loan program or other appropriate forms of
subsidy.

56. The federal government should ensure that, for specialized   241
recordings only, subsidy programs are established to assist
Canadian-owned companies to produce recordings by Canadian performers, with special consideration given to recordings
of which the material is written by Canadians.

57. The CBC should increase its production of quality recordings   242
     by Canadian artists and improve its promotion and distribu-
     tion of such recordings, extending these services to suitable
     recordings made by independent Canadian producers.

58. The federal government should assist Canadian record   243
     producers to improve the international marketing of their
     recordings through various means including attendance at
     marketing fairs.

59. Canadian-owned sound recording studios should be assisted   243
     to acquire and upgrade recording equipment through an ex-
     pansion of existing loan programs, possibly established in
     association with the Federal Business Development Bank.

60. The federal government should empower a nongovernment,   244
     Canadian cultural products marketing organization to ad-
     minister a discount voucher scheme, based on a levy on sales
     of blank audiotapes and videocassettes, to stimulate the sale
     and production of Canadian sound recordings and film and
     video productions.

Chapter 9 – Film

61. The Canadian Film Development Corporation should have its   259
     role and budget substantially enlarged so that it may take
     bolder initiatives in financing Canadian film and video produc-
     tions on the basis of their cultural value and professional
     quality.

62. The Capital Cost Allowance tax incentive for investment in   260
     Canadian film production, or at the very least some equivalent
     incentive, should continue to be used in order to channel
     private capital into Canadian filmmaking.

63. The federal government should provide the Canadian-   262
     controlled film distribution industry with the economic
     strength to market Canadian films successfully to Canadian
     and foreign audiences through all channels of exhibition and
     sales.

64. The National Film Board should be transformed into a centre   264
     for advanced research and training in the art and science of
     film and video production.

Chapter 10 – Broadcasting

75. The CRTC should require private broadcasters to allocate sub-   300
    stantial percentages of their programming time, programming
    budgets and gross revenues to new Canadian program pro-
    duction.

76. The CRTC should permit the establishment of new, private   300
    local television services in those communities able to absorb
    them, and use its licensing powers to ensure that these new
    services contain almost exclusively Canadian programs.

77. Any CRTC policies on multi-level, or tiered, cable service must   302
    continue to ensure that the first priority on the basic cable
    service is given to designated Canadian services. In addition, a
    substantial portion of all other tiers of service offered to cable
    subscribers must be Canadian.

78. The CRTC should encourage cable companies to improve their   303
    community channel operations, but cable production must re-
    main limited to such programming.

79. Cable television operators, as a condition of licence, should be   304
    required by the CRTC to allocate a significant percentage of
    gross revenues toward the facilities and programming of com-
    munity channels.

80. The CRTC should encourage the establishment of Local   304
    Programming Leagues wherever community channels are
    available to the local community.

81. The Canadian government must develop a clear and coherent   306
    policy for the orderly development of satellite capabilities and
    put such technologies and the funds they can generate to the
    service of new Canadian production.

82. The CRTC must strictly enforce conformity to all conditions of   307
    licence.

83. The proposed new Broadcasting Act should give clear authori-   307
    ty to the CRTC in matters related to the CBC.

84. The proposed new Broadcasting Act should confirm the total   307
    independence of the CRTC from political intrusion in matters
    relating to licensing, but permit direction by the minister on
    matters of general policy, under certain specified conditions.

85. The CRTC should continue to license provincially and   308
     municipally based broadcasting undertakings.

86. Federal and provincial governments should seek ways to   309
     assist community and campus-run radio stations to alleviate
     their financial difficulties and to stabilize their operations.

87. The CRTC should set up Advisory Committees in each province   310
     to assist in performance evaluation of licensees and to provide
     advice and reaction from a local perspective on all broadcast
     activities.

Chapter 11 – International Cultural Relations

88. The Department of External Affairs should extend federal-   319
     provincial consultation on international cultural affairs to
     include officials of other federal departments and agencies
     concerned with education, provincial departments of
     education, representatives of the Council of Ministers of
     Education – Canada, and the academic community.

89. The composition of the advisory committee designated to   320
     review applications from Canadian artists, performers and
     craftspeople seeking financial and administrative assistance to
     present their talent outside Canada should be expanded to
     include, when appropriate, knowledgable individuals from the
     professional creative arts community.

90. Among the Canadian companies, groups or artists eligible to   322
     receive federal support for international tours and projects, the
     following should be given priority:
     Canadians who have received recognition in Canada and who
     will benefit materially and professionally by foreign experience;
     Professionals, in the broadest sense, meaning not only those
     whose principal employment is the pursuit of their art but
     also those who have demonstrated excellence in performance;
     Canadian artists and performers representing the cultural tradi-
     tions of Canada's Native peoples and ethnic communities who
     can introduce foreign audiences to their specialized art forms.

91. The Department of External Affairs should formally designate   323
     cultural affairs as a distinctive career stream within the foreign
     service and provide appropriate recruiting standards and train-
     ing facilities to ensure its development and continuation.

92. The Department of External Affairs and the Department of   326
     Indian and Northern Affairs should explore methods by which
     barriers preventing the free exchange of cultural materials be-
     tween Canadian Inuit and their fellow Inuit in the circumpolar
     world may be removed.

93. Multilateral and bilateral cultural exchanges with countries of   328
     the Third World should be actively sought by all federal
     cultural agencies in cooperation with the Canadian Interna-
     tional Development Agency, the Department of External Affairs
     and the Canadian Commission for Unesco.

94. The Canadian Commission for Unesco should strengthen its   328
     direct contacts with government agencies concerned with
     cultural policy. Additional resources should be allocated to
     permit this expansion of its activities.

95. It is imperative that the editorial independence of Radio   329
     Canada International be maintained in any new financial
     arrangements that may arise from changes in the operation
     of the Canadian Broadcasting Corporation.

96. Radio Canada International should extend shortwave broad-   330
     casts as soon as possible to countries in the Pacific and Asia
     through transmission facilities in Western Canada.

97. The extension of knowledge of Canada in other countries is a   331
     fundamental element in federal cultural policy. The Depart-
     ment of External Affairs should therefore assign additional
     specialized staff and increased financial resources to the
     Academic Relations division to permit the development of
     innovative Canadian Studies programs in new geographic
     areas as well as to strengthen Canadian Studies programs now
     in place.

98. The Bureau of International Cultural Relations of the Depart-   334
     ment of External Affairs should involve itself more actively in
     the promotion of Canadian artists in other countries. In doing
     so, it should take full advantage of the expertise that exists in
     the International Trade divisions of the department and that is
     available on contract from professional arts managers in
     Canada and abroad. It should seek the active cooperation of
     interested private sector corporations in the promotion of
     cultural activities in those countries where such collaboration
     is likely to advance both trade and cultural objectives.

99. Although federal funding for the presentation of Canadian   336
     cultural activities in other countries has some relevance for the
     achievement of diplomatic and trade objectives, substantially
     increased expenditures would be justified for reasons relating
     to the professional development of artists, to the opportunity
     to increase their financial rewards and to the pride of all Cana-
     dians in their achievements.

100. The Cultural Affairs – Arts Promotion division and the   339
     Academic Relations division of the Bureau of International
     Cultural Affairs should be separated from the Department of
     External Affairs and given independent status as the Canadian
     International Cultural Relations Agency, reporting directly to
     the Secretary of State for External Affairs.

101. The proposed independent but associated agency of the   339
     Department of External Affairs, the Canadian International
     Cultural Relations Agency, should be directed by a chief
     executive officer with the rank of deputy minister, guided by
     an advisory board drawn from the Canadian cultural and
     academic community. It should be given adequate resources
     in dollars and person years to permit it to represent effectively
     not only the diplomatic interests of the Secretary of State for
     External Affairs but also the interests of Canadian artists and
     scholars seeking to present their work in other countries.

Minority Comments
by Committee Members

Minority Comments
by Committee Members

Comment by Albert Breton

Three general principles have guided the Committee's reflections, deliberations and policy recommendations:

i) The core of cultural policies and the measure of their fullness is
creativity and creative artists, and the extent to which audiences
participate in that creativity;

ii) Cultural policies so defined are sufficiently meaningful to stand
by themselves: their significance does not rest on their contribution to Gross National Product, employment, export or economic
growth, to national unity, identity, control or ownership; their
success cannot be gauged by the size of the physical and
material base supporting cultural and artistic activities, or by the
dimension and sophistication of the hardware that serves to diffuse or retrieve cultural messages;

iii) The notions that a larger quantity and more sophisticated hardware, and that Canadian ownership of that hardware are necessarily congruent with the pursuit of cultural objectives as defined
in (i) are naive and as often wrong as right.

The reader can verify how fundamental these principles have been to
the Committee. They are to be found on almost every page of the Report and
can be seen at the root of many recommendations. They are also documented in a number of places, sometimes clearly, sometimes more dis-
creetly: in the fact that the achievement of complete Canadian ownership in
private broadcasting, at the cost of a large volume of resources, has not produced a system that is culturally Canadian or one that can be compelled to
present shows that are Canadian in content; in the fact that the acquisition

by Canadians of Odeon Theatres has not helped the distribution of Canadian films, and may possibly have hindered it; in the fact that the dissallowance of advertising expenditures on foreign broadcasting stations in calculating taxable income and the allowance of such expenditures on foreign programs transmitted by Canadian stations has acted as an incentive to present foreign shows domestically; in the fact that "cultural hardware" seems to have an advantage over "cultural software" in the competitive struggle for investment resources. The list could easily be extended, but these examples are sufficient to underline how radical the Committee's view of cultural policies really is.

But in two areas the Committee has, in my view, reneged on its principles. Since I believe that the Committee's recommendations in these two instances run counter to what it itself defined as true cultural objectives, and that its failure to hold to these principles indicates how hard it is to give priority to cultural and artistic endeavours, I am compelled to register my dissent.

The two areas are publishing and sound recording. The Committee has decided to recommend that only Canadian-owned publishers, and record producers and distributors be eligible for help (subsidies, loans and other support programs) from the federal government. I believe that these recommendations run counter to the interests of Canadian writers and musicians, that they are recommendations which result from a confusion between what is truly cultural and what is only incidentally so. I hold to the view that all publishing companies and all record producers and distributors – irrespective of the origin of their ownership – should be eligible for public support aimed at getting writers published and read and musicians recorded and sold, if these companies accept all the conditions attached to the support programs.

To argue, as is done in Chapter 7, that very few foreign-owned publishing companies publish Canadian novelists, poets or playwrights is to miss the point. Foreign-owned companies are not currently eligible for government support and consequently do not have the inducement that domestic publishers have to publish Canadian writers. But the point is even more basic. If, in the absence of government help, foreign companies were more efficient than Canadian companies as publishers and merchandisers of Canadian writers, a policy that supported only the latter would be one which in effect assumed that publishing is more important than writing and getting the work of writers to audiences. It would be a counter-cultural policy.

Because the presumption cannot be that foreign-owned companies are less efficient as publishers and as producers and distributors of records than are domestically-owned companies, a cultural policy that gives priority to creativity and to creative writers and musicians would not discriminate against foreign-owned Canadian companies. To so discriminate is to give priority to nationalistic objectives to the detriment of arts and culture.

I therefore recommend that in designing support programs for book publishing and for record production and distribution, all companies – irrespective of ownership – should be equally eligible, if they satisfy the conditions and requirements attached to the programs.

Comment by Joy Cohnstaedt

Throughout the Broadcasting chapter, the separation of production and facilities from programming is commented upon. In this dissenting comment I make particular reference to the texts titled "CBC Television Programming," "Regional and Local Programming," "Local Television Programming."

The opening paragraphs on "Local Television Programming" attest to our common goals: "the development of local talent", "the stimulation of new production", and "further opportunities for production talent".

In this context, however, the Report does not comment on the impact of technology on culture in small communities, low-density regions, or highly diversified nations; or the political impact of a continuum of "local" – "regional" – "national"; or the need to overcome political, economic and social obstacles in order to enhance opportunities for indigenous francophone production outside of Quebec, and anglophone production outside of Toronto.

Whatever the cause or the adjective used (technical, economic, integrated, centralized, political), the "centre-hinterland" historical relationship remains anti-creative for opportunities affecting indigenous talent. Because facilities cannot be as widely dispersed as is local talent or the diverse cultures of Canada, the dichotomy regarding production opportunities will remain. Further, our nation's experiences with newspapers and railroads do not support the assumption that finances will automatically flow to wherever "demand" is claimed to exist.

The responsibility for ensuring that Canadians have access to opportunities to express themselves, and to share this expression with Canadians elsewhere, remains a public initiative.

Strong indigenous production is the foundation of a national broadcasting network. For many geographical and language communities, the evolution of CBC production facilities throughout Canada represents potential opportunities for local and regional expression, skill development, and platforms for new talent to gain exposure. The particular significance of each facility differs with the community it serves.

In Saskatchewan, the CBC facility, to be opened shortly, represents the conclusion of a struggle begun over 30 years ago for an equal opportunity to participate in our broadcasting network and to share the indigenous cultural expression with other Canadians. This building will be a visible acknowledgment of the differences between this province and the neighbouring ones which were originally grouped in the "Prairie Region."* For the arts, culture, and production community, this CBC facility represents an intent to develop and sustain employment opportunities for those who wish to live and work in Saskatchewan.

Policy statements do not lend themselves to articulating regulatory practices; they are expressions of desires and goals. Equal access cannot be guaranteed by direct manipulation. Only evolutionary growth encouraged and developed over time will achieve our goals. The Saskatchewan facility and other local and regional CBC facilities, provided with the necessary financial and personnel support, must evolve into opportunity centres, developing and encouraging new in-house and out-of-house production and artistic talent. A national broadcast network will only be as vital and strong as its parts – the local and regional productions.

Comment by Guy Robert

1.   Having been given responsibility for preparing design ideas for the Final Report in the fall of 1980, I presented five or six different formats to the Committee ranging from a book similar to that of the Massey-Lévesque Report released in 1951, to a half-hour documentary animated film. Each of these proposals was aimed at a different public: to whom do we wish to direct our recommendations in order to best influence decision-makers? Our Committee decided on a 300-page book of which several thousands of copies will be produced. I still prefer the idea of a short film which could have presented perhaps a dozen general recommendations to more than five million Canadians on television. Without excluding the preparation of a detailed written report, this film would have intended to show that culture and the arts touch almost everyone, which must be brought out to the public through today's means, namely, television.

2.   If we assume that we live in a rapidly evolving pluralist society, and if federal cultural policies ought to avoid imposing an official culture, then these policies must aim at making federal institutions and programs more flexible by adapting to rapid social, ideological, aesthetic and economic change. Too often our Report stresses the institutional role by recommending, for example, an increase in the budgets and duties of the Canada Council. In my opinion, this risks increasing bureaucracy, centralization and power-mongering by officials, which is why I disagree with the approach. If we are to serve more effectively the cultural aspirations of the public in general and artists in particular, then I feel it would be preferable to reduce the number and size of large administrative structures, to increase the programs aimed at specific

---

* The headquarters for the Prairie Region has been based in Winnipeg. Following a public lobby, Alberta formed its own region 10 years ago. The creation of a new Saskatchewan region confirms the view that the traditional concept of region is no longer viable for the constituency served. The concept of region has been narrowed to what has been called "local" or "sub-regional," and these require strengthening.

and immediate problems (and there are some!), to listen to regional needs and to coordinate our activities with those by the provinces and municipalities. It would then be easier to evaluate, correct or modify, expand or abolish programs depending on their effectiveness and changes in the cultural life of the country. It must be asked, for example, whether the current grant structure does not merely promote grasping dependence and artificial and excessive artistic production in theatre, publication, museums and perhaps other fields.

3.   This same desire to see the general public more actively involved in arts and culture leads me to the matter of the Canadian Broadcasing Corporation. I feel there is a more urgent and easier solution than reforming this vast organization: namely, that the CBC give priority to artistic and cultural information and to related programming, as there is a significant need in these areas and the CBC is the only Crown corporation in a position to fulfil this role. Surely such a role would not be contrary to its basic mandate and would fulfil a legitimate expectation held by a large part of the public. Our Report mentions this solution but does not give it priority.

4.   In the case of our national museums, which Ottawa has finally decided to provide with suitable facilities, I feel that they must be used to advantage to make the nation's capital a veritable showplace of museums as is happily the case in other capital cities. The spin-off from these museums would lead to increased attention in all other museums in the country to the benefit of all Canadians.

5.   As for the Canada Council, I have already been too vocal in my criticism of its jury system, particularly as regards the visual arts and the Art Bank, to support the conciliatory recommendations of the Committee: I feel that a thorough study should be made of the complaints of favouritism and that all of the collections and functions of the Art Bank should be transferred to the future Contemporary Arts Centre proposed by our Committee.

6.   Contrary to the statement made in our Report in Chapter 2, under the sub-heading "Ministerial Coordination," I feel that the work of our Committee should be continued and built upon by an appropriate body which would gather extensive documentation on the arts and on culture, hear complaints and suggestions from the arts community and from the general public, stimulate consultation and debate, evaluate the effectiveness of existing programs, undertake detailed studies and make the information available in order to stimulate public interest. This body would advise the minister responsible and the government on federal cultural policy, as a cultural development institution or a national culture and arts council (similar to other national councils).

7.   Among other things, I do not feel that our Report attaches enough importance to recent cultural conflict movements, to various counter-culture options, nor to the young people who will be the beneficiaries or victims of our recommendations and their application by politicians, bureaucrats, managers and institutions. In short, I feel that the Report devotes too much

attention to reviewing the activities of the past 30 years, often viewed through the rose-coloured glasses of one looking back in time, and not enough attention to accepting the challenge of the coming 30 years. This decreases our chances of attracting the attention of the general public who might even ignore the existence of some thousands of printed copies of our Report. This will undoubtedly limit debate and decisions to a very small circle.

These comments do not mean that I disassociate myself from the Report but they are comments that I feel are useful.

Historical Notes

Historical Notes

The Federal Cultural Policy Review Committee was established in its present form in August 1980 by the Honourable Francis Fox, Minister of Communications and Secretary of State. It grew out of an earlier group, the Advisory Committee on Cultural Policy, under the chairmanship of Louis Applebaum, which had been appointed by Mr Fox's predecessor, the Honourable David MacDonald.

The members of the Advisory Committee on Cultural Policy were all appointed to the new Federal Cultural Policy Review Committee, and other members were added. Jacques Hébert was named co-chairman in August 1980. In the following few months, six more members joined the Committee: Robert E. Landry of Toronto, Mary Pratt of Mt. Carmel, Newfoundland, Jean-Louis Roux of Montreal, Sam Sniderman of Toronto, Max Tapper of Winnipeg and Rudy Wiebe of Edmonton. A further change of membership occurred when Alex Colville left the Committee at an early stage to serve on the search committee for a new director of the National Gallery of Canada. Pierre Juneau and Léo Dorais, deputy minister and assistant deputy minister of Communications, respectively, who had both been members of the original Advisory Committee, felt it appropriate to withdraw from the Review Committee on the completion of the public hearings and the publication of the *Summary of Briefs and Hearings*, since many of the recommendations in the Committee's final Report would necessarily touch on programs for which they had responsibility.

In announcing the formation of the Committee with a renewed and enlarged mandate at the National Arts Centre on 28 August 1980, Mr. Fox defined the scope of the policy review. It should be, he said, "broad and include all the main programs of the Federal Government." He went on to indicate those cultural areas that should be included in the review: the visual and performing arts, heritage, publishing, sound recording, film, broadcasting, the National Library and Archives, international cultural relations, the respective roles of the federal cultural agencies and the government itself. Recognizing the broad nature of the subject matter, and the large number of Canadians concerned with it, the minister stressed the need for "wide public consultation."

To fulfil this mandate, the Committee scheduled public hearings in 18 centres throughout the country, in every province and territory. In preparation for these hearings, it published and distributed in December 1980 some 50,000 copies of a Discussion Guide, entitled *Speaking of Our Culture.* The Discussion Guide introduced the Committee, defined the field of inquiry, reviewed some of Canada's cultural achievements in the past 30 years, outlined challenges and options facing Canadian cultural policy in the years ahead and invited people to submit briefs.

The public response was gratifying. By the time of the deadline for submission of briefs, 9 March 1981, more than 1,100 briefs had been received from individuals, associations and institutions. (Eventually, 1,369 briefs were submitted.) Between 13 April and 10 July 1981, the Committee heard 512 of these in open, public session.

At the conclusion of the public hearings, the Committee undertook to prepare a report on what it had read and heard throughout this phase of its work. The document, entitled *Summary of Briefs and Hearings*, was intended as a synthesis of the written and oral presentations made to the Committee. It was completed in November 1981 and published in January 1982. The Summary pointed out some general themes: the global context of Canadian culture; Canadian cultural pluralism; the status of the artist; the importance of training and education; the need for financial resources; and the role of the federal government in culture and the arts. But, for the most part, the Summary allowed the intervenors to speak for themselves. It did not draw conclusions nor make recommendations.

These were left to the Committee's final Report. Even while the Summary was being prepared, work began on the Report. This phase of the project included: a careful analysis of the briefs received; an assessment of the three months of hearings; consultations with a variety of experts in each field; study of background papers prepared by staff and consultants; and much debate. The Report was substantially completed by 2 September 1982 and published in November 1982.

Biographical Notes

Louis Applebaum, composer, conductor and administrator, began his career in 1941 with the National Film Board where he was music director and composed some 250 film scores. After scoring many feature films in Hollywood and New York, be became the first music director for the Stratford Festival. He was part of the planning group of the National Arts Centre and wrote reports which led to the foundation of the National Arts Centre Orchestra and the department of music at the University of Ottawa. He was a founder of the Canadian League of Composers, was executive director of the Ontario Arts Council from 1971 to 1979, and was named an Officer of the Order of Canada in 1977. He holds an honorary LLD from York University.

Jacques Hébert, author and publisher, has founded two Montreal publishing houses, les Editions de l'Homme, and les Editions du Jour, and for many years served as president of l'Association des éditeurs canadiens. He founded Canada World Youth and is its president, and is co-chairman of Katimavik. He has traveled extensively throughout the world and is the author of more than 15 books on travel, civil rights and problems of industrially developing countries. Between 1970 and 1980, Jacques Hébert was a member of the Canadian Radio-television and Telecommunications Commission. He has been named an Officer of the Order of Canada.

Albert Breton is a professor of economics and research associate at the Institute for Policy Analysis at the University of Toronto. He is also a member of the Canadian Economic Policy Committee and the C.D. Howe Research Institute. Author of several books and numerous articles on economics and social policy, Albert Breton has been the frequent recipient of social science research grants. He was awarded two Canada Council Killam Senior Research scholarships. A native of Saskatchewan, Professor Breton was educated in Manitoba and the United States. He holds a PhD in economics from Columbia University, New York.

Ted Chapman, broadcaster, is president of CFCN Communications Limited in Calgary, a radio and television subsidiary of Maclean-Hunter Limited. He is a past president of Theatre Calgary and has been a member of the Board of Governors of the National Theatre School in Montreal. He is currently a member of the Chancellors Club at the University of Calgary.

Joy Cohnstaedt is deputy minister of cultural affairs and historical resources for the province of Manitoba and, prior to August 1982, was executive director of the Saskatchewan Arts Board. In 1978 and 1980 she was a member of the culture and communications sector of the Canadian delegations to the 20th and 21st Unesco general assemblies on culture and communications, in France and Yugoslavia. She has also been a delegate to the Commonwealth Conference of Arts Agencies in England. Joy Cohnstaedt trained as a visual artist and has completed postgraduate studies in art education, in the social sciences and in administration at various universities in Canada, the United States and Britain. She now lives in Winnipeg.

John M. Dayton, of Vancouver, was president in 1979 and 1980 of the Vancouver Opera Association and in 1970 and 1971 president of the Vancouver Symphony Society. He has been a member of the board of the Canadian Conference of the Arts, the Community Arts Council of Vancouver and the Cultural Advisory Committee of the Vancouver Foundation. A graduate of the University of Manitoba, John Dayton is a practising architect. From 1967 to 1968, he was president of the Architectural Institute of British Columbia.

Denis Héroux is a film director and producer, and president of the International Cinema Corporation. His recent feature film credits include *Les Plouffe*, *Atlantic City* and *Quest for Fire*. A former professor of history at Collège Sainte-Marie, he has published two books on historical subjects. In 1982, Denis Héroux received "Le Mérite annuel de l'Université de Montréal," of which he is an alumnus. He has been president of l'Association des réalisateurs de films du Québec, and l'Association des producteurs de films du Québec.

Robert E. Landry, vice-president, Imperial Oil Limited, is a director and vice-president of the Toronto Symphony and a member of the board of the National Theatre School. He is also a former vice-president of the Edmonton Symphony. A graduate of McGill University, Robert Landry was the first chairman of the Council of Public Affairs Executives of the Conference Board in Canada and a director of the Canadian Manufacturers' Association.

Elizabeth Lane, of Vancouver, is former president of the Canadian Conference of the Arts, 1976 to 1978. Educated at the University of British Columbia and long active in community arts organizations, she is a former president of the Community Arts Council of Vancouver and the Vancouver Museums Association, and was the first chairman of the British Columbia Arts Board. She has also served as a member of the Canada Council, and has been a member of the executive committee of the Canadian Commission for Unesco and chairman of the Commission's Advisory Committee on Culture and Communications. She is a member of the Order of Canada and holds an honorary LLD from Simon Fraser University.

Hilda Lavoie-Frachon, from Nigadoo, New Brunswick, is a painter and printmaker and the founder and director of Le Centre de Créativité Fine Grobe, which provides workshop and exhibition space for the creative works of visual and applied artists from northeastern New Brunswick. The centre is devoted to continuing the heritage of Acadian arts in Canada. Hilda Lavoie-Frachon holds degrees in fine arts and in art education from l'Ecole des Beaux-Arts de Montréal. She specialized in museology at l'Ecole du Louvre in Paris. She was founder-director of the visual arts department at the Bathurst Campus, University of Moncton, 1966-1975.

Mary Pratt is a painter and member of the Royal Canadian Academy. The Aggregation Gallery in Toronto has hung three solo shows of her paintings and drawings – in 1976, in 1978 and, most recently, in 1981. She was included in the National Gallery of Canada's major 1975 exhibition "Some Canadian Women Artists," and has had two shows tour nationally. Mary Pratt lives in Mount Carmel, Newfoundland. She has been a member of the board of Grace Hospital, St. John's, and has been a lay bencher for the Law Society of Newfoundland and Labrador. In 1973, Mary Pratt served on the Newfoundland provincial task force on education.

Guy Robert is an art historian, professor, lecturer, contributor to radio and television programs, author of some 40 books, art consultant, and publisher of limited editions of original etchings. A founder of the Montreal Museum of Contemporary Art, he is a member of the International Association of Art Critics and l'Union des écrivains québécois. Educated in Montreal and France, he holds a doctorate in aesthetics from the University of Paris. He has written numerous articles, books of poems, essays on art and literature, a history of painting in Quebec, *La peinture au Québec depuis ses origines*, and monographs on Canadian artists such as Riopelle, Pellan, Borduas, Jordi Bonet, Fortin, Dallaire. He received the Grand Prix littéraire de Montréal for his second book on the painter Jean-Paul Lemieux. He lives in Mont-Royal, Quebec.

Jean-Louis Roux, Director General of the National Theatre School, has been awarded the Prix Victor Morin and the Molson Prize, and has been named an Officer of the Order of Canada for his work in theatre. Co-founder with Jean Gascon in 1951 of Montreal's Le Théâtre du Nouveau Monde, he worked with the company as playwright, actor, producer and artistic director until 1982. Jean-Louis Roux has been president of the Société des auteurs dramatiques, the Canadian Theatre Centre and the Canadian Conference of the Arts. He has also been chairman of the board of the National Theatre School. He has served as vice-chairman of the National Film Board, vice-president of l'Union des artistes, and as a member of the executive committee of the International Theatre Institute.

Sam Sniderman, a member of the Order of Canada, is better known as "Sam the Record Man." He is president of Roblan Distributors Limited of Toronto which has established record stores throughout Canada. He is vice-president of the Canadian Academy of Recording Arts and Sciences and is a director of the Canadian Independent Record Production Association. He is also a director of CHIN Multicultural Radio and of the Canadian National Exhibition. He has contributed extensively to the music archives collection of the University of Toronto's music faculty, which was recently renamed as the Sniderman Recordings Archives. Sam Sniderman is a member of the board of the National Theatre School. He lives in Toronto.

Alain Stanké, author and journalist, has been a publisher for 20 years. Head of Les Editions de l'Homme for 10 years and a founder of Les Editions La Presse, he is now head of Les Editions Internationales Alain Stanké Ltée. Born in Lithuania, he was educated in France and in Quebec and has written several books, including his autobiography, first published in French under the title *Des barbelés dans ma mémoire* and later in English as *So Much to Forget*. Alain Stanké is also a scriptwriter and host of various radio and television programs in Montreal. He won the Wilderness Award Medal for the best Canadian television film of 1967. In 1971 he was honoured by the Government of Quebec for his contribution to Quebec journalism and publishing. He is a member of the board of the Montreal Symphony Orchestra.

Thomas H.B. Symons, Vanier professor at Trent University and chairman of the Commission on Canadian Studies, is vice-president of the Social Sciences and Humanities Research Council. Professor Symons's report on Canadian studies, *To Know Ourselves*, volumes I and II, was published in 1976. He was the founding President and Vice-Chancellor of Trent University, 1962-72. He is a historian – a graduate of the University of Toronto and Oxford University – whose interests have led him into the broad fields of Canadian studies, education, human rights (he was chairman of the Ontario Human Rights Commission from 1975-78), Native peoples' affairs, northern studies and the arts. His work in these and related areas, both in Canada and abroad, has earned him recognition from a number of universities and colleges in Canada and other countries, and in 1982 he received the Distinguished Service to Education Award, of the Council for the Advancement and Support of Education. He was named an Officer of the Order of Canada in 1976.

Max Tapper, of Winnipeg, is director of development for the Royal Winnipeg Ballet. He is a member of Canadian Actors' Equity and the Association of Canadian Radio and Television Artists, and has performed in the theatre and on radio and television. For seven years, Max Tapper worked with the Manitoba Theatre Centre in administration, publicity and promotion before assuming his present position with the Royal Winnipeg Ballet. A specialist in performing arts administration, Max Tapper has lectured for the Canada Council's Touring Office, the Banff Centre's Cultural Management Program and the Manitoba Arts Council.

Rudy Wiebe is an author and 1973 winner of the Governor General's Literary Award for his novel *The Temptations of Big Bear*. His long publishing record includes 16 books, among them the 1982 collection of short stories, *The Angel of the Tar Sands*. Rudy Wiebe is currently a professor of English and creative writing at the University of Alberta. He lives in Edmonton and was the founding president of the Writers' Guild of Alberta and a former vice-president of the Writers' Union of Canada. Since 1980 he has been on the Publishers and Writers Advisory Panel to the Alberta Minister of Culture.

Appendix C

Staff

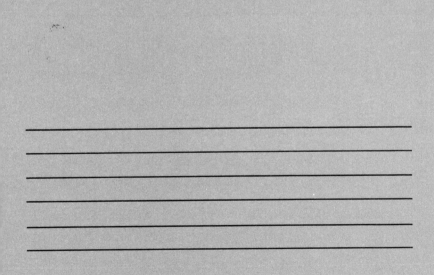

Appendix C

Staff

Secretary to the Committee*
Paul-Emile Leblanc

General Editors**
Norman Dahl
David Ellis

Senior Writers and Editors
Gordon Galbraith
Roy MacSkimming
Frank Milligan
Helen Small

Consultants
Ann Davis
Linda Gaboriau
Ninon Gauthier
Dinah Hoyle
Chloe McKinney
Michael Spencer
Francis Spiller

Managing Editor
Michelle d'Auray

Editor/Researchers
Guy Hurteau
Maureen Korp
Donna Lebo

Word Processing
Ilene Mitchell
Nicole Cadieux, Word Processor/
Receptionist

Administration
Louise Allard
Anita Haché

Secretary to the Chairmen
Jan Glyde

Documentation
Sylvie Mercier

Production
Information Services,
Department of Communications
Jackie Smith, Manager

Design
Wendesigns

French Text
Alphascript Ltée

*David Bartlett served as Secretary General between April 1981 and March 1982.
Ralph Heintzman and Germain Cadieux were respectively Director of Research and Director of Operations until March 1981. A list of staff members responsible for organizing the public hearings held in 1981 and for preparing the hearings report is included in the *Summary of Briefs and Hearings*, published in January 1982.
**David Ellis served as General Editor until the end of July 1982, when he was succeeded by Norman Dahl.

Index

Index

Recommendations relating to major subject categories are indicated in bold face type. A complete list of recommendations may be found in Chapter 12.

78-79, 215-219, **Rec. 50**, 220-221. *See
also* Communications, Department of
Canadian Brass, 238
Canadian Broadcasting Corporation (CBC),
20-22, 24-27, 46, 72-76, 274-280,
289-297, **Rec. 65 to 72**; chief executive
officer, 45, **Rec. 6**; CRTC, relations with,
307, **Rec. 83**; facilities, 295; film
distribution, 265, 294, 297, **Rec. 72**;
film production, 249, 251, 294; in-
house talent, 276-277; International
Relations section, 320, 332; mandate,
274, 277, 311; music recording, 236,
241-242, **Rec. 57**; Northern Service,
275, 294-295; official languages, broadcasting in, 296, 297, **Rec. 71**; personnel administration, 39, 276-277;
political control, 27-28, 35-36, 38,
Rec. 2; Radio Canada International
(RCI), 295, 329-330, **Rec. 95, 96**;
revenues, 76, 91, 93, 272-273,
278-280, 290-291, 297, **Rec. 72**, 300,
304. *See also* CBC Enterprises; CBC
radio; CBC television; programming,
Canadian Broadcasting Corporation
(CBC); Public Archives of Canada (PAC);
Radio Canada International (RCI)
Canadian Commission for Unesco, 113, 316,
325-328, **Rec. 93, 94**, 338-339
Canadian Conference of the Arts (CCA), 21,
49, 198
Canadian Conservation Institute (CCI), 108,
Rec. 16, 113-114, **Rec. 21**, 117,
119-120, 125, 128; as part of Canadian
Heritage Council (proposed), **Rec. 16**,
114, **Rec. 21**, 117, 127, 137. *See also*
conservation; heritage, National Programmes (NMC)
Canadian content, 21, 30, 76, 83, 89-90,
300, **Rec. 75, 76**; AM radio regulations, 236-239, **Rec. 54**, 276; broadcasting, 269, 272-274, 281-282, 300,
302, **Rec. 77**; cable operators, 284-285,
Rec. 79, 302-305; Canadian Radio-
television and Telecommunications
Commission (CRTC) regulations, 237,
285-288, 299-301, **Rec. 75, 76**, 307;
Department of External Affairs,
321-322, 330-331, **Rec. 97**; film,
254-257, 258-259, **Rec. 61**, 266; FM
radio regulations, 239, 276, **Rec. 54**;
performing arts, 170-172, **Rec. 39**;
publishing, 221, 224, 226, **Rec. 52**;
sound recording, **Rec. 55 to 60**,

240-243; visual and applied arts,
146-151, 164-166, **Rec. 34 to 36**
Canadian Council for Design and the Applied
Arts (proposed), 162-166, **Rec. 37, 38**
Canadian Crafts Council, 154, 158, 162, 163,
164; Third World countries, 328
Canadian Cultural Property Export Review
Board, 111-113, **Rec. 19, 20**, 132, 139;
associated with proposed Canadian
Heritage Council, 113, **Rec. 20**
Canadian Film Development Corporation
(CFDC), 20, 24-25, 27, 253-256, 316;
budget, 258-261, **Rec. 61**, 262; Film
Canada, 262, 332; personnel ad-
ministration, 38, **Rec. 3**; political con-
trol, 36, 38-39, **Rec. 2**; resource alloca-
tion, 38-39, 80, **Rec. 10**, 250, 260-261,
263
Canadian Government Photo Centre, 265
Canadian Government Publishing Centre,
222. *See also* Supply and Services,
Department of
Canadian Heraldic Authority, 136
Canadian Heritage Council (proposed), 59,
107-108, **Rec. 15, 16, 21**, 119, 120,
121, 123, 127, 131, 136-139, **Rec. 32**;
political control, 38-39, **Rec. 3**; role of,
36, 114, 116-117, **Rec. 22**, 119-120,
Rec. 23, 135, **Rec. 31, 33**
Canadian Independent Record Production
Association (CIRPA), 242, 244
Canadian Institute for Historical
Microreproductions, 134-135
Canadian International Cultural Relations
Agency (proposed), 124, 153, 336-340,
Rec. 100, 101; advisory board, 338,
339; mandate, 338, 340; relations with
Canada Council Touring Office, 188;
role of Department of External Affairs,
336-340
Canadian International Development Agency
(CIDA), 316, 326-328, **Rec. 93**, 339
Canadian Inventory of Historic Buildings,
115-116, **Rec. 22**
Canadian League of Composers, 183
Canadian Library Association (CLA), 133, 134
Canadian Mediterranean Institute, 331
Canadian Motion Picture Distributors'
Association, 258
Canadian Museums Association (CMA), 106,
120
Canadian Music Centre, 184, **Rec. 42**, 242
Canadian Periodical Publishers' Association,
223, 225